This important work refutes a currently fashionable consensus, which maintains that the English Civil War can be seen as primarily the result of a Laudian and Arminian assault on a previously dominant Calvinism. According to this picture, the isolation of the court from Calvinist opinions, and the aggressive Arminian policies pursued during the reign of Charles I, ultimately drove previously law-abiding Calvinists into counter-resistance to the king and the church hierarchy. Arguing for tensions within a continuing spectrum rather than a sharp polarity, Peter White denies any clearly defined 'Calvinist consensus' into which 'Arminianism' made deep and fateful inroads. The doctrinal evolution of the English Church is thus seen as a story to which theologians of contrasting churchmanship contributed.

Predestination, policy and polemic

Predestination, policy and polemic

Conflict and consensus in the English Church from the Reformation to the Civil War

Peter White

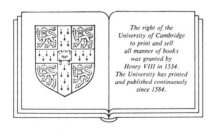

The right of the
University of Cambridge
to print and sell
all manner of books
was granted by
Henry VIII in 1534.
The University has printed
and published continuously
since 1584.

Cambridge University Press

Cambridge   New York   Port Chester
Melbourne   Sydney

Published by the Press Syndicate of the University of Cambridge
The Pitt Building, Trumpington Street, Cambridge CB2 1RP
40 West 20th Street, New York, NY 10011-4211, USA
10 Stamford Road, Oakleigh, Melbourne 3166, Australia

First published 1992

Printed in Great Britain at the University Press, Cambridge

A catalogue record for this book is available from the British Library

Library of Congress cataloguing in publication data

White, P. O. G. (Peter O. G.)
Predestination, policy and polemic: conflict and consensus in the English Church
from the Reformation to the Civil War / P. O. G. White.
    p.   cm.
Includes index.
ISBN 0 521 39433 3
1. Predestination – History of doctrines – 16th century. 2. Predestination –
History of doctrines – 17th century. 3. Church of England – History – 16th
century. 4. Church of England – History – 17th century. 5. Anglican Communion – England – History – 16th century. 6. Anglican Communion –
England – History – 17th century. 7. England – Church history – 16th century.
8. England – Church history – 17th century. 9. Puritans – England. I. Title.
BR757.W455 1991
283' .42' 09031 – dc20   91 – 1255   CIP

ISBN 0 521 39433 3 hardback

GG

Contents

Preface   *page* ix

Acknowledgements   xiv

1 The polemics of predestination: William Prynne
   and Peter Heylyn   1

2 The theology of predestination: Beza and Arminius   13

   Beza's doctrine of predestination   13
   The theology of Arminius   22

3 Early English Protestantism   39

   Hooper and Latimer   39
   Continental influences: Bucer and Martyr   44
   The Edwardian formularies   52

4 The Elizabethan church settlement   60

   Returning exiles and doctrinal definition   60
   John Jewel   69
   Henry Bullinger   74

5 Elizabeth's church: the limits of consensus   82

   Veins of doctrine   82
   The changing face of Elizabethan Calvinism   90

6 The Cambridge controversies of the 1590s   101

   The Lambeth Articles   101
   Peter Baro   110
   Matthew Hutton   117

7 Richard Hooker   124

8   The early Jacobean church   140

    The Hampton Court Conference   140
    The debate on Calvin   152
    Remonstrants, Contra-Remonstrants and the English
       Church   159
    Falling from grace   167

9   The Synod of Dort   175

    The evolution of royal policy   175
    Preliminaries   180
    Doctrinal definition: the Five Articles   183
    The first head: election and reprobation   184
    The second head: the extent of the Atonement   187
    The third and fourth heads: free will and conversion 192
    The fifth head: perseverance   195
    The closing sessions   199

10   Policy and polemic, 1619–1623   203

11   A gag for the Gospel? Richard Montagu and Protestant
    orthodoxy   215

    The *New Gagg*   215
    The York House Conference   224
    The defence of 'orthodoxy'   230

12   Arminianism and the court, 1625–1629   238

13   Thomas Jackson   256

14   Neile and Laud on predestination   272

15   The personal rule, 1629–1640   287

    Licensing policy   287
    The regulation of doctrine   299
    The personal rule in retrospect   307

Select bibliography   313

Index   327

Preface

This book is an attempt to chart the development of the doctrine of predestination in the English Church in the century between the Reformation and the English Civil War, but, as its title suggests, it seeks to locate that development in its contemporary political and often polemical setting. The challenge of a time-scale so lengthy and a canvas so broad may well be considered over-ambitious, especially for the author of a first book. Since the reasons for accepting the challenge have in large part determined the structure of the argument, it may be helpful to the reader to know what they are.

It is of course a commonplace that the links between church and state in the early-modern period were so close that no historian of the one can afford to ignore the other. The political setting of doctrinal evolution was above all monarchical. As the preamble to the Act in Restraint of Appeals of 1533 put it, 'this realm of England is an Empire . . . governed by one supreme head and king . . . unto whom a body politic, compact of all sorts and degrees of people divided in terms and by names of spiritualty and temporalty, be bounden and owe to bear next to God a natural and humble obedience'. Throughout the period covered by this book, the royal supremacy proclaimed under Henry VIII continued to operate as a powerful determinant of theological development, and the principle of *cuius regio eius religio* was accepted throughout Europe.

It was not merely the workings of the royal supremacy that forged inseparable links between church and state. In the century after the Reformation, religious belief was at a number of points linked with national identity. Under Elizabeth, for example, anti-Catholic meant anti-Spanish, and (at least after the papal bull of excommunication of 1570) it was not merely government propaganda that blurred the distinction between heresy and treason. As presented by John Foxe, patriotism became the keynote of Protestantism. That tradition continued to exercise a powerful influence in the seventeenth century, as is evident both from the pressure on James I to intervene in the Thirty Years War and the suspicions of popish plots under Henrietta Maria.

While the need for a broad canvas may be clear enough, the choice of time-scale and of predestination as a central theme may not. The answer lies in the recent historiography of Tudor and Stuart politics. Standard 'Whig' interpretations presenting it as a 'high road to civil war' between a monarchy committed to the divine right of kings and a would-be absolutist exercise of the royal prerogative on the one hand, and a House of Commons committed to the defence of individual liberties and representative government on the other, have been challenged by 'revisionist' historians. They have demonstrated how much the Whig-liberal picture presupposes a nineteenth-century view of politics which simply did not obtain in the early-modern period, in which all government tended to be aristocratic, which knew no political parties, and in which (it is claimed) there was no underlying constitutional conflict. Although the revisionists' case has not won universal acceptance, there can surely be no question of the importance of their insights for students of the period.

But if we must reject the traditional constitutional explanation of the Civil War, what remains to put in its place? The answer is that an increased weight has been placed on religious factors. To stress religious issues is in itself by no means novel: the concept of a 'Puritan Revolution' has long been familiar to historians. Paradoxically, however, current historiography appears in this field only too ready to embrace a Whig – indeed, a Radical – version of the issues in question. It refuses not merely to cast Puritans in the role of revolutionaries, but even to accept that there was an 'Anglican' moderate mainstream. The very existence of 'Anglicanism' prior to the Restoration of 1660 is rejected as anachronistic, and Puritans have been moved so far to the centre stage that, as will be apparent, some historians have doubted the utility of the distinction between 'Puritan' and 'Protestant'. Even those who grant that there were tensions on matters of liturgy and organization deny that they extended to matters of doctrine. Doctrinally, it is asserted, the English Church was uniformly 'Calvinist' from the beginning of the reign of Elizabeth, held there not only by theological commitment but by the underlying 'political realities' of Catholic plots at home and external threats.

This 'Calvinist' consensus is said to have centred on the doctrine of predestination, double and absolute: of the saints (or elect) to salvation and of the reprobate to damnation. Books and sermons of the period are said to evidence the ubiquity of the doctrine. It was buttressed by the teaching of the popular Geneva Bible, and evident in a number of wills in which the testator claimed to be an elect saint. It was not, it is argued, until the 1590s that it was first challenged. The attack came from those who have been called Arminians *avant la lettre*, because they anticipated the arguments of the Dutch theologian Jacobus Arminius, whose works were published in the first decade or so of the seventeenth century. Arminianism, it is asserted, represented a 'systematic refutation of Calvinism', but in England 'Calvinism remained dominant . . . throughout the first two decades of the seventeenth century.'

Seventeenth-century Arminianism, we are informed, was associated above all with William Laud. Although he did not become archbishop until 1633, he 'came out against Calvinism' as early as 1616, and 'the overthrow of Calvinism' followed the accession of Charles I in 1625. It was achieved by a fundamental redefinition of Puritanism to include the Calvinist doctrine of predestination. As a result, what had been the 'de facto religion of the Church of England under Queen Elizabeth and James I' was blackened and outlawed. The Civil War was not a Puritan Revolution but a counter-revolution against that Arminian takeover.

This book has been conceived as a challenge to this interpretation of the history of the Church of England in the post-Reformation period. It begins with a discussion (for the benefit especially of readers whose knowledge of the period is primarily of its theology) of the polemical writings of William Prynne in order to demonstrate how much current historiography has taken up Prynne's arguments, and follows with Peter Heylyn, again in order to show how much even hostile portrayals of Laud have been influenced by his would-be apologist. Precisely because the conceptual dichotomy is said to have been between Calvinism and Arminianism, it proceeds with a review of Beza's doctrine (unquestionably of importance in England) and then that of Arminius, which (as will be seen) was developed as an answer to Beza. It centres on the doctrine of predestination because that is taken to be the characteristic doctrine of Calvinism. Its review of doctrinal development starts in the mid-Tudor period because that is when the doctrine is said to have become normative. The importance of the debates that led to the Lambeth Articles, and of the place of Hooker in the development of English theology, needs no explanation. Similarly, the stress placed upon the revolutionary character of the accession of Charles I explains the space granted in this book to the last years of James I's reign and the early years of Charles's, and the need, here above all, to study the court politics of that period.

One result of the evidence considered here is to suggest that 'Arminianism', just as much as 'Puritanism', was vulnerable to redefinition. At first a doctrine of predestination, it was soon used both in the Netherlands and elsewhere as a polemical counter in the conflict between different schools of Protestantism. In English polemic it became 'a bridge to usher in Popery' and even a plot to introduce arbitrary government. While one aim of this study is to highlight the process of redefinition, to avoid misunderstanding it should be stressed that theologically the book remains a study of predestination. Conclusions are not drawn (and the reader is not invited to draw them) with respect to other doctrines, still less to matters of liturgy and church government. As to Puritanism, it will be argued here that, whatever the history of contemporary usage, there were from the early Elizabethan period doctrinal tensions between moderate and radical Protestants. Provided that is accepted, I am content for present purposes not to use the word 'Anglican'. The word 'Catholic' is used here as James I used it, to mean 'in accordance with what has been believed everywhere, always and by all' (i.e., according to the test of Catholicity associated with St Vincent of Lerins).

Again in order to avoid misunderstanding, it should be said that although 'Calvinist' is used in this book with reference to the doctrine of predestination, it is by no means intended to imply that Calvinism is thereby sufficiently defined. That a man believed himself elect is no evidence of 'Calvinism', for the doctrine of election (and indeed predestination) was shared by Calvinists and non-Calvinists alike. The tension, at any rate in the English Church, was not so much between 'Calvinist' and non-Calvinist theories but about the centrality or otherwise of predestination within a much larger doctrinal whole, about the precise interpretation of commonly accepted biblical insights, and about whether it was profitable that predestination should be preached. There was unquestionably a large body of opinion which thought that it should not. It should not be forgotten that the study of printed books and sermons disfranchises that constituency. To place too much stress on predestination, furthermore, fails to do justice to the rich complexity of Calvinism: it overlooks the profound ways in which Calvinists were influenced by what has been called experimental predestinarianism; and it ignores other doctrines arguably more important, such as the nature of the church, and concepts of doctrinal authority. Calvinism was in any case not an ossified series of propositions but a living organism capable, within recognizable continuities, of development and changes of emphasis; not just a system of beliefs, but a complex of aspirations.

Independently of these considerations, the current emphasis on the doctrine of predestination is unsatisfactory. Even granting that there were two extremes of churchmanship, the evidence considered here suggests that perceptions of the doctrine of predestination are probably the least helpful and most misleading way of trying to analyse them. Recent attempts to extend the scope of the argument by suggesting that the Arminians not only devalued predestinarian grace, but correspondingly overvalued sacramental, certainly fail to do justice to Calvin and to English Calvinists like Whitaker, for whom the sacraments were ordained means of grace. The English Calvinist Cornelius Burgess defended the baptismal regeneration of elect infants and attacked those who scorned baptism – including the Arminians!

For all these reasons, and for others that will appear in the body of the argument, the model of a polarity between Calvinist and Arminian is here rejected in favour of a spectrum. Although a spectrum does indeed imply a middle ground, it is not intended to suggest that any one group had a monopoly of moderation. Moderation on predestination did not necessarily imply moderation on other issues. If it be objected that individuals are often not placed on that spectrum, the reason is precisely that the evidence considered – the constellation of approaches to the doctrine of predestination, in which each divine modifies and emphasizes different aspects – does not lead to a meaningful classification. Indeed, so complex is the psychology of religious belief, that it may be questioned whether even broader doctrinal criteria would be much more satisfactory. It is, after all, from the revisionists themselves that we have learned to be suspicious of party labels. This book has been written to carry that insight into the study of religious history.

Acknowledgements

The ideas at the heart of this book were given their first airing in a paper read to the Maitland Historical Society at Downing College, Cambridge, in February 1982. I owe thanks to many scholars and friends for help in its preparation: to Kevin Sharpe, who suggested that I should write it, and who has continued to take an interest in its progress; to Harry Porter, whose own *Reformation and Reaction in Tudor Cambridge* was both inspiration and exemplar, and who also has continued to encourage and advise; to Nicholas Tyacke and Peter Lake, from whom I have learned much while begging to differ; and for particular kindnesses to John Adamson, George Bernard, Robert Buttimore, Julian Davies, Kenneth Fincham, Ian Green, David Keep, Anthony Milton, John Morrill, John Platt, Vicky Raymer, Howard Tomlinson and Hugh Trevor-Roper.

I am indebted to the British Academy for making me a grant for personal research, and to David Newsome, late Master of Wellington and the Governors for allowing me time to pursue it; more recently his successor, Jonty Driver, has generously allowed me a term's leave to complete the preparation of the text. My thanks are due also to the staff of the learned libraries, and especially those of Duke Humfrey's Library at Oxford and the Manuscripts and Rare Books Rooms at Cambridge, for continuing help and courtesy. In the final stages I have benefited from the expert guidance of Alex Wright, Religious Studies editor and Pauline Marsh, copy-editor, of Cambridge University Press: it is an especial pleasure that the book carries the imprint of my own university.

I owe a debt of a different kind to my wife Joy, who has accepted without resentment my preoccupation for over a decade with the ideas of a world apart.

1 The polemics of predestination: William Prynne and Peter Heylyn

'The task of the religious historian of England between the Elizabethan Settlement and the Civil War', it has been said, 'is . . . one of daunting complexity, if he is to confront the entire scene.' Somehow he must describe the simultaneous emergence of two 'almost antithetical processes': an increasing diversity of religious allegiance on the one hand, and the growth of a Protestant consensus on the other, closely linked with a sense of national identity and a hostility to Catholic foreign powers and to the Pope himself.[1]

One answer to this dilemma has been to assert the existence of a doctrinal consensus usually labelled Calvinism as a 'theological cement' which held the Elizabethan and Jacobean church together. The Lambeth Articles of 1595, agreed to by Archbishop Whitgift and sent by him to Cambridge to be imposed upon the university, are held to be conclusive evidence of that consensus. The English Civil War is then seen as primarily the result of a Laudian or Arminian assault on a previously triumphant Calvinism. From that perspective, the Arminian assertion of 'the free will of all men to obtain salvation' was, in a society as steeped in Calvinist theology as England, revolutionary, and is the main reason why religion became an issue in the Civil War crisis. Differences over rites and ceremonies or over church government were not too divisive while Calvinist predestinarian ideas provided a 'common and ameliorating bond', as they did under Elizabeth and even more under James I. James's education in Scotland had left him favourably disposed towards Calvinist teaching. The majority of the clergy and probably most of the laity were convinced predestinarians. The harmony that ensued was symbolized by the attendance of English divines at the Synod of Dort.

Unfortunately this Calvinist heritage was overthrown in the 1620s by Arminianism. A small group of clergy – Neile, Andrewes, Buckeridge and Overall, with Laud in the background – captured the minds first of the ageing king, then of Buckingham and the heir to the throne.

---

[1] P. Collinson, 'The Elizabethan Church and the New Religion', in C. Haigh (ed.), *The Reign of Elizabeth* (1984), 175.

1

Their manifesto was Richard Montagu's *New Gagg*, published in 1624. The accession of Charles was decisive, for the new king became within a few months the architect of a revolution. Doctrinal Calvinists, humiliated in front of Buckingham at the York House Conference, were excluded from royal counsels and from ecclesiastical preferment. The isolation of the court from Calvinist opinions, and the aggressive Arminian policies pursued during the personal rule, ultimately drove previously law-abiding episcopalian Calvinists, both in England and Scotland, into counter-resistance to the king and the church hierarchy: but it was unquestionably the king and Laud who were the innovators, and the Puritans, the reactionaries; and even in 1640 the essential issue was doctrinal.[2]

This understanding of the doctrinal evolution of the English Church is by no means unsupported by contemporary evidence. That evidence comes, however, very largely from the latter part of the period, and from by no means disinterested sources. It derives above all from William Prynne. Prynne's *Anti-Arminianisme* has, it is claimed,[3] 'never been answered' as a demonstration of the comprehensive commitment of the Elizabethan and Jacobean church to Calvinist orthodoxy. It was Prynne who, in seeking to demonstrate that commitment, first appealed to the output of the printing presses and to the content of university theses. It is Prynne, furthermore, who first advanced the view, often repeated but seldom argued, that there was a connection between 'Arminian' error in doctrine and 'Popish' ceremony in worship. The claim that until 1640 Prynne was a moderate should deceive no one.[4] *Anti-Arminianisme* was written, as its author himself acknowledged, to persuade King Charles's third Parliament into passing an Act against it.[5] Prynne had wanted action before the 'poisonous works of Aquinas, Lombard, Scotus, Suarez, Bellarmine and such like Popish schoolmen . . . read by too many, whence they smell and stink of Popery and Neutrality ever after, to their own perdition' did any more damage. The Dutch Arminians had been dealt with too leniently at Dort; English ones should be eliminated root and

---

[2] The argument here summarized is best known from N. Tyacke, 'Puritanism, Arminianism and Counter Revolution', in C. Russell (ed.), *The Origins of the English Civil War* (1973), 119–43, since elaborated in *Anti-Calvinists: The Rise of English Arminianism c. 1590–1640* (1987). Dewey Wallace 'is in the strongest possible agreement with his conclusions that Arminianism in England represented an utterly radical theological innovation'. D. Wallace, *Puritans and Predestination: Grace in English Protestant Theology* (Chapel Hill, 1982), 220.
[3] N. Tyacke, in a letter published in *History Today* 34 (1984), 49.
[4] W. Lamont, *Marginal Prynne* (1963), 13.
[5] William Prynne, *The Church of England's Old Antithesis to the New Arminianisme* (1629), sig. c2ʳ; it appeared 'much enlarged' as *Anti-Arminianisme* in 1630. Prynne's reply to Montagu, *The Perpetuitie of a Regenerate Man's Estate* (1626), was independent of either (*pace* Wallace, *Puritans and Predestination*, 85–6). Prynne's other specifically anti-Arminian book was *God, No Impostor or Deluder: An Answer to a Popish and Arminian Cavil, in the defence of Free Will and Universal Grace* (1629).

branch. 'This infernal monster, which . . . breaks the golden chains of salvation in pieces . . . (whatever some may vainly dream) is but an old-condemned heresy, raised up from hell of late, by some Jesuits and infernal spirits, to kindle a combustion of all Protestant states and Churches.' It was the heresy of Pelagius, revived after lying dead for over a thousand years 'by a kind of Pythagorean metempsychosis' in the shape of Arminius and his followers. In its new form 'it is but a bridge, an usher unto Popery and all Popish ceremonies, which wind themselves into our church apace'.[6]

Prynne claimed that Anti-Arminianism was 'the pith and marrow of divinity'. 'The whole fabric of our salvation' depended on it.[7] Far from being superfluous, nice or curious speculations, the truths of predestination had saved England from the Spanish Armada in 1588 and from the Gunpowder Plot in 1605.[8] Prynne posed as a truly orthodox Anglican. Although translations of Calvin and Beza proved that the Church of England had 'indenizened and adopted these foreign authors', the only proper appeal was to the Articles of Religion, the Homilies and the Book of Common Prayer, supplemented by the 'authorized writings of all the learned orthodox writers of the Church of England from the Reformation to this present'.[9] To these Prynne added the Lambeth Articles, which far from being the resolutions of private men had been approved by both archbishops and the whole University of Cambridge. It was wrong to say that they had been revoked by Queen Elizabeth, and in any case they were included in the Irish Articles of 1615, issued under the Great Seal. Thirdly, appeal could be made to the conclusions of the Synod of Dort, 'convented by the pious care and providence of our late sovereign King James', to which the English delegates had subscribed not as private persons but as representatives of the Church of England. Finally, Prynne claimed a unanimity of doctoral theses in both universities for his anti-Arminian tenets. 'Scarce a graduate in divinity, but hath either in lectures or disputes, defended them in the school.' There had been 'not one authorized or approved writer of our Church (for I count not Barrett, Thomson, Montagu or Jackson such) who did ever once oppugn them. Yea all such who have formerly but barked against them in their inconsiderate sermons, have been forced to sing a public palinode for their pains.'[10]

According to Prynne, Arminianism meant first the denial of an absolute, immutable and irrevocable decree of predestination. There was no

[6] W. Prynne, *The Church of England's Old Antithesis*, sig. c2^r–c3^v.
[7] Ibid., sig. ¶¶2^v.
[8] Ibid., 139.
[9] Ibid., 2.
[10] Ibid., sig. a2^v–a3^r.

predestination of particular persons, but generally a predestination of believers and unbelievers. Their respective numbers might therefore be increased or diminished. Election was conditional upon divinely foreseen faith, perseverance and good works. The only cause of reprobation was foresight of sin. Sufficient grace was granted to all men by which they might be saved if they would. Christ died for all men, without any intent to save any particular persons more than others. Men might either finally or totally resist the grace of God. True justifying faith was neither a fruit of election nor even exclusive to the elect alone, being often found in reprobates. The elect might fall both totally and finally from a state of grace.[11]

In order to refute these positions, Prynne took each doctrine in turn, contrasting it with its orthodox antithesis. He dealt first, therefore, with the eternity and immutability of election. His case for unanimity, beginning with Tyndall and ending modestly with his own *Perpetuity of a Regenerate Man's Estate*, is overdrawn but convincing enough. Unfortunately it is irrelevant to the theological debate between Calvinists and Arminians, since they both accepted that common biblical premiss. Prynne implies otherwise, but it was no part of his purpose to be fair to those who had doubts about the more uncompromising presentations of predestinarian belief, and he did not consider it necessary to quote them.

Other points were nearer the heart of the matter. In asserting the mere will and pleasure of God to be the only cause both of election and reprobation Prynne was indeed defending an interpretation of the 17th Article strongly argued by Cambridge Calvinists like Whitaker in the 1590s against William Barrett and Peter Baro. But it was much more difficult to demonstrate a universal consent to that interpretation. All Prynne could say about Bradford and Hooper was that they were demonstrably anti-Pelagian, and therefore 'must have' been anti-Arminian. 'These writers . . . make wholly for us, not against us, if rightly understood.'[12] It was on contentious issues like this that appeal had to be made – as was usual in 1628 – to the Articles of Ireland and the Synod of Dort.

In turning to consider universal grace Prynne was even less concerned to do justice to the opposition. He dismissed it as merely the assertion of free will, 'the only centre upon which the whole fabric of Arminianism is erected; by the undermining of which alone, the superstruction, both of Pelagianism, Popery, Arminianism and Libertinism, are utterly subverted'.[13] And now Prynne dropped all pretence that he was not engaged in routine polemic. 'Our Arminians to support this rotten idol

[11] Ibid., 49–51.
[12] Ibid., 71, 118–19.
[13] Ibid., 78. *Anti-Arminianisme*, 113.

of free will, are forced to maintain a conditional, mutable, general and confused decree of predestination only . . . If no predestination, then no vocation, no justification, no faith, no salvation, predestination being the original fountain of all these, and the main foundation both of grace and glory.' Free will made the fickle will of man the basis of the divine decrees; it made 'the great controller of the world a bare spectator'; it deified the will of man, pulled God out of heaven, destroyed the essence and nature of grace, suspended the efficacy of Christ's death, falsified Scripture, opened a gap to licentiousness,[14] and 'lastly, it would make the most of all our Arminian sticklers (who are generally the very proudest, the sloth-fulest, the most ambitious, envious, lascivious, voluptuous and prophanest of our clergy, making no conscience for to feed their flocks, with which they are seldom resident, but when some tithes or gains come in) exceeding obstinate and graceless sinners. For if they have this power to convert, repent and leave their sins (as they pretend to have) why are their actions and their lives so vicious?'[15]

The Church of England's Old Antithesis to the New Arminianisme was a lawyer's brief rather than a work of theology. To argue that because the 'ancient Church of England' was unanimous in its rejection of Pelagianism, it was therefore necessarily anti-Arminian was mere polemic. Prynne refused to recognize the evident existence within both the Protestant churches abroad and the Church of England of differences of opinion on the doctrine of predestination. His assertion of unanimity involved him in a gross distortion of the teaching of Bradford, Hooper and Latimer, to mention no others. His discussion of the doctrine of reprobation was vitiated by his assumption that 'predestination' normally denoted both election to life and reprobation to death, but in sixteenth-century scholarly usage it was usually a synonym for election, and excluded reprobation. Prynne used the ambiguity to argue, illegitimately, that because the church taught unconditional election it therefore taught unconditional reprobation. Because the 17th Article does not mention reprobation, Prynne had to appeal both to the Lambeth Articles and the Synod of Dort, and to pretend that they represented official orthodoxy. But there is a much more profound reason why Prynne's discussion is wrong-headed. The essence of theology is the resolution of the great antinomies, of nature and grace, of freedom and necessity, of faith and works, of divine love and divine justice, of the command to preach the Gospel to all the world in the face of the rejection of that Gospel by the world, of hope and despair, of assurance and doubt, of good and evil. In proclaiming the reconciliation of God and man, it finds itself reconciling opposites. It is a search

[14] *The Church of England's Old Antithesis,* 79–85, *Anti-Arminianisme,* 114.
[15] *The Church of England's Old Antithesis,* 87, *Anti-Arminianisme,* 136.

for equipoise, the pursuit of the middle way. For Prynne there was no middle way. Montagu was condemned because he was a neuter, a Proteus, a chameleon. His religion was a weather-cock.[16] Prynne's attack on him is a classic example of an excluded middle.

The ecclesiastical pastures which nourished 'anti-Arminianism' also produced anti-Calvinism. Where Prynne was William Laud's most prolific opponent, Peter Heylyn, only to a degree less prolific in controversy, was his first biographer: the Laud with whom the modern student is familiar remains substantially Laud seen through Heylyn's eyes. Most of Heylyn's controversial church histories date from the 1640s and 1650s, and several of them were not published until after his death in 1662. Harassed by Prynne in 1640, Heylyn lost all his money and his library early in the war, and spent much of the rest of it wandering from house to house in disguise.[17] The attack on episcopacy and the Prayer Book, together with the execution of Laud and later of Charles I, confirmed all the warnings that farsighted Anglicans like Bancroft and Montagu had issued earlier concerning the evil designs of the 'Calvinian faction.'

Heylyn's conspiracy theory reached maturity in *Aerius Redivivus, or The History of the Presbyterians*. The 'faction' had been the chief source of civil discord ever since the 'Genevians' had returned from exile. The Genevan Bible was a preparative to the introduction of 'the whole body of Calvinism, as well in reference to government, and forms of worship, as to points of doctrine'. Some of the Puritans 'in their zeal to the name of Calvin, preferred him once before St Paul'. They had received encouragement from persons near the queen, and especially from Leicester. A fatal step was the setting up of the French Calvinist Church in England by Grindal at the request of Beza: it was both a model for Presbyterians like Cartwright ('the very Calvin of the English') and one of the reasons for the alienation of church papists. It was primarily as a result of Cartwright's activities that the faction arrogated to themselves titles like 'the godly', 'the elect' and 'the righteous', to distinguish themselves from orthodox Christians, who were dubbed 'carnal Gospellers', 'the prophane' and 'the wicked'. Their divisiveness was reflected even in their repudiation of heathen names for their children, who instead were christened 'Accepted', 'Consolation', 'Discipline', 'Kill-sin' and so forth. Similarly

[16] W. Prynne, *Perpetuitie of a Regenerate Man's Estate*, 250–1. Similarly, Laud 'was another Cassander, or middle man between an absolute Papist and a real Protestant'. W. Prynne, *Rome's Masterpiece* (1644), 28–9. But by then Prynne was significantly less confident of the doctrinal charge: 'an absolute Papist in all matters of ceremony, pomp and external worship . . . if not half a one at least, in doctrinal tenets'.

[17] Biographical details from *Ecclesia Restaurata, or The History of the Reformation of the Church of England by Peter Heylyn . . . with a life of the author by John Barnard . . .* ed, J. G. Robertson (2 vols., Cambridge, 1849).

with their dress. The 'turkey gowns' worn by the delegates to the Hampton Court Conference reflected their subscription to Cartwright's opinion that in outward ceremonies 'we ought . . . rather to conform . . . to the fashion of the Turks than to the Papists'. Meanwhile, 'in the Low Countries all things prospered with the Presbyterians, who thrive best when they involve whole Nations in blood and sacrilege'.[18]

Heylyn's fullest discussion of matters doctrinal was reserved for his *Historia Quinquarticularis*. The burden of his attack on Calvin was familiar from Romanist polemic: he made God the author of sin.[19] In arguing a necessity in Adam to commit sin, because the Lord has so decreed it, Calvin maintained that God had sentenced millions of men to everlasting damnation necessarily, inevitably and without respect to their moral condition. Having ordained the end, He must ordain the means. 'The odious inferences which are raised out of these opinions I forbear to press, and shall add only at the present, that if we grant this doctrine to be true and orthodox, we may do well to put an *Index expurgatorius* upon the Creed and quite expunge the Article of Christ's coming to judgement.'[20] Beza and his followers made the doctrine even 'wilder' by placing the decree of predestination before the Fall, 'which Calvin had more rightly placed in the corrupted mass of mankind'.[21] The differences between them were reflected at the Synod of Dort, where arguments between the delegates had been quite as bitter as at the Council of Trent. Those differences did not, however, prevent the condemnation of the Arminians, who were looked on as mortal enemies. The supralapsarians, by contrast, were gently treated as erring brethren, Maccovius receiving no other reprimand for calling God the author of sin 'and many other expressions of a like foul nature' than a friendly warning to forbear such language in future.[22] Although Heylyn conceded that the canons were sublapsarian, his summary of the decrees ('the shortest and withal the most favourable summary . . . I have . . . met')[23] was unscrupulously designed to arouse his readers' moral outrage. 'God by an absolute decree hath elected . . . a very small number of men, without any regard for their faith or obedience whatsoever; and secluded from saving grace all the rest of mankind, and

[18] P. Heylyn, *Aerius Redivivus, or The History of the Presbyterians* (2nd edn, 1672), 213–15, 221–4, 254, 289, 334.
[19] P. Heylyn, *Historia Quinquarticularis, or a Declaration of the Judgement of the Church of England in the Five Controverted Points, Reproached in these Last Times by the Name of Arminianism* (3 vols, in 1, 1660), I. 6, citing Calvin's *Institutes*, III. 23, 7.
[20] Ibid.
[21] Ibid., I. 37. But cf. 38, where supralapsarianism is said to have been 'first broached by Calvin'.
[22] P. Heylyn, *Historia Quinquarticularis*, I. 66–7.
[23] Heylyn's authority was the noted anti-Calvinist Laurence Womock, *The Examination of Tilenus before the Triers . . . to which is annexed the Tenets of the Remonstrants* (1658).

appointed them by the same decree to eternal damnation, without any regard to their infidelity or impenitency.' Christ had died exclusively for the elect, 'having neither had any intent or commandment . . . to make satisfaction for the sins of the whole world'. Man had lost free will by Adam's Fall, and thereafter whatever he did or did not do was by an 'unavoidable necessity'. The elect were unable to reject grace, the reprobate unable to accept it. Once having received grace, the elect could never fall 'finally, or totally, notwithstanding the most enormous sins they can commit'.

Heylyn maintained that Arminianism, far from being novel, was older than Calvinism. Even in the Netherlands Arminius was by no means the first who had protested against the more rigorous doctrines brought in by the French ministers who settled there under the protection of William of Nassau.[24] Arminius had spread the doctrines; but there was no more reason for calling them Arminianism than for calling the great western continent America. Really they were the views held by all the ancient Fathers, both Greek and Latin, until St Augustine's time, by the Jesuits and Franciscans in the Church of Rome (the Dominicans holding views comparable to those of Calvin) and by Melanchthon and all his followers in the Lutheran churches. Among the Reformed, the Zwinglian doctrines were the same as the Calvinists. Heylyn did not accept that St Augustine provided support for Calvin, even though harsh expressions had escaped his pen in his writings against Pelagius.

In the Church of England, the Melanchthonian views had been held by Hooper and Latimer in the reign of King Edward. For Heylyn these 'old English Protestants' understood the true Anglican doctrine, represented by the Thirty-nine Articles, the Homilies, and the first Liturgy of King Edward VI ('the key to the whole work').[25] These were complete before either Bucer or Martyr arrived in England, and 'I am sure that our first reformers were too old to be put to school unto either of them.'[26] In any case Bucer approved of the first Book of Homilies, and the second Prayer Book marked only liturgical, and not doctrinal, development. Even under Elizabeth, there was nothing in Nowell's Catechism 'which a true English Protestant or a Belgic Remonstrant may not easily grant, and yet preserve himself from falling into Calvinism in any of the points disputed'.[27]

The 'first great breach' in the true doctrine, after the returning exiles

[24] Heylyn instanced Isbrandius, Snecanus, Holmanus, Meinhardius and Wiggerius as 'professed anti-Calvinists before Arminius was ever even heard of'. *Historia Quinquarticularis,* I. 48. Cf. P. Heylyn, *Certamen Epistolare* (1659), 22–3.
[25] Heylyn, *Certamen Epistolare,* 164.
[26] Heylyn, *Historia Quinquarticularis,* II. 4–34; *Certamen Epistolare,* 162–3.
[27] Heylyn, *Historia Quinquarticularis,* III. 24–6.

('though otherwise men of good abilities in most parts of learning . . . so altered in their principles, as to points of doctrine, so disaffected to the government, to forms of worship here by law established, that they seemed not to be the same men at their coming home as they had been at their going hence'),[28] was the work of Foxe. Even Foxe, however, agreed that we should rest in God's general promise, and not cumber our heads with any further speculations. William Perkins's *Armilla Aurea* (1592), first in Latin then (*The Golden Chain*) in English, marked the arrival of the fully fledged supralapsarian doctrine derived from Beza, though set forth more methodically. It became 'wondrously acceptable amongst those of the Calvinian party', the Latin edition being reprinted fifteen times in the space of twenty years. The defence of Perkins, 'though otherwise a godly and learned man', 'hath given the church some more than necessary troubles . . . not without manifest scandal to it'.[29]

In his comments on the two universities, Heylyn was prepared substantially to concede Prynne's case that Calvinism was triumphant. He gives a graphic *tour d'horizon* of its hegemony at Oxford:

The face of that university was so much altered, that there was little to be seen in it of the Church of England, according to the principles and positions upon which it was at first reformed. All the Calvinian rigours in matters of Predestination, and the points depending thereupon, received as the established doctrines of the Church of England; the necessity of the one sacrament, the eminent dignity of the other, and the powerful efficacy of both unto man's salvation, not only disputed, but denied; the article of Christ's local descent into hell . . . totally disclaimed, because repugnant to the fancies of some foreign divines . . . Episcopacy maintained by halves, not as a distinct order from that of the presbyters, but only a degree above them, or perhaps not that, for fear of giving scandal to the churches of Calvin's platform; the Church of Rome inveighed against as the whore of Babylon . . . the Pope as publicly maintained to be Antichrist, or the Man of Sin, and this as positively and magisterially as if it had been one of the chief articles of the Christian faith . . . the visibility of the church . . . no otherwise maintained, than by looking for it in the scattered conventicles of the Berengarians in Italy, the Albigenses in France, the Hussites in Bohemia, and the Wycliffites among ourselves. Nor was there any greater care taken for the forms and orders of this church, than there had been for points of doctrine, the surplice so disused . . . and the divine service of the Church so slubbered over in most of the colleges . . . And in a word, the books of Calvin made the rule by which all men were to square their writings, his only word (like the *ipse dixit* of Pythagoras) admitted for the sole canon to which they were to frame and conform their judgements . . . so as it might have proved more safe for any man . . . to have been looked upon as an heathen or publican, than an anti-Calvinist.[30]

[28] Ibid., 48.
[29] Ibid., 62–5.
[30] P. Heylyn, *Cyprianus Anglicus, or, The History of the Life and Death of William [Laud]* (1668), 51–2.

All the more credit, therefore, to Harsnett, to Barrett and to Baro for defending at Cambridge the 'genuine doctrine of the church', which by 1595 'was beginning then to break through the clouds of Calvinism, wherewith it was obscured, and to shine forth again in its former lustre'.[31] At Oxford, Heylyn, confessed, he could find no evidence of anyone who had been prepared to oppose Calvinism publicly in the university until after the turn of the century. The best he could do was to speculate that in all probability 'some hundreds' had held anti-Calvinist opinions without making them known! Yet even if Buckeridge, Howson and Laud were the sole witnesses to the cause, they would still be sufficient to show that the church had not lost altogether possession of her primitive truths. *Apparent rari nantes in gurgite vasto.*[32]

Heylyn was not quite sure what to make of James I. For all his boasting of his 'king's craft', Heylyn thought that usually he allowed himself to be manipulated by others.[33] To his credit were his handling of the Millenary Petition ('no less tedious than it was impertinent') and the Hampton Court Conference. On the debit side was his approval of the Irish Articles of 1615. Worst of all were the hostile expressions the king had used against Vorstius (Prynne had made much of the reference to that 'enemy of God, Arminius'), which Heylyn had to explain by reference to James's education in Scotland, the influence of George Abbot and James Montagu, the 'transport of affection' he had for the Prince of Orange which clouded 'the clear light of his own understanding', but most probably to *raison d'état*, which made the unity of the Netherlands vital to his foreign policy.[34]

Notwithstanding all that, James's preferments, especially of Bancroft, Barlow, Neile, Buckeridge, Harsnett, Overall, Howson, Cary and Laud were encouragements 'by which . . . the anti-Calvinians or old English Protestants took heart, and more openly declared themselves'.[35] The rise of Dutch Arminianism helped the Church of England to recover the true interpretation of its Articles. In the universities the king's directions of 1616 to study the church Fathers were a great blow 'which most apparently conduced to the ruin of Calvinism'.[36] The outbreak of the Thirty Years War was the final turning point. The Calvinists — and none more than Abbot — saw it as their opportunity to dethrone the Pope and set up Calvin in his chair, if necessary by pawning the crown jewels. But the king now

---

[31] Heylyn, *Historia Quinquarticularis*, III. 87.
[32] Ibid., 92 (printed 74).
[33] P. Heylyn, *Observations on The History of the Reign of King Charles published by H.L. Esq.* (1656), 13–14.
[34] Ibid., 23–4.
[35] Heylyn, *Historia Quinquarticularis*, III. 103.
[36] Ibid., 106–7.

finally decided that the only way to suppress the Presbyterians was to let Richard Montagu loose on them, 'a man of mighty parts and undaunted spirit' who knew better than any how to 'discriminate the doctrines of the Church of England from those which were peculiar to the sect of Calvin'. The accession of Charles I and the supremacy of Laud completed the triumph of the 'anti-Calvinist party'.[37]

This book re-examines the story that Prynne and Heylyn tell. Underlying that re-examination is the conviction that church history is worth studying for its own sake, and not merely as a tool of political explanation. It attempts to distinguish theology from polemic, and to demonstrate that theological development had a momentum of its own, which was sometimes at odds with political circumstances and the interests of the court. It seeks to do justice to the continuing power in the Reformation period of what was considered authoritative in the past, made in response to perceptions of paramount concerns in the present. Above all, however, it reflects the conviction that the model of a theological dichotomy between 'Calvinism' and 'Arminianism' is simply inadequate for understanding either the overall development of doctrine in the Reformation period, or of personal allegiances within it. This is by no means to deny the existence of polarities, but rather to suggest that they were concurrent and evolutionary rather than abruptly linear, that there was development within a continuing spectrum, a development to which theologians of contrasting churchmanship contributed, in spite of their indulgence from time to time in the language of polemic against each other.

A spectrum, however, includes a middle area. Where Prynne denied one altogether, Heylyn's lay between popery and Puritanism.[38] Interestingly, neither made more than a passing reference to John Jewel. Prynne gives only two references to Hooker – slender enough evidence for assimilating him to his prevailing orthodoxy: yet Heylyn cited him not at all.[39] Neither Prynne nor Heylyn made use of the British 'Suffrage' to Dort, surely a better indication of what the delegates thought were the doctrines of the Church of England than the canons of that synod. Heylyn was only lukewarm in his references to John Overall.[40] He did

[37] Ibid., 110.
[38] Prynne and others complained that Heylyn's 'Puritans' included all the 'real Protestants'. Hence the charge, repeated by Baxter, that the Laudians redefined Puritanism to include conformists 'who in doctrine were not Arminian'. For Heylyn's reply, see *Certamen Epistolare*, 1–19.
[39] Heylyn was reduced to suggesting that Hooker's *Discourse on Justification* must have been either a product of his misinformed youth, or alternatively doctored after his death, *Historia Quinquarticularis*, III. 90.
[40] 'He did not Arminianize in all things, but I am sure he Calvinized in none', P. Heylyn, *Respondet Petrus* (1658), 175. In the *Historia Quinquarticularis* Heylyn compared the 'invincible constancy of Barrett' – Heylyn denied that he had recanted – with the 'slender opposition' of Overall, III. 87.

not quote the views of Lancelot Andrewes. Even the Richard Montagu of the *New Gagg* was too hesitant to serve his purpose.[41] This book argues that protestations of moderation should not invariably be dismissed as mere rhetoric.[42] Perhaps there was a middle ground that neither Prynne nor Heylyn could see.

[41] Ibid., II, 85–6, on Montagu's admission in the *New Gagg* that the Church of England had left the doctrine of perseverance 'undecided'.

[42] P. Lake, 'Calvinism and the English Church, 1570–1635', *Past and Present* 114 (1987), 69. Cf. P. White, 'The *Via Media* in the Early Stuart Church', in K. Fincham (ed.), *The English Church under the Early Stuarts* (forthcoming).

2 The theology of predestination: Beza and Arminius

Beza's doctrine of predestination

Romanist polemic, then, condemned Protestants for making God the author of sin. Protestants in their turn accused not only papists, but any of their own number whose sails they thought too heavily trimmed to the winds of that polemic, of Pelagianism. There would be less reason to rake over the embers of their quarrels if fewer historians, at any rate of the English Church, did not accept at least the Protestant side of that polemic. The Arminians are accordingly said to have taught 'the free-will of all men to win salvation'; and that they denied the doctrine of predestination has become at any rate an undergraduate orthodoxy. Predestination itself is assumed to be, if not the invention of John Calvin, at any rate the defining characteristic of Calvinism. It is therefore necessary to repeat that all parties to the theological debate accepted the doctrine of predestination: it was after all integral to both the Old and New Testaments, and fundamental to the teaching of St Paul. Arminianism was nothing if not a doctrine of predestination. An attempt will be made to explain the theological issues at stake, first by examining the theology of Theodore Beza. Beza's teaching became normative for late sixteenth-century Calvinists, and Arminianism was conceived as a direct response to Beza's doctrine.

Beza's teaching on predestination is associated especially with his *Tabula praedestinationis* of 1555,[1] the book which contained his influential diagram of the order of predestination, later adapted by William Perkins (see figure 1). According to that work, predestination was the *summa totius Christianismi*. The diagram was revised in 1582, the year in which Beza published his *De praedestinationis doctrina*, another work in which

---

[1] The *Tabula* is printed in Theodore Beza, *Tractationes Theologicae* (3 vols., Geneva, 1570–82), I.170ff. The first English version, translated by William Whittingham, appeared in 1575 [?] as *A Brief Declaration of the chief points of Christian Religion, Set forth in a Table*. In spite of the title, it lacks the table. Another version, which includes the table, appeared in 1576 under the title *The Treasure of Truth, touching the groundwork of man his salvation . . . with a brief summe of the comfortable doctrine of God his providence, comprised in 38 short Aphorisms, written in Latin by Theodore Beza, and newly turned into English by John Stockwood.*

13

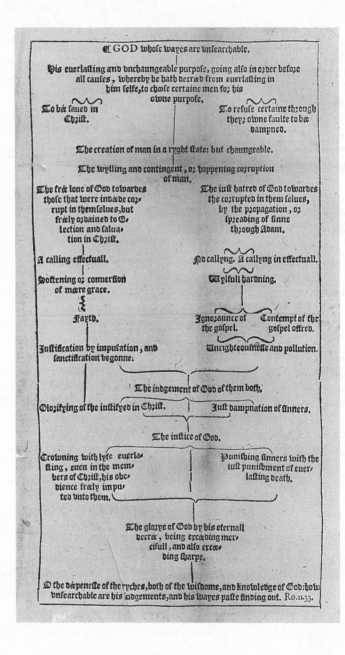

Figure 1   Beza's table of predestination, taken from *The Treasure of Truth* (STC 2049) 1576

predestination was treated as a fundamental doctrine. The lectures on Romans ix, also published in 1582, reflect the same emphasis. In other works, and especially in his Sermons, predestination was not given the same prominence, and it has been argued that neither in his ecclesiology nor in his eucharistic doctrine[2] is it the organizing principle or central dogma. There was nevertheless an ambivalence within Beza's own thought. In a letter to Calvin of 1555 he argued that all events were subordinated to the divine purpose of predestination; elsewhere the divine decree was stated to be the basis and cause of all redemptive history, and in saying that Scripture, when dealing with that history, ascends beyond the level of Christ to that eternal purpose which God has determined only in Himself, Beza himself is plainly asserting that the doctrine is an organizing principle. It may of course be true that Beza was mistaken about the importance of predestination in his own theology,[3] but that insight would hardly have commended itself to his followers in the sixteenth or seventeenth century.

Beza believed that predestination should be preached.[4] It was true that some hearers might use the doctrine as an excuse for a lax and immoral life, but that had always been a danger. Nor should the topic of reprobation be passed over in silence: there were benefits in preaching it for the elect, who would thereby hold God in greater fear and awe, and in learning that it is not in the power of every man to repent, would become more receptive to the special gift of faith. Beza conceded that the preacher should be careful not to go beyond the limits of Scripture, and that he must be careful to set forth the doctrine in a spirit of edification. Nevertheless, his own discussions, not only in the *Tabula* and other polemical works, but also in the annotations he added to his Latin translation of the New Testament published in 1556, reflect a desire to systematize and rationalize biblical texts into an intellectually coherent defence of the doctrine. To provide that defence with a visual aid in the form of the *Tabula* was indirectly to suggest that man's reason was indeed capable of apprehending these divine mysteries.

Beza's doctrine started from Romans ix.

So then he hath mercy on whom he will, and whom he will he hardeneth. Thou wilt say then unto me, Why doth he still find fault? For who withstandeth his will? Nay but, O man, who art thou that repliest against God? Shall the thing formed say to him that formed it, Why didst thou make me thus? Or hath not the potter a right over the clay, from the same lump to make one part a vessel unto honour, and another unto dishonour?[5]

[2] J. S. Bray, *Theodore Beza's Doctrine of Predestination* (Nieuwkoop, 1975), 84.
[3] As ibid. suggests.
[4] Ibid., 81.
[5] Romans ix, 18–21.

That 'lump' (*massa*) referred to mankind conceived as not yet created, much less fallen (*homo creabilis et labilis*). Beza's doctrine was not merely what was later called supralapsarian; it is creabilitarian.[6] It is important to be clear what is at stake. Supralapsarianism is often wrongly defined as the doctrine that the decree of predestination preceded the Fall of Adam; sublapsarianism even more wrongly as the doctrine that the decree of predestination came after the Fall.[7] That misses the point of the theological debate. Predestination was agreed to be 'before the foundation of the world' (Eph. i, 4). No competent theologian could suggest that the eternal decrees were the improvisation of a God confronted unexpectedly by the Fall! The point at issue is the conceptual order of the decrees, considered as antecedent to the fact of creation; it is not about succession in time. Supralapsarianism is correctly defined as the doctrine that the decree to predestinate was logically prior to the decree to permit the Fall; creabilitarianism is the doctrine that the decree to predestinate is logically prior even to the decree to create. Another way of expressing the difference is to say that for sublapsarians man as the object of predestination was conceived *in the divine mind* as both created and fallen. The response of most readers will probably be that to raise these questions is to seek to search into God's secrets. Beza did not agree. He was clear ('I do say and plainly avouch') that in using the similitude of the potter, Paul

mounteth up to the said sovereign ordinance whereunto even the creation of mankind is submitted in order of causes, and therefore much less doth the Apostle put the foreseen corruption of mankind before it.[8]

The decree of predestination thus conceived was double, absolute and unconditional:

God, whose judgments no man can comprehend, whose ways cannot be found out, and whose will ought to stop all men's mouths, according to the determinate and unchangeable purpose of his will, by the virtue whereof all things were made, yea even those things which are evil and execrable (not in that they be wrought by his divine counsel, but forasmuch as they proceed from the prince of the air,

---

[6] The words 'supralapsarian', 'infralapsarian' and 'sublapsarian' began to be used at about the time of the Synod of Dort. The controversy as Arminius expressed it was whether man as object of predestination was *creabilis* but *labilis* (not yet created but liable to fall), *creatus* and *labilis* (as having been created and liable to fall), or *creatus* and *lapsus* (as both created and fallen). Different sequences of divine decrees are implied in these distinctions.

[7] Cf., e.g., F. L. Cross and E. A. Livingstone (eds.), *The Oxford Dictionary of the Christian Church*, sub voce.

[8] Theodore Beza, *A Book of Christian Questions and Answers . . . translated into English by Arthur Golding* (1574), f. 84ᵛ. Beza goes on to say that 'if the lump betokened men corrupted, then they were vessels of dishonour already, and the potter should not be said to make them'.

and that spirit which worketh in the children of disobedience) hath determined from before all beginning with himself to create all things in their time, for his glory, and namely men: whom he hath made after two sorts, clean contrary one to the other. Whereof he maketh the one sort (which it pleased him to choose by his secret will and purpose) partakers of his glory through his mercy, and these we call, according to the word of God, the vessels of honour, the elect, the children of promise, and predestined to salvation: and the others, whom likewise it pleased him to ordain to damnation (that he might show forth his wrath and power, to be glorified also in them) we do call vessels of dishonour and wrath, the reprobate and cast off from all good works.[9]

Beza specifically denies that reprobation is for sin:

Likewise when mention is made of the damnation of the reprobate, although the whole fault thereof be in themselves: yet notwithstanding sometimes when need requireth the Scripture to make more manifest by this comparison the great power of God, his patience and the riches of his glory towards the vessels of mercy leadeth us into this high secret which by order is the first cause of damnation, of the which secret no other cause is known to men, but only his just will, which we must with all reverence obey, as coming from him who is only just, and cannot by any means, nor of any man, in any sort be comprehended.[10]

In defending himself against critics of the harshness of this doctrine, Beza insisted that God must have a goal for His creation. That goal had to be certain and independent of the will of man. But there was an unresolved antinomy in his thinking which is reflected in the phrase 'just and incomprehensible'. The justice of God was in the last resort dependent on the assertion that 'the will of God is the only rule of righteousness'.[11] Beza nevertheless attempted to argue it by pointing to the mercy of God in saving the elect, whose sins were punished in the person of His Son. The damned have no just cause for complaint that God has shown mercy on some. It was wrong to say that God hated the reprobate: He hated sin. Certainly, no one is damned except God ordain him to damnation, but equally no one is damned except those who are found to have in themselves just causes of damnation. It was at this point that Beza had recourse to the incomprehensibility of the divine justice. It was impossible for the human reason to penetrate the mystery of the divine decree.

As has been pointed out,[12] the very inconsistency between Beza's attack on speculation and his own inclination to engage in it provides us with a key to an important aspect of his thought. He drew a sharp dis-

[9] I have here as elsewhere used Whittingham's translation. *A Brief Declaration,* sig. A3ᵛ translating Beza, *Tractationes,* I. 171.

[10] Ibid., sig. Avʳ, translating the *Tractationes,* I. 176.

[11] Theodore Beza, *Quaestionum et responsionum Christianarum libellus,* 5th edn (2 vols., Geneva, 1577, 76), I. 121.

[12] Bray, *Beza's Doctrine of Predestination,* 89–91.

tinction between the decrees of predestination and the execution of those decrees. It has already been seen in his insistence that the first cause of the damnation of the reprobate was 'the secret decree of God'. It is the will of God that this secret remains hidden from us. The hatred of Esau (Rom. ix, 13) is not to be traced to his own sin, but to the will of God: human reason says that it is undeserved.[13] At the same time, God's word reveals the secondary causes of reprobation: corruption, lack of faith, and sin. 'For between the ordinance and its execution, sin intervened, and what is more appropriate than that God should punish sin?'[14] The distinction thus made by Beza in developing Calvin's contrast between the secret and the revealed will of God was to have enormous influence. The body of the *Tabula* was devoted to the explication of the secondary causes of predestination. It is understandable that in the works of his Protestant scholastic followers 'there are practically no acknowledgements of the difficulty of probing the divine mind'.[15]

A similar dualism is evident in Beza's discussion of the cause of election.

In similar fashion, when we describe the causes of salvation of the elect, we must draw a distinction between the decree of election itself, which God has determined in himself, and the execution of election which has been appointed in Christ. The decree goes before all the things that follow upon it.[16]

Reason can show us nothing concerning the *decree* of election. Beza specifically denied that it was founded 'as some say, because God did foresee their faith or good works'. It is part of 'that eternal purpose which God hath determined only in himself'. In such contexts Beza emphasizes the inscrutability of the will of God. Scripture tells us only of 'second causes', those which have to do with the execution of the decree, among which he included not merely faith and calling by the Gospel, but even Christ himself, 'in whom notwithstanding we are as our head elected and adopted'.[17] In other places Beza employed a scholastic analysis into efficient, material, formal or instrumental and final causes of salvation. He can speak of the efficient cause as the good pleasure, or free mercy of God. The material cause is invariably stated to be Christ. The instrumental cause is variously faith, the preaching of the Gospel, or the imputation of Christ's righteousness. The final cause is usually said to be the glory of God the Father.[18] Underlying all the formulations there are tensions, not merely between reason and revelation,[19] but of course also in the Pauline epistles to which much of Beza's exposition relates.

[13] Whittingham, *A Brief Declaration*, sig. A5^r, translating the *Tractationes*, I. 176.
[14] Beza, *Quaestiones*, I. 125.
[15] B. Armstrong, *Calvinism and the Amyraut Heresy* (Madison, 1969), 194.
[16] Beza, *Tractationes*, I. 178.
[17] Whittingham, *A Brief Declaration*, sig. A4^v, translating the *Tractationes*, 175.
[18] Bray, *Beza's Doctrine of Predestination*, 52.
[19] Ibid., 94.

The execution of the decrees is reflected in the historical process. Creation was the first stage in that process, a necessary event in order that the elective decree might be fulfilled. Man was not created a sinner, but in God's own image,[20]

to wit, in innocency, purity and holiness, who notwithstanding, without constraint of any, neither yet forced by any necessity . . . willingly and of his own accord rebelled against God, binding by this means the whole nature of man to sin. Yet we must confess that this Fall came not by any chance or fortune seeing his providence doth stretch forth even to the smallest things, neither can we say that anything doth happen that God knoweth not, or careth not for neither yet by any bare or idle permission or sufferance, for seeing he has appointed the end, it is necessary also that he should appoint the causes, unless we affirm with the wicked Manichees that this end happeneth at all adventures, or by means or causes ordained by some other God. Furthermore we cannot think that anything happeneth contrary to God's will, except we deny blasphemously that he is omnipotent and almighty.

At no point is the tension in Beza's theology more acute. God was the author of all things, but He is not the author of sin. Adam's sin was necessary, but at the same time the result of his own will.

We conclude therefore that this fall of Adam did so proceed out of the motion of his will that notwithstanding it happened not without the will of God, whom it pleaseth by a marvellous and incomprehensible meane, that the thing he doth not allow (forasmuch as it is sin) should not happen without his will . . .[21]

Beza could even claim that it 'was good that sin and death should enter into the world'[22] on the grounds that it was a necessary step before the benefits of the work of Christ. In that sense Adam's Fall was 'the best and the most profitable thing that could be done for us'.[23]

Again Beza was obliged to have recourse to the difference between the decree of reprobation and the execution of that decree. It enabled him to claim that the causes of reprobation were 'both necessary and voluntary'.[24] While, however, in election the secondary causes of the execution of the decree could be traced back to the first cause (election was the cause of faith), the same could not be said of reprobation, where the secondary causes arise from man himself, and the decree is executed by allowing man to do that which he wills. It is a significant lack of parallelism.[25] The sin of Adam has infected all men in such a way that they are driven by their will to sin, 'producing bad fruit in as many as God decides to leave in

---

[20] Whittingham, *A Brief Declaration*, sig. A7ᵛ–A8ʳ, translating the *Tractationes*, I. 177–8.
[21] Beza, *Tractationes*, I. 179.
[22] Beza, *Quaestiones*, I. 103–7.
[23] Ibid.
[24] Beza, *Tractationes*, I. 176.
[25] Bray, *Beza's Doctrine of Predestination*, 116–17.

their own lust in order that they may be the cause of their own damnation'.[26] They sin because God leaves them to their own devices and does not give them the faith that He gives to the elect. Yet the execution of reprobation remains under the divine control. In some, 'God executes just wrath as soon as they are born.'[27] For the rest, 'he observes two ways clean contrary the one to the other'. Some are not granted even the favour of hearing the Gospel, and their ignorance 'is the just punishment of that corruption wherein they are born'. The remainder hear the Gospel, but their fall is 'more terrible' in that they 'cannot believe, because it is not given unto them'. They are called, but because they are not among the elect, they do not hear. Worst of all is the plight of those whom God allows to hear the Gospel with that 'general faith whereby the Devils believe and tremble'. They are allowed to 'climb a degree higher, that their fall might be more grievous'. They receive 'some grace', and even 'seem to have received the seed', sometimes 'even shewing the way of salvation to others', but because the spirit of adoption is not given them, they 'return to their vomit, and fall away from the faith, are plucked up by the roots to be cast into the fire'.[28] In defending himself against the charge that his view effectively denied free will Beza pointed out that freedom does not demand a real choice between good and evil, for if it did God, who cannot choose evil, would not be free. Man sins by necessity, but not by compulsion.[29]

Only the elect experience effectual calling. Having said that the will of man is free, but incapable of choosing the good, Beza is consistent in denying that the Holy Spirit, as the effecter of faith, restores free will so that man may choose Christ.[30] Faith, which Beza distinguishes from intellectual assent, and defines as 'a certain persuasion and assurance that every true Christian man ought to have that God the father loves him for the sake of his son Jesus Christ',[31] is wholly a gift of grace, whereby the Holy Spirit changes men's 'hard hearts of stone into soft hearts of flesh, draws them, teaches them, enlightens them, opens their senses, their hearts, their ears and their understanding'.[32] The Spirit continues to work in the elect by increasing their faith and enabling them to persevere. In that sense Beza can speak of faith as the cause of both justification and sanctification. It is a faith which is sealed in baptism and the Eucharist.

Faith is a sure sign of election. Beza argues that it is possible to have

[26] Ibid. Beza. *Tractationes*, I. 179; *Quaestiones*, I. 120.
[27] Whittingham, *A Brief Declaration*, sig. Bvi^r, translating the *Tractationes*, I. 190.
[28] Ibid., sig. Bvi^v, translating the *Tractationes*, I. 192–3.
[29] Bray, *Beza's Doctrine of Predestination*, 117.
[30] Ibid., 104.
[31] Ibid., 105.
[32] Ibid., 104–5; Beza, *Tractationes*, I. 185.

assurance of salvation − to be as certain of it as if one 'had heard from God's own mouth'.[33] True faith (Beza contrasts it with temporary faith) is known not from the eternal decree but from its secondary effects. The testimony that one is justified and sanctified is therefore twofold: good works and the witness of the Spirit. 'One discovers in Beza's works a bald, almost brutal, demand for good works.'[34] The witness of the Spirit is shown in a strong desire to please God and to bring forth fruits pleasing to Him.

Beza did not, however, claim that the elect were without sin. The elect would certainly fall into sin, but when they did so the Spirit would work in them a revulsion against it. Beza appealed to the words of St Paul to illustrate the conflict between the desire to do good and the will to do evil which characterizes the life of the believer. That conflict is a sign of his adoption. The bewailing of our sins, the hatred of self, the desire to amend and the confidence to call upon God: all these come from grace.[35]

Beza acknowledged, therefore, that the believer's good works might be few and the testimony of the Spirit within him might be weak. In seeking at such times to buttress his assurance he should turn to whichever is the stronger; if both are lacking, he should remember that Christ does not expect a perfect faith but only a true faith. But how to distinguish a weak but true faith from a strong but temporary one? It is another point of tension that marks his theology and that of his followers. To the extent that his theology of assurance was based upon works, it was less appropriate for him to have recourse to Calvin's emphasis that those seeking certainty must turn their gaze to Christ. Instead Beza recommended that believers should remember that saints had experienced periods of barrenness in their lives. They should follow the example of David and meditate on godly fruit of early periods of their lives and remember that the divine decree does not change: God is immutable. No doubt as a pastoral recourse that response was helpful, but in making it Beza was in danger of forsaking the secondary causes on which he has stressed the believer should concentrate for an apprehension of the divine decree which he has said is hidden. The basic question, how to distinguish true from temporary faith, remained unanswered.[36]

Another strength from which the godly might gain encouragement in time of adversity was, according to Beza, the preaching of the doctrine of reprobation. It was a spur to godliness and a reminder of the sovereignty

[33] Bray, *Beza's Doctrine of Predestination*, 107; Beza, *Tractationes*, I. 200.

[34] Bray, *Beza's Doctrine of Predestination*, 108; Beza, *Tractationes*, I. 186, 188.

[35] Bray, *Beza's Doctrine of Predestination*, 109; Beza, *Tractationes*, I. 200. Beza takes Romans vii to refer to man as regenerate. For Arminius' interpretation, see below, p. 22–3, and Carl Bangs, *Arminius: A Study in the Dutch Reformation* (Nashville, 1971), 140–9.

[36] Bray, *Beza's Doctrine of Predestination*, 110.

of God over all things.[37] Beza agreed with Calvin that one could never be certain who belonged to the ranks of the reprobate. In this way he was able to rebut the charge that the preaching of the doctrine might induce despair, and he admitted that there was therefore a sense in which the Gospel should be preached to all.[38] But Beza denied that Christ had died for all men. Only the elect were able to partake of the benefits of His death, and Beza was firm in asserting a limited atonement. Given that the decree to send Christ was logically subordinate to the decree to predestinate, no other conclusion was possible. Christ had been sent to redeem the elect. Under the influence of that logic, the doctrine of a limited atonement became a key component in the theology of those who looked to Beza as the guardian of Calvinist orthodoxy.[39]

The theology of Arminius

James Arminius

Opposition to the Calvinist doctrine of predestination as taught by Beza is above all associated with James Arminius.[40] After graduating at Leiden University, Arminius studied under Beza at the Geneva Academy, and was personally recommended by him to the city of Amsterdam.[41] Predestination was starting to become an issue by the time Arminius became a minister there in 1587. The war against Spain had sharpened differences already evident between the Protestantism of the northern Netherlands, which was biblical, eirenic and conservative, and the strongly confessional, dogmatic high Calvinism of the south.[42] Arminius first drew attention to himself in 1591, by preaching that in Romans vii St Paul was talking of man before he is regenerated. That touched Calvinist orthodoxy at a tender point. Another of the Amsterdam ministers, Peter Plancius, accused him of Pelagianism, and of deviating from the Belgic

[37] Ibid., 113; Beza, *Tractationes*, I. 204.
[38] Bray, *Beza's Doctrine of Predestination*, 104; Beza, *Quaestiones*, I. 116–17.
[39] Bray, *Beza's Doctrine of Predestination* 111–12; Armstrong, *Calvinism and the Amyraut Heresy*, 137–8.
[40] 'Arminius' is the Latinized form of the Dutch 'Hermanns' (or 'Hermanson'). Arminius was the son of a cutler of Oudewater in south Holland.
[41] John Guthrie, *The Life of James Arminius, translated from the Latin of Caspar Brandt* (1854), 23–4.
[42] Bangs, *Arminius*, 51–4; and for a broader view of tensions in the Dutch Church, see Alastair Duke, 'The Ambivalent Face of Calvinism in the Netherlands, 1561–1618', in Menna Prestwich (ed.), *International Calvinism 1541–1715* (Oxford, 1985) and W, Nijenhuis, 'Variants within Dutch Calvinism in the Sixteenth Century', *Acta Historiae Neerlandicae* 12 (1979).

Confession[43] and Heidelberg Catechism.[44] The quarrel was patched up
after Plancius had been rebuked for rash accusations and Arminius had
promised not to broach 'new doctrines'.[45] Doctrinal controversy revived
in 1593 when Arminius preached on Romans ix. Plancius again made
charges. The consistory finally accepted Arminius' explanations, and urged
peace until a general synod should determine the proper interpretation
of the disputed articles. It is from 1593 that Arminius was associated with
dissent from the Bezan doctrine of predestination, and pressure for a revision of the Belgic Confession.[46]

In 1602, Arminius was invited to become a professor of theology at
Leiden. One of the existing professors, Francis Gomarus, pointed to his
disputes on the subject of predestination, and tried to block the appointment. He failed, but Arminius' career at Leiden was punctuated by controversy. In 1604, Gomarus complained that he was trespassing on his
sole right to expound the New Testament. Later in the same year Arminius
held a public disputation on predestination; Gomarus responded with an
unscheduled disputation of his own on the ground that error was abroad,
and that truth must be defended.[47] In 1605 the classis of Dordrecht complained of the controversies in the university and church at Leiden. Plancius continued his attacks on Arminius from Amsterdam. In 1607 it was
said that Arminius had received the offer of a large sum of money from
the Pope, and that he recommended Jesuit writings while vilifying those
of Calvin and Beza; in the following year he was accused of saying that

---

[43] The Belgic Confession, or *Confession de Foi des Eglises Réformées Wallonnes et
Flamandes*, was drawn up by Guido de Brès on the basis of the Gallican Confession of
1559 and printed in 1561. It was translated into Dutch, when the Synod of Antwerp in
1566 instructed Junius to revise it; the revised version was apparently sent to Geneva for
approval. A. Cochrane, *Reformed Confessions of the Sixteenth Century* (1966), 186.

[44] The Heidelberg Catechism was compiled for the Church of the Palatinate by Ursinus
and Olevian in 1563 and subsequently adopted by the Dutch Church.

[45] Bangs, *Arminius*, 147.

[46] Although Arminius denied that either the 14th or the 16th Article of the Belgic Confession was consistent with Beza's doctrine, and quoted Article XVI in support of his own
doctrine, he objected to the marginal notes in the Geneva version. In the 14th Article,
he objected to the words 'Nothing is done without God's ordination' on the grounds that
they might be construed to imply that God was the author of sin. He favoured a revision
which stated the fundamentals of doctrine as briefly as possible; all explanations, so often
a source of controversy, should be omitted. *Harmonia Confessionum Fidei Orthodoxarum, et Reformatarum Ecclesiarum* (Geneva, 1581), 96. See also Guthrie, *Life of
Arminius*, 58–61; Bangs, *Arminius*, 223–4.
Arminius argued that if the Heidelberg Catechism was regarded as a 'formula of concord' between the Reformed Churches, then it too should be 'subject to examination';
if not, then provided that subscription to it was not required and a reasonable liberty
of interpretation allowed in explanation of it, it could be left as it stood. 'Declaration
of the Sentiments of Arminius . . . before the States of Holland', in James Arminius,
Works, tr. and ed. J. and W. Nichols (3 vols., 1825–75), I. 558–9, 637–66.

[47] Bangs, *Arminius*, 263.

the Pope was a member of the body of Christ, and that the fourth book of Bellarmine was irrefutable.[48] Political factors played their part. Pressures were mounting early in the seventeenth century for a settlement of the war with Spain, especially in Holland, the province which bore the major financial burden of the war. Predestination became not only the subject matter of a theological debate, but the language in which a staunchly Calvinist war party, militantly anti-Catholic and strongly consistorial in discipline, confronted a dogmatically tolerant, Erastian peace party which espoused 'Arminianism'.[49] There was pressure for a National Synod to settle the disputes, and lobbying for foreign support by both sides.

Arminius provided his own diagnosis of the disputes in the Netherlands, and his suggestions as to how they should be healed, in an address of February 1606. He rejected the prohibition of controversy. It was folly to attempt to erect a superstructure of religious concord on a foundation of 'stupid ignorance'.[50] He rejected the papist answers of appeal to the authority of the church, of the Fathers (an endless, time-consuming and fruitless excursion which would eventually lead to the acceptance of the authority of the Pope) or of former councils. The only acceptable remedy was a synod of the dissenting parties, with free and frank discussion of differences, by delegates chosen for their spirituality, ability and integrity. His natural idealism and optimism, his confidence in the appeal to reason and good-will, are apparent. He was confident that agreement could be reached: if it could not, differences of opinion should be tolerated without polemic, and without compulsion. In the last resort, this was a plea for toleration, or in the language of the day, *libertas prophetandi*.[51] It was fundamentally out of tune with the urge towards increasing doctrinal definition, said little for Arminius' grasp of realities, and became another source of controversy. By the time Arminius died, in 1609, there was no prospect whatever of the sort of National Synod he wanted. When one eventually did meet, a decade later, at Dordrecht, it ended with the condemnation of the doctrines he was supposed to have held, the dismissal of the ministers who had followed him, and the execution of their political leader, Oldenbarnevelt.

---

[48] Guthrie, *Life of Arminius*, 234–5, 262–65. The majority of the population of Holland were still Catholic. Duke, 'Ambivalent Face of Calvinism', 109–10.

[49] Bangs, *Arminius*, 273–4.

[50] 'On Reconciling Religious Dissent Among Christians', in Arminius, *Works*, I. 401.

[51] The phrase *libertas prophetandi* was widely used to signify the right to interpret and expound Scripture at private meetings and in sermons. It was justified by reference to 1 Cor. xii, 9–10; xiv, 2–6; 1 Thess. v, 19–20 etc. The prophesyings for refusing to suppress which Grindal was suspended from his archiepiscopal functions by Queen Elizabeth in 1577 were justified by reference to the same texts, and in England it was the Puritans who asserted *libertas prophetandi* against an unsympathetic hierarchy.

Objections to Bezan predestination

If it is fair to point to the highly rationalistic confidence of Protestant scholasticism as developed by Beza and his followers, it must be admitted that Arminius' confidence in the capacity of human reason exceeded even that of Beza. Perhaps, indeed, the fundamental difference between them is that Arminius believed that the human reason must be able to justify the ways of God to man. He refused to take refuge in the inscrutability of God; if a doctrine was incomprehensible, it ought to be repudiated. Arminius complained that Beza's doctrine was both logically and morally incomprehensible: logically because it made the object of predestination a nonentity;[52] morally because if the decree to save some men and damn others precedes all others, then the decree of creation and the decree concerning the Fall (however formulated) become means to the fulfilment of the prior decree, and God must be the author of sin. Arminius rejected all Calvin and Beza's attempts to avoid that implication.

He took first the argument that God ordains the 'act', but not the 'criminality in the act'. The mercy and the justice which are integral to the divine decrees of election and reprobation require, said Arminius, not merely the bare act but the sin in the act, for mercy means *pardon* and justice means *punishment*. Both presuppose *sin*.[53] Another device was to distinguish between necessity and compulsion. Compulsion was a kind of necessity, Arminius answered. The same act cannot be both necessary and contingent. Similarly with the distinction between the decree and the execution of the decree. 'I answer, that the execution following upon sin does not excuse from blame Him who by His own decree ordained that sin should be committed, which He might afterwards punish.'[54]

Beza had refused to explain the Fall by distinguishing between what God permits and what He desires, for fear of violating divine omnipotence. Similarly, he had held that to subordinate the decree of predestination to the decree to permit the Fall was to make the judgments of God depend upon contingents. Arminius had a different starting point. Underlying his own explanation of the Fall was the basic premiss that the nature of God circumscribes His acts. God cannot lie, for His nature is truthful; God cannot commit injustice, for His nature is just. 'God can do many things by His absolute power which He cannot do by right.'[55] On the one hand, by requiring a certain action, God obliges Himself to provide the

---

[52] 'Examination of The Theses of Dr. F. Gomarus Respecting Predestination', in Arminius, *Works*, III, 530, 539.
[53] 'Friendly Conference with Dr F. Junius', in Arminius, *Works*, III, 80.
[54] Ibid., 81–2.
[55] Ibid., 85.

power and strength without which that action cannot be performed.[56] On the other hand, by granting man liberty, God obliges Himself not to infringe that liberty, even if the effect is to permit the Fall. 'For the cause why God permits sin is to be taken not merely from the consequent, but also from the antecedent. *From the antecedent*, because God so constituted man that he should possess a free will, and so might be able either to render obedience, or to recoil from it, according to the liberty of His will: which appointment of His own God could not rescind, on account of His own immutability, as Tertullian beautifully explains . . . *From the consequent*, because He saw that He could from the occasion of sin demonstrate the glory of his own grace and justice.'[57] Only along such lines can 'permission' of the Fall be explained without making it the efficient cause of sin. Arminius described it as 'a middle act between willing and not willing'. In the sense that God has foreknowledge of it, He may be said to will it. Nevertheless, the Fall can be called a 'happy fault' only by what Arminius describes as a 'catechrestical hyperbole; which, though it may find a place in declamations, panegyrical orations, and ornamental flourishes, is to be removed proportionately far from a solid disquisition on the truth'.[58]

The same insistence that God must be consistent with His own moral nature determined Arminius' criticism of Beza's account of election and reprobation. While agreeing that the end of predestination is God's glory, he insisted that predestination must have foreknowledge of sin, of Christ and of reconciliation. 'If the act of predestination is a preparation of the forgiveness of sins, or of the punishment of the same, then it is certain that predestination can have no place except in reference to sinners.'[59] Mercy means the grace whereby the elect are granted remission of their sins. Justice is represented by the punishment of those who reject the grace offered, whereby they are left in their wickedness.

Arminius did not deny reprobation from eternity, the right of God to consign sinners to eternal punishment, or even the fact that the elect are few.[60] Where he disagreed with Beza was firstly with the contention that the object of reprobation was man *creabilis* and *labilis* — man conceived in the divine mind as not yet created, much less fallen.[61] 'What is not capable of life and death, cannot be destined to death.' God cannot will

[56] 'Modest Examination of Dr Perkins's Pamphlet', in Arminius, *Works*, III. 283–4.
[57] Ibid., 284–5. The scholastic distinction between the 'necessity of the consequent' and the 'necessity of the consequence' was here invoked to defend the possibility of divine foreknowledge of contingents. Cf. ibid., 386–7 and 'Examination of The Theses of Dr F. Gomarus', 552–3. Gomarus eventually conceded the possibility.
[58] Arminius, *Works*, III. 287.
[59] Ibid., 281.
[60] Ibid., 302, 313, 351.
[61] 'Examination of The Theses of Dr. F. Gomarus', ibid., III. 588.

the impossible. Secondly, God's first action with regard to any object cannot be its condemnation to eternal misery. Because He is the highest good, His first action towards any object must be the communication of good. (How easy, he interjected, to lapse into Manicheism, when anyone is incautiously avoiding Pelagianism.) Thirdly, reprobation is separation from God; but this separation is effected by sin. Beza's attempt to accommodate his doctrine to the fact of sin by distinguishing between the decree and the execution of the decree was 'most futile'. If God does not damn any except a sinner, then 'it is necessary for Him to have appointed to damn none except a sinner; otherwise the decree will be changed'.[62]

Beza and his followers referred reprobation to the divine good pleasure ($\epsilon\dot{\upsilon}\delta o\kappa\dot{\iota}\alpha$). Arminius objected that every good pleasure of God towards man is in Jesus Christ. Scripture teaches that it is the 'good pleasure' of God that everyone who sees the Son, and believes on Him, should have eternal life.[63] Even worse, Beza had suggested that the reprobate are admonished in order to render them inexcusable, because God has determined by the divine decree not to grant them penitence and faith, and also because that is the *intention* of the divine admonition, and God is never frustrated in His end. Arminius rejected both explanations. Scripture shows plainly that the decree to exhort men to faith and repentance precedes the decree not to grant repentance and faith, the former belonging to the antecedent will of God, the latter to the consequent will.[64] Secondly, the explanation makes God guilty of hypocrisy by exhorting to repentance and faith those on whom He has decreed not to bestow either. The fact that preachers do not know who is elect and who reprobate made no difference to the argument.[65] Thirdly, Scripture shows plainly that God is often frustrated in His end.[66] The proclamation of the Gospel, and the faith, repentance and obedience which God requires of those to whom it is preached are all ends not always attained. Arminius again invoked the distinction between the antecedent will of God, which is often frustrated, and the consequent will, which is always attained.[67]

Another objection to both Bezan (and Thomist) accounts of reprobation was that they did not explain why, if it is necessary for God to punish sin, it is not necessary for Him to punish all sinners. In placing the decree to reprobate some men before the decree to send Christ as

---

[62] Ibid., 592.
[63] 'Modest Examination of Dr Perkins's Pamphlet', in Arminius, *Works*, III. 321.
[64] Ibid., 312, where Arminius cites Acts xxviii, 26, 27; Ps. lxxxi, 11, 12; Luke vii, 30; Acts xiii, 46; Rom. ix, 32 and 1 Pet. ii, 7, 8 in support of this crucial contention.
[65] Ibid., 313.
[66] Ibid., 317.
[67] Ibid., 318.

Mediator of the elect, they are *either* tied to conceding that for some the divine justice requires both the death of Christ and the eternal punishment of the sinner, *or* they are saying that Christ died only for the elect. Beza and his followers drew the latter conclusion. Arminius rejected it. Scripture is plain and says in simple language that Christ died for all, even for those who perish.[68] He granted that the redemption is not effectual for all. That is because sin is not actually remitted except to those who believe in Christ. Any other conclusion makes the command to believe and the promise of remission of sins, as applied to the reprobate, a command to believe a lie, for refusal to obey which they are then convicted on the grounds of their unbelief and stubbornness.

The contention that the death of Christ was for all took Arminius back to the scriptural evidence for the doctrine of predestination. All the New Testament passages, he asserted, reinforced his contention that predestination is 'in Christ.' Ephesians i, for example, demonstrates that the predestination of which the Scriptures teach is of men as they are sinners, made in Christ, and to spiritual blessings which to some extent are communicated even in our temporal life.[69] Again, in expounding Romans viii, 29–30, Arminius claimed that no one becomes conformed to the image of the Son of God, except the man who believes upon Him. 'Therefore no one has been predestinated by God to that conformity, unless considered as a believer. Unless, indeed, any one wish to include faith itself in that conformity which believers have with Christ: which is absurd; because that faith cannot be attributed to Christ at all; for it is faith in Him, and through Him in God; it is faith concerning reconciliation, redemption, remission of sins: then again, because faith is the means of arriving at that conformity.'[70] As to Ephesians ii, 8–9 ('For by grace are ye saved through faith; and that not of yourselves: it is the gift of God: not of works, lest any man should boast'), that passage is about whether we have salvation from grace and faith or from man and works. It is 'absurd' to take it as discussing whence we have faith, from God's gift and grace, or from ourselves and works. Romans iii, 27 makes this clear – 'Boasting is excluded, not by the law of works, but by the law of faith' – meaning simply that if salvation is not from works, there is no boasting.

Beza based his doctrine above all on Romans ix. It was common ground[71]

[68] Ibid., 421. The texts cited are Rom. xiv, 15; 2 Pet. ii, 1; Heb. xi, 9 and John vi, 51.

[69] 'Modest Examination of Dr Perkins's Pamphlet', in Arminius, *Works*, III. 275.

[70] Ibid., 297.

[71] Arminius' 'Analysis of Romans IX' was first published as an appendix to his *Examination of Dr Perkins's Pamphlet on Predestination* in 1602. He had originally written it as a treatise privately communicated to Gellius Snecanus, whose own *Introduction to the Ninth Chapter of the Romans* had appeared in 1596. In defending a Melanchthonian intepretation, Snecanus argued that the harsher doctrine had been unknown in Friesland at the beginning of the Reformation. Arminius acknowledged his debt: 'I freely admit that that part [of Scripture] always seemed to me enveloped in deepest shade . . . until the light shed upon it in this way dispersed the darkness, and gave my understanding a clear view of the place lit up by its brilliance.' 'Analysis of Romans IX', in *Works*, III. 485.

that in that chapter St Paul was trying to explain why, in spite of the promises of the divine covenant, most of the Jews were rejected. But Beza was utterly mistaken in understanding Paul's answer to be that the promises were overridden by an eternal, absolute and irrespective decree. On the contrary, Paul's answer is that the promises are still valid: but the Jews have misunderstood them. The promise was not, as they claim, without condition. It was 'that He would reckon as His sons those only of the Jews who would strive to obtain righteousness and salvation from faith; but that he would hold as strangers those who should seek after the same from the law'. That this is indeed St Paul's meaning is shown by the reference to Esau and Jacob, designed precisely to overcome any Jewish appeal to ancestry or righteousness according to the law: the promise to Rebecca was made 'before they were born', and therefore before they could have 'done any good or evil', whereby the one could deserve to be rejected, the other to be adopted.[72]

St Paul then asked 'Is there unrighteousness with God?' (verse 14). According to Beza's interpretation, his answer was merely to say 'God forbid' and to insist that the divine justice is incomprehensible to man. Arminius would have none of that. If indeed the question is why He hates Esau and loves Jacob then perhaps no other answer is possible, but the real question is why He hates the 'children of the flesh' and loves the 'children of the promise', and St Paul's answer is to assert that God could without any injustice have left men in the misery of their disobedience. Instead, He had *mercy*. The very word shows 'that the change of purpose was not made by any fault of God, but because its condition had been violated by transgression of the law'. Mercy, as Arminius never tired of saying, presupposes sin. Verse 15 ('He saith to Moses, I will have mercy on whom I will have had mercy . . .') is the expression in the Hebrew idiom of the truth that God is free to determine on whom He will have mercy, 'justice of course regulating that determination' — otherwise the Pauline argument would collapse.[73]

The justice of God is shown by His glory as well as His mercy. This is demonstrated by the example of Pharaoh, who is cited as an example of the just hardening and punishment of the children of the flesh. Arminius did not deny that some are hardened. What he emphatically denied is that the reason can be found only in the hidden will of God. 'Nothing is plainer in Scripture than that sinners persevering in their sins against the patience of God, who invites them to repentance, are those whom God wills to harden.'[74] What is hidden is who they are who are thus

[72] Ibid., 487, 492–3.
[73] Ibid., 498–500.
[74] Ibid., 506.

reprobated. That does not, however, imply that there is a difference between the secret and the revealed will of God ('it is wonderful in what
labyrinths they involve themselves').[75] The will of God is one. We must
assume (it is typical of Arminius' confidence in human reason) that St
Paul believes that he can provide a rational explanation.[76]

Vessels are made for a purpose. They are instruments which exist for
some end. Scripture tells us that the end is the glory of God. The glory
of God is comprehensible to man in terms of His attributes of goodness,
justice, wisdom and power. Those attributes were reflected in the creation of man under the law, but man through disobedience 'made himself
a bad vessel, that is, a sinner' and wisdom and justice alone would have
made him indeed a vessel of wrath. Goodness, however, moved towards
mercy ('which is the affection of goodness towards the miserable') and
wisdom conceived Jesus Christ as Mediator. 'But here again, *justice*, mind-
ful of its office, interposed, and showed that communication of justice
by mercy should not be made *without condition* in this state any more
than in the former.' The vessels of mercy are those who fulfil the condition; the vessels of wrath are those who persist in transgressing it. What
St Paul is saying is that

God has the power of making men out of shapeless matter, and of enacting a
decree about them, by the mere judgment and pleasure of His will, ratified by
certain conditions, according to which He makes some men vessels to dishonour,
others vessels to honour; and that therefore man has no just ground of expostula-
tion with God because He has made him to be hardened by His irresistible will;
since obstinacy of sins intervenes between the determination of His will and the
hardening . . . If any one simply say that God has the power of making man a
vessel to dishonour and wrath, he will do the greatest injustice to God, and will
contradict clear Scripture.[77]

Even Beza drew back from saying that *simply*. Instead, he invoked his
distinction between decree and execution, the execution being delayed until
man, having become a sinner, has made himself deserving of the divine
wrath. In making the execution depend on the decree, however, Beza took
back what he had thus conceded. Arminius insisted on plain language.
The Apostle's teaching is that God 'does not harden any who have not
already become vessels of the most just wrath by their own fault'.[78]
Hardening is the effect and sign of divine wrath. Wrath (like mercy)
presupposes sin. The mode of hardening, as stated by St Paul, makes this
clear, for God is said to have 'endured with much long-suffering' those

[75] Ibid., 505.
[76] Ibid., 507.
[77] Ibid., 514.
[78] Ibid., 516–17.

vessels fitted to destruction. What St Paul teaches is that God, using patience and long-suffering towards the vessels of wrath, hardens them according to that irresistible will by which he has decreed that He will deal with man according to equity.

The order of the divine decrees

Arminius accepted that the decrees of predestination are from eternity.[79] Where he differed from Perkins and Beza was in arguing that the decree of predestination is subordinate to the decree of creation and of permission of the Fall.[80] It would be wrong to conclude, however, that he was merely what would later be called a sublapsarian.[81] In Arminius' formulation of the divine decrees *of predestination* the Fall had no place at all. Certainly, mercy is to sinners; the non-election of others, their reprobation in wrath, presupposes persistence in sin and rejection of grace offered. But the first decree of all is the offer of Christ as Mediator to all men. If there is one distinctive feature of 'Arminianism', it is this.

I. The FIRST absolute decree of God concerning the salvation of sinful man, is that by which he decreed to appoint his Son Jesus Christ for a Mediator, Redeemer, Saviour, Priest and King, who might destroy sin by his own death, might by his obedience obtain the salvation which had been lost, and might communicate it by his own virtue.[82]

Unless that offer is to all men, the preaching of the Gospel is hypocrisy and its promise of salvation must to the reprobate be a command to believe a lie. God as *subject* of predestination is God in the fullness of His nature, including His wisdom, goodness, mercy and justice.

II. The SECOND precise and absolute decree of God, is that in which he decreed to receive into favour *those who repent and believe*, and, in Christ, for HIS sake and through HIM, to effect the salvation of such penitents and believers as persevered to the end; but to leave in sin and under wrath *all impenitent persons and unbelievers*, and to damn them as aliens from Christ.

III. The THIRD Divine decree is that by which God decreed to administer *in a sufficient and efficacious manner the MEANS which were necessary for repentance and faith; and to have such administration instituted (1) according to the Divine*

---

[79] 'Friendly Conference with Dr F. Junius', in Arminius, *Works*, III. 89.

[80] 'Man is the object of predestination: Therefore man is prior to the act of predestination. But man is what he is by creation: creation therefore is prior to predestination. (Understand, in the Divine mind)'. 'Modest Examination of Dr Perkins's Pamphlet', in Arminius, *Works*, III. 282.

[81] 'Declaration of the Sentiments of Arminius', in Arminius, *Works*, I. 587–9. Sublapsarianism in the form here criticized by Arminius would imply a general decree to predestinate as logically prior to the decrees of creation and 'permission' of the Fall, to which the decrees of election and reprobation of particular persons would then be subordinate.

[82] Ibid., 589, as for the subsequent decrees.

Wisdom, by which God knows what is proper and becoming both to his mercy and his severity, and (2) according to *Divine Justice*, by which He is prepared to adopt whatever His wisdom may prescribe and to put it in execution.

IV. To these succeeds the FOURTH decree, by which God decreed to save and damn certain particular persons. This decree has its foundation in the foreknowledge of God, by which he knew from all eternity those individuals who *would*, through his preventing grace, *believe*, and, through his subsequent grace *would persevere*, – according to the before described administration of those means which are suitable and proper for conversion and faith; and, by which foreknowledge, he likewise knew those who *would not believe and persevere*.

Predestination, thus explained, 'is the sum and matter of the gospel; nay, it is the gospel itself, and on that account belief in it is necessary to salvation, as far as the two first articles are concerned'.[83] So stated, the doctrine was in harmony with the goodness and righteousness of God, and with the creation of man as an expression of that goodness. It did justice both to the grace of God and to the freedom of the human will, in representing God as the cause of all good, and man as the cause of sin and of his own damnation.[84] It promoted the salvation of men by encouraging solicitude and preventing despair. In promising remission of sins, the grace of the Spirit and eternal life on condition of repentance and faith it confirmed 'that order according to which the gospel ought to be preached'.[85] Finally, Arminius claimed, predestination so understood 'has always been approved by the great majority of professing Christians, and even now, in these days, it enjoys the same extensive patronage'.[86]

Grace and free will

Arminius denied that he taught the free will of all men to win salvation; he denied, even, that he taught sufficient grace to be granted to all those to whom the Gospel was preached by which, 'if they will, they may believe'.[87] He pointed to our Lord's repeated warnings that some would reject the Gospel when it was preached to them.[88] The words attributed

---

[83] Ibid., 590 (retranslated from Latin original).

[84] Ibid., 591.

[85] Ibid. It was at this point that Arminius thought that Perkins's *Golden Chain* was in conflict with the rest of his works. 'You seem to me, most learned Perkins, to have forgotten your own self, and to be altogether another man . . .' 'Modest Examination of Dr Perkins's Pamphlet', in Arminius, *Works*, III. 308.

[86] 'Declaration of the Sentiments of Arminius', in Arminius, *Works*, I. 592.

[87] 'The Apology against Thirty-one defamatory Articles', in Arminius, *Works*, I. 699. See also *Works*, II. 19, for Arminius' response to the charge that he had said God did not deny His grace to anyone who does what is in him.

[88] E.g., Matt. xi, 25; x, 11–13.

to him were a crude formula designed to carry the imputation of Pelagianism, as though he taught that once sufficient grace had been bestowed 'the Holy Spirit and Divine Grace remain entirely quiescent, waiting to see whether the man will properly use the power he has received'.[89] He accepted the distinction between common grace, which is given to all men, and special grace, which is given to the elect alone. The common or sufficient grace which is given to all men was in his view the work of divine providence; special grace was the work of predestination. He was quite happy to concede to Perkins that if a man apprehended the offered common grace with the aid of special grace, then God has shown him greater love than him to whom He has given common grace only. His only reservation was that we ought not to teach special grace in such a way that it precluded free will, or common grace in a way inconsistent with divine justice.[90]

Grace was defined first as a 'gratuitous affection' of God towards sinners, according to which He has determined to adopt as sons believers in Christ. Secondly, it was an 'infusion' into the human understanding, will and affections of those gifts of the Spirit which appertain to regeneration (Arminius here includes faith, hope and charity, without which man is 'not sufficient to think, will or do anything that is good').[91] Thirdly, grace was that '*perpetual assistance*' of the Holy Spirit 'according to which God may then will and work together with man, that man may perform whatever he wills'.[92]

In this manner, I ascribe to grace THE COMMENCEMENT, THE CONTINUANCE AND THE CONSUMMATION OF ALL GOOD, and to such an extent do I carry its influence, that a man, though already regenerate, can neither conceive, will nor do any good at all, nor resist any evil temptation, *without this preventing and exciting, this following and co-operating grace.* – From this statement it will clearly appear, that I am by no means injurious or unjust to grace, by attributing, as it is reported of me, too much to man's free will.[93]

Man as first created was endowed with power to perform 'the true good', but not without the assistance of divine grace. After the Fall, man was unable either to think, to will or to do 'that which is really good' until regenerated by God in Christ through the Holy Spirit. Thus regenerated, 'I consider that, since he is delivered from sin, he is capable of thinking, willing and doing that which is good, but yet not *without the continued*

---

[89] 'The Apology against Thirty-one defamatory Articles', in Arminius, *Works*, I. 701.
[90] 'Friendly Conference with Dr F. Junius', in Arminius, *Works*, III. 168; 'Modest Examination of Dr Perkins's Pamphlet', ibid., 445.
[91] 'Declaration of the Sentiments of Arminius', in *Works*, I. 600.
[92] Ibid.
[93] Ibid.

aids of Divine Grace.[94] The nub of the question was whether that grace was irresistible or not. That was a controversy, Arminius claimed, about its *mode of operation*, and not about what actions or operations should be attributed to it. It was, however, plain from the Scriptures that many people reject the grace that is offered them; it could not, therefore, be offered irresistibly. The decree of predestination itself, however, he granted was immutable and its execution irresistible:

nay, irresistible power cannot but be placed over the execution of that decree. For damnation, as it is the infliction of punishment, and therefore against the will of the person about to be damned, ought to be inflicted by a power which cannot be resisted by that person . . . Salvation also, to which all the gates of hell oppose themselves, ought to be conferred by a power which the demons cannot resist, and which the person saved neither can resist, nor wishes to resist.[95]

It was perhaps more understandable that Arminius should be charged with saying that faith was not the gift of God.[96] He strongly denied it. he denied even that it depended *partly* on free will. He conveyed his own understanding by using the analogy of a beggar receiving alms. The alms did not cease to be a gift because the beggar extended his hand to receive it. Nor could it be said that just because the beggar stretched out his hand, he could have the alms just as he pleased. 'It is not our wish to do the least injury to Divine Grace, by taking from it any thing which belongs to it: But let my brethren take care, that they themselves neither inflict an injury on Divine Justice, by attributing to it that which it refuses; nor on Divine Grace, by transforming it into something else, which cannot be called Grace.'[97]

Faith and assurance

Arminius spoke of faith both as the condition of election and as the gift of God. He was walking a tight-rope here, and some of his earlier formulations lack precision. As finally developed, however, his views are reflected in the carefully enunciated difference between the second and third decrees of predestination as he states them, the decree to justify and adopt as sons believers in Christ, and the decree to bestow faith by certain means on some but not on others. Failure to recognize the difference

[94] Ibid., 596. The problem of the concurrence between divine grace and human free will drew from Arminius an uncharacteristic confession of perplexity; it was a 'labyrinth . . . which, to confess the truth, exceeds my powers', 'Modest Examination of Dr Perkins's Pamphlet', in Arminius, *Works*, III. 272.
[95] 'Examination of The Theses of Dr. F. Gomarus', in Arminius, *Works*, III. 545, 550.
[96] 'The Apology against Thirty-one defamatory Articles', in Arminius, *Works*, II. 51.
[97] Ibid., 52.

was, he thought, the main reason why Perkins made the commandment to believe more general than the promise of a Mediator.[98] Faith is 'the act of the man that apprehends the promise',[99] but 'no one can perform this act except through the grace of God'.[100] In examining the response of sinful men to Christ (saving faith belongs only to sinners), Arminius pointed out that saving or justifying faith is also called *the obedience of faith*.[101] That obedience has three parts, repentance, faith in Christ and in God through Christ, and the observance of God's commands, 'in which consists holiness of life, to which believers are called, and without which no man shall see God'.[102] The evangelical faith which is the second part of that obedience is 'an assent of the mind, produced by the Holy Spirit ... in sinners who ... are penitent ... by which they are not only fully persuaded within themselves, that Jesus Christ has been constituted by God the author of salvation to those who obey Him ... and by which they also believe in Him as such'.[103] Elsewhere Arminius defines the assent as that of the *affections*, which occurs when a proposition is believed both as true 'and when it also proposes a good that must be performed by us'.[104]

Assurance (*fiducia*) springs out of that assent of the affections. It is a feeling of confidence or trust. Arminius quoted approvingly the scholastic definition of it as 'strong or corroborated [*robusta seu roborata*] hope'. We do not have the same assurance or certainty of our own salvation as that by which we know there is a God, and that Christ is the Saviour of the world. Arminius pointed out that 'it is notorious ... that Augustine and his followers hold that no-one in this life becomes certain of his own election to salvation; a few excepted, to whom this befalls from special revelation'.[105] Arminius distinguished carefully between our assurance that Christ has *power to save* and *actual salvation*:

If therefore I believe, as I am bound to do, that Christ is constituted a Saviour, that is, possesses the power, ability and will to save, and if I thus through Faith deliver myself up to him, I shall in this case actually obtain salvation from him ... In these expressions, therefore, *I believe that Christ is the Saviour of the world, yea that He is the Saviour of believers and OF ME*, the following are not included, *I believe that I have remission of sins, I believe that I have eternal life;* but this is included in them, *I believe that I shall have these in His name.* For

---

98 'Modest Examination of Dr Perkins's Pamphlet', in Arminius, *Works*, III. 305–6.
99 Ibid.
100 'On the Predestination of Means to the End', in Arminius, *Works*, II. 394.
101 From a letter to Uitenbogaert of January, 1605, quoted in Arminius, *Works*, I. 179–80.
102 'On the Repentance by which Men answer to the Divine Vocation', in Arminius, *Works*, II. 398.
103 'Of Faith in God and Christ', ibid., 400.
104 From a letter to Uitenbogaert of August, 1604, in Arminius, *Works*, I. 176–7.
105 'Examination of The Theses of Dr. F. Gomarus', in Arminius, *Works*, III. 650.

since I believe that I shall obtain these blessings on my believing in Him, I believe in him that I may actually have them, and then I actually receive them.[106]

Yet a believer could, through his conscience and the witness of the Holy Spirit (Arminius stresses '*if his heart condemn him not*'), be 'in reality assured', of his adoption as a son of God, 'and yet this person should constantly pray, *O Lord, enter not into judgment with thy servant*'. He did not quarrel with the 'practical syllogism', but insisted that it must be based on a correct definition of election. The conclusion 'Therefore I have been elected to life' should rest, he said, on the major premiss 'The gospel teaches that believers and penitents have been elected to life eternal' and on the minor premiss 'But I am a believer and a true penitent; for so my conscience witnesses to me, and so the Holy Spirit witnesses at the same time with my heart.'[107] That conclusion could not be properly derived from predestination as defined by Beza. Arminius thought that the doctrine of assurance was a fit subject for a synod to discuss further.

Perseverance

Arminius was accused of saying that it was possible for believers finally to decline and fall away from faith and salvation.[108] He was under pressure here. He granted that he said it (with a qualification); but he had not asserted that they actually do fall away. He nevertheless confessed that there were passages of Scripture which seemed to point to the conclusion *that a true believer can either totally or finally fall away from the faith and perish*,[109] and he was not convinced by such arguments against them as he had seen; nevertheless, there were other passages which seemed to point to unconditional perseverance, and he confessed that they were 'worthy of much consideration'. It was another of those doctrines on which a National Synod might well adjudicate.[110]

As he pointed out, the answer depends on whether justifying faith is peculiar to the elect. He quoted St Augustine:

It is wonderful, and indeed most wonderful, that God does not bestow perseverance on certain of his sons, whom He has regenerated in Christ, and to whom he has given faith, hope and love; while he pardons such great acts of wickedness in sons that are alienated from him, and, by imparting his grace, makes them his children.[111]

---

[106] Arminius, *Works*, I. 179–80.
[107] 'Examination of The Theses of Dr. F. Gomarus', in Arminius, *Works*, III, 650. For a discussion of the practical syllogism as formulated by Perkins, see R. T. Kendall, *Calvin and English Calvinism to 1649* (pb. edn, Oxford, 1979), 8–9, 69–76.
[108] 'The Apology against Thirty-one defamatory Articles', in Arminius, *Works*, I. 674.
[109] 'Declaration of the Sentiments of Arminius', in Arminius, *Works*, I. 603.
[110] Ibid., 601–2.
[111] 'The Apology against Thirty-one defamatory Articles', in Arminius, *Works*, I. 676.

Prosper, too, lamented the 'many examples' of the regenerated relinquishing their faith. Among Protestant churches, the Lutherans were firm that faith was bestowed on the non-elect. Arminius' own final formulation was cautious:

Those persons who have been grafted into Christ by true faith, and have thus been made partakers of his life-giving Spirit, possess *sufficient powers* to fight against Satan, sin, the world, and their own flesh, and to gain the victory of these enemies, – yet not without the assistance of the grace of the same Holy Spirit. Jesus Christ also by his Spirit assists them in all their temptations, and affords them the ready aid of his hand; and, provided they stand prepared for the battle, implore his help, and be not wanting to themselves, Christ preserves them from fall: so that it is not possible for them, by any of the cunning craftiness or power of Satan, to be either seduced or dragged out of the hands of Christ.[112]

The place of Arminius in Reformed theology

There is controversy about whether Arminius may be described as 'Calvinist' or 'Lutheran'. There is no evidence of any direct link with Lutheranism, though there may have been an indirect influence. Plancius and others inevitably accused him of anti-Calvinism. The charge is a reflection of that hardening of Reformation theology into schools which is surely alien to the first-generation Reformers. Arminius said that he accepted everything Calvin said about justification in the third book of the *Institutes*. In reply to the accusation that he recommended his students to read the works of Jesuits, Arminius said it was a lie:

so far from this, after the reading of Scripture, which I strenuously inculcate, and more than any other (as the whole Academy, yea the conscience of my colleagues will testify) I recommend that the Commentaries of Calvin be read, whom I extol in higher terms than Helmichius himself, as he owned to me, ever did. For I affirm that in the interpretation of the Scriptures Calvin is incomparable, and that his Commentaries are more to be valued than anything that is handed down to us in the *Bibliotheca* of the Fathers; so much so, that I concede to him a certain spirit of prophecy in which he stands distinguished above all others, above most, yea above all. His *Institutes*, so far as respects *Commonplaces*, I give out to be read after the Catechism, as a more extended explanation. But here I add – *with discrimination*, as the writing of all men ought to be read.[113]

There is no reason to doubt the truth of that. Richard Neile, writing in 1629, commented: 'by what I have heard of him, take him out of the question of predestination and reprobation he is held in all other respects to be a rigid Calvinist'.[114] Even his doctrine of predestination, it has been

112 Ibid., 600–1.
113 Guthrie, *Life of Arminius*, 235–6.
114 See below, p. 274.

claimed, was 'truer to the more liberal spirit of Calvin'[115] represented by the *Institutes* and the Genevan Catechism. To claim, however, that 'had he been forty years earlier his teaching would have caused as little scandal as that of Anastasius, Bullinger or Melanchthon'[116] is to forget how much his thought belongs to the late sixteenth century. Arminius' theology evolved as his mind, independent, rationalistic, ethical and pietistic, yet bred within the traditions of early Dutch Protestantism, wrestled under the impact of Bezan Calvinism.

However unexceptionable its origins, in its impact his theology was divisive. What was acceptable in Amsterdam (and Arminius' exposition of Romans ix *was* acceptable there) was less so in the more academic and influential arena of the University of Leiden, and more controversial still when debated publicly by the States. Apart from the political implications, it was in any event too late to assert so confidently that Calvin and Beza were wrong. It was especially divisive to call for a revision of the Confession and Catechism. Calvin, admittedly, would have agreed with Arminius that too much authority should not be ascribed to them, and that there was no reason why they should not be altered. But to press for revision in the late sixteenth century gave colour to the accusation that Arminius was broaching new doctrines. The call to revise implied that earlier formulations had been wrong, and it undermined that claim of a confessional consensus by which Protestants set so much store in their apologetic against Rome. Such considerations help to explain how Bogerman, subsequently the president of the Synod of Dort, could in 1607 declare that the Scripture must be expounded according to the Confession and the Catechism.

It is therefore easy to understand why to many of his contemporaries Arminius appeared as a disputatious 'novelist' bent on destroying the confessional harmony of the Reformed churches. Irrespective of his doctrine of predestination, he was associated with another unpalatable claim, the assertion of *libertas prophetandi*, the right of the individual to interpret Scripture. If the demand for a National Synod and the revision of the formularies was Arminianism on the offensive, the claim to liberty of prophesying was Arminianism under pressure. Both were out of tune with contemporary Protestantism, whether in the Netherlands or elsewhere. In England, as will be seen, neither found many sympathetic echoes, whether among conservative or among more militantly Protestant churchmen.

[115] H. D. Foster, 'Liberal Calvinism: The Remonstrants at the Synod of Dort in 1618', *Harvard Theological Review* 16 (1923), 1–37.

[116] G. J. Hoenderdaal, 'The Debate about Arminius outside the Netherlands', in Th. H. Lunsingh Scheurleer and G. H. M. Posthumus Meyes (eds.), *Leiden University in the Seventeenth Century* (Leiden, 1975), 138. For Melanchthon's doctrine of predestination, see C. L. Manschreck, *Melanchthon, the Quiet Reformer* (New York, 1958), 293–302. Melanchthon did not have that confidence in the human reason which makes Arminius' theology so unmistakably a product of the late sixteenth century.

3   Early English Protestantism

Hooper and Latimer

Heylyn claimed that 'Arminianism' was nothing more than old English Protestantism revived. Just as, liturgically, Puritan objections to the 1559 Prayer Book were met by an increasing interest in that of 1549, so doctrinally the influence of Calvin and Beza was countered by an appeal to indigenous Henrician and Edwardian Protestantism. Given the strongly chauvinistic strain running through much English Calvinism, that argument had to be taken seriously. It was vital for each side to demonstrate that the foundation documents of the English Church, the formularies of belief, the Homilies, the Prayer Book, and the writings of those who had made the original break with Rome supported its understanding of the doctrinal stance of the English Reformation.

It would be naive to expect a reconsideration of the evidence to yield a conclusive verdict. Debates about grace and free will, justification and predestination are as old as Christian theology. As the Reformers soon discovered, the Fathers and the schoolmen provided them with endless material as they worked out the full implications of their protest against a theology of merit. They did not, it need hardly be said, speak with a unanimous voice.[1] For this reason, and also because the primary concerns of that first phase of English Reformation theology were different from those of a century later, neither Prynne nor Heylyn found exactly what he wanted when they combed the works of the early English Reformers.

In spite of that, John Hooper was undoubtedly an embarrassment for Prynne, and a correspondingly valuable quarry for Heylyn. As has often been observed, Hooper followed Tyndale in emphasizing a covenant theology in which the offer of divine grace becomes almost a reward for obedience.[2] It is because Hooper saw a continuity between the covenant

[1] C. W. Dugmore, *The Doctrine of Grace in the English Reformers* (Hulsean Lectures, 1960, unpublished).
[2] See J. G. Møller, 'The Beginnings of Puritan Covenant Theology', *Journal of Ecclesiastical History* 14 (1963), 46–67. In Møller's view, the ethical emphasis in Tyndale 'endangers his basically Reformed theology'.

of law and that of grace that he insisted so strongly that the promises of
the Gospel are to all men. To restrict them in any way would be to make
Christ inferior to Adam. How then do we explain that not all – indeed,
that few – are saved? Hooper's answer was to say that men exclude
themselves:

> the promise of grace appertaineth unto every sort of men in the world, and com-
> prehendeth them all; howbeit within certain limits and bounds, the which if men
> neglect or pass over, they exclude themselves from the promise in Christ: as Cain
> was no more excluded, till he excluded himself, than Abel; Saul than David; Judas
> than Peter; Esau than Jacob; though Mal. i., Rom ix, it seemeth that the sentence
> of God was given to save the one and to damn the other, before the one loved
> God, or the other hated God. Howbeit these threatenings of God against Esau,
> if he had not of his wilful malice excluded himself from the promise of grace,
> should no more have hindered his salvation, than God's threatenings against
> Nineve, Jonah i.; which notwithstanding that God said should be destroyed in
> forty days, stood a great time after, and did penance.[3]

Like Arminius, Hooper argued that St Paul's use of the example of Esau
and Jacob was designed to do no more than take away from the Jews
their confidence in their lineal descent from Abraham.[4] His whole purpose was to show that man can be saved from sin only by the merits of
Christ, and that those merits may be apprehended only by faith. Such
is man's servitude to sin, that he is incapable of the faith that God requires. We are nevertheless accounted faithful, 'except we transgress the
limits and bounds of this original sin by our own folly and malice, and
either of a contempt or hate of God's word we fall into sin, and transform
ourselves into the image of the devil'. The promise extends to all who repent. 'It is our office therefore to see that we exclude not ourselves from
the general grace promised to all men.' He warned of the danger of moving from one heretical extreme to another:

> It is not a christian man's part to attribute his salvation to his own free-will, with
> the Pelagian, and extenuate original sin; nor to make God the author of ill and
> our damnation, with the Manichee; nor yet to say, God hath written fatal laws,
> as the Stoic, and with necessity of destiny violently pulleth one by the hair into
> heaven, and thrusteth the other headlong into hell.[5]

The cause of reprobation is sin in man, which makes him unwilling to
hear or to accept the promise of the Gospel; or, having received it, to fall
into contempt or hate of it. 'This sentence is true, howsoever man judge
of predestination.'[6] The cause of election, by contrast, is the mercy of

---

[3] From the preface to 'A Declaration of the Ten Commandments', in S, Carr (ed.), *The
Early Writings of Bishop Hooper* (Parker Society, Cambridge, 1843), 259.
[4] Ibid., 260.
[5] Ibid., 263.
[6] Ibid., 264.

God in Christ. Nevertheless, Hooper warned against interpretations of John vi, 44 ('No man cometh unto me, except my Father draw him') which would make God require 'in a reasonable man no more than in a dead post'. 'God draweth with his word and the Holy Ghost; but man's duty is to hear and learn, that is to say, receive the grace offered, consent unto the promise, and not repugn the God that calleth. God doth promise the Holy Ghost unto them that ask him, and not to them that contemn him.'[7]

God's mercy, Hooper stressed, is constant. 'Let us think verily that now God calleth, and convert our lives to it. Let us obey it, and beware we suffer not our foolish judgements to wander after the flesh; lest the devil wrap us up in darkness, and teach us to seek the election of God out of the scripture.'[8] It was a warning against a 'carnal' consideration of the doctrine of predestination which was to be echoed by other English Reformers. We can judge of election only 'by the event or success that happeneth in the life of man': that meant firstly knowledge of our faith in Christ, and secondly the amendment of life that would follow from our rejection of sin and our obedience to the commands of God. Without that amendment of life, 'it is not lively faith that we have, but rather a vain knowledge and mere presumption'.[9] Fear of presumption is a recurring theme with Hooper; hence his repeated warnings of the need for obedience and the dangers of falling. He was equally concerned to warn men against the dangers of desperation. His answer was to insist that God's mercy is unlimited: 'God will always forgive how many and how horrible soever the sins be.'[10] A thoroughgoing doctrine of predestination would not have sat comfortably with either of those concerns, and it is absent from Hooper's writings.

Hugh Latimer, too, said that the Gospel must be preached to all the world, because the promises are for all. Individually, our salvation depends upon God. 'If thou wilt, thou canst make me clean.' But generally we may not doubt, but must 'apprehend God by his promise, saying "Lord, thou hast promised that all that believe in thee shall be saved."'[11] To doubt that promise would be to make God a liar.[12] Unfortunately, most men reject the promise made to them:

O what a pitiful thing it is, that man will not consider this, and leave the sin and pleasure of this world, and live godly; but is so blind and mad, that he will rather

[7] Ibid., 265.
[8] Ibid.
[9] Ibid., 264–5.
[10] Ibid., 423.
[11] G. Corrie (ed.), *Sermons and Remains of Hugh Latimer* (2 vols., Parker Society, Cambridge, 1844–5), II. 173–4.
[12] Ibid., I. 513.

have a momentary, and a very short and small pleasure, than hearken to the will and pleasure of Almighty God! That might avoid everlasting pain and woe, and give unto him everlasting felicity. For that a great many of us are damned, the fault is not in God; for *Deus vult omnes homines salvos fieri*, 'God would have all men saved': but the fault is in ourselves, and in our own madness, that had rather have damnation than salvation.[13]

Latimer makes salvation conditional on belief, but at the same time acknowledges that faith comes from the goodness of God. He was fond of repeating the prayer 'Lord, I believe; help thou my unbelief', but was in no doubt that the divine help would come only after a human initiative in response to the hearing of the word.[14] Belief begins with repentance. Contrition by itself, however, is not enough: mere abhorrence of ourselves and of our sins would leave us in desperation at the gates of hell. It must be followed by faith, or belief: 'we must believe Christ, we must know that our Saviour is come into this world to save sinners . . . And this faith must not be only a general faith, but it must be a special faith . . . I must believe for myself, that his blood was shed for me.'[15] Thirdly, Latimer says, we must thereafter 'wrestle with sin'.[16] That he was able so strongly to stress the human response to grace was because for him faith was above all opposed to pride. It was for pride that Lucifer was cast into hell. In seeking to explain the nature of faith Latimer took the example of the leper:

Now, when thou art in distress, in misery, in sickness, in poverty, or any other calamity, follow the ensample of this leper; run to Christ; seek help and comfort only at his hands; and then thou shalt be delivered and made safe, like as he was delivered after he came to Christ.

But what brought he with him? Even his faith. He believed that Christ was able to help him, and therefore according to his faith it happened unto him. Then it shall be necessary for thee to bring faith with thee; for without faith thou canst get nothing at his hands: bring therefore, I say, faith with thee; believe that he is able to help thee, and that he is merciful and will help thee. And when thou comest furnished with such a faith, surely thou shalt be heard . . . For faith is like a hand wherewith we receive the benefits of God, and except we take his benefits with the hand of faith, we shall never have them.[17]

Latimer would have thought it absurd if anyone had objected that this

---

[13] Ibid., II. 192.
[14] 'For his passion is profitable only to them that believe; notwithstanding that his death might be sufficient for all the whole world, yet for all that no man shall enjoy that same benefit, but only they that believe in him; that put their hope, trust and confidence in him.' Ibid., II. 3.
[15] Ibid., 10.
[16] Ibid., 11.
[17] Ibid., 170.

emphasis on the human response of faith was semi-Pelagian. Nor was he afraid to warn his congregation that they must not 'utterly set aside the doing of good works'.[18] Faith was what was needed in order to achieve that; Latimer compared it to the oil which the wise virgins had in their lamps. Good works do not save us, but God nevertheless requires them:

For man's salvation cannot be gotten by any work; because the Scripture saith, *Vita aeterna donum Dei*; 'Life everlasting is the gift of God.' True it is that God requireth good works of us, and commandeth us to avoid all wickedness. But for all that, we may not do our good works to the end to get heaven withal; but rather to shew ourselves thankful for that which Christ hath done for us, who with his passion hath opened the gate of heaven unto all believers.[19]

Latimer warned his hearers not to trouble themselves with 'curious questions of the predestination of God'. In particular, he condemned a 'lewd opinion of predestination' based on Acts xiii ('as many as were ordained to life everlasting believed') that 'therefore it is no matter whatsoever we do; for if we be chosen to everlasting life, we shall have it'. That Anabaptist doctrine was against the true meaning of Scripture; if most men are damned, the fault is not in God, but in themselves. If instead of troubling ourselves with dangerous questions we remember that God would have all men saved, and that He has chosen those who believe in Christ, 'let us have good hope that we shall be amongst the chosen, and live after this hope; that is, uprightly and godly; then thou shalt not be deceived'.[20]

Latimer acknowledged that our faith may be weak. Many think they have faith when they do not; others think they have none when they have some.[21] The best evidence that we have it is that we are conscious of fighting and striving with sin.[22] But we must always ask God to increase our faith and pray with the centurion (Luke xvii): 'O Lord, help my unbelief'.[23] One of the most striking passages in Latimer's Sermons is his answer to the question 'How do I know that I am in the book of life?'

I answer: First we may know, that we may one time be in the book, and another time come out again; as it appeareth by David, which was written in the book of life; but when he sinned, he at that same time was out of the book of the favour of God, until he had repented and was sorry for his faults. So we may be in the book one time, and afterward, when we forget God and his word, and do wickedly, we come out of the book; that is, out of Christ, which is the book.[24]

18 Ibid., 194.
19 Ibid., 200. Cf. ibid., I. 521: 'We must do good works . . . yet for all that, we must not trust in our doings.'
20 Ibid., II. 174–5.
21 Ibid., 186.
22 Ibid., 194.
23 Ibid., 187.
24 Ibid., 175.

The three special signs by which we may know that we are in Christ, and therefore in the book of life, are a consciousness of sin and a revulsion towards it; secondly an unfeigned and steadfast belief that God will cleanse us from that sin through the blood of Christ; and 'thirdly an earnest desire to leave sin and fly the same'. If we are sure of these three signs, we may be confident that we are elect and predestinate to everlasting life. Elsewhere Latimer reinforces his teaching that we may be 'in the book' (elect) at one time, and out of it at another by advising us to pray continually because a faithful man is tried by afflictions; by counselling us not to be too ready to condemn our neighbours 'when they do fall' – Christ bore with his disciples, in spite of their unbelief; and by warning us that 'in what state soever a man dieth in, in the same shall he arise again': those who die in repentance, to everlasting life; and those who die without a repentant heart, or with no faith, to everlasting damnation.[25]

It would have been impossible for any Protestant theologian to preach in the manner of Latimer subsequent to the maturing of Calvinism under Beza. In attacking the 'Anabaptist' doctrine of predestination he went further than Arminius in the Netherlands, or Richard Montagu ever did. Of course there is nothing in either Hooper or Latimer of that elaborate academic interest in the doctrine of predestination that characterized Arminius. There is no speculation upon how to define God as the subject or man as the object of predestination; no attempt to discuss or to formulate the logical order of the divine decrees. The early English Reformers were content with a relatively unsophisticated Protestantism which countered the merit theology and 'mass mongering' of Rome on the one hand, and guarded itself against Anabaptist excess on the other. The subsoil thus constituted would remain an uneasy foundation for any attempt to build an uncompromisingly rigid predestinarian superstructure. And it was the world of Hooper and Latimer that gave birth to the Anglican formularies.

Continental influences: Bucer and Martyr

Martin Bucer

Bucer arrived in England in 1549 to take up Cranmer's offer of a professorship at Cambridge. Although his influence was cut short by his early death, it was profound, not merely because of his immense reputation and strong personality, or even because he was resident during the formative period of Edwardian Protestantism, but also because even at that early date he was valued as a unifying influence among the continental

[25] Ibid., 185, 187, 191–2.

Reformers. When confessional differences hardened in the later sixteenth century, Bucer's influence remained strong, and not just among moderates: even the more extreme laboured to demonstrate his patronage of their standpoint. Historians preoccupied with the defence of 'Lutheranism' or 'Calvinism' have often overlooked it, but Bucer exercised a more intimate and a more powerful influence in England than Luther, Calvin or Zwingli.

It has been argued that the doctrine of predestination shapes the whole of Bucer's theology.[26] That may be misleading unless it is understood that for Bucer predestination meant predestination to life. He preferred to speak of election, of *praefinitio* rather than *praedestinatio*. In expounding the Pauline doctrine, Bucer argued that election means the separation of the saints from the unredeemed before they even exist. The point, he stresses, is both that the will of God is certain and immutable, and that it is without respect to any merit of our own.[27] Although election is from eternity, it is in Christ, and to final sanctification.[28] Bucer denied that anyone can be effaced from the book of life.[29]

Election would have no meaning unless some men are reprobate. Bucer could not believe that God has no control over them. He concluded that evil men must be His instruments for good purposes. Pharaoh, whom He gave over to a reprobate mind, and Esau, whom He hated before he had done anything evil, were both His creatures: who then could deny that God foreknew them before He created them, and that He had ordained them to His own ends? In the same way, we must believe that God uses all evil to a good purpose.[30] Bucer conceded that scriptural teaching to the effect that God blinds men, hardens them and gives them over to a reprobate mind is a mystery to human reasoning, but he refused to accept any escape — as by asserting that there is merely a permissive decree. Yes, God does allow those to fall whom He alone is able to prevent from falling. That judgment must to us remain an abyss — but God is just in all His ways, and we must remember that Scripture teaches the glory of God to be the final end of evil.[31]

Bucer then turned to the uses of the doctrine, and here he commended the teaching of Melanchthon. Its purpose was above all to make us more certain of our salvation, and to give us a stronger hold on the promises of the Gospel, 'for they who truly believe, have eternal life, and are not able to doubt that they have it, since our Lord's promise cannot be

[26] W. P. Stephens, *The Holy Spirit in the Theology of Martin Bucer* (Cambridge, 1970), 23.
[27] Martin Bucer, *Metaphrasis et Enarratio in Epistolam D. Pauli Apostoli ad Romanos* (Basle, 1562), 409.
[28] Stephens, *Bucer*, 14–16.
[29] Ibid., 40.
[30] Bucer, *Metaphrasis ad Romanos*, 410.
[31] Ibid., 410–11.

doubted, "Whosover believeth on me, hath everlasting life." ' On that promise rests our trust (*fiducia*), our love of Christ and good; just as doubt of our election is the source of all evil. 'Let us, therefore', says Bucer — the exhortation threatening to annihilate the strict logic of his position — 'be really predestinated.' We must presume, as the foundation of our faith, that we are all of us foreknown, fore-appointed, separated from the rest and selected to serve Him to eternity, that this purpose of God is unchangeable, and hence our every thought and care must be that we respond to this predestination in order to co-operate with those powers which our Lord always provides towards eternal life, for the increase of which we must not cease to pray.[32] And what of texts like 'Many are called, few are chosen' and 'Not every one that sayeth unto me, Lord, Lord shall enter into the kingdom of heaven'? The first refers to those who hear the Gospel, but who do not come to Christ because they are not chosen. Bucer exhorts his reader to believe; he has then come to Christ, and cannot thereafter doubt that he is foreknown, called according to the divine purpose, and elect. The second text is to encourage us to be more diligent in serving the Lord, not to make us doubt of our election. Our own righteousness is so weak, that it is only from a real trust in the promises of God that we have any hope of our salvation and hence of performing those good works, the Lord being our helper, which are the result of our election.

Although, therefore, Bucer has argued that God does not simply will all men to be saved, and has followed St Augustine in supposing that 1 Tim. ii, 4 must mean 'all sorts of men', for practical purposes he tells his Christian hearers that they must take hold of Christ's promises as though all are elect. The same note is struck even more decisively in the Lectures on Ephesians delivered at Cambridge. In that epistle, the whole doctrine of our eternal salvation is set forth clearly and without ambiguity. We can there learn of our adoption as sons of Christ Jesus our Saviour before the foundations of the world were laid. Election in this epistle means, Bucer says, the appointment of some men from the common mass to knowledge of God, and finally their designation to eternal life, through the mere grace of God.[33] It is the *memoria* and *meditatio* of our election which *alone* enables us to resist the Devil. That is why the doctrine of election was so important to Bucer. Election is not by foresight of faith, because the natural man is incapable of responding to the Holy Spirit. Yet the final cause of our election is to make more abundant the goodness

---

[32] Ibid., 411–12. The entire section is wholly in the spirit of Melanchthon. Bucer regretted that Wittenberg theologians were not more persistent in courting the English; G. Rupp, *Journal of Theological Studies* 48 (1947), 116.

[33] Martin Bucer, *Praelectiones . . . in Epistolam . . . ad Ephesios . . . habitae Cantabrigiae in Anglia Anno MDL et LI* (Basle, 1562), 21.

of God, and the righteousness of Christ towards all men, 'not because God needs our praises, but that in our praise many may come to that salvation and blessedness which is offered to all, when the Gospel is preached among the nations'.[34] And even though election is not dependent on foresight of faith, we are not to suppose, says Bucer, that the free will which we have through the Spirit is thereby annulled; when God draws us to Him, He does not draw us as a block of wood or as a lump of stone, but He enables us both to will and to do.[35]

Bucer is less decisive than might be expected, given his emphasis on sanctification, on how to distinguish between the elect and the reprobate. The problem as he confronts it is not how the Christian may know that he is elect – as he says, if we take the promise seriously, doubt is almost inconceivable – but how we may know whether others are elect. That is not easy. The difference lies in the Holy Spirit. The elect, however much they may be tempted, always have the seed of God, that is, the Holy Spirit, within them. By contrast, the sin against the Holy Spirit is a sure sign of the reprobate. Bucer was forced to qualify that apparently clear distinction. He admits that appearances may be deceptive. He concedes that the reprobate may have the gifts of the Spirit, but denies that they have its fruits: by this he would appear to mean that their lives are not inwardly transformed in the way that the elect are transformed. Alternatively, he says that the reprobate are those who participate in the Holy Spirit, but without regenerating or justifying faith. These distinctions are not fully worked out, and in another context Bucer concedes that there is no way we can be sure who is elect and who is reprobate, and that God alone knows.[36]

There are parallel ambiguities in Bucer's treatment of perseverance. It is absolutely certain that the elect will persevere. To be blotted out of the book of life is the same as to be rejected, and such people were never written in it, he says.[37] It is only the elect who will believe (otherwise, our assurance that we are indeed elect if we believe would be groundless). Equally, it is certain that having been called, we shall also be justified,

---

[34] Ibid., 22. The double emphasis on the universality of the promise is notable.

[35] See I. Backus, ' "Hercules Gallicus" et La Conception du Libre Arbitre dans le Commentaire sur la quatrième évangile de Martin Bucer', in I. Backus et al. (eds.), *Martin Bucer, Apocryphe et Authentique*, Cahiers, Revue de théologie et philosophie 8 (Geneva, 1983), in which it is argued that Bucer followed Erasmus rather than Luther in interpreting John vi, 44.

[36] Stephens, *Bucer*, 32–3.

[37] Ibid., 40. Bucer makes these remarks in commenting on Ps. lxix, 28 ('Let them be blotted out of the book of life, and not be written with the righteous'). His argument is that this text, and others like it, must be interpreted in the light of Romans viii, 29: such prayers are 'absurd', and God will reject them. Martin Bucer, *Psalmorum libri quinque . . . enarrati* (1554), 296.

and having been justified, then sanctified and finally glorified. Yet Bucer concedes that there are more who are called than who are elect.[38] His answer was to distinguish between a general vocation and the particular vocation of the elect, by which lives are transformed. But Bucer admits that we may see some of the elect 'living as though lost' and leading lives which undoubtedly conflict with the truth of the Gospel. In dealing with the example of Peter, Bucer argues that he sinned out of fear, and that all the time he knew inwardly that what he did was wrong. That is different, he argues, from conscious and deliberate sin. But Bucer's claim that we may always discern some 'seed of God' in the elect is grounded, one feels, more on his conviction that the purposes of God are immutable than on his pastoral experience.

The contrasting emphases evident in Bucer's doctrine of election are only partly explained by the paradoxes implicit in the scriptural material. The works in which there is more emphasis on the uncompromising elements of predestinarian doctrine were directed against Catholics; in his later works he was more concerned to refute Anabaptists. He defended infant baptism, for example, by reference to his doctrine of election. To some extent, however, the unresolved antinomies in his exposition reflect not merely a thinker who saw both sides of every question[39] but a struggle between heart and head. His thinking, more perhaps than most people's, cannot be isolated from his personality. An example is his response to the argument that preaching predestination leads to desperation: so deeply conscious was he of the Gospel promises of free grace to sinners, so completely did his thinking presuppose a commitment to Christ as Lord and Saviour, that he was at bottom unable to take the objection seriously. Similarly, his teaching on assurance, conditioned by a deep spiritual humility, could never be mistaken for a doctrine of security. Bucer was remembered at Cambridge as having said as his final word on this as on other controversies that he was content just to know Jesus Christ, and Him crucified.[40]

Peter Martyr

Peter Martyr was invited to England in 1547, and he and Cranmer became close friends.[41] He stayed six years, and had considerable influence

---

[38] Stephens, *Bucer*, 33

[39] Rupp, in the *Journal of Theological Studies* 48, 119.

[40] M. Parker, *How we ought to take the death of the godly, a sermon made in Cambridge at the buriall of the noble clerk, D. M. Bucer* (1551), sig. F ii. In praising Bucer's skill in reconciling differences of opinion, Parker had in mind above all the controversy over the Eucharist. 'Howsoever the one can bear with another in all other matters of question, yet in this one matter only, no concord . . .'. Ibid., sig. E viii.

[41] J. P. Donnelly, *Calvinism and Scholasticism in Vermigli's Doctrine of Grace* (Leiden, 1976), 174.

in the development of Edwardian Protestantism, indirectly on the Prayer Book and directly on the drafting of some of the Forty-two Articles, and he played a part in the writing of the *Reformatio Legum Ecclesiasticarum*. The homily on drunkenness and gluttony is in large part a translation from Martyr's commentary on Judges. His influence continued in the reign of Elizabeth, through the friends he had made while Regius Professor of Divinity at Oxford, through those he welcomed in the reign of Mary at Strasburg and then at Zurich, and more widely through English translations of his commentaries.[42]

Martyr's doctrine of predestination derived, after Scripture, largely from St Augustine, but more immediately from Bucer, with whom he had formed close links while they resided at Strasburg together from 1542 to 1547. Like Bucer's (and, indeed, Calvin's) it was worked out in opposition to the Catholic theologian Albert Pighi's defence of free will. This may well explain the similarities between Martyr's doctrine and Calvin's: Martyr approved of Calvin's treatise *De Aeterna Dei Predestinatione* of 1552, and wrote to tell him so, but he reached his own conclusions independently.[43] Beza wrote to Martyr for advice when he was preparing his *Tabula*; Martyr replied that he wholeheartedly approved of the table, and he advised Beza to expand and buttress his arguments with scriptural quotations – advice which Beza followed in the published version.

All this would suggest that Martyr's doctrine was uncompromising. In some respects that is true. It has indeed been claimed that predestination is more central for him than for Calvin.[44] Like Bucer, Martyr developed an emphasis on the total depravity of unregenerate man, and like Bucer he was not able to give an unequivocal 'no' in answer to the question whether God is the author of sin.[45] Although his views did not reach full maturity until his conflict with Bibliander at Zurich, his lectures on Romans at Oxford show substantially the same treatment. He rejected the interpretation that God merely permits sin. When Scripture says that God hardens sinners, that must be taken literally; God is the cause of sinful acts, but the actions are good in so far as they proceed from Him, and evil in so far as they result from human perversity. Sinners are necessitated but not forced to sin. Martyr claimed that the main Protestant theologians agreed with him; he admitted Melanchthon – 'venerabilem virum . . . quem amo et suscipio' – to be an exception.[46]

Like Bucer, Martyr followed St Augustine's interpretation of 1 Tim.

---

[42] Ibid.
[43] Ibid., 126–9.
[44] Ibid., 57.
[45] Ibid., 117–18.
[46] Ibid., 118.

ii, 4. The preaching of the word is for the predestined. The obstinacy of the reprobate is a spiritual help to the elect. Martyr dealt with the scriptural statement that God does not desire the death of the sinner by invoking the scholastic distinction between the *voluntas signi* and the *voluntas beneplaciti*; it is the former that wills the life of the sinner, just as it is the former that wills that all men keep the commandments, but much that happens is contrary to it. The *voluntas beneplaciti* which alone is efficacious does desire the death of the sinner.[47]

If the doctrine of predestination adumbrated thus far was central to Martyr's theology, that was because, as for Bucer, it made it impossible for man to glory in himself and led him to glorify God. It was integral to his refutation of Pighi's neo-Pelagian exaltation of human merit. Martyr defended the preaching of the doctrine against those who asserted that it would lead men to despair by arguing, following Augustine, that on the contrary by teaching Christians that their salvation does not depend on their own efforts it increases their trust in God and is a source of comfort and joy.[48] Each part of his definition of predestination was supported by scriptural references. It was

the most wise resolve of God by which he has steadfastly decreed before all eternity to call those he has loved in Christ to the adoption of sons, to justification by faith, and finally to glory through good works – a resolve by which they are made conformed to the image of the son of God so that in them may be declared the glory and mercy of the creator.[49]

Martyr argued that predestination relates to the divine goodness, wisdom and power. The resolve to save reflects the goodness; wisdom is reflected in the saving plan, and power in the saving action.

In dealing with the reprobate, Martyr pointed out that according to Scripture, only the elect are predestinate. Although God's foreknowledge extends to all His creatures, His will extends only to the elect.[50] In commenting on Romans ix, he argued that God was not obliged to be merciful to anyone; all men by their fallen nature are enmeshed in sin. Although, as we have seen, he approved of Beza's table, his own definition of reprobation implies merely a passing over of the reprobate: it is 'the most wise resolve of God by which he steadfastly decreed from all eternity, but without any injustice, not to have mercy on those whom he has not loved, but has passed over, that he might by their condemnation show his wrath towards sin and his glory'.[51] The ultimate purpose of reprobation is to declare the justice of God.

[47] Ibid., 122–3.
[48] Ibid., 130.
[49] Ibid., 131, 176.
[50] J. C. McClelland, 'The Reformed Doctrine of Predestination according to Peter Martyr', *Scottish Journal of Theology* 8 (1955), 262.
[51] Donnelly, *Calvinism and Scholasticism*, 132, Donnelly's translation of 'absque ulla iniustitia eorum non misereri quos non dilexit' ('without any injustice on their part . . .') is in error, and misrepresents Martyr's doctrine.

Just as Martyr denied that foreseen works, or even faith, are causes of election, so he denied that foreseen sin is the cause of reprobation. And although his definition of predestination emphasized that election is in Christ, he denied that the incarnation and death of Christ were causes of predestination: they were rather the first and greatest effects of predestination. There is much in Martyr, therefore, with which Arminius would have quarrelled, but there is a good deal less than later English Calvinists contended. In the first place, he rejected Luther's argument that divine foreknowledge precluded human freedom,[52] though he failed to explain satisfactorily how they may be reconciled. Secondly, he was markedly less emphatic than Bucer on the question of perseverance. According to Martyr, there could be no true faith without good works; hence a man may lose justification if he falls into sin; it may be regained by truly assenting to Christ's promises.[53] There is no emphasis on the certainty of salvation in Martyr. Instead, he argued that the happy mean between desperation and false security is hope, which he defined as 'the faculty given by the Holy Spirit by which we expect with certainty and calmness that the salvation begun in us through Christ and realised through faith shall eventually be perfected in us by God's mercy and not by our own merits'.[54] Finally, Martyr did not assert the irresistibility of grace in the form associated with many later Calvinists. Although man does not have the power to accept or reject justifying grace, even the strongest graces are said not to force the will, which falls in freely with the divine impulse. Once a man has been justified, Martyr insisted that he must co-operate with grace.[55]

Such were the major continental influences on emerging Edwardian Protestantism. Although Bucer and Martyr have much in common which provides an obvious contrast with Hooper and Latimer, there were significant differences between them. There was a spectrum of opinion on the doctrine of predestination in the Edwardian Church which cannot be neatly categorized into indigenous and continental, or 'Calvinist' and 'Lutheran' influences. It would seem, in particular, that Melanchthon's influence may have been seriously underestimated: Martyr, who disagreed with him, respected his views, and anyone who read and admired Bucer's commentary on Romans would have been indirectly influenced by him: as we have seen, for pastoral purposes Bucer saw eye to eye with Melanchthon. But in order to assess more fully the results of this complex of

---

[52] Ibid., 140.
[53] Ibid., 154.
[54] Ibid., 156.
[55] Ibid., 159–60.

ideas on the English Church, it will be necessary to turn to its early doctrinal statements.

The Edwardian formularies

'The Reformed Church of England occupies an independent position between Romanism on the one hand, and Lutheranism and Calvinism on the other, with strong affinities and antagonisms in both directions.' So Philip Schaff, from a late nineteenth-century German/American Lutheran standpoint, characterized the doctrinal position of the English Church and her relation to other churches.[56] We may well agree with Schaff that Anglican theology has been as much embodied in her episcopal polity and in her liturgy as in her doctrinal formularies, although not everyone will follow him in saying that while 'the Book of Common Prayer is catholic, though purged of superstitious elements, the Articles of Religion are evangelical and moderately Calvinistic'. In their earliest versions they were after all substantially the work of one man, working on existing models where available and taking advice and counsel from a wide variety of sources, to produce as far as he was able what was representative of the best Reformed scholarship as he knew it.[57] The mind that worked on those twin endeavours late in Henry VIII's reign and early in Edward VI's would surely have regretted attempts to categorize its thinking in the interests of subsequent Protestant sectarianism – whether Lutheran, Calvinist or Tractarian. Political influences, furthermore, operated against too precise a definition of doctrinal standards.[58]

The review here of the Articles of Religion (as first published in 1553, the Forty-two Articles) which have to do with the doctrine of predestination will concentrate on the relation of each article to problems then current, and interpret them as far as possible by contemporary evidence. The general line that emerges from this approach is Cranmer's desire to achieve a consensus of Reformed thinking against scholastic merit theology on the one hand, but guarding against Anabaptist excess on the other. At the same time, however, the sixth session of the Council of Trent had

---

[56] P. Schaff, *A History of the Creeds of Christendom* (1877), 598.

[57] As is well known, Cranmer invited Calvin, Bullinger and Melanchthon to join in framing a statement of doctrine which would settle differences among the Reformers and serve as an answer to the Council of Trent. H. Robinson (ed. and tr.), *Original Letters relative to the English Reformation* (2 vols., Parker Society, Cambridge, 1846–7), I. 17, 21–5. The Articles when published were 'agreed by the bishops and other learned men', and their conclusions described as 'a godly concord in certain matters of religion'. E. Cardwell (ed.) *Synodalia (A Collection of Articles of Religion, Canons and Proceedings of Convocation in the Province of Canterbury, 1547–1717)* (2 vols., Oxford, 1842), I. 18.

[58] A. G. Dickens, *The English Reformation* (1964), 179–80.

already produced (in January 1547) trenchant criticisms not only of the 'Lutheran' doctrine of justification but also of the doctrines of assurance and perseverance that were held to be implicit in it.[59] Thereafter, the Forty-two Articles, like all other Protestant formularies, could do no other than respond whether by refutation, reformulation or (just as significant) silence. In interpreting the Articles, the student is assisted by the Homilies, to which some articles specifically refer; but very helpful also is the neglected *Reformatio Legum Ecclesiasticarum*.

Article VIII: Of Original Sin or Birth Sin
Original sin standeth not in the following of Adam, as the Pelagians do vainly talk, which also the Anabaptists do nowadays renew, but it is the fault and corruption of the nature of every man, that naturally is engendered of the offspring of Adam, whereby man is very far gone from his former righteousness, which he had at his creation, and is of his own nature given [1563: 'inclined'] to evil, so that the flesh desireth always contrary to the Spirit, and therefore in every person born into this world, it deserveth God's wrath and damnation. And this infection of nature doth remain, yea in them that are baptised, whereby the lust of the flesh called in Greek $\Phi\rho\acute{o}\nu\eta\mu\alpha$ $\sigma\alpha\rho\kappa\acute{o}\varsigma$ (which some do expound the wisdom, some sensuality, some the affection, some the desire of the flesh) is not subject to the law of God. And although there is no condemnation for them that believe, and are baptised, yet the Apostle doth confess, that concupiscence, and lust hath of itself the nature of sin.[60]

This article was directed primarily against the Anabaptists, who had revived the Pelagian heresy referred to.[61] It was modelled on Article II of the Augsburg Confession through the medium of the Thirteen Articles agreed upon between English and German Divines in 1538. But Cranmer did not go so far as that Confession in defining the state of fallen man as 'born with sin, that is, without the fear of God, without firm confidence toward God, and with concupiscence' – which is further defined as an 'original disease or flaw' inevitably leading to damnation and eternal death in those who are not reborn by baptism and the Holy Spirit. In thus moderating the doctrine of total depravity[62] Cranmer showed himself independent of both Bucer and Martyr and left to the Church of England a teaching nearer to that of the Council of Trent that Adam and his successors lost the original righteousness and sanctity in which he had been constituted, and incurred the divine anger, and a corruption of his whole nature.[63]

---

[59] A. L. Richter (ed.), *Canones et Decreta Concilii Tridentini* (Leipzig, 1853), 28–9.
[60] I have used Grafton's original English version of June 1553, reproduced in C, Hardwick, *A History of the Articles of Religion* (3rd edn, Cambridge, 1859), 286ff.
[61] Ibid., 375.
[62] Cf. John Calvin, *Institutes* II.2.3; 'ex corrupta hominis natura nihil nisi damnabile prodire'.
[63] Dugmore, *Doctrine of Grace in the English Reformers*, II. 14.

Article IX: Of Free Will

We have no power to do good works pleasant, and acceptable to God, without the grace of God by Christ preventing us, that we may have a good will, and working in [1563: with] us, when we have that will.

Article X: Of Grace [omitted in 1563]

The grace of Christ, or the Holy Ghost by him given, takes away the stony heart and giveth an heart of flesh. And although those that have no will to good things he maketh them to will, and those that would evil things, he maketh them not to will the same, yet nevertheless he enforceth not the will. And therefore no man when he sinneth can excuse himself, as not worthy to be blamed or condemned, by alleging that he sinned unwillingly, or by compulsion.

Article IX is quoted almost verbatim from St Augustine.[64] As the *Reformatio* makes clear,[65] it was designed to assert the necessity for prevenient and co-operating grace against the Anabaptists. The 10th Article was directed against another school of Anabaptists who would appear to have believed human actions to be involuntary, and evil actions the result of a necessitating decree of God.[66]

Grace 'enforceth not the will'. There is compelling evidence of a consensus among Edwardian Protestants that divine grace may be spurned and rejected, that it is not irresistible; human free will must play its part, first to accept or reject, to obey or not to obey, and having obeyed, then to co-operate. The concern of the *Reformatio* was to refute those who placed such confidence in human free will that they believed that 'by it alone, without any special grace of Christ', man could live uprightly.[67] The *Necessary Doctrine and Erudition* of 1543 had spoken of man's free will as 'wounded and decayed', that it 'hath need of a physician to heal it, and to help repair it; that it may receive light and strength, whereby it may see, and have power to do those godly and spiritual things, which before the fall of Adam it was able and might have done'.[68] While it was asserted that the initial impetus to any good thing was 'of the grace of God only', it was necessary that men did not 'wilfully refuse' that grace; and their continuance in goodness depended on both 'the grace of God' and also 'our free will and endeavour'.[69] The *Paraphrases* of Erasmus, ordered by the king's Injunctions to be provided in every parish, spoke

[64] St Augustine, *De Gratia et Libero Arbitrio*, 17.
[65] *Reformatio Legum Ecclesiasticarum* (1571), 'De Haeresibus', c. 7.
[66] Hardwick, *Articles of Religion*, 100–1. Cf. Hooper to Bullinger, 25 June 1549: 'How dangerously our England is affected by heresies of this kind, God only knows.' *Original Letters relative to the English Reformation*, 1. 65–6.
[67] *Reformatio Legum Ecclesiasticarum*, 'De Haeresibus', c. 7.
[68] *A Necessary Doctrine and Erudition for any Christian Man* (1543), f. 85^r.
[69] Ibid. 'All men be also nourished and chiefly preachers that in this high matter they looking on both sides so attemper and moderate themselves that neither they so preach the grace of God that they take away thereby free will nor on the other side so extol free will that injury be done to the grace of God'. f. 86^r.

to the same effect. On Matt. xxiii, 37 for example, after stressing that our Lord 'of his goodness would have no man utterly to perish', Erasmus adds 'but to whom free will is once given, he cannot be saved against his will'.[70] Finally, the inclusion in the Prayer Book of ancient Collects such as that for Easter Day ('as by thy special grace preventing us thou dost put into our minds good desires, so by thy continual help we may bring the same to good effect') ensured a continuity on the doctrine of grace in the teaching of the English Church. It is the authentic Augustinian doctrine that all is of God: grace is that divine initiative of love which, if not rejected, becomes the response of faith.[71]

Article XI: Justification of Man.
Justification by only faith in Jesus Christ, in that sense in which it is declared in the Homily of Justification, is a most certain and wholesome doctrine for Christian men.

Article XII: Works before justification.
Works done before the grace of Christ, and the inspiration of his Spirit, are not pleasant to God, forasmuch as they spring not of faith in Jesus Christ; neither do they make men meet to receive grace or (as the School authors say) deserve grace of congruity: but because they are not done as God hath willed and commanded them to be done, we doubt not but they have the nature of sin.

Article XIII: Works of Supererogation.
Voluntary works besides, over and above God's commandments which they call works of supererogation, cannot be taught without arrogance and iniquity: for by them men do declare, that they do not only render to God as much as they are bound to do, but that they do more for his sake than of bounden duty is required: whereas Christ says plainly, When ye have done all that are commanded to you, say, We be unprofitable servants.

According to the Council of Trent, faith was not alone sufficient for justification; it must be accompanied by hope and love. The homily to which the 11th Article refers (it is the Homily of Salvation) steered a middle course by explaining that 'faith doth not shut out repentance, hope, love, dread, and the fear of God, to be joined with faith in every man, that is justified, but it shutteth them out from the office of justifying'.[72] At the same time, the Homily makes clear that faith is not a human work. 'The true understanding of this doctrine, we be justified freely by faith without works, or that we be justified by faith in Christ only, is not, that this our own act to believe in Christ, or this our faith in Christ, which is within us, doth justify us . . . (for that were to count ourselves to be

---

[70] *The First Tome . . . of the Paraphrases of Erasmus upon the New Testament* (1548), xc–xci.
[71] Dugmore, *Doctrine of Grace in the English Reformers*, II. 20.
[72] *Certaine Sermons or Homilies appointed to be read in churches in the time of Queene Elizabeth* (1623), 14–15.

justified by some act or virtue that is within ourselves) but . . . that . . . although we have faith, hope, charity, repentance, dread and fear of God within us, and do never so many works thereunto; yet we must renounce the merit of all our said virtues of faith, hope, charity, and all other virtues and good deeds . . . as things that be far too weak and insufficient and unperfect to deserve the remission of our sins.' Instead, we must trust in God's mercy, and in the merits of Christ's sacrifice, 'once offered upon the Cross, to obtain thereby God's grace, and remission as well of original sin in baptism, as of all actual sin committed by us after our Baptism, if we truly repent, and turn unfeignedly to him again'. According to the homily, therefore, repentance is ruled out as a meritorious cause, but it remains as a necessary condition, of our justification. The Homily upon Faith, similarly, distinguished between idle, unfruitful and dead faith, and the faith that 'worketh by charity . . . which as the other vain faith is called a dead faith, so may this be called a quick or lively faith'.[73] Such a lively faith included 'an earnest trust and confidence . . . that our offences be continually washed and purged, whensoever we (repenting truly) do return to him, with our whole heart, steadfastly determining with ourselves, through his grace, to obey and serve him in keeping his commandments, and never to turn back again to sin'.[74] Furthermore, the homily warned, 'When men hear in the Scriptures so high commendations of faith . . . if they then fancy, that they be set at liberty from doing all good works, and may live as they list, they trifle with God, and deceive themselves.'[75]

Article XV: Of Sin against the Holy Ghost.
Every deadly sin willingly committed after baptism, is not sin against the Holy Ghost, and unpardonable. Wherefore the place for penitents is not to be denied to such as fall into sin after Baptism. After we have received the Holy Ghost, we may depart from grace given, and fall into sin, and by the grace of God we may arise again and amend our lives. And therefore they are to be condemned, which say, they can no more sin as long as they live here, or deny the place for penitents to such as truly repent, and amend their lives.

The concern of this article was to condemn the Anabaptist doctrine that it was impossible, once justified, to lose the Holy Spirit.[76] As the *Necessary Doctrine* had asserted, 'it is no doubt, but although we be once justified, yet we may fall therefrom by our own freewill and consenting unto sin . . . And here all phantastical imagination, curious reasoning, and vain trust of predestination, is to be laid apart'.[77] The opposite

---

[73] Ibid., 17.
[74] Ibid., 22–3.
[75] Ibid., 23.
[76] Hardwick, *Articles of Religion*, 382.
[77] *A Necessary Doctrine and Erudition for any Christian Man.* ff. 88ᵛ–89ʳ.

extreme, to assert that any post-baptismal sin amounted to a sin against the Holy Ghost, and was therefore unforgivable, was described as 'Novatian' by the Confession of Augsburg, which likewise condemned it. There would appear to have been a good deal of common ground here with the Council of Trent, which had also condemned those who held that 'once justified a man cannot any more sin, or lose grace, and so that he who falls and sins has never been truly justified'.[78] The teaching of this article that the justified may fall from grace provoked intermittent hostility in Puritan circles during the reign of Elizabeth, for example from Cartwright in 1572.[79]

Article XVII: Of Predestination and Election.
Predestination to life, is the everlasting purpose of God, whereby (before the foundations of the world were laid) he hath constantly decreed by his own judgement [1563: 'counsel'] secret to us, to deliver from curse and damnation those whom he hath chosen [1563: 'in Christ'] out of mankind, and to bring them to everlasting salvation by Christ, as vessels made to honour. Whereupon such as have so excellent a benefit of God given unto them, be called according to God's purpose, by his spirit working in due season, they through grace obey the calling, they be justified freely, they be made sons by adoption, they be made like the image of God's only begotten son Jesus Christ, they walk religiously in good works, and at length by God's mercy, they attain to everlasting felicity.

As the Godly consideration of predestination, and our election in Christ, is full of sweet, pleasant, and unspeakable comfort to godly persons, and such as feel in themselves the working of the spirit of Christ, mortifying the works of the flesh, and their earthly members, and drawing up their mind to high, and heavenly things, as well because it doth greatly stablish and confirm their faith of eternal salvation to be enjoyed through Christ, as because it doth fervently kindle their love towards God. So, for curious and carnal persons, lacking the spirit of Christ, to have continually before their eyes the sentence of God's predestination, is a most dangerous downfall, whereby the devil may thrust them either into desperation, or into recklessness of most unclean living, no less perilous than desperation. Furthermore, although the decrees of predestination are unknown to us [omitted in 1563], yet we must receive God's promises in such wise, as they be generally set forth to us in holy scripture, and in our doings, that will of God is to be followed, which we have expressly declared unto us in the word of God.

Much effort has been devoted to searching for the origins of this article, without conspicuous success. Attempts to trace the first part to Luther's preface to the Epistle to the Romans, and the latter part to Melanchthon,[80] have not won general acceptance. Still less convincing, however, is a recent judgment as to its 'immoderate Calvinism' and rigorous supralapsarianism'.[81] If Beza may be taken as representative of

---

[78] Richter, *Canones et Decreta Concilii Tridentini*, 32.
[79] W. H. Frere and C. E. Douglas (eds.), *Puritan Manifestoes* (1907), 118.
[80] Hardwick, *Articles of Religion*, 383.
[81] Dickens, *The English Reformation*, 252.

what that means, then it is difficult to find any of the doctrines to which Arminius objected in Article XVII. The claim, put forward by Whitaker in the 1590s, and by Gomarus at Dort, that it implies supralapsarianism failed to win general support on either occasion. May the article then reasonably be claimed, as by Schaff, to be 'moderately Calvinistic'?[82] There is certainly no evidence that English Calvinists ever wanted to quarrel with anything the article says; but the story of the Lambeth Articles shows that for many of them it did not go far enough. As has often been pointed out, nothing is said in the article of any decree of reprobation, which would seem to have been an essential part of Calvin's doctrine. In the *Reformatio*, the whole chapter on predestination (as, indeed, all the chapters dealing with the detail of the doctrine of grace) are included not in the first section, *De Summa Trinitate et fide Catholica*, but in the second, *De Haeresibus*. That would seem to be quite incompatible with Prynne's claim that the doctrine of predestination was at the heart of English Protestantism.[83]

It has been argued that the 'cautions' against abuse of the doctrine are consistent only with a Calvinistic interpretation.[84] That is surely a misunderstanding. The cautions, as the *Reformatio* makes very clear, were directed against Anabaptist doctrines of predestination: no one, presumably, would argue that therefore the article must be Anabaptist! The Council of Trent, too, stressed that the decree of predestination was a 'secret mystery'. It had condemned any 'presumptious certainty of salvation', warning that no one (unless by a special revelation) can know for certain that he is among those who have been predestinated to life. He who is once justified cannot be sure, either that he will not fall again into mortal sin or that if he does he has been promised repentance.[85] The Forty-two Articles are silent as to the doctrines of assurance and perseverance. They were designed 'for the avoiding of the diversities of opinions, and the stablishing of consent, touching true religion'. That is why, surely, the language of Article XVII contains such strong echoes of the scriptural passages on which the doctrine was founded – Ephesians i and Romans viii and ix – echoes which are even stronger in the Latin than in the English. The purpose of the article was to limit doctrinal

---

[82] Schaff, *Creeds of Christendom*, 623.

[83] In the *Harmonia Confessionum Fidei Orthodoxarum, et Reformatarum Ecclesiarum*, agreement on the doctrine of predestination had to be limited to the Second Helvetic, Basle, Gallican and Belgic confessions. Article XVII of the Thirty-nine Articles was significantly not quoted, and it was even more awkward that the Augsburg Confession (Article XX, *De Fide*), had affirmed that the doctrine was not necessary to the truth of justification by faith.

[84] Schaff, *Creeds of Christendom*, 635.

[85] Richter, *Canones et Decreta Concilii Tridentini*, 28–9.

definition to what was beyond dispute — that could be achieved only by keeping as closely as possible to the words of Scripture, and by avoiding any of the issues over which differences of Reformed opinion were beginning to appear — and specifically to guard against Anabaptist abuse. Any unmistakably 'Lutheran' or 'Calvinist' slant would have been inconsistent with that main purpose. Bucer and Martyr[86] may well have contributed directly or indirectly to the evolution of the Edwardian Articles, but they would surely have approved of that purpose, and if they did so, they contributed nothing to which Hooper and Latimer would not readily have agreed.

[86] Donnelly sees Martyr's hand in Article XVII but concedes that in so far as Article XVII avoids the issue of reprobation, 'it cannot be called Vermiglian'. Most of the key phrases of both may be found in the Vulgate. Donnelly, *Calvinism and Scholasticism*, 176.

4   The Elizabethan church settlement

Returning exiles and doctrinal definition

A sharp discontinuity between the old English Protestantism of Edward's reign and the theology of the Elizabethan church underlay Heylyn's understanding of the English Reformation. His assumption that the return of the Marian exiles marked the triumph of Calvinism has been widely accepted. A typical judgment is that the exiles consisted mainly of those who 'set least store on the bonds that tied them to historic catholicity . . . In more or less degree they came under the spell of Calvin's genius.'[1] Other historians, it is true, have recognised that in liturgical matters many of the exiles 'were openly opposed to Calvin and his influence',[2] that they were in no sense a single party, and that those who went to Zurich and Strasburg were independent of, if not actually opposed to, Geneva; but they have nevertheless conceded that in doctrinal matters 'the Anglican Church, from the time of Archbishop Parker to the end of the century, was Calvinistic. The Lambeth Articles cannot otherwise be interpreted.'[3] Those conclusions were in harmony with studies of the political role of the exiles which suggested that they constituted a radical opposition group both in and out of Parliament, the nucleus of a Puritan party.[4] As a result of their activities, it appeared, the queen was forced to accept a much more radically Protestant church than she had wanted or intended.[5]

Recent scholarship demands a major revision of this picture. Politically, it is clear, returning exiles played an insignificant role in the Parliament of 1559. At most, there were nineteen members who had been in exile, of whom eleven had resided mainly in Italy as political and not religious exiles. Of over two hundred exiles at Geneva, only one was returned for either of Elizabeth's first two Parliaments, and the city continued to

[1] W. H. Frere, *The English Church in the Reigns of Elizabeth and James I* (1911), 8.
[2] W. M. Southgate, 'The Marian Exiles and the Influence of John Calvin', *History* 27 (1942), 148–50.
[3] Ibid., 151.
[4] C. H. Garrett, *The Marian Exiles: A Study in the Origins of Elizabethan Puritanism* (Cambridge, 1938).
[5] J. M. Neale, *Elizabeth and Her Parliaments* (2 vols., 1953–7), I. 1–77.

provide the fewest MPs of any major exile community.[6] More fundamentally, the hypothesis that the queen originally intended only to pass a supremacy bill, but was forced in addition to revive Edward's second Prayer Book as part of a much more Protestant settlement than she had originally envisaged, has been subjected to fundamental revision.[7] Even if it is going too far to claim an identity of outlook between the queen and her Protestant advisers,[8] there can be no doubt that the major threat to the settlement came not from radical Protestants but from Catholics in the Lords.

The assumption of discontinuity, which for Heylyn was axiomatic, does not bear scrutiny. Common to Elizabeth's first advisers, both clerical and lay, was a shared Edwardian Protestantism. Significantly, however, there were for the first time no clerical members of the Privy Council. The dominant figures were university-trained laymen. Although some of them had served under Mary, there were no committed Catholics. Equally, however, 'extremists of what was to be called the Genevan camp were not represented'.[9] Most were identified with the 'moderate Protestantism associated with Thomas Cranmer, Martin Bucer, and Peter Martyr'. That was certainly true of Cecil, and also of Bacon. Almost all the members, furthermore, had held office under Edward; many had served under Henry.

Most of the clerics who played a part in the settlement represented the same standpoint. Many of them had like Cecil himself been students at Cambridge of Cecil's brother-in-law John Cheke, the Regius Professor of Greek in the 1540s who was tutor to Edward VI and friend of the foreign Reformers in England, especially Martin Bucer. Pre-eminent was Cecil's Cambridge friend Matthew Parker, Master of Corpus Christi. Returned exiles similarly identified with a return to Edwardian Protestantism were Grindal, William Bill, William May, James Pilkington, Richard Cox and John Jewel. The tradition they shared was of course compatible with differences over matters of detail, and even more with different perceptions of what was politically possible, but there is evidence that at bottom they appreciated that the church settlement 'could only be a pragmatic act of statesmanship'.[10] Whatever the personal religious outlook of the queen,

---

[6] K. R. Bartlett, 'The Role of the Marian Exiles', in P. W. Hasler (ed.), *The House of Commons 1558–1603* (3 vols., 1981), I, app. XI, 102–10.

[7] N. L. Jones, *Faith By Statute: Parliament and the Settlement of Religion, 1559* (1982).

[8] See, for example, P. Collinson, *Archbishop Grindal, 1559–1583: The Struggle for a Reformed Church* (1979), 85–6.

[9] W. Hudson, *The Cambridge Connection and the Elizabethan Settlement of 1559* (Durham, North Carolina, 1980), 25.

[10] N. M. Sutherland, 'The Marian Exiles and the Establishment of the Elizabethan Regime', *Archiv für Reformationsgeschichte* 78 (1987), 264. Although Dr Sutherland does not discuss the doctrinal settlement, her conclusions parallel those reached here.

the settlement would have to be acceptable both to the Edwardians who were advising her and to those Marians who, she hoped, could be reconciled to it. It could therefore 'neither be doctrinally crypto-catholic nor too obtrusively reformed'.[11]

If, as seems likely, the *Device for the alteration of religion and divers points of religion contrary to the church of Rome* represents Cecil's perspective of the planned settlement,[12] and of the major threats to its achievement, then both the fact of continuity with Edwardian Protestantism, and the need for careful compromise, are confirmed as crucial. Caution was reflected in the advice 'that there should be no often changes in religion which would take away authority'.[13] The clergy nominated to review the Book of Common Prayer were Bill, Parker, May, Cox, Whitehead, Grindal and Pilkington – all associates of Cecil; three Protestant peers were to be made privy to their proceedings. Yet there would have to be compromise, as the document makes clear. Quite apart from conservative objections, there would be opposition, it anticipated, from those who 'when they shall see peradvanture that some old ceremonies shall be left still, or that their doctrine is not allowed and commanded only and all other abolished or disproved, shall be discontented, and call the alteration a cloaked papistry or mingle-mangle'.[14] The very language of what would later be called Puritanism was thus anticipated, and it was expected to be concerned with doctrine as well as ceremony.

What must be stressed, however, is that notwithstanding the frustration of at least some of the queen's clerical advisers with the slow progress of the settlement, and with their failure to achieve a greater degree of ceremonial reform,[15] their doctrinal stance was studiously moderate. Fortunately, evidence has survived which enables us to describe it in their own words. In or about May 1559, those of them who had preached before the queen[16] presented her with a long declaration of their doctrines and opinions.[17] It was written to justify themselves against hostile criticism after their disputation at Westminster with Marian Catholics[18] 'most untruly reporting of us that our doctrine is detestable heresy, that we are fallen from the doctrine of Christ's Catholic Church, that we be subtle sectaries, that we dissent among ourselves, and that every man nourisheth

---

[11] W. P. Haugaard, *Elizabeth and the English Reformation* (Cambridge, 1968), 37–42.
[12] Sutherland, 'The Marian Exiles', 267.
[13] British Library, MS Cotton Julius F6, ff. 161f., printed in Henry Gee, *The Elizabethan Prayer Book and Ornaments* (1902), 195–202.
[14] Ibid., 197.
[15] Jones, *Faith by Statute*, 67–8, 138–9.
[16] They included Edwin Sandys, Richard Cox and John Jewel.
[17] Printed in R. W. Dixon, *History of the Church of England* (6 vols., 1878–82), V. 107–16, from Corpus Christi College, Cambridge, MSS CXXI, 20.
[18] Jones, *Faith by Statute*, 123–9.

and maintaineth his own opinion'.[19] 'We do justly vindicate and challenge to ourselves the name of Christian Catholics.' They defined 'Catholic' as 'that which is founded and grounded upon the doctrine of the prophets and apostles'.[20]

They proceeded to set forth their doctrine in a series of articles, modelled on the Forty-two Edwardian Articles: the document is thus part of the history of the evolution of the Thirty-nine Articles. If the exiles had been doctrinal Calvinists, then we should expect this document, when compared with the Forty-two, to show signs of movement in that direction. The opposite is the case. In the first place, there is a move away from doctrinal definition in general, towards a less 'precise' standpoint. This was achieved by separating the first seven of the Forty-two Articles as the important ones, the denial of which would amount to heresy. These seven articles were combined into a confession of faith in order to rebut that charge. It was on these articles that the writers of the Declaration rested their claim to be called Catholics. In the rest of the document, other articles were enumerated, beginning at Article I: the enumerated articles 'were not such that no variation of opinion on them could be allowed by men of catholic mind'.[21] In other words, the returned exiles had a more generous concept of doctrinal *adiaphora* than that exhibited by the Forty-two Articles.

None of the articles of the Forty-two that deal with the doctrine of grace was included in the preliminary confession of faith: they were all placed in the enumerated articles. The conclusion would seem inescapable that, whatever else they had learned in Frankfurt, Strasburg, Zurich or Geneva, the exiles had not returned with the conviction that the doctrine of predestination was in any sense the foundation of the Gospel. Their first article, 'Of original or birth Sin', repeated Article VIII of the Forty-two; their second, 'Of Free-will and Grace', combined Article IX with the first part of Article X of the Forty-two. Their third article, 'Of Predestination and Election', repeated Article XVII of the Forty-two, and then added a long apology.

This Article of God's predestination and election, as it is most true, so it is a high and weighty matter and a most deep mystery: and therefore when just cause is offered to entreat of it either in sermons or otherwise, it is to be done with great consideration and discernment; and the hearers or readers of books written in these matters ought to lay apart all carnal curiosity, as it is aforesaid in the Article. For whosoever gathereth upon the consideration of God's election or the weakness of man's nature either encouragement to carnal or ungodly life, either a dulness or slothfulness to piety and godly exercises, let him assure himself that he hath no right consideration neither of himself nor of God's merciful goodness promised

[19] Dixon, *History of the Church of England*, V. 110–12.
[20] Ibid., 115.
[21] Ibid., 108–9.

us in Christ. For those agitations which proceed from God's Spirit tend always to the overthrow of the Devil's work and sin, and not contrariwise to minister provocations unto sin. And although many godly men in these our days will think that in this our corrupt age, in the which men are given to all rashness of judgement and dissoluteness of life, and do not weigh the mysteries of our faith with such Christian humility as they ought to do, it were best that such Articles should be passed over in silence (indeed we do think that discreet ministers will speak sparely and circumspectly of them, and that upon the considerations before rehearsed), yet notwithstanding, seeing some men of late are risen which do gainsay and oppugn this truth, we cannot utterly pass over this matter with silence, both for that the Holy Ghost doth so often make mention of it in the Scriptures, especially in St Paul's Epistles, which argues it to be a thing fruitful and profitable to be known: and also being occasioned by the same reason which moved St Augustine to write of this matter of predestination: whose words are these . . . from *De Bono Perseverantiae cap. 26. Let the truth therefore,* saith St Augustine, *be spoken, especially when any questioning requireth it to be spoken, lest peradventure while it is kept in silence for their sakes which cannot receive it, they which are able to receive the truth and thereby avoid falsehood be not only defrauded or kept back from the truth, but also be caught with falsehood and error.* These and many other like causes, which St Augustine writeth in the book aforenamed, wherein he answereth to the objections of them that are of contrary mind, have moved us also at the time not to pass over this Article (and yet not without a charitable admonition), seeing that some even in these our days (who also pretend the name of the Gospel) do oppugn this and other Articles touching the doctrines of grace and our free justification and salvation by Christ, for the which we are right sorry. Notwithstanding we do not despair but that such are curable; and through fair and open preaching of the Gospel will be brought to see and understand the truth better than they have hitherto done. For truth it is that these and other most grievous errors have increased in this realm in these late years for want of preaching. Experience declareth that even as in other countries, where the preaching of God's words is not permitted, all horrible heresies and sects do most flow and abound.[22]

Had the exiles been bent on introducing doctrinal Calvinism into England, they would have written in very different terms from these. Instead, they would seem to have been divided between those ('the many godly men') who favoured the omission of the article and others who agreed with St Augustine that to omit it altogether would not be consistent with scriptural truth taken as a whole, and might indeed lead to heresy, falsehood or error. Given that standpoint, it is hard to imagine any exposition more cautious or moderate.

Other articles reflect the same perspective. In treating of justification, for example, the exiles defined faith as 'a certainty and full persuasion wrought in the heart of man through the Holy Ghost, whereby he is assured of the mercy of God promised in Christ, that his sins are forgiven him, that he is made the Child of God, and inheritor of everlasting salvation,

---

[22] Ibid., 109–10.

and that freely of God's good will and mercy, without all respect of works and deserving of our parts', but they were at pains to refute the allegation that they condemned fasting, prayer and all other good works, which indeed 'necessarily follow' our reconciliation to God, because 'the Spirit of God in the just is no idle Spirit, but continually moveth and striveth to work the will of God, acknowledging to that end they are made just, to exercise and practise the works of justice'. Although John Jewel, in a letter to Peter Martyr, claimed that the Declaration did not depart 'in the slightest degree from the Confession of Zürich',[23] there is nothing in it which would lend support to the image of a pressure group of returned exiles in favour of further doctrinal definition. There is no evidence, furthermore, that the failure for the time being of the government to take any official steps towards a revised statement of doctrine occasioned them any disquiet, even though it was bound to diminish the appearance of fundamental reform.

The sense of continuity with the Edwardian past, and of careful moderation, was reinforced by the Injunctions which followed the completion of the statutory settlement early in 1559, in the preparation of which clerical advisers, Cecil and perhaps the queen herself shared. Many of them repeated the Edwardian Injunctions with little if any alteration. Among those in that category were Injunction VI, which required the *Paraphrases* of Erasmus in English to be provided along with the Bible in every parish church, and also XVII, which exhorted[24]

That the vice of damnable despair be taken away, and that firm belief and steadfast hope may be surely conceived of all their parishioners being in any danger; they shall learn and always have in a readiness such comfortable places and sentences of scripture, as do set forth the mercy, benefits and goodness of almighty God towards all penitent and believing persons; that they may at all times when necessity shall require, promptly comfort their flock with the lively word of God, which is the only stay of man's conscience.

At the parochial level, therefore, there can be no doubt that official teaching was from the first anxious to stress the infinite value of the death of Christ to all believers, and to guard against unacceptable formulations of the doctrine of reprobation.

[23] H. Robinson (ed. and tr.), *Zürich Letters* (2 vols., Parker Society, Cambridge, 1842–5), I. 21, Jewel to Peter Martyr, 28 April 1559.

[24] Printed in E, Cardwell (ed.), *Documentary Annals of the Reformed Church of England (A Collection of Injunctions, Declarations, Orders, Articles of Enquiry, etc,) 1546–1716* (2 vols., Oxford, 1844), I. 210ff. A curious provision was included in the 'Interpretations and further Considerations' for the better direction of the clergy (preserved in Parker's papers) to the effect that 'incorrigible Arians, Pelagians, or Free-will-men, be sent into some one castle in North Wales or Wallingford; and there to live of their own labour and exercise: and none other be suffered to resort unto them but their keepers, until they be found to repent their errors'. Ibid., 237.

When tentative steps were taken towards a revision of the formularies, they were fully in harmony with the Declaration. In 1561, both the Latin 'Principal Heads of Religion'[25] and the English Eleven Articles[26] in different ways illustrated the forces making for comprehension rather than definition. The 'Principal Heads', for example, go further than the Forty-two Articles in asserting the reality of sacramental grace in general and of the presence of Christ in the Eucharist. The Eleven Articles, authorized by the bishops and not superseded even by the Thirty-nine Articles, generally avoided controversial topics, and went little further than endorsing the Prayer Book 'for doctrine' as well as a liturgy. Both bear witness to the power of forces making for comprehension rather than division in the early Elizabethan church.

The adoption of the Thirty-nine Articles in 1563 was a further step in the same direction. Minor alterations only were made to those of the Forty-two which had to do with the doctrine of grace. In Article VIII, 'Of Original or Birth Sin', where Cranmer had described fallen man as 'given' to evil, Parker substituted the still softer 'inclined'; that apart, the article was left as it stood. Article IX, 'Of Free Will', now began 'The condition of man after the fall of Adam is such, that he cannot turn and prepare himself by his own natural strength and good works, to faith and calling upon God, wherefore . . .': a rebuttal of Pelagianism, but making no concessions to any doctrine of total depravity; and in the rest of the article, 'the grace of God by Christ preventing us, that we may have a good will' was now said to work 'with [1553 'in'] us, when we have that will'. This insistence that grace co-operated with the will but did not 'enforce' it made possible the omission of Article X, which had been anticipated in the Declaration. Two minor alterations were made to Article XVII. The words 'in Christ' were added to the description of the elect 'chosen out of mankind', and the words 'although the Decrees of predestination are unknown to us' were omitted. Both changes were designed to discourage speculation ('carnal curiosity') and to reinforce the teaching of the last paragraph that men ought to content themselves with God's will 'expressly declared unto us' – namely, the promise of salvation in Christ. A new article (XII) 'Of good works' was added, partly drawn from the Württemberg Confession, echoing the Declaration's repudiation of extreme solifidianism.[27] In all, it is hard

---

[25] Text in J. Strype, *Annals of the Reformation under Elizabeth* (7 vols., Oxford, 1824), I, i, 323–5; Haugaard, *Elizabeth and the English Reformation*, 240–1.

[26] Haugaard, *Elizabeth and the English Reformation*, 240–1; text in Hardwick, *Articles of Religion*, 337–9.

[27] 'Albeit that good works which are the fruits of faith, and follow after justification, can not put away our sins, and endure the severity of God's judgement; yet are they pleasing and acceptable to God in Christ, and do spring out necessarily of a true and lively faith, in so much that by them, a lively faith may be as evidently known, as a tree discerned by the fruit.'

not to agree with the verdict that in their final form the Articles, while pleasing to continental Protestants in their renewed repudiation of Rome, contained little ammunition for inter-Protestant battles.[28] Together with changes noted earlier, they reflected above all caution and moderation. In doctrine as well as in liturgy, the Elizabethan settlement was a return to late Edwardian Protestantism with judicious concessions to conservatives.

When the first Latin edition of the Articles was published, they were printed with two changes that had not been discussed in Convocation and which appear to have been made on the queen's initiative. A sentence asserting the power of the church to decree rites and ceremonies was added to Article XX, and Article XXIX, which denied the participation of the wicked in the sacrament of the Lord's Supper, was omitted altogether.[29] Both changes reflected the queen's anxiety not to alienate conservative opinion. In 1571, all thirty-nine were again confirmed by the bishops in Convocation and subsequently 'approved and allowed' by Elizabeth. In canons approved by the same Convocation, the clergy were required to subscribe the Articles, and preachers were to teach doctrine agreeable to the 'catholic fathers and ancient bishops'.[30] Clerical subscription to the Articles was, in addition, required by a statute of 1571.[31]

This amounted to a modest doctrinal requirement by continental standards. As anticipated, it did not meet the aspirations of all zealous Protestants, some of whom prepared proposals for the 1563 Convocation entitled 'General notes'.[32] They asked that the Edwardian Articles (as about to be revised) and Jewel's Apology and Nowell's Catechism be combined in one volume and be made the doctrinal standard of the Elizabethan church. Alexander Nowell was Dean of St Paul's, and prolocutor of the Lower House of Convocation. His Catechism, although moderate on predestination,[33] was modelled closely on Calvin's: Nowell's definition of the church, for example, followed Calvin in describing it as the society of the elect, and he envisaged a godly discipline in the hands of the local congregation. Although the bishops 'allowed' the Catechism, they refused to give it the official status which the Lower House requested for it. In 1571, the canons required schoolmasters to use Nowell's Catechism in teaching the young, but the bishops declined to go any further in

---

[28] Haugaard, *Elizabeth and the English Reformation*, 272.
[29] STC 10035: *Articuli, de quibus in synodo Londiniensi MDLXII ad tollendam opinionum dissensionem & firmandum in vera religione consensum, convenit.*
[30] Cardwell, *Synodalia*, I. 126–7.
[31] 13 Eliz. c. 12. See also G. R. Elton, *The Parliament of England, 1559–1581* (Cambridge, 1986), 210–14.
[32] Haugaard, *Elizabeth and the English Reformation*, 277.
[33] See W. P. Haugaard, 'John Calvin and the Catechism of Alexander Nowell', *Archiv für Reformationsgeschichte* 61 (1970), 50–65.

implementing proposals for imposing doctrinal standards on either clergy or laity.[34]

In making that decision, the bishops had before them a petition from a group of former Marian exiles who, while affirming their continued abhorrence of all papistry, stated that they could not accept the convictions of many of their Protestant brethren about predestination.[35] Denying that God's predestination was in any sense 'the occasion or cause at all in anywise of the wickedness, iniquity, or sin that ever was, is, or ever shall be', on the grounds that this would make Him 'the chief author and occasion thereof', they maintained that 'God doth foreknow and predestinate all good and goodness, but doth only foreknow, and not predestinate, any evil, wickedness or sin.' They claimed that their views were in accordance with those of 'all the learned fathers unto this our age', but that they were being subjected to the slander that they were 'free-will men, Pelagians, papists, epicures, anabaptists, and enemies unto God's holy predestination and providence, with other such like opprobrious words and threatenings'. They asked that in future disputes about predestination should be 'had and made only by writing, and not by word of mouth, for the avoiding of all unreverend speaking . . . and to avoid all contention and brawling, and other uncharitable behaviour'.[36]

In declining to accede to demands for a more thoroughgoing definition of doctrine, and the sanctions to enforce it, the bishops ensured that the strength of conservatism, reflected already in the preservation of an episcopal church order and many of the outward observances of traditional worship, was reflected in its doctrinal settlement. The continental Reformers themselves recognized that reality, and the consequent limitations on their influence. In January, 1559, Calvin's gift to the queen of his commentaries on Isaiah had been coldly received, and Cecil too had been severe to the point of discourtesy.[37] Peter Martyr declined to be drawn into direct confrontation over ceremonial. 'I do not think that any letter of mine will have much weight.'[38] Two earlier letters, he said, had remained unacknowledged, and he was discouraged by the reported determination of the English to embrace the Augsburg Confession and make an alliance with the German Protestants.[39] Assurances to the contrary by the returned exiles were received with scepticism, and one of the main reasons why the Swiss leaders eventually counselled conformity on ceremonial was, as Rudolph Gualter admitted in a letter to Beza of 1566,

---

[34] Haugaard, *Elizabeth and the English Reformation*, 288.
[35] J. Strype, *Annals of the Reformation*, I. i, 494–8.
[36] Ibid., 496–7.
[37] *Zürich Letters*, II. 34–5.
[38] Ibid., 48.
[39] Ibid.

that otherwise 'we well knew that either avowed papists, or Lutherans, would succeed unto their places, and introduce greater follies, and corruption of doctrine at the same time'.[40] Beza had already written to Bullinger of the 'very wretched state' of the English Church, 'altogether beyond endurance'. He asked Bullinger to do what he could. 'Yours, my father, is the only church by whose authority both the queen and the bishops seem likely to be influenced . . . For as to our own church, it is so hateful to that queen that on this account she has never said a single word in acknowledgement of the gift of my Annotations.' He gave two reasons: the one, Knox's books, the other 'because we are accounted too severe and precise, which is very displeasing to those who fear reproof'.[41] It was an unsympathetic way of saying that the English Church and his own were crucially different, not only in polity and worship, but also in their approach to the definition of doctrine.

John Jewel

In John Jewel, the early Elizabethan church found its first and only major apologist. First at Merton under John Parkhurst, and then at Corpus under Richard Foxe, Jewel's theological studies (in the last years of Henry's reign) had been centred on the patristic works made available by Erasmus: Jerome, Augustine, Ambrose and Origen. At the same time, his prodigious memory was employed on the Greek and Latin classics then becoming popular in humanist circles. He soon acquired a reputation as a leading member of Oxford's radical intelligentsia, attracting a considerable circle of students, and becoming Reader in Humanity and Rhetoric in 1548. That was the year in which Martyr was appointed Professor of Divinity, and Jewel soon became his secretarial assistant; intellectually and temperamentally they had much in common. Their friendship deepened under Mary after Jewel had joined Martyr at Strasburg. He was one of the large number of exiles identified with the preservation of unity on the basis of the second Edwardian Prayer Book. Under the pressure of events, that had become a conservative standpoint.[42]

When, in 1556, Bullinger invited Martyr to Zurich, Jewel went too. The

---

[40] Ibid., II. 143. The exiles themselves occasionally admitted their despair of the 'irreligious lukewarmness of the English in regard to religion', which seemed likely to lead them 'to fall back again into Popery, or something worse'. Ibid., II. 77. England had many more 'Samaritans, limping on both feet' than 'sincere professors of the gospel', said William Turner in a letter to Bullinger of 1566. Ibid., II. 125. Between the lines, the strength of doctrinal conservatism is apparent.

[41] Ibid., II. 131.

[42] W. M. Southgate, *John Jewel and the Problem of Doctrinal Authority* (Cambridge, Mass., 1962), 6–19.

personal and theological bonds between him and the Zurich Reformers became close. On his return to England, Jewel wrote to Martyr as 'my father, my pride, and even the half of my soul'.[43] In November 1559 he could assure him that, whatever the difficulties over the queen's ceremonial conservatism ('as to ceremonies and maskings, there is a little too much foolery. That little silver cross, of ill-omened origin, still retains its place in the queen's chapel'), everywhere the doctrine was 'most pure'.[44] Just over two years later, his preoccupation was still ceremonial, but this time with 'that linen surplice'. 'As to matters of doctrine, we have pared every thing away to the very quick, and do not differ from your doctrine by a nail's breadth.'[45] In that and perhaps other respects Jewel's optimism was gradually being challenged by the extent of English conservatism. Although at first he assured Martyr of the queen's high regard, and explained the slowness of reform by the need for due processes of law, he discouraged him from coming again to England. 'You know the character and disposition of us islanders.'[46]

Jewel's claims of doctrinal purity must therefore be treated with caution. They were in any case designed primarily to assure Martyr that England was free from Ubiquitarianism, and therefore stood on matters of eucharistic doctrine with the churches of Switzerland. In a different context he revealed to Martyr that Francis Baldwin (Professor of Civil Law at Paris) had commented favourably on the moderation of the Elizabethan settlement, 'but that your preciseness, as well as that of Geneva, is by no means agreeable unto him. In this respect he is, I think, rather unjust to Calvin.'[47]

The truth is that Jewel's anti-Roman apologetic stance made the claim to a consensus on fundamentals of doctrine between the Lutheran, Reformed and English Churches almost mandatory. Historians have sometimes taken that claim at its face value, while regarding as largely rhetorical Jewel's other assertion, the claim to true catholicity. Originally made in his Paul's Cross sermon of 26 November 1559, this took the form of a challenge. 'If any learned man of all our adversaries, or if all the learned men that be alive, be able to bring any one sufficient sentence out of any old catholic doctor, or father, or out of any old general council, or out of the holy scriptures of God, or any one example of the primitive church' whereby they were able to prove the teachings and practices of the Roman Church, 'I promised then I would give over and subscribe to them.'[48] The

---

[43] *Zürich Letters*, I. 16.
[44] Ibid., 55.
[45] Ibid., 100.
[46] Ibid., 46.
[47] Ibid., 118–19.
[48] John Jewel, *Works*, ed., J. Ayre (4 vols., Parker Society, Cambridge, 1845–50) I. 20–1.

challenge was subsequently developed in the *Apologia Ecclesiae Anglicanae* of 1562 (English version, 1564), designed to expose the calumny (on the basis of which the Pope had excluded the Protestant churches from the Council of Trent) that 'we are all heretics and have foresaken the faith . . . while they [Rome] have held and kept still . . . all things as they were delivered from the apostles and well approved by the most ancient fathers'.[49]

In the *Apology* and in all his controversial works Jewel took the line that Scripture was the final authority in all matters of doctrine.[50] But the Holy Spirit is needed for the understanding of the word of God.[51] 'We may not take the letter in all places of the Scripture as it lieth. The scriptures stand not in the reading, but in the understanding',[52] and for that purpose the patristic writings were essential. 'Throughout the whole discourse of this Apology, in defence of the catholic truth of our religion, next unto God's holy word, [we] have used no proof or authority so much as the expositions and judgements of the holy fathers.'[53] The assertion of a Protestant consensus could be maintained only by ignoring or by glossing over points of contention. The claim to true catholicity, by contrast, was fundamental to both principle and method of Jewel's apologetic.

The *Apology* was received with enthusiasm by the Zurich divines. Peter Martyr told Jewel that they 'can make no end of commending it'.[54] Readers approaching it for the first time, however, will be surprised to find that it says nothing about predestination. Its main preoccupation – like that of the challenge sermon which preceded it – is the Roman doctrine of the Mass. By contrast, little is said even upon the doctrine of justification by faith: Jewel was well aware that the appeal to the Fathers was much less clear-cut in that territory.[55]

In the elucidation of Jewel's understanding of the doctrine of grace, therefore, recourse has to be made to some of his lesser-known writings. Predestination, it is evident, was in no sense central to his understanding of the Gospel. On none of the points in dispute did he favour the more uncompromising stance. In reacting against the doctrine of merit, for

---

[49] J. E. Booty, *John Jewel as Apologist of the Church of England* (1963), 11; Jewel, *Works*, III. 53–4.

[50] Ibid., III. 57; cf. 601.

[51] Ibid., II. 685, 882.

[52] Ibid., I. 1112.

[53] Ibid., I. 225; see also II. 810, III. 191–2.

[54] *Zürich Letters*, I. 339. The ambassador to France, Throckmorton, who had hoped to use the Apology to encourage the French, who disliked Lutheranism and were fearful of Calvinism, towards a Reformed position, was disappointed to find that while the papists were well answered, the Calvinists had not been dealt with. Booty, *John Jewel as Apologist*, xxxii.

[55] Southgate, *John Jewel and the Problem of Doctrinal Authority*, 51; Jewel, *Works*, I. 27–8.

example, his response was 'I say not that nature alone is able to lead us into the perfection of faith.'[56] Christ himself said 'No man cometh unto the Father, but by me.' Though 'the heart of man is naturally inclined to religion; notwithstanding, being blinded with original sin', our proneness to evil will 'continue in us whiles the world lasteth'.[57] As Augustine taught, 'this same concupiscence . . . is forgiven in baptism, but is not utterly taken away'.[58] In thus echoing Article VIII of 1553, Jewel distanced himself both from a doctrine of total depravity and from the indefectibility of grace. His response to Harding's jibe as to the Reformers' 'presumptuous certainty of salvation' was grounded on Romans viii and on a catena of quotations from Ambrose, Theodoret, Gregory of Nazianzus, Origen, Chrysostom, Augustine and Aquinas: 'If it be so presumptuous a matter to put affiance in the merits of Christ, what is it then to put affiance in our own merits?'[59] It was trust rather than certainty for which he contended.

Similarly, Jewel was firm that Christ died for all men. Expounding the First Epistle to the Thessalonians, he urged the importance of preaching, 'for faith cometh by hearing, and hearing by the word of God'. In his quotation of 1 Tim. ii, 4 there is no hint that Jewel followed St Augustine in construing that verse to mean all kinds of men. On the contrary, he follows it with a citation of James i: 'It is not the will of my Father that one of these little ones should perish. Whosoever believeth, and shall be baptized, shall be saved.'[60] Conspicuous by its absence here is any suggestion that the Gospel must be preached to all simply because the preacher does not know who are elect, who reprobate. The reprobate for Jewel are those 'who have refused the word of reconciliation', for 'though God be patient and long-suffering, because he would have all men come to repentance; yet, in whom his mercy taketh no place to work their amendment, upon them he poureth out his wrath and indignation to the utmost'.[61]

In the same spirit, Jewel urged that belief is not enough. Faith that has no works is dead. He quotes Titus, ii: 'For the grace of God hath appeared, that bringeth salvation unto all men, and teacheth us that we shall live soberly, and righteously, and godly, in this life.'[62] Certainly, the God who has called us has promised to keep us faithful, but Jewel has no

[56] Jewel, *Works*, III. 198.
[57] Ibid., II. 1084; cf. II. 885: 'For, as God hath given us reason to see what is good, so hath he given us will to seek after that which is good.'
[58] Ibid., III. 464.
[59] Ibid., III. 243–6.
[60] Ibid., II. 840.
[61] Ibid., 841–2.
[62] Ibid., 849.

hesitation in warning that without the right response from ourselves the gift of the Holy Spirit may be lost. 'We must pray with David that the right spirit is renewed within us, and the Holy Spirit not taken from us. For 'if we have the word of God before our eyes, and regard it not, nor be thankful for it, nor set price by it, God in his justice will withdraw it from us'.[63] It is those who have heard the word and who then despise it whom God gives over to a reprobate mind.[64] Jewel quotes a whole series of New Testament texts to announce the preaching of the Gospel throughout the whole world, and then follows them with Romans x: 'They have not all believed our gospel' and Proverbs i: 'I have called; and ye refused: I have stretched out mine hand; and none would regard.' 'Let us not despise the gospel of Christ, whereby the whole world is saved.'[65]

There is a delicate balance, therefore, between our knowledge that God has chosen us from the beginning, that our calling and election are sure, and the requirement that we take heed lest we fall; between faith as the gift of God, and the need to work out our own salvation in trembling and in fear.[66] In a sermon on 1 Corinthians vi, 1 Jewel warned his congregation against 'receiving the grace of God in vain', and invited them to consider what it is 'to be striken out of the book of life'.[67] If we ask how we may know that God has chosen us, how we may 'see' or 'feel' our election, Jewel's answer is that it is through our sanctification and the credit we give to the Gospel. The promise of salvation by grace through faith we take to be true because it is God's word. 'Without faith it is impossible to please God.' We believe both that 'faith cometh by hearing', and that 'it is the gift of God'.[68] We need those assurances during temptation. And again Jewel warns us. 'Remember Lot's wife.' 'A terrible example to those which have set their hand to the plough, and look back again, and make themselves unworthy of the kingdom of heaven. God will forsake such, and make their hearts hard as a stone.'[69]

In 1609 Bancroft saw a wish fulfilled when Jewel's works were collected into one volume so that every parish church could have a copy. A preface was provided by John Overall, and a short life included by Daniel Featley. In a sermon preached before James I and Prince Frederick in 1613, Lancelot Andrewes linked the Apology 'vere Gemmeam' with the Catechism and the Thirty-nine Articles as containing in essence the teaching of the English Church.[70] And if, by that date, the unity of that

[63] Ibid., 924.
[64] Ibid., 925.
[65] Ibid., 1089.
[66] Ibid., 933–5.
[67] Ibid., 1089.
[68] Ibid., 934.
[69] Ibid., 935.
[70] Lancelot Andrewes, *Opuscula Posthuma*, ed. J. P. Wilson and J. Bliss (Anglo-Catholic Library, 1852), 91.

church was being threatened in a way that Jewel would have deplored, it is nevertheless true that there was much in his writings to which each side could legitimately appeal. For Featley there was Jewel's sense of identity with continental Protestantism and his emphatic evangelism. For Bancroft, Overall and Andrewes, there was a triumphant vindication of the claim to true catholicity. There was, however, nothing which would have helped the Cambridge opponents of Baro and Barrett in the conflict that led to the Lambeth Articles.

Henry Bullinger

The survival in John Jewel and in other returned exiles of moderate views on predestination raises the question of the theological influence of their continental hosts. Judging by the *Zürich Letters*, pre-eminent among these was Henry Bullinger. The question is all the more significant if Bullinger, as is often asserted, was a thoroughgoing 'Calvinist' in holding to a theory of unconditional, double predestination.[71] In that case, Jewel's moderation might merely be a temporary survival of indigenous English Protestantism, soon to be overtaken by a continental Reformed orthodoxy as Bullinger's *Decades*, Calvin's *Institutes* and the Geneva Bible bcame the staple diet of the Elizabethan church.

The truth is more complicated. The very notion of a single Reformed stance on predestination must be questioned. A recent study of Bullinger's theology draws a clear line of division between theologies of 'testament' and theologies of 'covenant'. Theologies of testament, like that of Calvin, emphasized the unilateral, unconditional nature of the divine action in human history, and led to an emphasis on double predestination. Theologies of covenant, like those of Zwingli and Bullinger, regarded the divine action as bilateral, mutual and conditional, preserving the doctrine of salvation *sola fide* and *sola gratia* in a carefully stated doctrine of single predestination.[72] Although covenant theology, 'the other Reformed tradition', came under pressure both in Bullinger's own lifetime and later in the sixteenth century, it survived in various ways as an alternative to a strict Calvinist orthodoxy.

As he developed it in the 1520s, Bullinger's teaching on predestination combined an emphasis that election is 'in Christ', and therefore totally of God's free grace, with the assertion that everyone is included under sin,

---

[71] The usual interpretation is that Bullinger's thought developed from the doctrine of single predestination to a Calvinistic double predestination in the 1560s. D. J. Keep, 'Henry Bullinger and the Elizabethan Church', Sheffield University Ph.D thesis, 1970, 256.

[72] J. Wayne Baker, *Heinrich Bullinger and the Covenant: The Other Reformed Tradition* (Ohio, 1980), introduction, xxii–iii.

so that God may show His mercy upon all.[73] In his comments on Ephesians, which date from the 1520s, Bullinger stressed that election is through grace alone, but warned against irreverent talk of a double predestination whereby some were saved, others damned by an absolute necessity. On the contrary, he argued, election must always be spoken of in scriptural terms, by saying that the elect are those who believe in Jesus Christ, and that He invites all to faith in Him: the will of God is that all men shall be saved and come to a knowledge of the truth. Bullinger therefore defined predestination as the election by God before the foundation of the world of those whom He foreknew, through no merit of their own, would be saved through belief in Jesus Christ. This remarkable and explicit anticipation of what was later called Arminianism was supported by reference to Erasmus' *Paraphrases* and buttressed with warnings against those who so talked of election that they regarded it as a preservative against falling in spite of any kind of wickedness, saying that those who had faith had been chosen by God in His eternal counsel. Bullinger never withdrew these remarks, which appeared in every subsequent edition of his commentaries upon the New Testament.[74]

Subsequent formulations carefully guarded against extremes. In an oration of 1536, for example, Bullinger spoke of God's gift of the means of salvation to those 'who struggle to life through Christ', and warned against those 'who cast all things back into absolute necessity so that they make God the author of all evil and of every sin'.[75] God foreknows who will refuse His offer of salvation: but they do not refuse because He foreknows; rather, He foreknows because they would refuse. Predestination to life, by contrast, rests on pure grace. Faith is the result of election.

Bullinger hesitated to talk of reprobation as part of predestination for fear of making God the author of sin. Where he did so, he was careful to safeguard himself by qualifications. In the *Decades*, for example, having said that God 'has pre-ordained those who must be saved or condemned', he goes on to insist that the end of predestination is Christ, 'for God decreed to save all, however many, who have fellowship with Christ'. To those who asked whether they had been elected to life or predestined to death, his only reply was 'if you have fellowship with Christ, you have been predestined to life . . . but if you are estranged from Christ, however strong you might appear to be in virtues, you have been predestined to death'.[76] That these words should not be used to father a doctrine of

[73] Ibid., 29.
[74] *Heinrici Bullingeri Commentarii in omnes Pauli Apostoli Epistolas* (Zurich, 1582), 310–11.
[75] Baker, *Bullinger and the Covenant*, 30.
[76] Ibid., 32; Henry Bullinger, *The Decades of Henry Bullinger*, ed. T. Harding (5 vols. in 4, Parker Society, Cambridge, 1841–52), IV, 185–7.

double predestination on Bullinger may be demonstrated from his sermon on the Gospel, where he proclaims unambiguously that the grace of Christ 'belongs to everyone'.

For we must not imagine that in heaven are laid two books, in the one whereof the names of them are written that are to be saved, and so to be saved, as it were of necessity, that, do what they will against the word of Christ and commit they never so heinous offences, they cannot possibly choose but be saved; and that in the other are contained the names of them which, do what they can and live never so holily, yet cannot avoid everlasting damnation. Let us rather hold that the holy gospel of Christ doth generally preach to the whole world the grace of God, the remission of sins and life everlasting.[77]

The reason why not all men are saved is that God requires faith for salvation, and many men reject the Gospel. 'Election promised inclusion in the kingdom of God, but it did not threaten exclusion.'[78]

As disputes on predestination began to disturb the Reformed churches, Bullinger came under pressure. When, for example, Jerome Bolsec appealed to Melanchthon and Bullinger's teaching to support his accusation that Calvin's doctrine made God the author of sin, Calvin and the Genevan ministers wrote to the pastors of Zurich for support. In a personal letter to Calvin, Bullinger repeated from St Paul the will of God that all should be saved, and concluded: 'however many men are saved, they are saved by the pure grace of God the saviour; those who perish do not perish by fated, compelled necessity, but because they willingly reject the grace of God. For there is not any sin in God; that and the blame of our damnation inheres in us.'[79] In a further letter, he warned Calvin: 'Believe me that many are offended by your statements about predestination in the *Institutes*.'[80] Calvin, in a letter to Farel, complained that 'Bullinger haughtily despises our necessities',[81] but subsequently asked Bullinger to explain in what respects he had departed from the doctrine clearly taught in God's word. In reply, Bullinger instanced the teaching that God not only knew, but predestined and arranged the Fall of Adam, and that the universal promises of the Gospel were meant only for the few. 'It is certain that not a few men zealous for the truth are offended by these things.'[82]

In his reply to Bartholomew Traheron, then Dean of Chichester, who

---

[77] Baker, *Bullinger and the Covenant*, 33; *Decades*, III. 32–4.
[78] Baker, *Bullinger and the Covenant*, 34.
[79] C. P. Venema, 'Heinrich Bullinger's Correspondence on Calvin's Doctrine of Predestination', 1551–1553', *Sixteenth Century Journal* 17/4 (1986), 435–50; John Calvin, *Opera quae supersunt omnia* (14 vols., Brunswick, 1863–1900), XIV, col. 208.
[80] Calvin, *Opera*, XIV, col. 215.
[81] Ibid., cols. 208, 210.
[82] Baker, *Bullinger and the Covenant*, 35–6; Calvin, *Opera*, xiv, cols. 289–90.

wrote to say that it was rumoured that Bullinger inclined towards Melanch-thon's views on predestination,[83] Bullinger sought to steer a middle course between Melanchthon's synergism and the extreme positions of Calvin.[84] He clung to what he called the 'sacred anchor in this disputa-tion', the principle that God is not the author of evil. Again he distin-guished between election, the only cause of which was the good and just will of God, and reprobation, the blame for which was 'not to be cast back on God and his predestination or compulsion or retention in faithlessness, but on the depraved will of those who refuse'.[85] After argu-ing that the reason why predestination had been revealed to men was to show God's will for the salvation of all men, Bullinger warned of the danger of disputing about God's secrets beyond the warrant of Scripture. Bullinger rejected the position of those who talked of a small number of the elect. 'We prefer to insist upon these universal promises and have a good hope for all.' He granted that the motive of Calvin's teaching was to protect the purity of God's grace, and he compared him with St Augustine, who had also gone to extremes in some of his writings against the Pelagians. When Calvin spoke of God 'raising up vessels of wrath' and of God 'blinding the heart of the unbeliever', he spoke in a way the church Fathers never condoned. Such exhortations were not required in order to honour God's mercy and grace.[86]

Bullinger found it more difficult to maintain his theological in-dependence of Calvin after the appointment of Peter Martyr as Professor of Old Testament at Zurich in 1556. Martyr soon became involved in public controversy with Theodore Bibliander,[87] as a result of which Bibliander was forced to retire on a pension. A similar controversy disturbed Strasburg, where Zanchi defended a highly dogmatic doctrine of double predestination against the Lutheran Johann Marbach. In arguing that there should be no fudging of disputed points in the pursuit of doctrinal truth, Zanchi was not afraid to say that in some senses God was the author of sin.[88] A compromise, based on the recognition that the boundaries of

---

[83] Robinson, *Original Letters relative to the English Reformation*, I. 325.

[84] Venema, 'Heinrich Bullinger's Correspondence', 444.

[85] Baker, *Bullinger and the Covenant*, 36–7.

[86] Calvin, *Opera*, XIV, col. 488.

[87] Theodore Bibliander became Professor of Old Testament in Zurich after Zwingli's death. His doctrine of predestination distinguished between God's predestination and foreknowledge (God knew some things that He had not predestinated) and rejected the election of individuals in favour of the predestination of two classes, believers and unbelievers. Bibliander thought that this was the only formulation which left scope for some exercise of the human will. In spite of all this, he was able to work at Zurich in harmony with Bullinger for nearly twenty-five years. Baker, *Bullinger and the Covenant*, 39–40.

[88] See C. J. Burchill, 'Girolamo Zanchi in Strasbourg, 1553–1563', Cambridge University Ph.D. thesis, 1979, 156.

theology were prescribed by Scripture, and a common allegiance to the Augsburg Confession, was suggested in an effort to resolve their differences, but it was not approved by Calvin, who thought that it obscured the clarity of the doctrine and undermined Reformed teaching.[89] When Zanchi appealed to Zurich for support, Bullinger was afraid that Marbach would be ejected, and the Strasburg Church lost to Lutheranism. He therefore asked Martyr to prepare a brief opinion for Zanchi's use. The resulting statement, which was signed by Bullinger, illustrates how far he was prepared to go in the interests of ecclesiastical politics. Zanchi had asserted: 'With God there is a definite number of those elected to life as well as of the reprobates predestined to destruction.' The Zurich reply, while granting the certainty as to number, restricted predestination to the elect; those who were not saved were 'forsaken'. Of Zanchi's claim that the elect are 'necessarily saved' and the reprobate 'cannot be saved and thus are necessarily condemned', Bullinger wrote to Martyr that 'if it were proposed so nakedly to the people, it would be proposed to more of them with offence than with edification', but eventually said that it could be accepted 'properly understood'. No difficulty was felt in granting that 'he who is once elected . . . cannot become a reprobate'. Finally, to Zanchi's assertion that 1 Tim. ii, 4 referred to 'all the elect', Zurich said that this interpretation, which had been the opinion of St Augustine, distorted Scripture the least. Zanchi's theses contained 'nothing either heretical or absurd. Indeed we embrace them partly as necessary, partly as probable.' They were in accordance with the teaching of Luther, Capito, Bucer and Brenz.[90]

Bullinger's role in promoting Martyr's statement, and his signing of it, has to be seen as the outcome of a crisis in ecclesiastical politics. This judgment is confirmed by his adherence to his earlier moderation on predestination in subsequent theological formulations, such as the Second Helvetic Confession, completed in 1564, revised in consultation with other Reformed churches in 1565 and 1566, and first published in 1566. In it Bullinger condemned 'all who make God the author of sin'. The decree to send Christ as the Mediator of the whole world was placed first: election is in Christ, and on account of Christ. Although God knows who are His, and although there are places in Scripture which say that the elect

---

[89] Ibid., 268–80.

[90] Baker, *Bullinger and the Covenant*, 42–4. Bullinger's own comments on 1 Tim. ii, 4 made no reference at all to St Augustine's interpretation: indeed, he used the text to argue that we ought to pray not merely for unbelievers but also for the heathen, with a reminder of the injunction to go into all the world and preach the Gospel to every creature. The reason why all are not saved is, he explains, St Paul's: that God wills all *believers* to be saved. Bullinger based his views on St Ambrose's *De vocatione omnium Gentium*. See *Bullingeri Commentarii in omnes Pauli Apostoli Epistolas*, 433.

are few, good is to be hoped for all men, and no one rashly numbered among the reprobate. Curious speculation should be avoided because it leads to a fatalistic attitude, either of 'security' or of desperation. The right approach is not to ask what God has decreed before all eternity, but to heed the proclamation of the Gospel: if you believe, and if you are in Christ, you are elect; the promises of the Gospel are universal.[91] Similar remarks are common to Bullinger's *Fundamentum firmum* of 1563, to the Isaiah commentary of 1567, and to his *Bekerung* of 1569.[92]

If Bullinger had a central dogma, it was the idea of covenant, and in works where he approaches salvation historically the emphasis on that idea is so strong as to come near to universalism.[93] An example is the *Summa* of 1556, Bullinger's simple exposition of the main points of the Christian faith. Apart from a general condemnation of Pelagianism, Bullinger ignored predestination altogether. Even when he is commenting upon passages like Ephesians 1, he made an explicit affirmation of universal atonement. Faith is indeed God's free gift, but we can pray for it, remembering that it is not God's will that any man should be lost (2 Pet. iii, 9) and that the sacraments help in the increase and maintainance of faith.[94] In arguing that baptism initiates the individual into the covenant community, Bullinger expounded an inclusive doctrine of election, making it the ground of assurance in the promises of the Gospel. Where, increasingly, Calvinist orthodoxy subordinated covenant to an abstract, speculative dogma of double predestination, Bullinger stressed it as the vehicle through which God dealt with man, God's election becoming binding only as individuals kept the conditions of the covenant.

At the Synod of Dort, the leader of the Swiss delegation, Johann Jacob Breitinger, claimed that Bullinger agreed with Calvin on predestination. The honour of the Zurich Church, which he represented, was at stake, and he was able to point to Bullinger's support of Zanchi against Marbach[95] in the disputes over predestination at Strasburg. In the Netherlands, both Remonstrants and Contra-Remonstrants had been claiming the authority of Bullinger since the late sixteenth century. He does seem to have had some direct influence on the forerunners of Arminius. Veluanus knew and respected his works; Snecanus, it has been said, 'sounds more like Bullinger on the covenant than any of the late sixteenth-century thinkers',[96] and Wiggertsz was also indebted to

---

[91] Latin text of Article X of the Second Helvetic Confession (1566), 'the most Catholic amongst the Swiss Confessions', in P. Schaff, *The Creeds of the Evangelical Protestant Churches* (1877), 254.

[92] Baker, *Bullinger and the Covenant*, 46–7.

[93] Ibid., 47–9.

[94] Ibid., 51.

[95] Ibid., 29.

[96] Ibid., 212.

Bullinger. It is perhaps a fair judgment that while Bullinger would temperamentally have been in sympathy with the followers of Arminius, he would have found the atmosphere of scholastic disputation pervading both sides at Dort regrettable and uncongenial.

In assessing Bullinger's influence in England, those who have not presented him as in essentials a high Calvinist have assumed that his moderate views on predestination were of little significance. Covenant theology in England has been presented as the preserve of a 'Puritan' tradition running from Tyndale and Coverdale to Hooper,[97] then to be superseded by a Calvinist theology of testament, especially in the theology of William Perkins. That is altogether to ignore Bullinger's influence on Jewel and other like-minded Marian *émigrés*. Far from being limited to a 'Puritan' theological tradition, Bullinger's moderation on predestination was embodied in the official formulations of the early Elizabethan church and was echoed in the first great defence of that church by Jewel. Bullinger was an establishment figure. It was therefore entirely appropriate that when, in 1570, the papal bull *Regnans in excelsis* branded the early Elizabethan church as 'Calvinist', Bullinger was asked to refute the claim. His *Confutation*,[98] with its claim of true catholicity for that church, stands theologically four-square with Jewel's *Apology*. As to the description of that church as 'Calvinist', Bullinger dismissed it as the 'spiteful interlacing' of a name merely to bring discredit. It was a feature of the popish church, not the English, to 'hang wholly upon men . . . and have a pleasure to be called Benedictines of Benet, Franciscans of Francis . . . therefore they imagine that we also would be called Lutherans of Luther, Zwinglians of Zwingli, and Calvinists of Calvin'.[99] St Paul had forbidden such reliance upon the ordinances of men, and the Protestant churches acknowledged them only so far as they were agreeable to Scripture. As for Elizabeth, 'the Queen of England's majesty never received of Calvin, or of any other excellent or well-learned men, any ordinances to follow, nor never regarded them: and yet by the way, if any of them have taught anything out of God's pure word, no godly man can take scorn thereof'.[100] That balanced and eirenic outlook became more difficult to sustain as theological conflict sharpened in the late sixteenth century, but Bullinger's example and teaching were far from forgotten. In 1586, Convocation required all inferior clergy to have a copy of

---

[97] For Bullinger's influence on Hooper, see Robinson, *Original Letters relative to the English Reformation*, I. 33–4, 54, 65–6, 92–3, 96. See also Baker, *Bullinger and the Covenant*, 209–10.

[98] Henry Bullinger, *A Confutation of the Pope's Bull . . . together with a defence of the said true Christian Queen, and of the whole realm of England* (1572).

[99] Ibid., 90.

[100] Ibid., 91.

Bullinger's *Decades* in Latin or in English.[101] It demonstrated the vitality in the Elizabethan church of 'the other Reformed tradition'.

[101] J. Strype, *The Life and Acts of John Whitgift* (3 vols., Oxford, 1821), III. 194.

5   Elizabeth's church: the limits of consensus

Veins of doctrine

Although no doubt some Elizabethans followed Traheron in claiming that the English Church was doctrinally Calvinist,[1] a more common argument was that the first generation of Protestants, whether Lutheran or Reformed, had all agreed on predestination: there was therefore no good reason to argue about it. Edmund Grindal, for example, writing to Conrad Hubert in 1562, found it 'astonishing that they [certain divines in Bremen] are raising such commotions about predestination. They should at least consult their own Luther on "the bondage of the will". For what else do Bucer, Calvin and Martyr teach, that Luther has not maintained in that treatise?'[2] Hubert would no doubt have agreed: he had recently republished Bucer's early works in an attempt to support Zanchi's position at Strasburg.[3] The claim that there was a consensus, whether Protestant or Reformed, was one way of inhibiting discussion.

Recent historiography has mirrored the change of emphasis: not very long ago it was still common to follow Traheron, but recent studies have reflected Grindal's standpoint.[4] There is considerable evidence, however, of a strong element of wishful thinking in both. The Reformed tradition, as has already been demonstrated, was more diverse than Grindal would have cared to admit. It may be argued, furthermore, first that the doctrinal Reformation generally made much slower progress in the Elizabethan church than has until recently been recognized;[5] secondly, that the extent

---

[1] Robinson (ed.), *Original Letters relative to the English Reformation*, I. 323–4, 328.
[2] Robinson (ed.), *Zürich Letters*, II. 73.
[3] Burchill, 'Girolamo Zanchi', Cambridge University Ph.D. thesis, 243.
[4] For Traheron's standpoint, see C. D. Cremeans, *The Reception of Calvinistic Thought in England* (Urbana, Illinois, 1949). Cf. N. Tyacke, 'Debate: The Rise of Arminianism Reconsidered', *Past and Present* 115 (1987), 205: 'the theology of the Church of England derived from the Swiss rather than from the German Reformation'. Wallace, *Puritans and Predestination*, 1–2, groups the Swiss and Rhineland Reformers together. He grants that it can be misleading to refer to the theological strain they represented as 'Calvinism', but nevertheless thinks they were basically homogeneous on predestination.
[5] See, for example, C. Haigh (ed.), *The English Reformation Revised* (Cambridge, 1988).

as well as the nature of Swiss as opposed to Lutheran influence has almost certainly been misunderstood; thirdly, that much early Elizabethan 'Calvinism' was carefully moderate in its assertion of predestinarian doctrine.

Calvinist dominance of the universities from virtually the beginning of Elizabeth's reign is, for a start, not confirmed by modern research. The most recent historian of Elizabethan Protestantism in Oxford concludes that for the first two decades of the reign, Zurich was at least as significant as Geneva.[6] Even the contacts with Zurich were those of a tiny and hardly representative circle: apart from Jewel and Parkhurst, now no longer resident, they were Thomas Sampson, Laurence Humphrey and William Cole. When Rudolph Gualter the younger arrived in Oxford in 1573, he found Magdalen the only exception to a prevailing religious conservatism and lack of interest in the writings of the Reformers.[7] Another small group of Swiss students, including Wolfgang Musculus the younger, was established in Oxford in 1577–9, but the first student from Geneva (John Castorllius) did not arrive until 1578.[8] It was not until the 1580s that Oxford was brought into the circle of Beza through the efforts of Jean Hotman and Isaac de Cardencia in making the university aware of the precarious situation of the city and people of Geneva.[9]

Recent work on the contents of college libraries, both in Oxford and Cambridge, confirms the picture of a slow reformation, to which a number of continental centres contributed. Not only was Zurich more important than Geneva, but until after the end of the century Lutheran books were more extensively acquired than Reformed. The standard divinity books were in any event, after the various bibles, the sixteenth-century editions of the Greek and Latin Fathers, usually in the Basle editions.[10] The impact of the Reformation was evident, not in the number of Protestant books, for at the beginning of Elizabeth's reign the colleges were altogether without them, but rather in the absence of the scholastic texts, the weeding out of which had been the work of the first phase of English Protestantism. The deficiency in Protestant books was not in the majority of cases soon remedied. At Oxford, 'twenty years after the accession of Elizabeth one could go into some college libraries and find no

[6] C. M. Dent, *Protestant Reformers in Elizabethan Oxford* (1983), 75.
[7] Ibid., 76; *Zürich Letters*, II. 217–19.
[8] Dent, *Protestant Reformers*, 78.
[9] Ibid., 79.
[10] P. Gaskell, *Trinity College Library* (Cambridge, 1980), 8. On Cambridge libraries generally, see H. M. Adams, *Catalogue of Books Printed on the Continent of Europe 1501–1600 in Cambridge Libraries* (2 vols., Cambridge, 1967) and E. S. Leedham-Green, *Books in Cambridge Inventories: Book Lists from Vice-Chancellor's Court Probate Inventories in the Tudor and Stuart Periods* (2 vols., Cambridge, 1986).

evidence that the reformation had occurred or that England was a Protestant country'.[11] At Oxford, the only exceptions were Magdalen, Merton, Corpus and Queen's. Magdalen was exceptional in not waiting for donors, but in buying (in 1562) five works of Musculus, and Calvin on the Minor Prophets and on Daniel. Merton chained works by Bucer, Oecolampadius, Musculus, Gualter and Borrhaeus in 1565, but Calvin's *Institutes* were not acquired until 1583, when they were included in a mainly Catholic collection (notably works by Ockham, Durandus, Scotus and other commentators on the *Sentences*) bequeathed by William Marshall.[12] The bequest was typical of the interest in the scholastics which revived in the early 1580s. 'By 1583 we have come to the time when people in Oxford had begun to attach importance to having the works of the Schoolmen and especially Aquinas in college libraries, together with the work of the modern Catholic theologians.'[13] Magdalen, for example, acquired the new twelve-volume edition of Aquinas in the early 1590s, together with two volumes of Bellarmine, at the same time that it acquired books of modern theology on the Protestant side. All Souls had no Protestant works before 1576, when Andrew Kingsmill, 'dying beyond the seas at Geneva', left the college £5 to purchase the works of Calvin and Martyr.[14] Christ Church was weak in Protestant literature until the beginning of the seventeenth century.[15]

The picture is similar at Cambridge. Libraries were more likely to have the works of Chrysostom than those of Calvin.[16] When Protestant books were acquired, they tended to be the biblical commentaries, and especially those of Zwingli, Oecolampadius, Musculus and Bucer. Few collections included much of either Luther or Calvin before 1580.[17] Calvin's commentaries were more widely used than his *Institutes*, and in the early part of the reign libraries were more likely to contain works by Melanchthon, Bucer, Bullinger, Peter Martyr or the *Loci Communes* of Wolfgang Musculus than those of Calvin. At Trinity, the Master, Robert Beaumont, who had been a member of Knox's congregation at Geneva and died in 1567, left two titles by Luther and nine by Calvin to the college library, but they had disappeared by the time the first inventory was taken in 1600.[18] By then the books included Knox, but nothing by Calvin, on

[11] N. P. Ker, 'Oxford College Libraries in the Sixteenth Century', *The Bodleian Library Record* 6 (1957–61), 501.
[12] Ibid., 500, 505.
[13] Ibid., 506.
[14] Ibid., 501.
[15] Dent, *Protestant Reformers*, 95.
[16] Leedham-Green, *Books in Cambridge Inventories*, II. 203–7.
[17] Gaskell, *Trinity College Library*, 8.
[18] The 1600 Inventory is printed ibid., appendix A.

predestination; and nothing at all by Beza.[19] Even the library of Emmanuel College held twice as many Lutheran books as Reformed when its first inventory was compiled, probably in the late 1590s. Beza was represented only by his *Theological Tractates*.[20] Private libraries were more likely to include the works of Calvin, but they were not among the books commonly owned by Cambridge men in the late sixteenth century.

Probably the most popular of all the Protestant books acquired in the early part of Elizabeth's reign was Musculus' *Common Places*. His English editor was the Warden of Merton, John Man. Its teaching is worth at least some comment, especially since the theology of the author, who was Reader in Divinity at Berne, has attracted no modern study. His popularity is easy to understand. The *Common Places* must have been the ideal handbook for the student and later for the preacher: comprehensive, clearly arranged, and homiletic in intent. It is an early and impressive example of the success which awaited works of practical divinity. Their use was not dependent on agreement as to every particular; in this case, for example, the editor included a preface excusing the author for disapproving of infant baptism.

A brief review of Musculus' doctrine of grace will illustrate its orientation towards practical piety, its relative unsophistication, its refreshing freedom from polemic, and its less than complete consistency. The grace of God is free, whether 'going before' or 'coming after'.[21] The will, being by natural corruption 'unclean', 'cannot of itself will that which is good, unless it be changed by heavenly grace . . . this changing is the work of the grace of God alone'. Once regenerated, the will 'travaileth in the good work whereunto it is disposed, but yet being as it is, it should work and travail to no purpose' without the grace of God's goodness. 'We do work with God.'[22] This moderate statement of the Protestant theology of grace is neither oppressed by a doctrine of total depravity nor so obsessed with the dangers of Pelagianism that it is afraid to admit the co-operation of the will with grace. Furthermore, just as the Fall was universal, so the grace of God 'is open unto all the world', although it comes only through Christ, and therefore through the Gospel. It is received 'by hearing, believing and obeying'.[23] Musculus quoted Mark xvi, 16: 'Christ said, Preach the Gospel unto all creatures. He that believeth and is baptised, shall be saved; he that believeth not, shall be condemned.'

[19] Leedham-Green, *Books in Cambridge Inventories*, II, 90–3; Adams, *Books in Cambridge Libraries*, I. 120–2 (Beza) and 227–30 (Calvin).

[20] S. Bush Jr and C. J. Rasmussen, 'Emmanuel College Library's First Inventory', *Transactions of the Cambridge Bibliographical Society*, 8/5 (1985), 516.

[21] Wolfgang Musculus, *Common places of Christian Religion* (1563), f. 126.

[22] Ibid., f. 127^v.

[23] Ibid., ff. 140^r, 141^r.

According to Musculus, 'we have power to believe grafted in us by God of nature'. Nevertheless, faith is a gift from God, and we must pray for it. Not the same measure of faith is given to all, but all have sufficient. Faith is not given to all, because all do not obey the Gospel.[24] Because it is not given 'in respect of our quality, merit or dignity', the giving of it must depend on the free choice of God's will, and here Musculus referred to Romans ix. Nevertheless, men are 'not to prate why it should be necessary to preach', and 'busy and curious reasoning' is to be avoided. Because faith is given only to the elect, 'it is a most infallible token of our election' – just as 'stubborn unbelief is the token that men be refused and cast off'. We must therefore 'try ourselves, whether we be in faith and Christ in us or no'.[25] There are echoes of both Bucer and Bullinger here, as also in Musculus' warning that none must be judged to be reprobate rashly: some are called very late.

In dealing with election, Musculus was aware that 'this matter, which is plain and clear of itself, is through the scrupulosity of our wits and desire of contention, made crabbed and intricate'.[26] Election comes first, faith afterwards. God has liberty to choose some. The fact that He chose us before we were is witness to His amazing grace and the ground of our assurance that He will not forsake us. St Augustine acknowledged that the number of the elect is certain. The Master of the Sentences discussed whether that number might be increased or diminished, but Musculus thought the question 'fond and foolish', 'too curious for a godly person'.[27] At the same time, Musculus was not happy with St Augustine's apparent identification of prescience and predestination in the first book addressed to Simplicius: while it was true God did not predestine what He did not foreknow, He did not predestine all that He foreknew. Election must be attributed to the goodness of God, and we must not ask for causes of causes.[28]

Contentions touching the reprobate were to be avoided. 'Surely I do so much esteem the grace of election . . . that I think it not necessary so much as to think upon the reprobate.'[29] Musculus claimed that St Paul himself 'did scarcely touch of them in one or two places'. But there must be some reprobate. The meaning of 1 Tim. ii, 4 must therefore be 'all sorts of men', otherwise the will of God would be made void, 'which

[24] Ibid., f. 200.
[25] Ibid., f. 201.
[26] Ibid., f. 208^r.
[27] Ibid., f. 208^v.
[28] Ibid., f. 209^r.
[29] Ibid., f. 213^v.

is altogether wicked'.[30] Reprobation, like election, is from eternity. Its cause is secret. Although Musculus says that it must not be attributed to the malice of the reprobate to come (he so interprets the reference to Esau), he follows St Augustine in claiming that it cannot be unjust, and Lombard in asserting that the reprobate 'can neither obey God when he calleth, nor believe, nor repent, nor be justified'.[31] 'And this we do say briefly, without the prejudice of any person that thinketh otherwise.' But only God knows the names of the reprobate. 'Let us as near endeavour as we can to save all men, lovingly embrace all men, and let us do good to all men, and not rashly despair of any man.'[32]

Like Bucer and Bullinger, Musculus was enthusiastic that the Gospel should be preached. His approach was, however, more practical, less academic than theirs. He is at his most typical in treating of such matters as 'the nourishments of faith' – he mentions especially the Eucharist – 'the increase of faith', the nature of repentance, the need for good works, and the Christian's hope (he avoids the word 'certainty'). The result is an emphasis on the covenantal elements in the Reformed tradition. His treatment of reprobation (which he presents almost reluctantly) has more in common with Bucer's than with Bullinger's, but seems to be drawn directly from St Paul, and St Paul as interpreted by St Augustine, St Ambrose and Peter Lombard. Its orientation is distinctly homiletic and edificatory rather than theoretical: it is presented as the necessary counterpart to the Gospel message of redemption, and not as part of a doctrine of God.

Another good example of the variety that was possible within the Reformed consensus in the Elizabethan church is provided by the Heidelberg Catechism, compiled by Ursinus and Olevianus in 1562. It became recommended reading for Oxford undergraduates by a university statute of 1579,[33] and its popularity is demonstrated by the many editions of the lectures upon it by Zacharias Ursinus entitled *The Summe of the Christian Religion*. It has been said to combine the intimacy of Luther with the charity of Melanchthon and the fire of Calvin. Ursinus had studied for seven years with Melanchthon at Wittenberg before going briefly to Zurich, where he came under the influence of Peter Martyr and Bullinger.

---

[30] Ibid., ff. 213^v–214^r. Nevertheless, Musculus elsewhere offers the alternative interpretation that 'God willeth all men to be saved, but under this condition, if they refuse not the truth', though he was aware that some of his readers would prefer the Augustinian exposition. Ibid., f. 392^v.

[31] Ibid., f. 214^v.

[32] Ibid.

[33] Dent, *Protestant Reformers*, 186.

Not surprisingly, there are unresolved tensions in his theology.[34] What immediately strikes the reader is the edificatory value of this attempt to resolve the controverted questions of divinity. It is a moderate presentation. Ursinus concedes, for example, the Scripture references that many of the reprobate are made partakers of the Holy Ghost for a time.[35] He is especially strong in insisting that destiny is no cause of sin, which comes from the Devil and the free choice of man, God only permitting.[36] Ursinus quoted Romans xi, 32: 'God hath shut up all in unbelief, that he might have mercy on all.'[37] In general Ursinus preferred to talk of the unregenerate rather than the reprobate.[38] He developed the doctrine that no work of man is pleasing to God without regeneration into the statement that many of the works of the unregenerate are morally good, but nevertheless not pleasing to God, and therefore sinful.[39] On a sounder and more typically Protestant footing was his teaching that the will is not merely passive or idle when subject to grace.[40]

There is an inconsistency in Ursinus between the discussion of the covenant between God and man to which conditions are attached[41] and the treatment of election, in which he denies that God's promises are to all on the condition of obedience. He nevertheless claimed that all who are not saved have only themselves to blame; they are 'unbelievers who embrace not the grace of Christ offered, but like ungrateful men reject it . . . in believers only doth God obtain his end and purpose'.[42] In spite of his claim to remove difficulties, there are other unanswered questions when Ursinus turns to discuss the four kinds of faith: historical (bare knowledge); temporary, or hypocritical; the faith that works miracles; and justifying faith. He argues that justifying faith is peculiar to the elect, temporary faith accordingly is limited to hypocrites, and the other two kinds of faith are common to both godly and ungodly. No one knows what justifying faith is unless he has it, yet it is in this life 'imperfect' and 'languishing', though never 'wholly extinguished'.[43] Anyone who feels in

---

[34] In spite of the claim which prefaces the lectures, 'wherein are debated and resolved the questions of whatsoever points of moment which have been or are controverted in Divinity'. Tyacke takes Ursinus' teaching that election and reprobation are 'according to the eternal counsel of God' and not dependent on whether 'a man is worthy' as evidence both of the author's Calvinism and that of Oxford University. 'Debate: The Rise of Arminianism Reconsidered', *Past and Present* 115 (1987), 203.

[35] Zacharias Ursinus, *The Summe of Christian Religion* (Oxford, 1591), 88.

[36] See esp. ibid., 97–105.

[37] Ibid., 109.

[38] See, for example, the discussion ibid., 169.

[39] Ibid., 95.

[40] Ibid., 167.

[41] Ibid., 241ff.

[42] Ibid., 253.

[43] Ibid., 270.

his heart 'an earnest desire of believing and a strife against doubts' may and indeed ought to conclude that he is endowed with true faith. While temporary faith 'breedeth a certain joy' it does not promote a 'quiet conscience, (because it ariseth not from the true cause) as also it maketh a show of confession, and some shew of good works, but that only for a season'.[44] His analysis may well have bred more doubt than assurance.

Ursinus, along with Bucer, is a good example of the way in which Melanchthon's doctrine of predestination was mediated through theologians anxious to reconcile the conflicting insights with which Christians from St Paul onwards have wrestled. An even clearer instance is the Danish Lutheran, Neils Hemmingsen. When Peter Baro was deeply involved in controversy over predestination in 1596, he wrote to Hemmingsen, who was a friend, that 'in this country we have hitherto been permitted to hold the same sentiments as yours on grace; but we are now scarcely allowed publicly to teach our own opinions on that subject, much less to publish them'.[45] Baro's words are usually quoted to illustrate a Calvinist monopoly of the late-Elizabethan press, but more significant perhaps is his claim that until 1596 there had been no difficulty. It may have been through the influence of Baro that a number of Hemmingsen's books had been made available in Cambridge, and some of them translated into English. *The Preacher*, a manual of pulpit rhetoric which was an important source of William Perkins's *Prophetica*, had appeared in 1574; his Latin commentary on Romans was published in London in 1577; *A Godly and Learned Exposition upon the xxv Psalm*, in 1580; and both the *Enchiridion Theologicum* and an English translation of a commentary on the Epistle to the Ephesians in 1581.

Hemmingsen had been a pupil of Melanchthon, and it is a Melanchthonian doctrine of predestination which is set forth in uncomplicated fashion in all his theological works. Predestination is a useful doctrine, provided that we keep to the Scripture and avoid speculation.[46] The promise of grace is universal. There is no conflict of wills in God. Grace must triumph over sin. As the Fall of Adam involves all men, so the promise is to all his posterity. No one is predestined to sin (*malum culpae*), but only to punishment (*malum poenae*). The order of predestination, following St Paul, is foreknowledge, election, calling, justification, glorification. Election, which is before the foundation of the world, is of those who believe in Christ. Their names are written in the book of life. Calling is 'from the beginning of the world, immediately after the fall of our first parents'.

---

[44] Ibid.
[45] Arminius, *Works*, I. 91–2.
[46] This account of his doctrine is derived from N. Hemmingius, *Enchiridion Theologicum, praecipua verae religionis capita breviter et simpliciter explicata* (1577). Predestination is discussed on pp. 217–31.

The use of this rule is to stop us provoking God to anger by either our security or our impenitence. The doctrine is full of consolation provided that we do not allow the Sophists to deceive us into Stoic opinions. No one is excluded from grace except those who exclude themselves by their own malice or contrariness (*dissidentia*). All are called to whom the Gospel is preached. The cause of our calling is only the good pleasure of God, who requires faith and holiness in those who are called. The final cause of election or predestination is the preaching of the grace and glory of God. Nothing is more absurd than the Sophist doctrine that the decrees of predestination are unknown. Election is known from its effects in us, from our calling itself, from faith and the Holy Spirit which we receive when we put on Christ, from the newness of life or sanctification which follows, and from the sacraments, which are signs of the grace of God. The 'use' of the doctrine of predestination is to remove faith in human merit, to make us value the preaching of the word through which we are called, to encourage us to be thankful, a 'spur to prick us forward to all exercises of godliness'[47] and to console and fortify us in temptation and persecution.[48]

Hemmingsen provides a valuable corrective to many misconceptions about predestinarian teaching in the reign of Elizabeth. Firstly, library inventories not merely at Cambridge but also at Oxford demonstrate the surprisingly wide dissemination of his books. Christ Church, Exeter, Magdalen, Queen's, St John's and Wadham all acquired the Geneva edition of his *Opuscula Theologica* (1586); Queen's, Pembroke, Trinity, Corpus, Christ Church, Exeter, Merton, St John's and Wadham all had a copy of his *Commentaria in omnes epistolas Apostolorum*.[49] Secondly, the doctrine of conditional predestination which he enunciates is set forth in unmistakably 'Protestant' terms as a corrective to the errors of the papists in making merit the ground of our salvation. Thirdly, there is no suggestion that Hemmingsen himself, or his books, were regarded with hostility in moderate Puritan circles. The doctrine of the universality of grace is shown to have origins deep in the heart of the Protestant tradition.

The changing face of Elizabethan Calvinism

To Traheron, the doctrine of predestination was at the heart of Calvinism. There are a number of indications that others who consciously

[47] Ibid., 230–1.
[48] Hemmingsen gave the chief testimonies to the doctrine of predestination as Ephesians i, Acts xiii, John xv and John x. Romans ix–xi was also relevant, but care had to be exercised 'lest we follow, as many do, disputations alien to the purpose'.
[49] Information derived from the *Inter Collegiate Catalogue of Continental Books held in Oxford Libraries*.

looked to Geneva early in the reign of Elizabeth did not attribute anything like the same importance to it. One example is Alexander Nowell. Nowell's Catechism, first published in 1570, makes clear the responsibility of the unfaithful for their reprobation, 'in refusing the promises offered them by God' and who therefore 'shut up the entry against themselves, and go empty away'.[50] Another, even more significant example is provided by Percival Wilburn's church at Northampton, which adopted its own standard of doctrine, discipline and liturgical practice in 1571, with the approval, it was claimed, of the Bishop of Peterborough, but in plain violation of the Elizabethan church settlement. According to these orders, Calvin's Catechism was used to instruct the youth of the parish, and a Confession of faith was appended which bears no relation to any official formulary. According to this Confession, the Bible is 'the infallible truth of God', valid not only for doctrine but for 'the trade of all men's lives', while the Pope was identified as the 'very Antichrist'. The Confession proceeded to repudiate a comprehensive list of popish errors, but there was no statement at all of the doctrine of predestination, still less of double predestination, in this early Elizabethan Calvinist summary of Protestant doctrine.[51]

The most convincing example of the moderation of early Elizabethan Calvinists on the doctrine of predestination is provided by the Geneva Bible. It is a popular misconception that as soon as it appeared in 1560, that Bible became the most widely read English Bible, and that it did so largely on account of its marginal notes, which are supposed to reflect an extreme Calvinist orthodoxy. In reality the Geneva translation got off to a slow start.[52] Parker discouraged publication; he wanted an edition without the 'bitter notes' of the Geneva,[53] and no Geneva Bible came off an English press before Parker died in 1575. The first complete Geneva Bible printed in England[54] followed in 1576. Thereafter, it rapidly achieved its ascendancy. Of the twenty-seven editions of the Bible in the decade 1576–85, 20 were Genevas; of the ninety-two editions in the years 1576–1611, 81 were Genevas.

The Geneva Bible was not, however, the Bible of the Puritans. Lancelot Andrewes almost always preached from it, even after the Authorized Version had been published. Laud used the Geneva Bible as late as 1624. The theological notes of the original Geneva Bible are at most moderately

---

[50] Nowell, 208. For the relation of Nowell's Catechism to Calvin's, see Haugaard, 'John Calvin and the Catechism of Alexander Nowell', 50–65.

[51] J. C. Cox (ed.), *The Records of the Borough of Northampton* (2 vols., 1898), II. 389–90.

[52] N. Shaheen, 'Misconceptions about the Geneva Bible', in F. Bowers (ed.), *Studies in Bibliography* 37 (1984), 156–8.

[53] From the instructions to the translators, printed in J. Bruce and T. T. Perowne (eds.), *The Correspondence of Matthew Parker* (Parker Society, Cambridge, 1853), 336–7.

[54] STC 2117.

'Calvinistic'. In commenting on Ezekiel xviii, 23, for example: 'He speaketh this to commend God's mercy to poor sinners, who rather is ready to pardon, than to punish, as his long-suffering declareth, chap 33. Albeit God in his eternal counsel appointed the death and damnation of the reprobate, yet the end of his counsel was not their death only, but chiefly his own glory. And also because he doth not approve sin, therefore it is said that he would have them to turn away from it that they might live.' On Romans iii, 27: 'The Law of Faith is the Gospel which offereth salvation with condition (if thou believest) which condition Christ also freely giveth us.' On Romans ix there are fewer notes than might be expected: no discussion, for example, of the crucial verses 21–3. Verse 15 is glossed 'As the only will and purpose of God is the chief cause of election and reprobation: so his free mercy in Christ is an inferior cause of salvation, and the hardening of the heart an inferior cause of damnation.' Although, as might be expected, 1 Tim. ii, 4 is glossed 'as Jew and Gentile, poor and rich', the treatment of predestination in Ephesians i is passed over without comment.

It is not definitely known who wrote these notes. If, as is possible, they are the work of Anthony Gilby,[55] their moderation was a matter of deliberate policy, for Gilby had written a treatise on predestination, published in Geneva in 1556,[56] in which his approval of Beza's doctrine is explicit. It is true that from 1576 some Geneva Bibles were published with the Geneva Catechism, and others with Beza's *Questions and Answers* appended,[57] but these variants were part of the marketing policy of the printer Charles Barker and his son, into whose hands control of the Bible had passed. The Geneva Bible was popular not because it was regarded as a test of party loyalty but because it was seen as a 'modern' and scholarly translation, grammatical and exact.[58]

It would seem, therefore, that not only the queen, but at least some English Calvinists recognized that the English Church accommodated conscientious Catholics at one extreme and Protestants desirous of further reformation at the other; and that they were prepared to temper doctrinal winds to the shorn lamb. The first threats to this delicate *modus vivendi* came from those least sensitive to the needs of the domestic establishment: the stranger churches in London.[59] Certainly in Calvin's own view their

[55] D. G. Danner, 'The Contribution of the Geneva Bible to the English Protestant Tradition', *Sixteenth Century Journal* 12/3 (1981), 5–18.

[56] Anthony Gilbie, *A Brief Treatise of Election and Reprobation: Answers to the Objections of the Adversaries of this Doctrine* (Geneva, 1556).

[57] These appeared from 1579. M. S. Betteridge, 'The Bitter Notes: The Geneva Bible and its Annotations', *Sixteenth Century Journal* 14/1 (1983), 44.

[58] L. Trinterud, *Elizabethan Puritanism* (New York, 1971), 202–8.

[59] P. Collinson, 'England and International Calvinism, 1558–1640', in Menna Prestwich (ed.), *International Calvinism* (Oxford, 1985), 197–223, esp. 201.

existence afforded an opportunity to exert indirect pressure for doctrinal conformity on the English church. Edmund Grindal, who, as Bishop of London, was responsible for their surveillance, was on the whole a willing agent of that purpose. Even Grindal, however, was embarrassed when he was obliged to accede to the sentence of excommunication passed by the Dutch church in Austin Friars on the martyrologist Adriaen van Haemstede. 'Calvinism' was threatening to become a narrowly conceived orthodoxy as yet uncharacteristic of the English Church, but not unwelcome to those members of it whose understanding of Protestantism was strongly coloured by their sense of identity with the continental Reformed churches.

The influence of the stranger churches is well illustrated by the fate of foreigners who came to teach in England, whether in Oxford or Cambridge. One was Francesco Pucci, who became a member of the Italian church in London shortly after his arrival in England in 1572.[60] Pucci, an advanced free-thinker who refused to subscribe to the confession of faith of any particular church, was soon in trouble after his arrival in Oxford a little later, the opposition to him being led by Humphrey and John Reynolds. Expelled from Oxford, he was then in conflict with the London French, this time for arguing that faith in God rested upon the divine good-will in general rather than on any specific promise, that the whole of humanity participated in the benefits of Christ's saving work, and that human reason was capable of accepting or rejecting that salvation. Not surprisingly these views, which subsequently developed into a thoroughgoing universalism defended by Pucci with consistent confidence in his own unaided reason, could not be tolerated even in Oxford.

Another example is provided by the story of the Spaniard Antonio del Corro.[61] Theologically, Corro was influenced by the ideas of Luther, Melanchthon and Bullinger, but he subsequently won the confidence of Calvin, who recommended him to the court of Navarre, and he took the oath as a Calvinist minister in 1562. In 1567 he arrived in London from Antwerp, whose church he likened to the Inquisition when he found that its confession of faith required him to condemn the Anabaptists. The French Church, already alerted, reported him to Grindal, who after examining him was prepared to say that he embraced 'the pure doctrine of the Gospel'. That, however, was not enough to avert a long-running conflict with the London French, in which his dislike of confessional tests, his readiness to bury a Jew, and doubts about his orthodoxy as to predestination were compounded, it seems, by an overbearing manner. In spite of all that, Corro was able to secure the patronage first of Cecil

[60] Dent, *Protestant Reformers*, 106f.
[61] Ibid., 110–22.

and then of Leicester in seeking a position in one of the universities. Corro's quarrels with the London French church were transferred to Oxford in 1576, when his application to be admitted to a DD was frustrated by Pierre L'Oiseleur de Villiers, minister of the church and himself an applicant. The accusations against him found a sympathetic ear in Reynolds, who feared that if he were admitted as a reader in the university, his Pelagian and universalist tendencies would corrupt the undergraduates and lead them to popery. Corro was forced temporarily to abandon his attempt to gain admission to Oxford, but in 1578 he was back, apparently with Leicester's help, to succeed Laurence Humphrey as Censor Theologicae at Christ Church. He became catechist in Gloucester Hall, Hart Hall and St Mary's Hall, and in 1581 published his *Epistola Beati Pauli*, a summary of his lectures as Reader of the Temple Church in 1574, and intended to be used in conjunction with the Prayer Book Catechism.[62]

Corro's difficulties may have owed more to his personality and to his nationality than to heterodoxy. In a declaration which, admittedly, he presented in self-defence against the charge of Pelagianism 'because I do often exhort my hearers to good works',[63] Corro affirmed the eternity, gratuity and immutability of election. His assertion that 'although God knows which are his, and that in some places mention is made of the fewness of the chosen, yet ought we to hope well of all men, and not to be rash in reckoning any man to be a reprobate' was well within the scope of the Reformed consensus. His declaration that he misliked 'of such as seek without Christ whether they be chosen from everlasting or no: and what God hath determined of them before all time' was similarly an echo of a common Reformed tradition. His reminder that 'we be greffed into Christ's body by baptism, and are often fed in his Church with his flesh and blood unto eternal life. Being confirmed with these things we be willed to work out our own salvation in fear and trembling' was another familiar catechetical lesson.

Peter Baro was yet another foreigner whose doctrinal orthodoxy was questioned in England as a result of the initiative of the stranger churches.[64] The difficulties in which he and Corro found themselves

---

[62] Ibid., 187.

[63] *The Articles of the Catholic Faith which Anthony Coranus Spaniard Student of Divinity professeth and always hath professed now set out in print*, esp. ff. 147–155. Appended to *A Theological Dialogue wherein the Epistle of St Paul to the Romans is expounded* (1575).

[64] On this see P. Lake, 'Laurence Chaderton and the Cambridge Moderate Puritan Tradition, 1570–1604', Cambridge University Ph.D. thesis, 1978, 179 n.2, where the campaign against Baro is shown to have originated not in Cambridge but in the London classis in its 'self-appointed role as guardian of the reformed conscience of the Church of England', acting in concert with the French Calvinist church in London.

illustrate the extent to which that preoccupation with heresy hunting which characterized international Calvinism could spread its tentacles in alien waters. International Calvinism, however, was more usually preoccupied with matters of foreign policy and fund raising, and it was never more than the concern of a minority.[65] Other explanations of the hardening of doctrinal definitions are needed.

One particular native development was the emphasis on personal piety which flowered in the theology of William Perkins and which has been dubbed 'experimental predestinarianism'.[66] It has recently been suggested that it is here rather than in credal predestinarianism that we should look if we wish to understand the polarities in the Elizabethan church,[67] on the grounds that the experimental predestinarians took the doctrine seriously enough to make it not only the foundation of their godly living, but also the basis of an exclusive doctrine of the true church as confined to the elect; and that this was sharply at odds with an inclusive institutional church consisting of the community of the baptized assumed to be co-extensive with parish and diocese. Many complex issues are involved here, but some salient points may be made. First, Perkins's emphasis on the practical syllogism was a natural growth out of that insistence upon the necessity for good works which, we have seen, was common both to the English Church and the continental Reformers. To insist that instead of trying to fathom the divine secrets we should seek to do the will of God was not only the conclusion of Article XVII but remained common ground, emphatically shared by Bancroft at the Hampton Court Conference and later by Laud. There were, however, possible points of tension. While in the case of Perkins himself, an acute sense of his own spiritual unworthiness before God made an emphasis upon the grounds of Christian assurance a desperately needed source of inner comfort, there was a danger that his preoccupation with the destiny of the individual soul might lead others, of different personality, either to spiritual pride or alternatively to despair. There was in consequence, as will be seen, much discussion of the doctrine of assurance in English theology from the 1590s. Whether, in addition, the logic of experimental predestinarianism was inherently separatist or presbyterian (not to say 'anti-nomian and subversive') seems much more doubtful; in any event, relatively few of Perkins's followers seem to have been prepared to follow that logic in practice.[68]

A more serious threat to the established church order came from that

---

[65] Collinson, 'England and International Calvinism', 210f.
[66] Kendall, *Calvin and English Calvinism to 1649*.
[67] P. Lake, 'Calvinism and the English Church, 1570–1635', in *Past and Present* 114 (1987), 40–1.
[68] Ibid., 40.

active minority who were 'Calvinists' in the more literal sense of admiring Calvin and Beza as the founders of a church polity they took to be indispensable to a full reformation. As Whitgift said in his reply to Cartwright in the Admonition Controversy, he included a long quotation from Beza precisely because Beza was an authority 'from whom you will be loath to disagree'.[69] Although he was prepared to 'reverence M. Calvin as a singular man, and worthy instrument of Christ's Church', he was 'not so wholly addicted to him, that I will contemn other men's judgements that in divers points agree not fully with him'.[70] Above all, according to Hooker, 'Calvin was honoured as the father of the discipline. This is the boil that may not be touched.'[71] The pressure to conform to Calvin extended to doctrine as well. As a result 'men are accused of heresy for that which the fathers held, and are never clear till they find out somewhat in Calvin to justify themselves'.[72] It was becoming 'safer to discuss all the saints in heaven than M. Calvin'.[73] Similarly, as Whitgift complained in a long letter to Beza of 1593,[74] cataloguing an extensive list of grievances which threatened to destroy the good relations between the English Church and the continental Reformed churches, Beza himself had argued 'that the purity of doctrine could scarcely be had without that discipline'.[75] Whitgift, aware of Beza's endorsement of the execution of Johannes Sylvanus of Heidelberg, can have been under no illusions as to what that would mean.[76] There was always a doctrinal subtext to the debate on church polity.

As these polarities developed, the doctrine of predestination began to harden into a Puritan grievance. In 1584, for example, the Puritans complained of both Article XVI, asking 'whether it be not dangerous to say: a man may fall from grace?' and of Article XVII, 'that maketh no mention of reprobation'.[77] Some of them objected that the Book of Common Prayer tended to favour 'the error of Origen, that all men shall be saved'.[78] Another Puritan complaint of the same year[79] included Article XVI among those which were in part 'untrue' and 'directly contrary to these places of Scripture: John vi, 37; iii, 9; ii, 19; Jer. xxxii, 39'.

[69] J. Ayre (ed.), *The Works of John Whitgift* (3 vols., Parker Society, Cambridge, 1851–3), III. 142–3.

[70] Ibid., I. 436.

[71] J. E. Booty, in *The Folger Library of the Works of Richard Hooker*, gen. ed. W. Speed Hill (5 vols., Cambridge, Mass., 1972–), IV, introduction, xliii.

[72] Hooker's autograph notes on *A Christian Letter* printed ibid., 3.

[73] Ibid., 57–8.

[74] Printed in Strype, *Whitgift*, II. 160–73.

[75] Ibid., 162.

[76] Collinson, 'England and International Calvinism', 201.

[77] A. Peel (ed.), *The Second Part of a Register* (2 vols., Cambridge, 1915), I. 197.

[78] Ibid., I. 256.

[79] Bodl. Lib., MS Rawlinson D 1349, 'Puritan Objections to the Thirty-nine Articles'.

On Article XVII it was objected that without reprobation the doctrine of predestination could not be soundly taught according to the Scriptures, much less 'take away the dissensions of opinions and confirm the consent of true religion concerning this point of doctrine when as the chiefest and hardest point of controversy concerning this article not only with the papists but some others also of ourselves consisteth of that part whereof they have never a word'.[80] At the same time the Book of Common Prayer, it was argued, ought to be purged of prayers like the last collect for Good Friday, which asked for mercy upon all Jews, Turks and Infidels and heretics that their ignorance and hardness of heart might be taken away, and the petition 'that it may please thee to have mercy upon all men' in the Litany. Among prayers which were said to be 'against the eternal predestination and diverse working of God' were that for the third Sunday after Easter, with its petition for 'all them that are admitted into the fellowship of Christ's religion' and its implication that God was willing to shew all that were in error the light of his truth in order that they might return and even, perhaps, repent.[81] However reluctant contemporaries were to admit it, the existence of doctrinal Puritanism can hardly be gainsaid.

Increasing polarity was reflected, too, in the history of the English Bible. On the one hand, the Rheims New Testament, published in 1582, was designed to correct the heresies of the existing English versions. On the other, changes were made to the Geneva Bible.[82] In 1592, Laurence Tomson's translation of the New Testament of 1576 (based on Beza's Latin text of 1574) was added to the existing Geneva Old Testament, and then in 1602 came the Geneva – Tomson – Junius version, in which Tomson's translation of Beza's notes on the Book of Revelation was replaced by a violently anti-papal diatribe of Francis Junius. In Tomson's notes there was a little more emphasis on the theological as opposed to the soteriological aspects of predestinarian doctrine, a note being added for the first time to Romans ix, 21.[83]

External factors contributed to these polarities. Religious wars in Europe were hardening the lines between Catholic and Reformed, making it much more difficult for a theology which claimed to be both Catholic and Reformed to survive. In England, the impact of foreign policy issues, the

---

[80] Ibid., f. 98ᵛ.
[81] Ibid., f. 102ᵛ.
[82] Betteridge, 'The Bitter Notes', 44.
[83] 'Alluding to the creation of Adam, he compareth mankind not yet made (but in the Creator's mind) to a lump of clay: whereof afterward God made and doth daily make, according as he purposed from everlasting, both such as should be elect, and such as should be reprobate.' Even that gloss avoids any of the contentious issues between Beza and Arminius. Not all Tomson's notes are polemical, and many Geneva Bibles were printed without any notes at all. Ibid., 55–6.

intrigues of Spanish ambassadors and the activities of Jesuits and seminary priests all contributed to a polarity upon which able theologians of the Counter-Reformation, notably Stapleton and Bellarmine, capitalized. As the polarity between Protestant and Catholic widened, so did that between Lutheran and Reformed. The failure of the discussions at the Colloquy of Montbéliard in 1586[84] had consequences throughout Europe.

A spate of books followed in which theologians defended extreme positions. The most significant for the English Church was of course Perkins's *A Golden Chain*. Whatever the differences in detail between Perkins's exposition and Beza's,[85] Perkins's purpose was avowedly to destroy any accommodation between Lutheran and Reformed doctrines. The various positions were set out and illustrated by tables. There were the 'old and new Pelagians', who by arguing that free will is able either to accept or reject the grace offered, placed the causes of predestination in man. There were the Lutherans, who attempted to combine a doctrine of gratuitous election with reprobation on account of foreseen rejection of grace offered. There were the 'semi-Pelagian papists', who ascribed predestination partly to mercy and partly to men's foreseen preparations and meritorious works. They were all unsatisfactory.[86] For Perkins, it is clear, the only consistent doctrine was a double decree, the sole cause of which was the divine will and pleasure, the sole purpose the divine glory, and to which both Creation and Fall were means. All other doctrines undermined the very nature of predestination. The doctrine of 'the writings of some later divines of Germany', for example, that God appointed all to be saved under the condition *if they believe* was 'absurd': it 'quite taketh away the certainty of God's decree'.[87] Similarly, Perkins would not allow the issue to be blurred over reprobation. 'We utterly deny, that the foreseeing of the contempt of grace in any, was the first and principal cause of the decree of reprobation.' He knew that this was 'an hard sentence', but the efforts of 'some divines' to mitigate it by arguing that man as the object of predestination was a reasonable creature were misguided; 'albeit

---

[84] The rival Lutheran and Calvinist delegations were led by Jacob Andreae and by Beza himself. They refused to shake hands at the conclusion of the proceedings, and published rival accounts of what had taken place.

[85] The best account of Perkins's doctrine of predestination is still H. C. Porter, *Reformation and Reaction in Tudor Cambridge* (Cambridge, 1958), 288–313. For a comparison between Perkins's diagram and that of Beza (in which both are reproduced), see Richard A. Muller, 'Perkins' *A Golden Chaine:* Predestinarian System or Schematized *Ordo Salutis?*', *Sixteenth Century Journal* 11/1 (1978), 69–81.

[86] Perkins's version of the spectrum was especially provocative in placing the papists' doctrine next to his own, then what he claimed was the 'Lutheran' doctrine, and at the other extreme assimilating the tradition represented by Hemmingsen to the old Pelagians. William Perkins, *A Golden Chain*, in *Works* (3 vols., Cambridge, 1616–18), I, 'To the Christian Reader', sig. B2.

[87] Ibid., 122.

they may seem to be subtle devices, yet they are not altogether true'.[88]
Indeed, it was 'preposterous that God did first foreknow mankind created,
fallen and redeemed in Christ and that afterward he ordained them so
foreknown to life or to death'. On the contrary, the decree was absolute
and unconditional, the means to execute it respective only of that absolute
decree.

While lip-service to a reformed consensus was indeed an ameliorating
bond, the doctrine of double-predestination as thus asserted was not.
A widespread reaction was to say that predestination should not be
preached.[89] A more forthright response was reflected in a sermon preached
at Paul's Cross in 1585 by Samuel Harsnett.[90] In taking as his text
Ezekiel xxxiii, 11, Harsnett set himself to counter the doctrine that

God should design many thousands of souls to Hell before they were, not in eye
to their faults, but to his own absolute will and power, and to get him glory in
their damnation. This opinion is grown huge and monstrous . . . and men do shake
and tremble at it; yet never a man reaches David's sling to cast it down. In the
name of the Lord of Hosts, we will encounter it; for it hath reviled, not the Host
of the Living God, but the Lord of Hosts.[91]

Harsnett proceeded to spell out the consequences of the doctrine: that it
turned the truth of God into a lie; that it implied the creation of millions
of men for no other purpose but to fry in hell; that it made God the author
of sin, and took away free will from Adam; and that it rested on a false
distinction between a secret and revealed will in God. He dismissed the
doctrine as contrary both to the laws of nations and the rule of reason.
The true cause of reprobation was sin, and no man was of absolute
necessity condemned to hell. The will of God was to save all men, and
His son was sent for that purpose. Effectual grace was offered through
Christ to all, and it was neglect of that grace, and not any 'privative decree',
which explained why not all are saved. The absolute will of God to save
was subject to a conditional will dependent upon our belief. In citing,
among other standard texts, 1 Tim. ii, 4[92] Harsnett dismissed the 'Gene-
vian conceit' which 'curtailed the grace of God at the stumps' in interpreting it to mean 'one or two out of every order and occupation . . .
For it would teach us to say God would have all to be saved, that is God

---

[88] Ibid., 122–3.

[89] In the preface to his translation of Beza's *Tabula* in 1576, John Stockwood wrote of those
who 'are utter enemies to this doctrine and do think all writings hereof more meet for
the fire than for the reading of God his children'. *The Treasure of Truth*, 'To the godly
reader'.

[90] Samuel Harsnett, *A Sermon preached at Paul's Cross*, appended to R. Stewart, *Three
Sermons* (1656).

[91] Ibid., 133.

[92] Ibid., 153.

would have a few to be saved: God would not have any to perish, that is, God would that almost all should perish: so God loved the world, that is, so God loved a small number of the world . . .' The spirit of Peter, which taught that it was not God's will that any should perish,[93] 'was a great deal wiser than that of Geneva'. The Calvinist appeal to a distinction between the sufficiency and efficiency of the death of Christ he dismissed as another 'silly shift'[94] which implied that God was a dissembler, and made Christ 'shed crocodile tears, to laugh and lament both at once'.[95]

To conclude, let us take heed and beware, that we neither (with the Papists) rely upon our free will; nor (with the Pelagian) upon our nature: nor (with the Puritan) *Curse God and die*, laying the burden of our sins on his shoulders, and the guilt of them at the everlasting doors: but let us fall down on our faces, give God the glory, and say, Unto thee O Lord belong mercy and forgiveness.[96]

Harsnett had broken the ground rules of Protestant apologetic by thus explicitly making Geneva his target. Not surprisingly, he was reprimanded by Whitgift, and instructed never again to preach on reprobation. When, in 1624, he was accused of being a papist, he wondered whether it was because of that sermon.[97] We do not, however, need to search for alien Lutheran or other foreign influences in order to explain Harsnett's reaction. It rested largely on a combination of familiar scriptural texts and moral indignation. It was the inevitable response to the changing face of Elizabethan Calvinism. If, for whatever reasons, it was becoming difficult to preach the will of God to save all men in the English Church, such explosions were bound to follow. Before long the University of Cambridge witnessed an even bigger one.

[93] Ibid.; 2 Pet. iii, 9.
[94] Harsnett, *A Sermon*, 157.
[95] Ibid., 164.
[96] Ibid., 165.
[97] *House of Lords Journals*, III. 389.

6 The Cambridge controversies of the 1590s

The Lambeth Articles

On 27 February 1595, William Whitaker, Master of St John's College in the University of Cambridge, and Regius Professor of Divinity, delivered a public divinity lecture 'against those who assert universal grace'.[1] Whitaker's target (although he did not mention him by name) was the Lady Margaret Professor of Divinity, Peter Baro, and his following in the university. The stage was set for a trial of strength between two rival academic factions, which before long involved both archbishops and the queen, with repercussions the importance of which it would be hard to exaggerate for the Church of England. The Lambeth Articles, which grew out of the crisis, have become a byword for a rigid Calvinism to which, it is usually claimed, both Whitgift (after, perhaps, some initial hesitation) and Matthew Hutton subscribed.[2] It will be contended here that on the contrary the archbishops were throughout theologically independent of the two factions, that neither was in any meaningful sense a Calvinist, and that the Lambeth Articles were intended by Whitgift to put a rein on both Calvinists and anti-Calvinists in the university.

[1] The lecture took as its text 1 Tim. ii, 4. In the printed version (Cambridge, 1600), the original Greek is followed by the Latin mistranslation 'Qui quosvis homines vult servari', a remarkable example of tampering with Holy Writ in the interests of Calvinist orthodoxy. Whitaker's attack on the doctrine of universal grace had been anticipated by Perkins, who associated it with 'some later Divines in Germany' (*A Golden Chain,* in *Works,* I. 109–11) and by Andrew Willett, who linked it with 'the Rhemish Papists'. *Synopsis Papismi* (1592), 554. In 1600, Willett identified three Protestant versions of universalism: that of Huber and Andreae, according to whom all men are actually saved by Christ sufficiently and effectively, but the reprobate refused the grace offered; that of Pucci, according to whom all men are saved, but not without faith, faith, however, being naturally given to all; and that of Hemmingsen and Snecanus, according to whom the divine purpose is to save all upon the condition of faith. The third version, said Willett, 'seemeth to be much approved by our own countrymen, and already hath gotten some patrons and defenders in our Church'. *Synopsis Papismi* (1600), 783–4.

[2] This chapter owes much to Porter, *Reformation and Reaction in Tudor Cambridge,* 344–390, and also to W. D. Sargeaunt, 'The Lambeth Articles', *Journal of Theological Studies* 12/46 (1911), 251–60 and 12/47 (1911), 427–36. For a different view, see Peter Lake, *Moderate Puritans and the Elizabethan Church* (Cambridge, 1982), 201–42.

Baro did not immediately reply to Whitaker, but a young fellow of Caius College, William Barrett, did. His sermon,[3] preached in the university church on 29 April, was a counter-attack on late sixteenth-century high Calvinism at what Barrett conceived to be its weakest points: its doctrines of assurance, perseverance and irrespective reprobation. Barrett denied that anyone, apart from a special revelation, could be so certain of his faith that he was 'secure' of his salvation. Final perseverance, he argued, was contingent; to hold otherwise was arrogant and impious. Barrett cast doubt on the distinction between true and temporary faith; there was no difference, he asserted, in faith but in believers.[4] Most provocatively of all, he denied that an individual could be certain of the remission of his sins. Lastly, in the case of those who were not saved, sin was the true, proper and first cause of reprobation. He ended his sermon with a violent attack on Calvin and other continental Reformers.[5]

Within a few days Barrett was called before the consistory court, and required to make a public retractation. He was made to say that those who are justified by faith are indeed rightly not merely certain but 'secure' by certitude of faith; that Christ's prayer[6] was efficacious for all true believers, and it was therefore impossible for their faith to fail. A true and justifying faith was proof against the temptations of the world, the flesh and the Devil, and it was therefore not possible that anyone who had it should not persevere to the end. Temporary faith was different, not merely in degree but in kind, from saving faith. The truly faithful were rightly certain of the remission of their sins. Finally, the reprobation of the wicked was from eternity, and what St Augustine had said was indeed true, namely, that if sin were the cause of reprobation, then no one would be elect. Calvinist doctrine, and Calvinist discipline to boot, appeared to have established itself in Cambridge.

The Barrett affair, however, was only just beginning. Barrett read his recantation deliberately parrot-fashion, and a petition signed by fifty-six dons (over half of them from St John's and Trinity) demanded further action. A libellous version of the original sermon was circulated, and Barrett was summoned yet again before the consistory court to be threatened with expulsion from the university.[7] It was at this stage that both sides began to represent their case to Whitgift, into whose hands

---

[3] Barrett's sermon has not survived. These points are derived from his retractation, in Trin. Coll. Camb. MS B 14/9, pp. 39–41; printed in Strype, *Whitgift*, III. 317–19.

[4] Barrett may merely have meant to say that some men's faith, however genuine, will prove temporary. Sargeaunt, 'Lambeth Articles', 251,

[5] Trin. Coll. Camb. MS B 14/9, p. 35 (Strype, *Whitgift*, III. 320).

[6] The difference of opinion hinged on the exegesis of Luke xxii, 32, according to whether Christ's prayer was for Peter, or for all the Apostles.

[7] Porter, *Reformation and Reaction*, 346f.

came Barrett's retractation. The archbishop submitted it to his chaplains, Adrian Saravia and Lancelot Andrewes, for comment.

Saravia was a scholar of some distinction. He had finally settled in England in 1585, having earlier been a pastor at Antwerp and later Professor of Divinity at Leiden. He had assisted in drafting the Belgic Confession, and on more than one occasion been asked to adjudicate in cases where Netherlands pastors were accused of unorthodoxy on predestination.[8] In a long memorandum,[9] Saravia supported Barrett on most of the points at issue, though he deplored his railing against Calvin. Barrett was right to deny that anyone ought to feel 'secure'; security, Saravia asserted, was the product not of faith but of arrogance and presumption, and there were numerous warnings in Scripture against it. A man might be 'certain', but only as long as he was also solicitous not only of faith but of perseverance. He was right to say there was no difference in quality between temporary and justifying faith, although of course some temporary faiths were feigned. Not all those who truly believed were proof against their faith failing ('suffulti, ut eorum fides nequeat deficere'), but only the elect, and no one had the right to assume that he was one of the elect.

Saravia turned to election and obduration, 'about which there is considerable controversy among theologians'. He argued that St Paul's intention in Romans ix was to teach nothing more than the free grace of God in election and justification. The cause of election is grace without any merit, while the cause of reprobation is the justice of God and the punishment of sin. Barrett was right to assert that sin was the true, proper and first cause of reprobation, and the Heads had erred both in their understanding of St Augustine and in making him retract the assertion. 'Some learned men write of the eternal decree of God, as if they themselves had been privy to the divine counsel.' Saravia flatly denied that there was any predestination of God whatsoever to disobedience, unbelief, apostasy or sin. Barrett and those who thought like him were wrongly labelled Pelagians; the churches had contained and still did contain many faithful men who thought differently on predestination without having to indulge in mutual accusations of heresy. Andrewes, consulted on the first point of the retractation, gave his judgment to similar effect.[10] He pointed out that the Scriptures nowhere urge security; rather 'they took the word in evil part'. Whitgift's chaplains, from such different backgrounds, were

8 W. Nijenhuis, *Adrian Saravia (c. 1532–1613)* (Leiden, 1980), 72.
9 The Latin text from which this account is taken, Trin. Coll. Camb. MS B 14/9, pp. 169–83; printed in Nijenhuis, *Adrian Saravia*, 330–42.
10 Text in Lancelot Andrewes, *A Pattern of Catechestical Doctrine*, ed. J. P. Wilson and J. Bliss, Anglo-Catholic Library (Oxford, 1846), 301–5.

agreed in rejecting the doctrine of irrespective predestination. The cause of reprobation was God's prescience of sin. A justifying faith was no absolute promise of any future state.

Whitgift, thus armed, sent a message to the Heads that in his opinion

in some points of his retractation they have made him affirm that which is contrary to the doctrine holden and expressed by many sound and learned divines in the Church of England, and in other Churches likewise, men of best account: and the which for my own part I think to be false and contrary to the Scriptures. For the Scriptures are plain, that God by His absolute will does not hate and reject any man, without an eye to his sin. There may be impiety in believing the one; there can be none in believing the other. Neither is it contrary to any article of religion, established by authority in this Church of England: but rather agreeable thereunto.[11]

He invited them to show him against what article Barrett's warning against security had offended, 'seeing security is never taken in good part: neither doth the Scripture so use it'. Again, to what article, he asked, was it contrary to say that the faith of the elect might fail totally, but not finally? 'It is a matter disputable, and wherein learned men do and may dissent without impiety.' Whitgift conceded that Barrett had been in error to assert that there was no distinction in faith, and to deny that remission of sins was special, of this man or that: but on neither count had it been necessary to proceed by means of a retractation. The message ended with the statement that there was no Article of Religion to prevent the conscientious criticism of Calvin, Beza or Peter Martyr, 'for the doctrine of the Church of England doth in no respect depend upon them'.[12]

The Heads were not prepared to agree that the matters in dispute were indifferent. On the contrary, they claimed, they concerned the 'substantial ground, and chief comfort and anchor hold of our salvation'.[13] Not only were they 'unyielding . . . in all the points of the recantation', but they denied the archbishop's authority over them 'either to determine what the doctrine is of the Church of England, or otherwise, howsoever; but stand peremptorily upon their privileges, which they take to be a sufficient warrant for all their dealing'.[14] Meanwhile, Barrett, encouraged by the disputes, had revoked his recantation, and the Vice-Chancellor (Robert Some) had taken the opportunity of a sudden vacancy in the list of university preachers to make a violent attack upon him.[15]

In those circumstances, Whitgift empowered Whitaker to examine

[11] Trin. Coll. Camb. MS B 14/9, p. 3.
[12] Ibid., p. 4.
[13] Heads to Whitgift, 7 July 1595. Ibid., p. 52.
[14] Ibid., p. 25, as reported to Whitgift by Richard Clayton, Master of Magdalene.
[15] Porter, *Reformation and Reaction*, 357–8.

Barrett further. He was presented with questions[16] which held traps for him. He was asked, for example, 'whether Christ prayed for Peter only, that his faith should not fail; or also for all the elect, that they fall not away from faith and salvation, either finally, or for a time totally?' To answer 'only for St Peter' would not only imply a denial of the doctrine of perseverance but could be held 'popish' in supporting St Peter's supremacy among the Apostles. He was asked 'whether justifying faith is not in reality distinct and diverse from a hypocritical, feigned and dead faith', whether it did not 'make us certain of our election and adoption, and persuade, without all doubt, that we shall be saved' and 'whether any godly and faithful Christian ought not to believe the remission of his sins'. To deny any of those propositions could be held to deny the doctrine of justification by faith. He was asked 'whether God from eternity hath predestinated certain men to life; and reprobated certain. And why?' He might be trapped into denying the doctrine of predestination altogether.

According to Whitaker, the whole tenor of Barrett's answers was evasive and popish. They were such 'as might be thought that he disliked the doctrine of justification by faith, approved in the Book of Articles; and the distinction he made of *fides formata* was Popish, and not only against Scripture, but the Book of Articles also; teaching that good works are the fruit of faith, and so must be the formal cause thereof'.[17] Whitgift took a different view. When he told Whitaker that 'in perusing Barrett's answers he was partly of their [the heads'] minds'[18] he did not mean that he had changed his own: it was a response to the finer sifting to which Barrett had been subjected. Whitgift thought the interpretation of Luke xxii doubtful, but 'elsewhere . . . that Christ prayed for all the elect, no man could doubt'. Barrett's distinction between *fides formata* and *fides informis* was indeed 'popish'; but before conceding that he had contradicted the doctrine of justification by faith as set forth in the Articles, he would need further information. He did not think that Barrett's doctrine of assurance contradicted any of the Articles of Religion. Whether it contradicted 'any other article of Religion professed in this Church of England, is questionable; and therefore requireth further conference of learned men'. It was 'common to him with some others and the question was of that nature, that men might answer . . . *pro et con*, without impiety'.[19]

There is nothing in Whitgift's reply to suggest any wavering in his

---

[16] Latin text in Trin. Coll. Camb. MS B 14/9, p. 59; English translation in Strype, *Whitgift*, II. 263. Sargeaunt may be right to suggest that these questions were framed by Whitaker and not by Whitgift. Whitgift was very uncertain as to some of the answers.

[17] Trin. Coll. Camb. MS B 14/9, p. 71.

[18] Ibid., p. 13.

[19] Ibid., p. 14.

rejection of the doctrines of irrespective reprobation, of the indefectibility of faith in the man once justified, and of absolute assurance of
perseverance and salvation. But he agreed that Barrett should retract his
lapses from the English Reformation views of justification by faith alone,
his assertion that remission of sins depended on the performance of
penitential acts, and his desire to distinguish Peter above the rest of the
Apostles. And he was prepared to submit the question of assurance of
salvation to further discussion. To that end, Whitgift suggested that during the forthcoming term there should come to Lambeth 'some one or
two of you' and 'likewise the parties offending', and that meanwhile 'no
man in pulpit within that university deal in these causes to or fro, until
further order be taken'.[20]

Whitgift's own account of his involvement in the Barrett affair, completed after it was all over, is worth careful study.[21] It began with
Barrett's sermon, which had contained 'divers unsound points of divinity
. . . to the offence of many'. Whitgift himself had intervened not only
in order that he 'might understand the causes of their [the Heads'] proceeding, being matters of Divinity' but also 'because I found some error
in that recantation, which they caused him to pronounce: which error also
was afterward confessed by some of them; and is manifest'. Some of the
things called in question were 'deep points of divinity, and wherein great
learned men did vary in opinion'. That was why the archbishop had
asked the Vice-Chancellor 'that some might be sent unto me instructed
in these causes; and that Barrett might come up likewise, to the end that
I might the better understand the controversies'.[22] As a result of the
ensuing discussions, Whitgift wrote

I found that Barrett had erred in diverse points. I delivered mine opinion of the
propositions brought unto me by Dr Whitaker: wherein some few being added,
I agreed fully with them, and they with me.
And I know them to be sound doctrines, and uniformly professed in this Church
of England, and agreeable to the Articles of Religion established by authority.
And I therefore thought it meet that Barrett should in more humble sort confess
his ignorance and errors: and that none should be suffered to teach any contrary
doctrine to the foresaid propositions agreed upon.
And this is the sum of all this action. And if this agreement be not maintained,
further contentions will grow, to the animating the common adversaries, the
Papists, by whose practice Barrett and others are set on, some of his opinions
indeed being Popish.

[20] Ibid., pp. 15–16.
[21] Ibid., pp. 79–80.
[22] Strype's transcription has 'end' for 'understand'. The correct text reinforces the point
that what was in debate was for Whitgift far from being a matter either of consensus
or of the essentials of the Christian faith as commonly understood.

According to the interpretation here offered, what Whitgift was saying is that unless the Heads were prepared to abide by the agreement, that is, if they persisted in proscribing opinions which were not contrary to the doctrine of the Church of England, as they had done in Barrett's case, others who shared his popish opinions would raise fresh contentions to the delight of the papists, the common adversaries – common, that is to say, to the Cambridge high Calvinists on the one hand and to himself and his advisers on the other. He would support the Cambridge authorities only so far as they were prepared to act on the basis of 'sound doctrines, and uniformly professed in the Church of England, and agreeable to the Articles of Religion established by authority',[23] but *no further*.

In order to provide a rule which might stand as a guide to their further conduct, giving them reasonable grounds to condemn 'Popish opinions', but no scope to impose high Calvinism upon those who declined to subscribe to it, Whitaker was invited to formulate propositions for the archbishop's approval. We should expect the Lambeth Articles – given that they were originally drafted by Whitaker – to spell out more explicitly the implications of Article XVII of the Thirty-nine, but to be so carefully phrased, at any rate in their final form, as to prevent further episodes like Barrett's retractation. That this was indeed the archbishop's intention is suggested by Matthew Hutton's subsequent observation that subject to three slight changes 'ipse Momus non haberet quod contra diceret'[24] – a revealing comment which suggests that he at least understood what his fellow archbishop was about. But the acid test is to look at the articles.[25]

1. God from eternity has predestined some men to life, and reprobated some to death.

The article was left as Whitaker drafted it. Andrewes raised no objection.[26] As he pointed out, election was, in the scriptural phrase, πρὸ καταβολῆς κόσμου, that is, 'from eternity'; election implied predestination; and if some were elected, those who were not were reprobated. So much was 'beyond controversy'. The article says nothing of the 'causes'

---

23 The limits of Whitgift's agreement with the Heads may be tested by reference to Barrett's second recantation, in Trin. Coll. Camb. MS B 14/9, pp. 75–6, composed with his approval, and containing no reference either to 'security' or to reprobation. See P. O. G. White, 'Debate: The Rise of Arminianism Reconsidered', 222. The only one of Barrett's original assertions which Whitgift believed to contradict the Articles was part of his 5th: 'Remissionem peccatorum non esse specialem, nec huius, nec illius'. See Sargeaunt, 'The Lambeth Articles', 259.

24 Trin. Coll. Camb. MS B 14/9, p. 150. Momus was the god of censure.

25 I have followed the translations of Whitaker's draft and of the final version of the Lambeth Articles in Porter, *Reformation and Reaction*, 365–6, 371.

26 For Andrewes's judgment of the Lambeth Articles, see *Catechestical Doctrine*, 295–300.

of predestination, but would serve to check anyone who denied the doctrine of reprobation altogether.

2. The moving or efficient cause of predestination to life is not the foreseeing of faith, or of perseverance, or of good works, or of anything innate in the person of the predestined, but only the will of the good pleasure of God.

Whitaker's draft spoke only of 'predestination'. The addition 'to life' clearly excluded the cause of reprobation, on which he and Whitgift so fundamentally differed, from the scope of the article. As to the cause of election, to which it was now limited, Whitaker's Calvinistic 'only the absolute and simple will of God' was changed to the scriptural and Augustinian 'only the will of the good pleasure of God.' There is nothing in this article to have hindered Barrett from repeating his belief that sin was the cause of reprobation.

3. There is a determined and certain number of predestined, which cannot be increased or diminished.

Whitaker no doubt meant that the irrespective choice of some and the irrespective rejection of others necessitated each man's fate, but it was open to Baro and Andrewes to understand the number to be determined and certain because foreknown. The controversy at the root of Arminius' difference with Gomarus, as to the possibility of infallible divine foreknowledge of contingents, was left untouched.[27]

4. Those not predestined to salvation are inevitably condemned on account of their sins (*necessario propter peccata condemnabuntur*).

Hutton would have deleted 'inevitably'; then *minus offenderet infirmos*.[28] But the inevitability need not be causal; it may derive from the infallibility of the divine foreknowledge. It was open to Whitaker, of course, privately to gloss the article and distinguish between damnation and reprobation along Bezan lines, but it gave him no licence to impose that gloss on others.

5. A true, lively and justifying faith, and the sanctifying Spirit of God, is not lost nor does it pass away either totally or finally in the elect.

Whitaker had written 'in those who once have been partakers of it'. The change was fundamental, enabling anyone who chose not to restrict justifying faith to the elect to hold that it might totally or finally be lost in others. Again, Whitaker would have deplored that interpretation, but was

---

[27] The Irish Articles attempted to repair the deficiency by including the statement that 'God from all eternity did by his unchangeable counsel ordain whatever in time should come to pass.' Schaff, *Creeds of the Evangelical Protestant Churches*, 528.
[28] Trin. Coll. Camb. MS B 14/9, p. 150.

left powerless to proscribe it. At the same time, Whitgift allowed himself
to be convinced, apparently for the first time, that faith cannot fail
totally in the elect, but Andrewes and Baro were content to understand
that to mean 'not so lost that it could not be recovered':[29] they did not
assert that faith could finally fail in the elect. The difference between them
and the high Calvinists is again that for them the truth of the article derives
from the infallibility of the divine foreknowledge, and not from the causal
necessitating of the divine decree. Nor, it should be added, would
Whitaker's draft have been changed if the archbishop and his advisers
meant to allow that any particular man might assume himself to be of
the elect.

6. The truly faithful man — that is, one endowed with justifying faith — is sure
by full assurance of faith of the remission of sins and his eternal salvation through
Christ.

Whitaker's *certitudine fidei* was changed to *plerophoria fidei*. Some
members of the conference wished it to be *plerophoria spei*, the phrase
subsequently preferred by Matthew Hutton.[30] The change was from the
Calvinist doctrine of certainty to the Pauline doctrine of assurance.[31] For
Andrewes and Baro, the assurance or certitude was conditional — *si
Christo ad finem usque adhaeserit*[32] — and Whitgift too, had distinguished it from the certainty attached to categorical statements like 'God
is almighty.'

7. Saving grace is not granted, is not made common, is not ceded to all men, by
which they might be saved, if they wish.

Whitaker had written 'Grace sufficient to salvation'. The change enabled
Andrewes to maintain, without contradicting the article, that although
offered to all, 'per homines autem ipsos stare quod oblata non con-
feratur'.[33] Whitgift and his revisers, however, were committing
themselves no more to that gloss than to Whitaker's Calvinist original.
All that the revised article asserts is — as do Articles X and XVIII of the
Thirty-nine — that the condition of man after the Fall is such that only
where the Gospel of Christ is preached have men any hope of salvation.
In that sense it was common ground. It gave Whitaker no scope for insisting that saving grace was denied to the non-elect.

8. No one can come to Christ unless it be granted to him, and the Father draws
him: and all men are not drawn by the Father to come to the Son.

[29] Andrewes, *Catechestical Doctrine*, 299.
[30] Sargeaunt, 'The Lambeth Articles', 432.
[31] Porter, *Reformation and Reaction*, 371.
[32] Trin. Coll. Camb. MS B 14/9, p. 85.
[33] Andrewes, *Catechestical Doctrine*, 300.

Andrewes and Baro, avoiding the obvious Calvinist gloss (because the Father does not so will), interpreted the article to mean 'so that they come' (ita ut veniant).[34] But all that the revisers were conceding is, as in Article VII, that the Gospel is not preached to all. The divine purpose for those like the Jews, Turks, infidels and heretics, from whom it is denied, must be left to God's mercy.[35]

9. It is not in the will or power of each and every man to be saved.

Andrewes and Baro were both content. Neither believed in the free will of all men to win salvation. Whitaker was entitled to think that it rebutted Pelagianism, but he was given no sanction to impose the doctrine that the non-elect, who were passed by without regard to their future sins or impenitence, were predestinated to continue to the end without grace.

The Heads themselves may have assumed that, because Whitgift had eventually been compelled to produce a theological rule on the basis of a draft submitted by Whitaker, their stance had been vindicated. That was to overlook the delicacy with which the stings had been withdrawn in the revision process. Whitgift's purpose of bringing peace to the university required that he should keep his own counsel. Lancelot Andrewes, however, knew they would be disputed over, rival parties reading into them their own doctrines.[36] The widespread misconception that they demonstrate 'rigid Calvinism' was the result of just that process, and of the immediate sequel, which concerned the Lady Margaret Professor. Baro had remained out of the limelight until the Lambeth Articles had been sent to Cambridge. He now became the centre of the Cambridge disputes.

Peter Baro

Baro had come to England as a French Huguenot refugee in 1572. In the following year he had been elected a fellow-commoner of Peterhouse, and then in 1574, at the age of forty, appointed Lady Margaret Professor of Divinity. He was thus senior to most of the other actors in the Cambridge controversies of 1595–6.[37] He was a well-known and much-respected member of the university. His lectures on the prophet Jonah had been published in 1579, together with two disputations, in one of which he had argued that 'God's purpose and decree taketh not away the

---

[34] Ibid.
[35] Cf. the prayer 'O Merciful God, who hast made all men, and hatest nothing that thou hast made . . . have mercy upon all Jews, Turks, Infidels and Hereticks . . . and take from them all ignorance, hardness of heart and contempt of thy word . . . that they may be saved among the remnant of the true Israelites.'
[36] Andrewes, *Catechestical Doctrine*, 300.
[37] Porter, *Reformation and Reaction*, 373.

liberty of man's corrupt will.' This had been followed in 1580 by a treatise on faith,[38] and in 1588(?) by *A Special Treatise of God's Providence.* Baro's theological views were therefore well known. Apart from a disputation with Laurence Chaderton in 1583 on the nature of faith,[39] they had not occasioned controversy; nor is there any indication that they suddenly changed in 1595–6: those who complained about him to Burleigh in 1596 admitted as much when they asserted that 'for the space of these fourteen or fifteen years' he had 'taught in his lectures, preached in sermons, determined in the Schools and printed in several books divers points of doctrine . . . contrary to that which hath been taught and received ever since her Majesty's reign, yet agreeable to the errors of popery'.[40] Baro became involved in the Cambridge controversies not because he was broaching new doctrines but because of a polarity between Calvinist and anti-Calvinist which was threatening to destroy the diversity and mutual tolerance which had previously characterized the hybrid Protestant tradition common to the Church of England and Cambridge divinity.

Although in the aftermath it was widely supposed that the Lambeth Articles had been primarily aimed at Baro,[41] that was in no sense part of Whitgift's purpose. His own summary of his reasons for intervention made no mention of Baro. Some of the Cambridge Heads, however, decided to use the Articles to intimidate him. The Vice-Chancellor, now Goad of King's, sent the Articles to the Heads of Colleges; and 'unto some particular persons, of whom I doubted, as namely Dr Baro the Frenchman, I gave knowledge and caveat by causing him to see and read over the propositions, as also the clause of the said letters that nothing should be publicly taught the contrary'.[42] Baro had already received warning that some of those who were attacking Barrett were aiming at him as well. On 9 July 1595, he had been summoned before the consistory court and asked to state his views on the questions of assurance that Barrett had raised.[43] The session ended inconclusively, but Baro may well have anticipated further proceedings in due course, for two days later he wrote to an unnamed friend setting out what he believed about predestination, asking for comments.[44]

There were fourteen theses according to which, he wrote, the mystery

[38] Peter Baro, *De fide, eiusque ortu & natura explicatio* (1580).
[39] Porter, *Reformation and Reaction*, 377–8.
[40] Trin. Coll. Camb. MS B 14/9, pp. 184–5.
[41] Cf. Tyacke, 'Debate: The Rise of Arminianism Reconsidered', 204: 'Hence the importance of the famous Lambeth Articles . . . which sought to quash emergent English Anti-Calvinism, especially in the person of Peter Baro'.
[42] Trin. Coll. Camb. MS B 14/9, p. 130.
[43] Ibid., p. 26.
[44] Bodl. Lib., MS Rawlinson C 167, f. 70ʳ.

of predestination must be expounded if the truth were to be maintained. First of all, 'Deum decernentem sibi exequenti dissimilem non esse nec exequentem decernenti.' Baro meant that propositions which hold good of God executing His decrees must hold good of God making His decrees. The distinction on which Beza's doctrine of predestination depended is rejected. All things are not determined by an inevitable necessity; God has left man a degree of free will. The divine promises are to be generally received, as they are in Scripture generally set forth. We must believe that God created Adam, and hence all men, for a good end: to have done otherwise would be inconsistent with His goodness. Baro concluded that no one has been predestinated to eternal death unless on account of sin, and that there was no decree whereby the first parents were not able to keep the command not to eat the forbidden fruit. God, having forbidden sin, cannot either have willed or decreed it: rather, foreknowing it, He permits it and ordains it to a good end. Just as the possibility of repentance was left to the first parents, so also it is left to all of fallen mankind. It is no more the fault of Christ that all are not saved than it is to the credit of Adam that all do not perish. Nevertheless, and in contradiction of the Pelagians, grace is not granted to men by their own will, nor is it given according to merit. We can neither will the good nor receive grace which is offered unless through grace. Finally, grace given and received by us imposes no necessity whereby we are not able to fall away (*recedere*) from it. Notwithstanding that, election is certain, it is of grace, and it is according to the eternal purpose of God's good pleasure in Christ.

In spite of Baro's repudiation of Pelagianism, the moderation of his concluding assertions and the familiarity of his doctrines, there was more than enough material here for dispute in Cambridge, where it was becoming ever more difficult to steer a middle course between a Bezan doctrine on the one hand and the tradition represented by Melanchthon and Hemmingsen on the other. Baro believed that all theories of predestination except his own made God the author of sin. In a treatise composed in 1594,[45] he drew no distinction between the doctrine of Calvin and that of Beza; it was also the doctrine, he claimed, of Luther, and of the mature St Augustine, and it was represented in Cambridge by Robert Some. According to this view God decreed from all eternity to create mankind for the express purpose of electing some and reprobating others, for no other reason than to show His mercy in the former, His justice in the later and His glory in both, without respect either to Christ or to faith in election, and without respect to sin, either original or actual, in reprobation. From that first decree, all else followed: the Fall of the first man, the

---

[45] P. Baro, *Summa trium de Praedestinatione Sententiarum* (1613). I have used the translation of James Nichols printed in Arminius, *Works*, I. 92–100.

corruption thereby of the whole human race, the gratuitous election of some, and the sending of Christ on their account, the desertion of the rest without the means of salvation and their just condemnation on account of the sins committed by them. But because, said Baro, the means to reprobation no less than the means of election alike follow from the same decree, 'it is scarcely (and not even *scarcely*) possible to understand how God may not be accounted the Author of that which is evil as well as of that which is good, and of men's destruction as well as of their salvation'.[46]

A second theory, according to Baro, was the opinion of St Augustine in his middle period, followed by Zanchi among the Protestants and shared by Bellarmine among the papists. According to this theory, predestination is to be 'computed only from the Fall of Adam'. Election and reprobation are both out of a corrupt mass. Baro claimed, like Arminius, that this theory represented no real improvement, in that it held, in common with the first, an eternal decree to elect some and to reprobate others; that Christ was sent only for the elect[47] and that some are saved, others damned by an inevitable necessity. Through the insistence that predestination depends upon the absolute will of God, 'this milder opinion . . . comes back in substance to the first which it is desirous to avoid'.[48]

The third opinion, that of Baro himself, was the theory of Melanchthon, Hemmingsen, Snecanus 'and not a few of other divines in various countries';[49] it was the theory of the Christian Fathers before St Augustine, and of Augustine himself before his conflict with Pelagius. 'God has predestinated such as he from all eternity foreknew would believe on Christ (who is the only way to life eternal) that they might be made conformable to him in glory. But he hath likewise from all eternity reprobated all rebels, and such as contumaciously continue in sin, as persons unfit for his kingdom.'[50] This theory, while agreeing with the first two that election and reprobation are eternal and determinate, differed from the other two both in asserting that Christ has died for all and in denying that God created the greater part of mankind for destruction (according to the first opinion) or decreed to leave them in their fallen state without any hope of pardon (according to the second). The two main axioms of the third opinion, said Baro, are the doctrines that it is the will of God that all men be saved, and that Christ has died for all. That in fact all are not saved is through the 'perverseness and depravity' of some, and here Baro

[46] Ibid., 93.
[47] Ibid., 94.
[48] Ibid., 95.
[49] Ibid., 96.
[50] Ibid.

invoked the distinction 'of the ancient Fathers' between the antecedent and the consequent will of God.[51]

The third view, according to Baro, while granting that predestination is 'immutable in the divine mind', denied such predestination as made the wills of men immutable. Since only one of the theories could be true, 'let everyone seriously consider which of the three he ought to reject, and which he ought to embrace . . . if it be his wish to have a proper regard for his own salvation'.[52]

Although Baro's tract was not to be published until 1613, it is further evidence of the polarity that had come to characterize Cambridge theology in the 1590s, divided between the Calvinists, whose *Summa* was Perkins's *Golden Chain* and whose leader was Whitaker, and an anti-Calvinist circle, which looked to Baro. Each side assimilated 'Lutheranism' to the views of its opponents. Each side claimed that the formularies of the English Church supported its own interpretation.

In spite of Whitgift's inhibition of further discussion pending agreement on the Articles, Whitaker saw fit to preach on the forbidden points.[53] Taking 1 Thessalonians v, 22 as his text ('Try all things; cleave to that which is good'), Whitaker warned of the dangers of false prophets and the need to deal promptly with present discords lest greater ones followed ('Non agam litigiose, sed quam placide possim et sedate et Christiane').[54] Like Baro, he identified three opinions of predestination, and like Baro he thought only one was acceptable. The first held the cause of predestination and reprobation to be foreknowledge of something in the predestined and the reprobate. The second held the cause of predestination to life to be the simple will of God, but that of reprobation to be sin, either original or actual. The third theory held the cause of both to be none other than the eternal and immutable will of God. Whitaker dismissed the first as tantamount to a denial of predestination. It was either explicit or (if stated as election *ex praevisa fide*) implicit Pelagianism. He likewise rejected the second theory. He granted that it had the support of certain passages in St Augustine, 'but here I know not whether St Augustine disagrees more with himself or with the truth'.[55] Reprobation cannot be on account of original sin, since that is forgiven in baptism, and both elect and reprobate are baptized. Furthermore, if original sin were the cause of reprobation, all men would be reprobated. Nor, said Whitaker, can reprobation be on account of sins actually committed,

[51] Ibid., 98. The distinction derived from John of Damascus, and was used by Aquinas.
[52] Ibid., 99.
[53] W. Whitaker, *Cygnea Cantio*, printed in *Praelectiones de Ecclesia* (1599).
[54] Ibid., 48.
[55] Ibid., 52.

for the divine permission of sin was a consequence of divine providence
and of the decree of reprobation.[56] The only possible conclusion was the
third theory, that no reason for predestination or reprobation on the part
of man can be given: it must be sought exclusively by reference to the
nature of God.[57]

But Peter Baro — Whitaker named him — thinks this is too hard, and
he and others therefore argue that God offers and gives grace to each mortal man by which he can be saved if he wills. A plausible opinion, but
close to Pelagianism. For what is common to all is natural, and grace is
thereby confounded with nature. Is the grace thus offered efficacious or
not? If efficacious, why are not all saved? If the answer is, because not
all are willing, then we are back in Pelagianism. Of what kind or quality
is this grace? Not, surely, faith, which St Paul expressly denies is granted
to all. Faith comes from hearing, and the Gospel has not been heard by
the thousandth part of the human race. There is no grace without faith,
and no faith without preaching. Is Baro suggesting that the Turks and
atheists have faith?[58] To teach that all are given saving grace is in fact
worse than Pelagianism, for Pelagius taught that nature suffices to salvation, never that grace was distributed as widely as nature.

Whitaker claimed that the English Church since the Reformation had
been consistent in holding the third opinion. Article XVII represented a
plain statement of it. Bucer, Martyr, the returning exiles, those in prison
under Mary had all shared it. 'Concerning Calvin I say nothing: although
if I place him above Hemmingsen I dare say no one will quarrel with my
judgment. As to Andreae, admittedly I do not think highly of him, so
turbulent, truculent and quarrelsome a theologian. It is no wonder that
the grace of Christ is prostituted to all by a man who argues with such
frenzy that the body of Christ is everywhere even in dungheaps — but
it is not my intention to be personal.'[59]

Whitaker's attack was so explicit that it was virtually certain that Baro
would reply. He may well have been fortified in his determination to do
so as a result of Whitaker's own tactical error in informing his patron
Burleigh of the events leading up to the Articles, and in showing him a
copy of them, together with his sermon. Burleigh's response was the

---

[56] Whitaker expounded Romans ix, 21 to mean predestination from an incorrupt mass, on
the grounds that if the corruption of the mass was why God made vessels to dishonour,
he would have made no vessels to honour. He argued, furthermore, that divine permission to sin was an effect of the decree of reprobation. Ibid., 54.

[57] Ibid., 59. Whitaker claimed Aquinas and Peter Lombard agreed — an indication,
perhaps, of the authorities to whom his opponents were inclined to appeal.

[58] This was a prominent complaint against Baro. Trin. Coll. Camb. MS B 14/9, p. 162.

[59] Whitaker's sermon went on unrepentantly to defend a 'Calvinist' doctrine of perseverance
(67–79) and the propriety of 'security' of salvation (79–82).

opposite of what Whitaker had anticipated: he 'seemed to dislike of the propositions concerning predestination, and did reason somewhat against Dr Whitaker in them, drawing by a similitude a reason from an earthly prince, inferring thereby they charged God of cruelty and might cause men to be desperate in their wickedness'.[60] It is likely that it was Burleigh who informed the queen of what had taken place, for soon Whitgift was reporting that the Articles had been reported to her 'in evil sense, and as though the same had been by me sent down to the university to be disputed upon, or (I know not how) published'.[61]

When, therefore, early in December, Baro commented publicly on the Articles, Whitgift had a double reason for reacting with hostility, and sent an order to him 'utterly to forbear to deal therein'.[62] Baro explained that he had only been insisting on two points, neither of them condemned by the Articles (and in both of which, as has been seen, Whitgift agreed with him): that God condemns men because of their sins, and that men cannot have security of salvation. He was nevertheless summoned to Lambeth and interviewed twice by Whitgift, who showed him the Articles, and demanded his opinion of them. Baro agreed (after 'some frivolous and childish objections against one or two')[63] that they were all true. They did not, he said, impugn any of his assertions.

But Baro had not yet replied to Whitaker. It mattered not that Goad vetoed the printing of Whitaker's sermon.[64] On 12 January 1596, Baro preached on the text of James i, 27, 'with more earnestness and vehemency, than is remembered that ever he shewed before'.[65] He began with the nature and purpose of God in the creation of all men to eternal life. Christ died sufficiently for all men, his offering being a 'perfect redemption . . . for all the sins of the whole world' (Article XXXI).[66] We must 'receive God's promises in such wise, as they be generally set forth' (Article XVII). By his antecedent will God created each and every man to eternal life. Reprobation is an act of the consequent will of God, a result of man's own rejection of the grace offered him. A king, Baro said, adapts his laws to the capacities of his subjects; a father does not beget his son for the gibbet; a farmer does not plant a tree only to uproot it. 'Men shut themselves out of heaven, not God.'[67]

In the Vice-Chancellor's view, the sermon was a flagrant defiance of

---

[60] Porter, *Reformation and Reaction*, 373.
[61] Trin. Coll. Camb. MS B 14/9, p. 117.
[62] Ibid., pp. 119–20.
[63] Ibid., p. 135.
[64] It was eventually printed in 1599.
[65] Goad to Whitgift, 13 January 1596; Trin. Coll. Camb. MS B 14/9, p. 131.
[66] Baro to Whitgift, 27 January 1596, Trin. Coll. Camb. MS B 14/9, pp. 95–9.
[67] Porter, *Reformation and Reaction*, 380–1.

the Lambeth Articles and of his own warning to Baro. A nucleus of dons who had played a significant part in the proceedings against Barrett drew up a formal complaint as a basis for action.[68] But Goad, who wrote to Whitgift for advice, learned that the archbishop suspected that Baro had been encouraged by those at court 'that seem to take some account of his judgement in these points' and that there was 'some misliking of the said propositions by some in authority'.[69] His advice was therefore that Baro should be interviewed, but that no formal proceedings should be taken against him without further consultation. In spite of that advice, Baro was summoned before the Heads in consistory ten days later (22 January). The main charge was that he had spoken against the Lambeth Articles. He denied it. It was just what Lancelot Andrewes had anticipated. Goad's frustration was complete when he wrote finally to Burleigh, to be told that the Chancellor was unable to take the same view. He thought the doctrine supported by the Heads 'dangerous and offensive', and that 'as good and as ancient are of another judgement'. Baro had been subjected to interrogation 'as if he were a thief. This seemeth done of stomach amongst you.' 'You may punish him if you will; but you shall do it for well doing in following the truth in my opinion.'[70]

The case against Baro was dropped. His tenure as Lady Margaret Professor, however, expired in December 1596, and as the new Vice-Chancellor, Jegon, wrote to Whitgift, 'he hath lately found some heavy friends among us, to the prejudice of his former credit and his present re-election'.[71] In spite, therefore, of Whitgift's 'good opinion' of him,[72] Baro anticipated defeat by not even standing. Thomas Playfere, a fellow of St John's, was elected to succeed him.

Matthew Hutton

Baro's failure to be re-elected to his professorship and the fact that he never returned to Cambridge have been interpreted to demonstrate his theological isolation, against a dominant Calvinism represented not only by the Heads, but by the two archbishops. That the balance in Cambridge was not entirely one-sided had been shown a year earlier, when Whitaker was succeeded as Regius Professor by John Overall. It is a mistake, however, to identify either Overall or Andrewes with Baro without reservation. Baro's communication of July 1595 spoke of predestination as a 'mystery', but so remorseless was his logic that by the time he

[68] Ibid.
[69] Trin. Coll. Camb. MS B 14/9, pp. 135–6.
[70] Ibid., p. 129.
[71] Porter, *Reformation and Reaction*, 390.
[72] Jegon's words, ibid.

had finished, not much of the mystery was left. Although he was right in thinking that Andrewes had similar reservations to his own about the doctrines defended by Whitaker, for Andrewes the doctrine did indeed remain a mystery, on which reticence and therefore a degree of agnosticism were in order.[73] The difference is illustrated by Baro's complaint to Hemmingsen that he was no longer able to publish his views. Andrewes, by contrast, was reluctant to discuss predestination even in a private memorandum to Whitgift. Overall similarly never attempted to publish on predestination: it was a matter for the schools, or for private correspondence, conducted exclusively in Latin. Consistently with his cautious approach, Andrewes remained firm to the distinction which he shared with Hutton, but which Hemmingsen and Baro rejected, between the secret will of God's good pleasure, the *voluntas beneplaciti*, and the revealed will, or *voluntas signi*. Andrewes was careful to avoid a doctrine of conditional predestination.[74] The furthest that he would go was to say that he thought the divine decree to be relative rather than absolute, because it was 'in Christ', Christ being first predestinated, and then us in Him; and if in Christ, it was, he thought, hard to argue that it was independent of the divine foreknowledge of faith in Christ, 'and it seems to me not detrimental [to divine sovereignty] if God chooses in us his own gifts in order that he may crown in us his own gifts'.[75]

It remains to consider the role of Matthew Hutton. Consulted by Whitgift, Hutton was in no doubt[76] that Baro's use of the distinction between antecedent and consequent will (as opposed to the usual, and very different, distinction between the *voluntas beneplaciti* and the *voluntas signi*) amounted to Pelagianism: Hutton saw it as a doctrine of conditional predestination, similar to that urged by the papists under Mary, he recollected. It granted too much to human works. Hutton also declined to follow Baro in the assertion that all men are created by God's absolute will in the divine image, and to eternal life — a novel opinion which he could not remember in any of the ancient writers. Baro's similitude of the earthly legislator, father or farmer was likewise popish and Pelagian. As to Baro's claim that the promises of the Gospel are universal, Hutton admitted that it must be preached to all, yet to some it brings life, to others death. To assert that Cain was no more rejected by God than Abel deserved

---

[73] Andrewes, *Catechistical Doctrine*, 294–5.

[74] Tyacke, *Anti-Calvinists*, fails to do justice to Andrewes's position. What Andrewes said was that he would not, like Beza, condemn the Fathers, almost all of whom had taught that the *voluntas beneplaciti* included *praescientia*. He was quite clear that the faith which God foresees was His own gift. Matthew Hutton agreed, as he pointed out. *Catechistical Doctrine*, 295–7.

[75] Andrewes, *Catechistical Doctrine*, 296–7.

[76] Trin. Coll. Camb. MS B 14/9, p. 151.

castigation from the censor rather than confutation by a theologian. As for Christ's death for all men, Hutton's reply was: sufficiently, yes, but efficaciously only for the elect and for those who believe.

In spite of his differences with Baro, however, Hutton was as far as Whitgift from approving the doctrines of the Cambridge Heads. Whitgift himself grouped his fellow archbishop with Andrewes. As early as August 1595, he wrote to Burleigh to say 'that the most ancient and best divines in this land, with whom I have conferred, whereof the Archbishop of York was one, were, in the chiefest points of opinion, against their [the Heads'] resolutions'.[77] Whitgift, therefore, took Hutton's comments as confirming the opinions of his two chaplains. They were the divines on whose judgment he was most inclined to rely.[78] A fuller understanding of Hutton's doctrinal position may be gained from the tract he sent to Whitgift,[79] which will serve to demonstrate how far it is from proving his commitment to a doctrine of double and absolute predestination.[80]

Hutton began by defining election and predestination. Election refers to the purpose of God to separate in Christ those He has chosen out of the corrupt mass. The reprobate are those who are left in the mass. Predestination, Hutton argued, refers partly to ends, partly to means. The end is double: ultimate (the divine glory, or the praise of His grace and mercy); and intermediate (eternal life). The means are calling, faith, justification, sanctification and good works. Predestination is not 'by a leap' but 'by stages, through the zeal for good works'.[81]

But what of reprobation? Hutton said that predestination was to punishment but not to blame, to suffering for sin but not to sin itself, to the end but not to the means. The end is the demonstration of the glory of God and the eternal punishment deserved by the reprobate. Hutton cited St Augustine,[82] who, he said, was far from saying that God is the author of sin. He quoted Prosper[83] to argue that the infidelity of those who do not believe the Gospel is not the result of divine predestination. God is not the author of sin, but He does not sit idly: He controls it to His own purposes.[84]

---

[77] Trin. Coll. Camb. MS B 14/9, p. 10.

[78] See White, 'Debate: The Rise of Arminianism Reconsidered', 222.

[79] Hutton's tract *Brevis et dilucida explicatio, verae, certae, et consolatione plenae doctrinae De Electione, Praedestinatione ac Reprobatione* was not published until 1613, when it was included in the first volume of Anthony Thysius' *Scripta Anglicana*, in order to refute the Remonstrant claim that their doctrines were supported by the Anglican formularies. Cf. Lake, *Moderate Puritans*, n. 53.

[80] N. Tyacke, 'Debate: The Rise of Arminianism Reconsidered', 205.

[81] Hutton, *Brevis et dilucida explicatio*, 3–4.

[82] St Augustine, *Ad Dulcitium*, 61; *De Civitate Dei*, lib. 22, cap. 24; *Tract. in Joh.* 48.

[83] Prosper, *Aquit. at Capit. Gallorum*. c. 14.

[84] Hutton, *Brevis et dilucida explicatio*, 10.

When did God distinguish? The Scriptures are in no doubt that election is from eternity. But if Jacob is loved from eternity, what has God loved? If not anything that Jacob has done, it must therefore be that which is His, that God was to give to him.[85] If election is from eternity, then reprobation must be from eternity. God hates nothing that He has made: what He hated in Esau was neither anything that He had done, nor anything that He had made in him. What God hated can therefore only have been original sin.[86] So we must assume that God elected and reprobated – and here Hutton differs fundamentally from Perkins and Beza – man as contemplated in a mass corrupted by sin.[87] Admittedly if original sin were the cause of reprobation, all men would be damned, and we must therefore explain the election of some by referring to the will of God, of which no cause can be predicated. Hutton agreed with the schoolmen in arguing that the order of predestination and reprobation are not the same. In election, God first sees Peter, then wills to give him eternal life, and thirdly wills the necessary means. In reprobation, He first sees Judas, then sees his evil works, and then decrees his eternal punishment.[88]

Hutton turned to the question of assurance. The salvation of the elect is certain as far as God is concerned, because the *voluntas beneplaciti* is always fulfilled.[89] With us, however, in this present life it is uncertain.[90] From the human perspective, the church includes those who are elect but but not elect (like Hymenaeus, Philetus and Judas), who have a temporary righteousness (*qui temporalem habent justitiam*),[91] and those who are both called and elect. The evidence here that Hutton differed from the Heads in granting that justifying faith may be lost is confirmed by his suggested addition to the final version of Article V of the Lambeth series, 'and called according to purpose'.[92]
series, 'and called according to purpose'.[92]

Only God, therefore, knows who are His. Hutton agreed with Bucer that once in the book of life, no one can be blotted out, and he follows Bonaventure in explaining Psalm lxviii to the effect that those deleted were never written in it.[93] However, since we do not know who is elect, we must avoid rash judgments on our neighbours and leave it to God who

---

[85] Ibid., 15.
[86] Ibid., 16.
[87] Ibid.
[88] Ibid., 17–18.
[89] Ibid., 23.
[90] Ibid., quoting St Augustine.
[91] Ibid., 24.
[92] Trin. Coll. Camb. MS B 14/9, p. 81, quoting *De Bono Perseverantiae*, 8. i – another explicit repudiation of Cambridge high Calvinism by an appeal to St Augustine.
[93] Hutton, *Brevis et dilucida Explicatio*, 28.

can and will bring sinners to repentance if they belong to His elect. As to judging our own state, Hutton again cited St Augustine[94] explicitly to deny that in this present life anyone can be 'secure' of his salvation. Lancelot Andrewes made exactly the same point in a sermon before the queen in 1595.[95] Great caution was necessary in order to avoid the extremes of presumption and desperation. Saravia had said the same in his judgment of Barrett's recantation. There was a certain measure of faith and of the gifts of the Spirit which is for a time common to the elect and the reprobate,[96] and to that extent the elect are not able to be more certain of their salvation than the reprobate. Yet we must believe that God has in some sense given His Spirit more generously to the elect. Hutton's answer was to distinguish between faith, which fluctuates greatly, and that *plerophoria spei* or persuasion that nothing can separate us from the love of God. The gulf separating Hutton's doctrine from that of the Heads at this point is demonstrated by the fact that William Perkins condemned precisely that phrase as the crucial difference between the Protestant and Papist doctrines of assurance.[97] It is further emphasized by what follows. 'The Gospel', said Hutton, 'is as it were a hand by which God offers from heaven salvation in his beloved Son to all who believe [*omni credenti*]; faith is as it were a second hand by which we take hold of the salvation which is offered us and apply it to ourselves.'[98]

In the context of this doctrine Hutton then expounded the practical syllogism. Although it is indeed the ground of assurance that God will not allow the faith of the elect totally or finally to fail, however frail and fragile, the tract ends with a repetition of his warning of the dangers of security. Certain with God as our salvation may be, with us it is made firm only by the fruits of election, by faith and hope and love, by prayers and fastings, and by continual meditation in the law of the Lord. We are predestinated not just to life, but also to the means, and only through the means do we come to the goal.[99]

This is a different language from that of late sixteenth-century Cambridge high Calvinism. To suggest that it represents 'an earlier style of Calvinism'[100] is to confuse the issue in order to save a theory. Perkins condemned the doctrine held by Hutton and Whitgift as Lutheran. Neither archbishop was prepared to accept the doctrines of irrespective reprobation, of security of salvation and the indefectibility of justifying faith.

---

[94] Ibid., 33, quoting St Augustine, *De Bono Perseverantiae*, c. 22.
[95] Andrewes, *Sermons*, II. 72.
[96] Hutton, *Brevis et dilucida explicatio*, 33.
[97] William Perkins, *A Reformed Catholic*, printed in *Works*, I. 565–6.
[98] Hutton, *Brevis et dilucida explicatio*, 34.
[99] Ibid., 42–3.
[100] Lake, *Moderate Puritans*, 224.

Of course they granted the perseverance of the elect, but the elect are known only to God, and they are distinguished from others not, as Whitaker would have held, because their faith is different in kind from temporary faith, but because of that interior witness of the Spirit which Hutton called a persuasion and which was grounded in good works. Whitgift shared Hutton's suspicions of Pelagianism, but there is evidence that he found some of the points at issue less clear-cut than Hutton did.[101] He chose not to act on Hutton's suggestion that his tract should be published; from his point of view the sooner the dispute on predestination was forgotten the better, and he would have much preferred the university not to have embroiled itself in it at all. Baro had certainly played a part in Whitgift's own discomfiture over the Lambeth Articles, but in spite of that and any reservations he had over his theology, there is no real evidence that the archbishop saw either as an obstacle to his re-election as professor, or that he desired his departure from Cambridge.[102]

Neither Hutton's tract nor Baro's *Summa* was published until 1613, when both were included in the Contra-Remonstrant Anthony Thysius' two-volume *Scripta Anglicana*, together with contributions from Chaderton, Robert Some, Andrew Willett and George Estye, William Whitaker's last sermon, and a detailed critique of Baro by the German theologian Johann Piscator. The purpose of Thysius' collection was to counter the Remonstrant claim that the formularies of the Church of England supported them, and he therefore prefaced the work with an account of the Cambridge debates which presented them as an unqualified victory for the Cambridge Heads, supported by Whitgift and Hutton, against Baro. The Lambeth Articles were taken to be an official statement of Anglican orthodoxy making explicit the doctrines implicit in the Thirty-nine, especially those of double and absolute predestination and the indefectibility of faith.[103]

Modern historiography has usually accepted this early piece of Contra-Remonstrant propaganda, but it was challenged almost at once by the Remonstrant J. A. Corvinus.[104] Corvinus pointed out the crucial modifications made to Whitaker's draft by the *Lambethani*. He drew attention to the points at which Hutton's tract plainly contradicted the assertions of the Cambridge Heads, and the implications of Whitgift's agreement with his fellow archbishop. Most damagingly of all, he pointed out the rejection by James I of the proposal that the Lambeth Articles be added to the Thirty-Nine, and he presented a rival account of the Cambridge

---

[101] Porter, *Reformation and Reaction*, 383.
[102] Lake, *Moderate Puritans*, 235–6.
[103] By 1613, however, even Thysius was soft-pedalling on irrespective reprobation.
[104] Jean-Arnold Corvinus was a Remonstrant minister, later to be deprived at the Synod of Dort.

disputes, according to which Whitaker had attempted to impose Bezan doctrines upon the university by exploiting Whitgift's fear of Pelagianism, a plan which nearly succeeded in spite of the modifications made to the nine articles. Corvinus proceeded to publish for the first time the story of Burleigh's intervention, of the queen's summons to her archbishop to explain how 'a few theologians' had dared presume to settle grave questions debated time out of mind without solution, of the threat of *praemunire* proceedings (deserving, of course, a heavy transfer of ecclesiastical wealth to the crown), and of Whitgift's abject and hasty suppression of the Articles.[105]

Thus rival accounts of the Cambridge debates were deployed in the quarrel between Contra-Remonstrants and the followers of Arminius in the Netherlands, and the theological debate developed a historiographical dimension, itself providing ammunition for further conflict. In the process, Whitgift's original purpose in sending the Lambeth Articles to Cambridge was forgotten. From the one perspective, they became instead the shibboleth of doctrinal Puritanism. Inexorably, from the other, they became the embodiment of a rigid predestinarianism, 'fatal doctrines' rightly suppressed by Queen Elizabeth and never countenanced by James I.

---

[105] For Corvinus' account, see his *Responsio ad Bogermanni annotationes, pro Grotio* (Leiden, 1614), 561–78. An MS version is in Brit. Lib., Harley MS 750, f. 83ff.

7 Richard Hooker

According to a tradition going back to Izaak Walton,[1] Richard Hooker was the archetypal 'Anglican' divine, whose celebrated defence of the established church against the Puritans, *Of the Lawe of Ecclesiastical Polity*, finally made explicit the principles of the Elizabethan church settlement as a *via media* between Rome and Geneva. The 'Anglicanism' he defended was implicit in that settlement, 'protestant but not Calvinist, episcopalian yet reformed, sacrament and ceremony centred although in no sense popish'.[2] 'Puritanism', by contrast, was the radical Protestant opposition to that mainstream.

The reaction against Walton has today gone so far that scholars refuse to accept even the categories he took for granted. It has become all but an orthodoxy that 'Anglicanism' did not exist under Elizabeth. 'Puritans', by contrast, have been moved so far to the centre of the stage that it is they, we are told, who represented the 'mainstream': English Protestant divinity is said to have been so much dominated by a word-centred, austerely simple ideal of piety that the small minority of those Protestants who wanted to retain some degree of ceremony can in turn be consigned to the sidelines, and the name 'Puritan' safely dispensed with, the more so as there were no significant differences of theology that divided them.[3] Others would not go so far, but nevertheless are convinced that the influence of Calvin was unquestioned, that his theology was a common bond in spite of all the other disagreements between Cartwright and Whitgift, and that even the continued existence of episcopacy was precarious.[4]

Where, then, did Hooker stand? From that perspective, implicitly if not explicitly outside the existing consensus. Hooker, we are told, was the first divine who 'broke with the mainstream of English Calvinism'. The

---

[1] Walton's *Life* (1665) is printed in J. Keble (ed.), *The Works of . . . Mr Richard Hooker*, I. 3–117.

[2] P. Lake, *Anglicans and Puritans? Presbyterianism and English Conformist Thought from Whitgift to Hooker* (1988), 4–5.

[3] C. H. and K. George, *The Protestant Mind of the English Reformation, 1570–1640* (Princeton, 1961).

[4] Lake, *Anglicans and Puritans?*, 10–11.

Ecclesiastical Polity was covertly if not overtly 'a full scale attack on Calvinist piety'. We should not be deceived by the appearance of conservatism, which was a mere 'ploy' to ensure the book would get printed: 'for all its judiciousness of tone', it was 'the conformist equivalent of the Marprelate tracts' and indeed 'by far the more novel for the future of English protestantism'. Underlying it was a novel reading of the theology of the English Church which sought to sever the close doctrinal links with the Reformed churches and which on a whole series of issues ranging from the authority of Scripture to the place of the sacraments in doctrine and worship adopted either 'novel' or 'rather novel' opinions. Above all, Hooker's doctrine of predestination, 'all but Arminian', 'represented the greatest barrier to the free passage of his ideas into the mainstream of English protestantism'.[5]

It will be contended here that Hooker's defence of the English Church does indeed represent a development, but that this development is intelligible only as an episode, albeit a major episode, in the continuing tensions between conservative and radical Protestant theology. That tension can be seen in microcosm in Corpus Christi College, Oxford, where Hooker had been admitted through the influence of John Jewel in 1567. Jewel had represented above all a tradition of patristic learning. Now, John Reynolds recommended his students 'to travail painfully in Calvin's *Institution of Christian religion*, not only to the understanding of the scripture, whereof it is a brief and learned commentary, but also to the perceiving of points of doctrine, whither all things do appertain, and may of us be applied'.[6] A still more divisive issue was the value to be attached to Aristotle and his medieval followers. Although in many respects Reynolds's outlook was humanistic and eclectic, and he lectured with enthusiasm on Aristotle, the enthusiasm ended where the study of Christian ethics and theology began.[7] Reynolds was also hostile to the schoolmen: it was becoming increasingly fashionable to study them, but in his opinion Scaliger was worth 'six hundred' times as much as a Scotus or even an Aquinas.[8] Hooker stood firmly on the other side. Like Jewel, he acknowledged the importance of patristic authorities, but where Jewel's defence of the English Church had been founded on its fidelity to the purity of the primitive church, stressing the authority of the Creeds, the first four Councils and the early Fathers, Hooker was ready to appeal to the church's medieval teachers as well. The evidence that Hooker's thought

[5] Ibid., esp. 67, 145–6, 151–3, 156–9, 182–6.
[6] Keble (ed.), *Works of Hooker*, I. 11.
[7] J. McConica, 'Humanism and Aristotle in Tudor Oxford', *English Historical Review* 94 (1979).
[8] As he told Hooker's friend George Cranmer in a letter printed in Keble (ed.), *Works of Hooker*, I. 106.

was steeped in the ancient and medieval past is so compelling as to render altogether implausible the claim that his theology was in its particulars as well as in their synthesis novel.[9]

Even in the context of the Reformation, the originality of the appeal should not be overstressed. English Protestant theology only gradually adjusted to a world picture in which Aristotelian and Thomist thinking still exercised immense influence. That picture assumed a cosmic harmony, that reality was teleological, that order was the servant of reason, that law was supreme, and that the will would function properly only when following the dictates of reason. These deeply entrenched views survived, however much at odds with the spiritual milieu of Protestantism, especially of radical Protestantism. 'The human mind never moves as fast as some of the ideas which, however powerful, must encounter enormous inertia within it.'[10] What Hooker attempted was to provide a rationale of the English Church on the basis of that medieval inheritance. True to the tradition he valued, he used it to shed light, clarify dilemmas, resolve disputes and deepen understanding. Walton was entirely justified to represent Hooker as in temperament eirenic.[11]

In 1585, Hooker was appointed Master of the Temple, where Walter Travers was lecturer. Travers had been in Geneva from 1571 to 1575, and had taken a leading part in the complaints against Peter Baro in 1579. According to Thomas Fuller, 'the pulpit spake pure Canterbury in the morning, and Geneva in the afternoon'.[12] The main issue between Hooker and Travers was the appropriate response to the Church of Rome, especially to the Counter-Reformation apologetic of William Allen, and the threats presented to the English Church by the conversion of many students to Rome while Hooker was at Oxford. The problem was heightened by the political tensions between Catholic and Protestant in Europe, to say nothing of the conspiracies surrounding Mary Queen of Scots. Whereas Travers responded with the traditional anathemas of radical Protestantism, Hooker seemed to contemplate Catholicism with equanimity if not positive good-will. Travers lost no time in complaining of 'sundry unsound points of doctrine' in his sermons.[13] Predestination was one

---

[9] O. Loyer, *L'Anglicanisme de Richard Hooker* (2 vols., Lille, 1979), I. 114, 683–5; W. D. J. Cargill Thompson, 'The Philosopher of the "Politic Society": Richard Hooker as a Political Thinker', in W. Speed Hill (ed.), *Studies in Richard Hooker: Essays Preliminary to an Edition of his Works* (1972), 20.

[10] J. Daly, 'Cosmic Harmony and Political Thinking in Early Stuart England', *Transactions of the American Philosophical Society* 69/7 (Philadelphia, 1979), 22–3.

[11] Loyer, *L'Anglicanisme de Richard Hooker*, 10–11, 18.

[12] T. Fuller, *The Worthies of England*, ed. P. A. Nuttall (3 vols., 1840), I. 423.

[13] Keble (ed.), *Works of Hooker*, I. 64–5.

issue, but of less importance than others, such as whether Rome was a true church.[14]

There was also the issue of doctrinal authority. Travers demanded to know who were Hooker's authorities, and when Hooker replied 'St Paul', asked what was his authority for an interpretation of St Paul so much at odds with 'all churches and all good writers', to which Hooker answered, 'his own reason':[15]

not meaning thereby mine own reason as now it is reported, but true, sound, divine reason . . . theological reason, which out of principles in Scripture that are plain, soundly deduceth more doubtful inferences, in such sort that being heard they neither can be denied, nor anything repugnant unto them received . . . and the true consonant meaning of sentences not understood is brought to light. This is the reason which I intended . . . as the most sure and safe way whereby to resolve things doubted of, in matters appertaining to faith and the Christian religion.[16]

To claim so much challenged Travers at more than one sensitive point in Protestant theology. In the first place it reflected a different doctrine of man. For Travers, as for Calvin, the reason as well as the will was corrupted, incapable of attaining any solid truth, whether ethical or metaphysical. In taking a more optimistic view, however, Hooker was not betraying the English Reformation. He was explicit that reason was not fully reason unless transfigured by grace,[17] and English Protestant theology had never committed itself to such a doctrine of the depravity of man as would have rendered his appeal to reason null and void. Jewel's answer to the problem was implicity the same as his.[18]

Another sensitive issue was the protestant principle of *sola Scriptura*. Hooker was firm that Scripture was the sole source of Revelation, and the sole rule of Faith, but objected to a biblicism which in denying any place to reason made it also the only rule of action and of *discipline*. To claim so much, he thought, was really to devalue it. In taking that line, too, Hooker had predecessors. In 1550, an English translation of Erasmus' 1529 *Colloquy* was published under the title *Cyclops, or the Gospel Bearer*, the theme of which was the danger of over-emphasis on the bare word of the Bible. Cranmer and Nicholas Ridley were probably responsible for that publication. The issue had been raised in practice over Hooper's refusal to wear a surplice, and Ridley's manuscript reply to Hooper had been kept by Whitgift.[19] Like other Protestant formulae, *sola Scriptura*

[14] Loyer, *L'Anglicanisme de Richard Hooker*, 45.
[15] Keble (ed.), *Works of Hooker*, III. 559.
[16] Ibid., 594–5. See the comments of W. Speed Hill, 'Doctrine and Polity in Hooker's Laws', *English Literary Renaissance* 2/2 (1972), 173–93.
[17] Loyer, *L'Anglicanisme de Richard Hooker*, 224.
[18] W. M. Southgate, *John Jewel and the Problem of Doctrinal Authority*, esp. 135–42.
[19] H. C. Porter, 'Hooker, the Tudor Constitution, and the *Via Media*', in Speed Hill (ed.), *Studies in Richard Hooker*, 91–2.

was in danger of becoming a mere shibboleth by endless repetition.[20]

To elevate the bare letter of Scripture and at the same time to denigrate the reason gave to faith the character of a once-for-all experience, abrupt, total, indivisible; it was hard to reconcile with the Christian experience of growth or with a theology of the sacraments as means of grace. Hooker's theology has been described as a theology of 'participation'.[21] In contrast to the radical Protestant stress on the rupture between man and God, its insistence on certainty, its search for proof of divine favour in conduct, and its heavy emphasis on sin, Hooker offered a theology of faith infused, a seed growing secretly, unknown at times perhaps by those who have it, of a sacramental sanctification not always evident to human observation. Faith was not necessarily a once-for-all experience: it could blossom gradually and yet not be immune to periods of doubt and despair. The object of faith was Christ the good news of the Gospel, not the biblical text.[22]

The differences are evident in Hooker's sermon on *The Certainty and Perpetuity of Faith in the Elect*.[23] When he argued 'that the assurance of what we believe by the word is not so certain, as of that we perceive by sense', he was trying to persuade his hearers not to despair if they experienced periods of doubt, for by its very nature our apprehension of Christian truth lacks the evidential certainty attaching to sense experience. For Travers, by contrast, the 'assurance of faith was greater' only because, in his view, our apprehension of it was 'contrary to all sense and human understanding', a merely passive acceptance of supernaturally accredited writ. For all Hooker's emphasis on the human reason, the 'certainty of adherence' for which he argued involved the heart as well as the head:

the faith of a Christian doth apprehend the words of the law, the promises of God, not only as true, but also as good; and therefore even then when the evidence which he hath of the truth is so small that it grieveth him to feel his weakness in assenting thereto, yet is there in him such a sure adherence unto that which he doth faintly and fearfully believe, that his spirit having once truly tasted the heavenly sweetness thereof, all the world is not able quite and clean to remove him from it; but he striveth with himself to hope against all reason of believing, being settled with Job upon this unmoveable resolution, 'Though God kill me, I will not give over trusting in him.'[24]

Hooker's message was intended to comfort and reassure those who

---

[20] Loyer, *L'Anglicanisme de Richard Hooker*, 16.
[21] Ibid., esp. 369ff, 668ff.
[22] Ibid., 395–406.
[23] The sermon, preached in the Temple Church in 1585–6, is printed in Keble (ed.), *Works of Hooker*, III. 469–81.
[24] Keble (ed.), *Works of Hooker*, III. 471.

'remained faithful in weakness, though weak in faith',[25] rather than to reinforce an invincible certitude which all too often led those who had it to a sense of their own superiority:

> Better it is sometimes to go down into the pit with him, who, beholding darkness, and bewailing the loss of inward joy and consolation, crieth from the bottom of the lowest hell, 'My God, my God, why hast thou forsaken me?' than continually to walk arm in arm with angels, to sit as it were in Abraham's bosom, and to have no thought, no cogitation, but 'I thank my God that it is not with me as with other men.'[26]

In conversation with Travers, Hooker promised in due course to make the controverted points 'as clear as light to him and to all others'.[27] Travers 'wished him and prayed him not so to do, for the peace of the Church, which, by such means, might be hazarded'.[28] It was not until after the publication of the first five books of the *Ecclesiastical Polity* in 1593–7, and the appearance in 1599 of the anonymous reply entitled *A Christian Letter,*[29] that Hooker decided to defend himself and fulfil his promise to Travers at the same time. The contemplated reply was unfinished at Hooker's death in November 1600, and the manuscript remained unpublished until 1836.[30]

A Christian Letter represents a further stage in the development of doctrinal Puritanism. Its authors, like Travers, attacked Hooker for his eirenic attitude towards Rome. They complained that 'under the shew of inveighing against Puritans, the chiefest points of popish blasphemy' were being propagated.[31] Like Travers, they claimed to represent 'the present state of religion authorized and professed in England',[32] and they

[25] Ibid., 476.

[26] Ibid., 474–5.

[27] From Hooker's *Answer to the Supplication that Mr Travers made to the Council,* ibid., 593.

[28] From *A Supplication made to the Council by . . . Walter Travers,* ibid., 559.

[29] STC 4707. On the authorship of *A Christian Letter,* see the discussion in *The Folger Library of the Works of Hooker,* IV, ed. J. E. Booty, xvii–xxv. It may indeed be questioned whether the man who wrote the scholarly *Synopsis Papismi* (Andrew Willett) could have written *A Christian Letter.*

[30] All the surviving material has now been printed, some of it for the first time, in volume IV of the Folger edition of Hooker's *Works,* together with the text of *A Christian Letter.* It consists of (1) Hooker's autograph notes, written on a copy of *A Christian Letter;* (2) a folio of notes in the manuscript collection of Trinity College, Dublin (MS 364, f. 80); and (3) three longer essays called by Keble 'Fragments of an Answer to a Christian Letter', also in the Dublin library (MS 121). Although Hooker may well have incorporated earlier unpublished material on predestination in the 'Dublin Fragments', it is the opinion of their Folger editor (introduction, xxxviii–xliv) that Hooker's mature views on predestination represent a clarifying and expanding of his teaching rather than any change in it.

[31] *The Folger Library of the Works of Hooker,* IV. 7.

[32] Ibid., 6.

buttressed that claim with references to the Thirty-nine Articles, and quotations from Jewel and Whitgift, but it is supported neither by the provenance of *A Christian Letter* nor by its contents. The book was anonymous, and printed without official permission at Middleburgh. The printer, Richard Schilders, was reputedly a member of the French Church, and well known as a channel for Puritan tracts. On point after point at issue it is Hooker who was closer to the early English Reformers.[33]

A telling example is the complaint about Hooker's doctrine of justification. In discussing faith and works, *A Christian Letter* quoted Article XI[34] and interpreted it to imply a doctrine of justification 'only by that naked faith which is the work of God in us'. Hooker was betraying the Protestant doctrine of *sola fide* by making 'not faith alone, but faith hope and love, be the formal cause of our righteousness' and flirting with the popish doctrine of merit 'to the disgrace of our English creed'.[35] Appalled by the misuse of scholastic terminology, Hooker's initial reaction was to write 'Ignorant ass' and 'Your godfathers and godmothers have much to answer unto God for not seeing you better catechised' in the margin. Yet again, adherence to a bare formula masked a crude distortion of Lutheran teaching.[36] As to English orthodoxy, the authors quoted only the first part of Article XII of the Thirty-nine, that 'Good works, which are the fruits of faith and follow after justification, cannot abide the severity of God's judgment', ignoring the second, 'yet they are pleasing and acceptable to God in Christ, and do spring out necessarily of a true and lively faith in so much that by them a lively faith may be as evidently known, as a tree discerned by its fruit', added by Parker specifically to guard against solifidian excess. Cranmer's homily *Of Good Works Annexed unto Faith* reinforced the point: 'Faith may not be naked without good works; for then it is no true faith.'[37]

In the first book of the *Ecclesiastical Polity*, Hooker had discussed the functions of reason and the will in men's knowledge of and obedience to the moral law. He had argued that man, 'in perfection of nature being made according to the likeness of his Maker resembleth him also in the manner of his working'. From that standpoint, the 'laws of well-doing are the dictates of right reason' and 'there is in the Will of man naturally

---

[33] And sometimes to Calvin. Loyer, *L'Anglicanisme de Richard Hooker*, 133, 403.

[34] *The Folger Library of the Works of Hooker*, IV. 19, quoting the first part of the article, 'Only for the merit of our Lord and Saviour Jesus Christ, through faith and not for works and our merits we are accounted righteous before God', but omitting the reference to the Homily of Justification.

[35] Ibid., 21–2.

[36] Loyer, *L'Anglicanisme de Richard Hooker*, 406.

[37] The homily cites St Augustine and St John Chrysostom; Hooker made a note to 'look up St Augustine's book de fide et operibus'. *The Folger Library of the Works of Hooker*, IV. 19.

that freedom whereby it is apt to take or refuse any particular object what-soever being presented to it'.[38] The authors of *A Christian Letter* found the 'whole discourse subtle and cunning'.[39] In their view, after the Fall of Adam, nature was perverted, the reason corrupted and the will powerless. 'We desire to be taught how such sayings overthrow not our English creed and the holy scripture in this matter', and they reminded Hooker of Article X. As Hooker noted, 'Nature, Reason, Will and such like' were 'bugs words'. Because they had heard that man's nature was corrupt, his reason blind and his will perverse, they excluded all three from any part at all in man's salvation.

Hooker restated[40] his own understanding of their proper relationship. Without God's preventing and helping grace 'we are nothing at all able to do the works of piety which are acceptable in his sight. But must the will cease to be itself because the grace of God helpeth it?'[41] Echoing Article X of the Forty-two, Hooker denied that grace (or prescience and predestination) imposed 'that necessity by force, whereof man in doing good hath all freedom of choice taken from him'.[42] 'If the grace of God did enforce men to goodness, nothing would be more unpleasant to men than virtue.'[43] The Pelagians erred in making man 'almost a God', the Libertines and Enthusiasts in making him 'little more than a block' in the work of His own salvation. If, in order to counter the error of Pelagius, 'we teach grace without necessity of man's labour, we use one error as a nail to drive out another'.[44] The only error blamed by the Catholic Fathers (and here Hooker quoted Prosper) was that of ascribing any laudable motion or virtuous desire 'to the naked liberty of man's will, the grace of God being severed from it'. He had said (following, as he pointed out, St Hilary and St Augustine)[45] that the will was 'apt', but had not claimed that it was 'able'.

In sum, the grace of God hath abundantly sufficient for all. We are by it that we are, and at the length by it we shall be that we would. What we have, and what we shall have, is the fruit of his goodness, and not a thing which we can claim by right or title of our own worth. All that we can do to him cometh far behind the sum of that we owe, all we have from him is mere bounty. And seeing all that we of ourselves can do, is not only nothing, but naught, let him alone have the glory by whose only grace, we have our whole ability and power of well-doing.[46]

[38] Keble (ed.), *Works of Hooker*, I. 220–2.
[39] *The Folger Library of the Works of Hooker*, IV. 19.
[40] Ibid., 101–13.
[41] Ibid., 101.
[42] Ibid., 102.
[43] Ibid., 103.
[44] Ibid., 112–13.
[45] Loyer, *L'Anglicanisme de Richard Hooker*, 363–5.
[46] *The Folger Library of the Works of Hooker*, IV. 112–13.

A recurrent Puritan complaint objected to the prayer that all men might be saved. Cartwright had raised it, and had been answered by Whitgift.[47] Hooker gave his answer in the *Ecclesiastical Polity*. He granted that the salvation of all and the endless perdition of some were contradictory. He granted that men were divided into the elect and the reprobate. Nevertheless, 'What portion either of the two hath, God himself knoweth; for us he hath left no sufficient means to comprehend, and for that cause neither given any leave to search in particular who are infallibly the heirs of the kingdom of God, who castaways.' The only safe assumptions which the rule of charity might make were 'He which believeth already is', and 'he which believeth not as yet may be the child of God'.[48] Hooker granted that our prayers ought to conform to God's will. The prayer that all might be saved was conformable to His *general inclination*, if not to His *occasioned will*. The Church of England was not the first to use such a prayer. Hooker quoted Prosper as witness to the invariable Christian practice to pray for idolators, Jews, heretics and schismatics. 'If the grace of him which saveth . . . overpass some, so that the prayer of the Church for them be not received, this we may leave to the hidden judgments of God's righteousness, and acknowledge that in this secret there is a gulf, which while we live we shall never sound.'[49] According to Izaak Walton, Hooker had given the same answer in a sermon preached at St Paul's Cross in 1581, the text of which has not survived.[50] Apparently this had not attracted adverse comment, and Bishop Aylmer, who had licensed Hooker to preach, raised no objection. When in 1585 Travers referred to the same doctrine in his list of complaints about Hooker,[51] Whitgift too ignored it.[52]

The authors of *A Christian Letter* claimed that Hooker's doctrine of predestination was contrary to Article XVII. His words implied 'some place unto chance and fortune', and a God 'as a man not of an all-sufficient knowledge, wisdom and counsel, but inclinable some one way, until he find a more better way'. They feared 'the witty schoolmen had seduced you' and 'the error of popery touching works foreseen'.[53] Hooker's answer represents the largest part of his reply to *A Christian Letter*. Echoing St Augustine (and unlike the authors of *A Christian Letter*), he

---

[47] Whitgift, *Works*, III. 383. Whitgift had replied 'We do so indeed; and what can you allege why we should not do so?' Whitgift's agreement with Hooker is not recognized by Lake, *Anglicans and Puritans?*, 161–2.
[48] Keble (ed.), *Works of Hooker*, I. 214.
[49] Ibid., 217.
[50] Ibid., 22–3.
[51] Ibid., I. 59–60.
[52] Ibid., 64–5.
[53] *The Folger Library of the Works of Hooker*, IV. 27.

'had not adventured to ransack the bosom of God and to search what is there to be read concerning every particular man as some have done'.[54] But in order to reply, he was compelled to enter into that 'gulf of bottomless depth, God's unsearchable purpose'.[55]

To start with, it was necessary to distinguish between things contingent and things necessary, avoiding the extremes of attributing all that happens to irresistible destiny, and leaving all 'to the loose uncertainty of chance and fortune'. Between those two errors, the only 'true mean' was a doctrine of divine providence which, while granting that the divine prescience is a 'large volume' in which all that happens is 'exactly registered', preserved the operation of things contingent. Hooker distinguished between 'real necessity', or God as cause, and the 'necessity in reason' (deriving from the infallibility of divine foreknowledge), whereby things casual inevitably happen 'because otherwise God were deceived'.[56]

Fundamental to the *Ecclesiastical Polity* was Hooker's contention that God does not act without law, and that 'the being of God is a law unto his working'.[57] Calvin had also said that 'God is a law unto himself', but where Calvin's priority was to the will, Hooker gave it to intelligence and wisdom. He wrote of God as 'an intellectual worker', and of law as having her seat in the bosom of God, her voice in the harmony of the world. Creation was the fruit of 'the natural desire which goodness has to show and impart itself'. God's own nature as Creator is good *and kind*, and therefore imposes love on the things created. God hates nothing that he has made. Like Hutton, Hooker included sin among the things that God has foreseen but does not cause: it was 'beyond the bounds of predestination but not those of prescience'.[58] Nevertheless, 'we must of necessity grant that there could be no evil committed, if his will did appoint or determine that none should be'.[59] The only solution was to accept 'certain special differences in God's will'. Hooker instanced not only the dis-

[54] Ibid., 28.
[55] Ibid., 123.
[56] Ibid., 128–9. In MS 364 Hooker used the distinction (derived from St Thomas Aquinas, ST 1a 14) between the divine *simplex intelligentia*, which precedes His act, and *visio*, which follows. Through *simplex intelligentia* God was aware of all contingent possibilities. Hooker used the distinction to reconcile eternal predestination and human free will. 'The divine knowledge is a book in which are written *the very names of all men*, than which nothing more contingent exists . . . The books which will be opened at the last judgment are not the consciences of men, but the separate knowledge which God has of good and wicked men . . . in one of which is written the names of the living, the other contains the names and deeds of the sons of death. From this book of life whatever they have done well in life will be produced in honour of God's elect and presented to the sight of all, but that which they have done ill will never be heard because Christ's blood will have wiped it out, as is clear in the Gospel.' Ibid., 85–6.
[57] Keble (ed.), *Works of Hooker*, I. 200–3.
[58] From MS 364, in *The Folger Library of the Works of Hooker*, IV. 86–8.
[59] Ibid., 131.

tinction between the positive will ('whatsoever himself worketh') and the permissive ('that which his creatures do'), but also the 'negative or privative will' 'whereby he withholdeth his graces from some, and so is said to cast them asleep whom he maketh not vigilant: to harden them whom he softeneth not: and to take away that, which it pleaseth him not to bestow'.[60] Hooker granted that there is in God an 'incomprehensible wisdom'; but 'there are no antinomies with God'. The concealed causes of His secret will are not repugnant to the causes of His revealed will. The antecedent will is that all men shall be saved: the occasioned will, whereby all are not, must therefore proceed from God 'as it were with a kind of unwillingness'.[61]

Hooker therefore refused to 'run into their error, who blend even with God's very purpose of creation a reference to external damnation and death'.[62] Angels and men were created with a liberty which was so essential to their nature that without it they would have been left uncreated. They had before their Fall the grace 'whereby they might have continued if they would without sin, yet so great grace God did not think good to bestow on them, whereby they might be exempted from possibility of sinning, because this latter belongeth to their perfection who see God in fulness of glory, and not to them who as yet serve him under hope'.[63] Where Perkins and Beza had argued that God the Creator was a God of justice as well as of love, Hooker believed that 'sin hath awakened justice, which otherwise might have slept'.[64] 'In the act of sinning, God hath the place of a mere patient.'[65] Sin is 'no plant of God's setting'; 'he seeth and findeth it a thing irregular'. He makes it an occasion of acts of mercy, and both an occasion and a cause of punishment. That mercy and that justice do indeed glorify God, 'yet is not this glory of God, any other in respect of sin, than only an accidental event', for punishment 'is to the will of God no desired end, but a consequent of ensuing sin'.[66]

The revealed, or signified, or principal[67] will of God is that all men might be saved. Willing that end, He has willed the means. The Fall presupposed, the only means are the merits of Jesus Christ.

---

[60] Ibid., 132–3.
[61] Ibid., 133.
[62] Ibid., 135.
[63] Ibid., 136–7.
[64] Ibid., 139.
[65] Ibid., 141. Hooker did not charge Calvin with making God the author of sin; on the contrary, he praised Him as the one to whose industry alone was due the refutation of the Libertines, who had revived the Manichaean heresy. Ibid., 138.
[66] Ibid., 142, and the notes on 256. Where Baro had used the distinction between antecedent and conditional will in preference to the conventional distinction between the *voluntas signi* and the *voluntas beneplaciti*, Hooker conflates them. Ibid., 133.
[67] Ibid., 143.

God being desirous of all men's salvation, according to his own principal or natural inclination, hath in token therefore for their sakes whom he loved, bestowed his beloved Son. The self-same affection was in Christ himself, to whom the wicked at the day of their last doom will never dare to allege for their own excuse, that he which offered himself as a sacrifice to redeem some, did exclude the rest, and so made the way of their salvation impossible. He paid a ransom for the whole world, on him the iniquities of all were laid, and as St Peter plainly witnesseth, he bought them which deny him, and which perish because they deny him . . . Nor do I think that any wound did ever strike his sacred heart, more deeply, than the foresight of men's ingratitude, by infinite numbers, of whom that which cost him so dear, would so little be regarded, and that made to so few effectual through contempt, which he of tender compassion in largeness of love had provided to be a medicine sufficient for all.[68]

According to Hooker, the ancient Fathers were unanimous that reprobation presupposes foreseen sin. 'The place of Judas was *locus suus* a place of his own proper procurement. Devils were not ordained of God for hell-fire, but hell-fire for them, and for men so far forth as it was foreseen, that men would be like them.'[69] All deserve that condemnation, but 'mercy hath found a way to triumph over justice, love how to bury the cause of hatred, grace how to save that which righteousness would destroy'.[70] 'The whole cause why such [the reprobate] are excluded from eternal life, resteth altogether in themselves.'[71]

But if reprobation is from ourselves, salvation and life 'proceedeth only both from God and of God'.[72] Hooker explicitly rejected the earlier view of St Augustine, which made election conditional on foreseen faith.[73] Following Prosper, 'it must ever in the election of saints be remembered, that to choose, is an act of *God's good pleasure, which*

---

[68] Ibid., 144.

[69] Ibid., 146. MS 364 shows that Hooker was aware of unsolved problems here. Was original sin or actual sin the cause of perdition in those who perish through retributive justice? Not original sin, presumably, because the whole human race is guilty of it; 'rather the antecedent evil in the damned is the cause of damnation'. He concluded that 'none of the wicked perish through God's decree . . . except those in whom a sin is foreseen as the true and just cause of their damnation according to the rules of His justice which has become known to us with the help of reason, although we perhaps might not be able to explain fully this cause'. Again, he had to concede that the cause of the withdrawal of special grace was not always clear, though we must believe that it pertains to retributive justice: 'for what is hidden is known to God alone'. Ibid., 95–6.

[70] *The Folger Library of the Works of Hooker*, IV. 147.

[71] Ibid., 152.

[72] Ibid.

[73] For Augustine's earlier view, see his *Expositio 84 propositionum epistolae ad Romanos* §§62 and 60; for his later change of mind, *Retractiones*, I. 22. 2–3, *The Folger Library of the Works of Hooker*, IV. 257–8. Given Hooker's familiarity with that development, it is implausible to suggest that his own mind was moving in the opposite direction (Lake, *Anglicans and Puritans?*, 182–6). Hooker proceeded to review the course of predestinarian debate in St Augustine's later works, and up to the Synod of Arles (475). *The Folger Library of the Works of Hooker*, IV. 148–51, 258–63.

presupposeth in us sufficient cause to avert, but none to deserve it'.[74] The decree of predestination to life includes the means of our salvation. Christ, appointed to suffer for the sins of the whole world, 'is a mean unto God for us'.[75] But there must also be 'the means of application which God requireth', and the decree includes these too, for 'if we taste not, it heals not'.[76]

Was grace offered to all men? Hooker distinguished between outward grace, which operates through the visible church ('a mean toward us') and inward grace which operates through the invisible ('a mean in us'). Outward grace was offered to the Jews when it was denied to other nations of the world.[77] Rejected by the Jews, it was offered to the Gentiles, 'who sought not him, but he them, as the one had no cause to grudge, so neither had the other any to boast'. So much, said Hooker, is proved by Paul in Romans ix–xi. Has God eternally rejected the Jews? 'Be it far from us so to think.' Perhaps 'as we being sometimes unbelievers, have at length obtained mercy; so they at the length may find mercy . . . This may suffice touching outward grace, whereby God inviteth the whole world to receive wisdom, and hath opened the gates of his visible Church unto all, thereby testifying his will and purpose to have all saved, if the let were not in themselves.'[78]

Inward grace is that grace of the Holy Spirit which brings men to eternal life. Since it is the will of God to save all, all men must be capable of it

because without that grace there is no salvation. Now there are that have made themselves incapable of both; thousands there have been, and are in all ages, to whose charge it may be truly laid, that they have resisted the Holy Ghost, that the grace which is offered they thrust from them, and do thereby, if not in word, yet in effect pronounce themselves unworthy of everlasting life, and of all effectual helps thereunto belonging.[79]

Although offered, therefore, in some cases men have made themselves incapable of receiving it. But inward grace was not even offered to the Devil, and Hooker elsewhere asks 'What if the malice of the greatest part do come so near diabolical iniquity that it overmatcheth the highest measure of divine grace?' He has to confess that 'we can yield no reason, why of all other wicked tyrants in Egypt, Pharaoh alone and the people under him should be made such a tragical spectacle'.[80] It may be, he suggests, that the divine purpose in the greater punishment of some is to

[74] Ibid., 152–3.
[75] Again following Prosper.
[76] *The Folger Library of the Works of Hooker*, IV. 153.
[77] Ibid., 154.
[78] Ibid., 157.
[79] Ibid., 159.
[80] Ibid., 161.

highlight His undeserved mercy to others. His confidence in human reason as a paradigm for understanding the mind of God is being tested here.

In the last few pages of the *Dublin Fragments*,[81] Hooker offered his own version of the Lambeth Articles. 'God hath predestinated certain men, not all men' demonstrates his refusal to include reprobation in the divine decree: it is a passing over, a dereliction. We have here a doctrine of single predestination. 'The cause moving him hereunto was not the foresight of any virtue in us at all.' There is no reason to suppose that Hooker was being evasive here, and implying election from foreseen faith: he is clear that the means of election are of God. Nevertheless, 'God is no favourer of sloth', and he denied any 'such absolute decree touching man's salvation as on our part includeth no necessity of care and travail'. Labour 'to concur on our part with the will of God' was necessary both in justification and in sanctification. 'To him the number of his elect is definitely known.' The Lambeth Articles failed to stress that the number is known only to God, but cannot have meant to imply that it was known to anyone else. 'It cannot be but their sins must condemn them to whom the purpose of his saving mercy doth not extend.' Hooker's wording confirms his preference to exclude reprobation from predestination, but he would not have denied the 'inevitability' of the Lambeth Articles. 'That to God's foreknown elect, final continuance of grace is given.' The main difference from the Lambeth Articles is that Hooker leaves open the possibility of a total loss of faith in the elect.[82] On this point Whitgift had originally agreed with him, but allowed himself to be persuaded by Whitaker. At the same time, Hooker believed in the possibility of final apostasy after inward grace, and interpreted Hebrews vi, 6 to refer to such. The grant of inward grace was not limited to the elect. 'Inward grace whereby to be saved is deservedly not given to all men.' Hooker again stresses the analogy between human and divine reason. His article leaves open the question whether inward grace is *offered* to all. Hooker then omits Article VI of the Lambeth Articles, on the question of assurance, altogether. 'No man cometh unto Christ whom God by the inward grace of his spirit draweth not.' Hooker's phrasing avoids the Lambeth wording 'all men are not drawn by the Father to come to the Son'. 'It is not in every, no not in any man's own mere ability, freedom and power to be saved, no man's salvation being possible without grace.' Where the last of the Lambeth Articles might be construed to mean that it was part of the eternal purpose of God

---

[81] Ibid., 166–7. For Keble's comments, see *Works of Hooker*, I. cii–cvi.

[82] Whitgift originally held the same view, but allowed himself to be persuaded otherwise in the course of the Cambridge debates: see above, pp. 104, 109. At Hampton Court, James I's opinion was the same as Hooker's, implying the possibility of total falling, but recovery after repentance. See below, pp. 144–7, 167.

that some should not be saved, Hooker's wording was designed to stress that salvation depends wholly upon grace. The difference, reflecting as it does his closeness to the central insight of the Protestant Reformation, is typical.

Although this examination of Hooker's thought has necessarily focussed on predestination, that doctrine was far from being central to the *Ecclesiastical Polity*, which was above all a defence of the means of grace, of the necessity and efficacity of prayer and of the sacraments, and therefore of the theology implicit in the Book of Common Prayer.[83] Those concerns reflected not only the liturgy as established by law, but also the underlying assumptions of the Elizabethan settlement: and they were entirely consistent with the theology of the English Reformers. Hooker was not deceiving himself when he assumed that he was defending a *status quo*. When he wrote that 'equity and reason, the law of nature, God and man, do all favour that which is in being, till orderly judgment of decision be given against it',[84] he signalled his preference not merely for the liturgy and church polity as they stood, but also for the generous attitude towards doctrinal definition that had marked the Elizabethan settlement. Just as there was 'no man of the Church of England who is not also a member of the Commonwealth', so there was no member of the Commonwealth who was not also of the Church of England.[85] Hooker's view reflected the *de facto* acceptance of a pluralistic religious society which, save in its periodic fits of anti-popery, marked the Elizabethan state.

A generously inclusive doctrine of the church was paralleled by an eclecticism which makes it impossible to assign Hooker too precise a place in the development of Anglican theology. His thought resembles a cathedral where contrasting and successive styles of architecture are successfully blended in the complete edifice. Partial readings have been adduced to support very different points of view, from Prynne's that he represented no departure from orthodox Calvinism to the claim that only disingenuity prevented him from declaring himself an Arminian.[86] They convince only in so far as they refute each other. Hooker shared some common ground with Baro, notably in their understanding of reprobation and redemption, and in their doctrine of God as Creator, though Hooker's was expressed through a combination of Thomist and

---

[83] Book V of the *Laws*, which is longer than the whole of books I–IV, was Hooker's defence of the Book of Common Prayer.

[84] Keble (ed.), *Works of Hooker*, I. 170.

[85] Ibid., III. 330.

[86] Lake, *Anglicans and Puritans?*, 182–6, 195, 234. But as Lake concedes, when Francis White came to defend Montagu, there was nothing in Hooker he could use in relation to the doctrine of predestination.

Neoplatonist insights. That common ground separated them both from orthodox Calvinism, but Hooker's closeness to St Augustine distinguishes him in turn sharply from Baro, as does his sense (notwithstanding his defence of the role of reason) of the ultimate mystery of the great antinomies and his dislike of controversy. A study of Hooker's sacramental theology might well demonstrate that there too he could appeal to St Augustine not indeed against Calvin, but against some radical Protestants.[87] Although Hooker despaired of those who made Calvin's books 'almost the very canon to judge both doctrine and discipline by', and a detailed knowledge of his writings the criterion above all others of skill in divinity,[88] he cited the *Institutes* not just because the Puritans revered him, but also because 'concerning the sacraments he found in Calvin a kindred spirit'.[89] The defence of the Book of Common Prayer inevitably implied fundamental differences with anyone whose doctrine of predestination threatened to deny their efficacy as means of grace.[90] Jewel had also defended them, in response to what he took to be a papist caricature of Protestant theology.[91] Hooker had to do the same, just because radical Protestants now defended the doctrines papal apologists had ridiculed.

[87] Loyer, *L'Anglicanisme de Richard Hooker*, 475ff., 887–8.

[88] From Hooker's preface to the *Laws, Works*, 1. 139. Cf. his autograph notes to *A Christian Letter*, in *The Folger Library of the Works of Hooker*, IV. 57–8: 'Two things there are which trouble greatly these later times, one that the Church of Rome cannot, the other that Geneva will not err.'

[89] J. E. Booty, in *The Folger Library of the Works of Hooker*, IV, introduction, xliii.

[90] The second of the Dublin Fragments treats of sacramental grace. *The Folger Library of the Works of Hooker*, IV. 117–21. See also pp. 31–48 for Hooker's autograph notes in reply to the objections of *A Christian Letter*, and especially 43–4 for Hooker's doctrine of baptism as 'a seal perhaps to the grace of election before received, but to our sanctification here a step that hath not any before it'.

[91] John Jewel, *Certain Sermons preached before the Queenes Maiestie, and at Paules Crosse. Whereunto is added a short treatise of the Sacraments* (1582), esp. sig. R^v–R2^r.

8 The early Jacobean church

It has been argued thus far that the theological polarity of the late-Elizabethan period represented a departure from a central tradition which kept the debate on predestination out of the limelight, steered a middle course between extremes, and avoided too precise a definition of controverted questions. The challenge to that tradition came first from those who pressed for Bezan orthodoxy, and then from Harsnett and the outspoken anti-Calvinist followers of Baro: but even in the 1590s, it has been suggested, characteristically mediating and moderating influences were represented by the two archbishops and their advisers.

The same spectrum was reflected in the early Jacobean church. 'Calvinists' and 'anti-Calvinists' (often called Arminians *avant la lettre* or even simply Arminians) represented extremes into which the majority of churchmen cannot without distortion be made to fit. Theologically most of them belonged in the centre, like Bancroft: and their standpoint was supported decisively by James I, who in the debates at Hampton Court rejected the attempt to modify the official formularies in a Calvinist direction.

The Hampton Court Conference

The fulcrum of all recent discussion of the Hampton Court Conference is an article by Professor Mark Curtis[1] which argued that William Barlow's contemporary record[2] has seriously misled historians in portraying it as a failure for the Puritan cause.[3] He drew attention to the importance of an alternative, anonymous, account[4] in which the king is

---

[1] M. H. Curtis, 'The Hampton Court Conference and its Aftermath', *History* 46 (1961), 1–16.

[2] William Barlow, *The Summe and Substance of the Conference . . . at Hampton Court* (1605), printed in E. Cardwell (ed.), *A History of Conferences and other Proceedings connected with the Book of Common Prayer, 1558–1690* (Oxford, 1840).

[3] See, for example, S. R. Gardiner, *A History of England from the Accession of James I to the Outbreak of the Civil War* (10 vols., 1883–4), I, chap. 4 and R. G. Usher, *The Reconstruction of the English Church* (2 vols., New York, 1910), I. 285–333.

[4] Printed in Usher, *Reconstruction*, II. 341–54, from British Library, Harleian MSS 828, f. 32ff.

represented as having acted independently of his bishops, and to have been more sympathetic to Puritan aspirations than Barlow's account would lead us to suppose. The king's independence bore fruit in the decisions made at the conference, which represented real concessions to the Puritans. It was only in the 'aftermath' that the conference was a failure, for the king failed to ensure that his bishops properly implemented the reforms that had been agreed.

Subsequent studies have on the whole accepted James's independence of his bishops, but have questioned the validity of a two-party model.[5] Professor Collinson[6] has demonstrated the serious differences between moderate and radical Puritans. Other studies have drawn attention to the broad spectrum of theological opinion[7] among the bishops, and the extent to which some of them identified with moderate Puritan aspirations. According to another recent discussion,[8] the king's distance from the rigid conformist position represented by Bancroft was reinforced by his complete agreement with Reynolds on doctrinal issues. Thus he 'responded to a tirade from Bancroft on the antinomian consequences of puritan preaching on predestination by backing the predestinarian article in question'. Similarly, the king 'agreed to alter the 16th of the 39 Articles in a more overtly Calvinist direction', and made a 'favourable response to John Reynolds' desire for clarification of article 17'. Although the authors have to concede that 'curiously, the changes to the 39 Articles were never implemented', the Puritans had the satisfaction of seeing Thomas Rogers, who was chaplain to Bancroft, 'publish a semi-official commentary' on them in 1608 'which gave a Calvinist reading to the articles on predestination'.[9] We are led to conclude, therefore, that in spite of the differences between the king and the Puritans on matters of ceremonial, church discipline or *iure divino* episcopacy, there was an underlying identity on doctrine between them which the prelates had no alternative but to stomach. The following discussion of the conference will test that reading of its doctrinal significance.

The Millenary Petition of April 1603 asked modestly for 'a uniformity of doctrine' to be prescribed and for 'no popish opinion to be any more

---

[5] The only exception is F. Shriver, 'Hampton Court Revisited: James I and the Puritans', *Journal of Ecclesiastical History* 33/1 (1982), 48–71.

[6] Collinson, *The Elizabethan Puritan Movement*, 448–67, and 'The Jacobean Religious Settlement: The Hampton Court Conference', in H. Tomlinson (ed.), *Before the English Civil War* (1983), 27–51.

[7] Tyacke, *Anti-Calvinists*, 9–28.

[8] K. Fincham and P. Lake, 'The Ecclesiastical Policy of King James I', *Journal of British Studies* 24 (1985), 169–207.

[9] Ibid., esp. 173–4, and 179–80.

taught and defended',[10] both requests being included under the first head of *desiderata* entitled 'In the church-service'. The mere implication that the doctrine or the discipline of the church was in any respect deficient was enough to condemn the petition in the eyes of the academic establishment. The university of Cambridge approved a grace that anyone who impugned either should be proceeded against and suspended from any degree held.[11] Oxford followed suit. A published reply addressed to the Council approved the Cambridge action. The Puritans had sought the support 'of they care not whom' for a petition that 'the Church may be further reformed . . . according to the rule of God's word and agreeable to the example of other Reformed churches which have restored both the doctrine and discipline, as it was delivered by our saviour Christ and his holy apostles'. The Oxford reply was indignant:

As if there were no uniformity, no consent of doctrine among us. (We refer to the Articles agreed upon in Convocation, 1562). As if there were some Popish opinions defended in our Liturgy (as they deem who are ready to make everything Popery which they do not fancy). These are the weapons with which Bellarmine and that brood are wont to wound, or rather falsely to reproach our faith and profession.[12]

Even before the Hampton Court Conference started, the strength of the opposition among the academic leaders of the Jacobean Church to any doctrinal revision is evident.

An anonymous reply to the Oxford answer[13] reflects Puritan sensitivity to that charge of rocking the doctrinal boat. They were issues 'which we could have been content had not been remembered if you had not forced us to make mention of them'. Their meaning had not been to imply popish opinions in the liturgy, 'but as you draw it in, yes, we desire indeed that the same were as free from those imputations as you pretend it to be'(!). After all, it could not be denied that private baptism and baptism by women implied the absolute necessity of that sacrament and also the doctrine that 'the sacraments confer and give grace for the work wrought'. More to the point, however, was the evidence of popish doctrines elsewhere, and here they produced a garbled account of 'two foreigners, one a Spaniard seating himself at Oxford, the other a Frenchman, entertained at Cambridge'. Corro 'was notoriously known to have been full of many erroneous and fantastical opinions'. Baro had 'taught the popish doctrine of co-operation of faith and works to justification (the terms are

[10] Printed in J. P. Kenyon, *The Stuart Constitution*, 2nd edn (Cambridge, 1986), 117–19.
[11] Strype, *Whitgift*, II. 483.
[12] *The Answere of the Vice Chancellor . . . and other Heads of Houses in the Universitie of Oxford . . . to the Humble Petition of the Ministers of the Church of England* (Oxford, 1603), 13.
[13] Bodl. Lib., MS Bodley 124.

indeed a little changed, but the doctrine is one and the same in effect). He laboureth also to make men believe that the Reformed Churches' doctrine is not so differing from popish doctrine.' Even worse, he had taught 'that the heathen may be saved without the faith of the Gospel', and 'brought the popish schoolmen into credit, and diminished the honour of the learned writers of this age'. Although eventually he had been removed from Cambridge, 'many in that university had been led astray'. Other false doctrines recently proclaimed included transubstantiation, consubstantiation, popish absolution, auricular confession and false teaching about Christ's descent into hell. As to popish books, they instanced the 'infamous libels' of Jesuits and seminary priests which had appeared 'of late years under pretence of policy and state wisdom'. A mixed metaphor concluded the document: 'So in many degrees was the Sun declined in our dial . . . and now we hope the Lord will bark again.'[14]

There were early signs that such hopes would be dashed. In a proclamation of 24 October,[15] the king declared that he was 'persuaded that both the constitution and the doctrine' of the church was 'agreeable to God's word and near to the condition of the Primitive Church'. It was a direct rebuttal of Puritan objections.[16] The king was willing to correct abuses, but made it clear that there would be no fundamental changes. Furthermore, any reforms would be effected not by the forthcoming conference, but by Privy Council, Parliament or Convocation, 'not doubting but that in such an orderly proceeding, we shall have the Prelates and others of our clergy no less willing, and far more able to afford us their duty and service, than any other, whose zeal goeth so fast before their discretion'.[17] The choice of Puritan representatives was another indication that there would no 'alteration of any substantial institutions':[18] none of the prime movers of the Millenary Petition was chosen. Instead, the selection of John Knewstub, Laurence Chaderton, Thomas Sparke and John Reynolds was enough to convince the radical Henry Jacob that the 'whole managing of it . . . was underhand plotted and procured by the prelates themselves'.[19] The exclusion of the radicals led them to formulate 'Ten Demands', which included a request that 'the articles of religion may be reviewed, and more particularly and plainly and fully set down, that so all erroneous doctrines may be prevented, and the doctrine of the

---

[14] Ibid., esp. ff. 57–9, 63.
[15] J. F. Larkin and P. L. Hughes (eds.), *Stuart Royal Proclamations* (2 vols., Oxford, 1973–83), I. 60–3; Shriver, 'Hampton Court Revisited', 54.
[16] Shriver, 'Hampton Court Revisited', 53–5.
[17] These words were not in the draft of the proclamation. Ibid., 55.
[18] Ibid., 56, quoting Bishop Matthew of Durham's impression after a conversation with Cecil, November 1603.
[19] Ibid., 58.

church touching all the points controverted at this day may be clearly known'.[20] The moderation of the Millenary Petition masked a much more radical programme, and the programme included doctrinal revision.

The first day's conference began with a deliberate snub to the Puritans, for when the bishops and their assistant clergy arrived in the presence chamber, they found the four 'agents for the millenary plaintiffs', as Barlow described them, 'sitting upon a form' expecting to be called in.[21] When the time came, however, only members of the Privy Council, together with the bishops and five deans, were admitted. For five hours the assembled company discussed current practices in relation to baptism, confirmation, absolution and excommunication. The most heated discussion was over the issue of lay baptism, especially baptism by midwives. Barlow's version omits the king's ripostes as the bishops attempted to defend existing practice, but there is no reason to doubt that the clergy were united behind Bancroft in urging the necessity of baptism – not, as he put it, 'as if God without baptism could not save the child; but the case put, that the state of the infant, dying unbaptised, being uncertain, and to God only known; but if it die baptised, there is an evident assurance that it is saved'.[22] The king, while admitting he thought 'you in England give too much to baptism', agreed that he too maintained the necessity, and had been accustomed to argue with his Scottish divines 'for ascribing too little to that holy sacrament'. That would appear from all accounts to have been the only doctrinal issue discussed on the first day. According to Dudley Carleton, the king was 'reasonably satisfied'. It was agreed that there should be some minor alterations in the wording of the Prayer Book, 'but the substance to remain'.[23]

The Puritan representatives were admitted to the second day of the conference, in the presence of the council but this time with only two bishops (Bancroft and Bilson) and the deans in attendance, a less than substantive body for the implementation of fundamental reform. It was only now that Reynolds was able to state the case 'that the doctrine of the church might be preserved in purity according to God's word'. He began with predestination, arguing that Article XVI appeared to contradict Article XVII, and he asked that the words 'neither totally nor finally' might be added to the former where it said 'after we have received the Holy Ghost, we may depart from grace'. He asked further that the 'nine assertions orthodoxal', as he called the Lambeth Articles,

[20] S. B. Babbage, *Puritanism and Richard Bancroft* (1962), 63.
[21] Barlow, *Summe and Substance*, 170.
[22] Ibid., 175.
[23] Ibid., 176; Shriver, 'Hampton Court Revisited', 59.

might be added to the Thirty-nine.[24] There followed other doctrinal points before Bancroft lost his temper and interrupted with the pronouncement (on his knees) 'schismatici contra episcopos non sunt audiendi' and uncomplimentary references to delegates in Turkey gowns[25] who in spite of all protestations to the contrary were seeking to overthrow the liturgy and discipline established. Although the king insisted that Reynolds should be heard, it was nevertheless agreed that discussion should proceed of his objections in order, and Bancroft

took occasion to signify to his majesty, how very many in these days, neglecting holiness of life, presumed too much of persisting of grace, laying all their religion upon predestination, If I shall be saved, I shall be saved; which he termed a desperate doctrine, shewing it to be contrary to good divinity, and the true doc-trine of predestination, wherein we should reason rather *ascendendo* than *descendendo*, thus; 'If I live in obedience to God, in love with my neighbour, I follow my vocations, &c., therefore I trust that God hath elected me, and predestinated me to salvation:' not thus, which is the usual course of argument, 'God hath predestinated and chosen me to life, therefore though I sin never so grievously, yet I shall not be damned: for whom he once loveth, he loveth to the end.'

Bancroft then showed the king Article XVII, pointing to the last paragraph:

'We must receive God's promises as they are generally set forth to us in Holy Scrip-ture; and in our doings, that the will of God is to be followed which we have ex-pressly declared to us in the word of God:' which part of the article his majesty very well approved and . . . after his manner singularly discoursed upon that place of St Paul, 'Work out your own salvation with fear and trembling.'[26]

The king then asked if Reynolds's point might be met by adding the word 'often' to Article XVI.[27] If Reynolds made any response it is not re-corded, but the answer must surely have been no: he had wanted to protect a doctrine of absolute perseverance by the addition of 'neither totally nor finally'. The king's concluding remarks show how far he was from accepting that doctrine, for he asked that the doctrine of predestina-tion 'might be very tenderly handled, and with great discretion, lest on the

---

[24] Barlow, *Summe and Substance*, 178. The account in Harley MS 828 (Usher, *Reconstruc-tion*, II. 344) is manifestly less accurate.

[25] Barlow, *Summe and Substance*, 179.

[26] Ibid., 180–1. Lake 'Calvinism and the English Church', 49, suggests that the point at issue here was experimental as opposed to credal predestinarianism, with James (and presumably Bancroft) prepared to accept credal but not experimental. What Bancroft was saying, however, was that the doctrine must not be made a matter of abstract specula-tion divorced from conduct: and that was the essence of experimental predestinarianism.

[27] Barlow, *Summe and Substance*, 181.

one side, God's omnipotency might be called in question, by impeaching the doctrine of his eternal predestination, or on the other, a desperate presumption might be arreared, by inferring the necessary certainty of standing and persisting in grace'.[28]

Other requests for changes met with an even less sympathetic response. A second reference to the Lambeth Articles made it clear that James had never heard of them, and when the circumstances had been explained, his answer was that 'when such questions arise among scholars, the quietest proceeding were, to determine them in the universities, and not to stuff the book with all conclusions theological'. He made it clear that he was against any attempt to extend the Articles by including condemnations of 'every position negative', recalling a similar attempt in Scotland which 'did so amaze the simple people, that they, not able to conceive those things, utterly gave over all, falling back to popery'.[29]

At this point the Dean of St Paul's, John Overall, asked leave to say something more of the Cambridge controversies. He explained how he himself had been involved in them,

upon a proposition which he had delivered there; namely, that whosoever (although before justified) did commit any grievous sin, as adultery, murder, treason, or the like, did become, *ipso facto*, subject to God's wrath, and guilty of damnation, or were in state of damnation . . . until they repented; adding hereunto, that those which were called or justified according to the purpose of God's election, howsoever they might, and did sometimes fall into grievous sins, and thereby into the present state of wrath and damnation, yet did never fall, either totally from all the graces of God, to be utterly destitute of all the parts and seeds thereof, nor finally from justification, but were in time renewed by God's Spirit unto a lively faith and repentance; and so justified from those sins, and the wrath, curse and guilt annexed thereunto, whereinto they are fallen, and wherein they lay, so long as they were without true repentance for the same. Against which doctrine some had opposed, teaching, that all such persons as were once truly justified, though after they fell into never so grievous sins, yet remained still just, or in the state of justification, before they actually repented of those sins; yea, and though they never repented of them, through forgetfulness or sudden death, yet they should be justified and saved without repentance.[30]

James at once declared his 'utter dislike' of that doctrine, and again discoursed on the doctrine of predestination at greater length than before, making clear

the necessary conjoining repentance and holiness of life with true faith: concluding that it was hypocrisy, and not true justifying faith, which was severed from them:

[28] Ibid.
[29] Ibid., 181–5.
[30] Ibid., 186. Harley MS 828 (Usher, *Reconstruction*, II. 344) is even more markedly inadequate.

for although predestination and election depend not upon any qualities, actions, or works of man, which be mutable, but upon God his eternal decree and purpose; yet such is the necessity of repentance, after known sins committed, as that, without it, there could not be either reconciliation with God or remission of those sins.[31]

Not surprisingly, this vehement vindication of Overall's stance is obscured in the Puritan account, which becomes at this point incoherent.[32] Had the king supported the Puritan understanding, he would have been sympathetic to their request to omit the prayer for deliverance from sudden death from the Litany (made in advance of the conference), as a prayer which gained its whole strength from the fear of dying unrepentant, and therefore in a state of damnation.[33] It is clear that James contemplated that possibility with the utmost seriousness, as did Archbishop Hutton in correspondence with Whitgift on the eve of the conference.[34] Attempts to drive a wedge between their doctrinal position and Overall's cannot be sustained in the face of this evidence.

Other doctrinal issues caused less difficulty. The king responded sympathetically to a request for a uniform Catechism, fuller than the Prayer Book's, but shorter than Nowell's, but here again he issued two warnings, both of them in tune with the moderation of his comments on predestination. Firstly, he required that 'old, curious, deep and intricate questions might be avoided in the fundamental instruction of the people'; and secondly, 'that there should not be any such departure from the papists in all things, as that because we in some points agree with them, therefore we should be accounted to be in error'.[35] It was then agreed (in spite of Bancroft!) that there should be a new translation of the Bible, the king being of the opinion that the Geneva version was the worst of all the English translations, and that it should be without marginal notes: but the objections discussed at Hampton Court were to the political notes.[36]

Accounts differ as to what exactly was agreed with reference to the doctrinal formularies. The question of revising or enlarging the Articles was not, apparently, mentioned when the bishops and Puritans were assembled together on the third day. One account, nevertheless (said to be in Bancroft's hand), states plainly 'one catechism to be made and used in all places' and 'The Articles of Religion to be explained and enlarged; and

---

[31] Barlow, *Summe and Substance*, 186.
[32] Usher, *Reconstruction*, ii. 344–5.
[33] Cf. White, 'Debate: The Rise of Arminianism Reconsidered', 228.
[34] For James I's views, see Barlow, *Summe and Substance*, 186; for Mathew Hutton's, Strype, *Whitgift*, III. 400–1.
[35] Barlow, *Summe and Substance*, 187.
[36] Ibid., 190.

no man to teach or read against any of them'.[37] Another list, while agreeing that there was to be a new Catechism, makes no reference at all to a revision of the Articles.[38] A third memorandum[39] of matters to be considered by the Council and the bishops, mentions only that there were to be some additions to the existing Catechism. In the event, that is all that happened. Shortly after the conclusion of the conference, the revised Prayer Book appeared, together with a proclamation (5 March 1604)[40] referring to the complaints which the king had received on his entry to the kingdom 'of the errors and imperfections of the church here, as well in matter of doctrine as of discipline'. Looking back on the conference, the king admitted that its success was typical of 'many other things, which moving great expectation before they be entered into, in their issue produce small effects'. The reason, he explained, was that 'vehement informations' were 'supported with so weak and slender proofs' that it had appeared to him and his council that 'there was no cause why any change should have been at all in that which was most impugned, the Book of Common Prayer . . . neither in the doctrine which appeared to be sincere, nor in the forms and rites which were justified by the practice of the primitive Church'. Nevertheless, he had agreed 'that some small things might rather be explained than changed'. It was made clear that no further alterations would be contemplated, and the proclamation concluded by stressing how necessary it was 'to use constancy in the upholding of the public determinations of States'. Whatever James had said at Hampton Court, by early March there was no hope whatever of any revision of the Articles.

The immediate sequel demonstrates that the Puritan case for doctrinal revision was in any case not fully thought-out, as would no doubt soon have become apparent. Reynolds had asked that the articles should be 'enlarged', but the traditional Puritan stance, that they should be asked to subscribe 'only' to the doctrinal articles, had implied that there were too many.[41] The contrasting approaches were reflected in the proceedings

[37] PRO, SP 14/6/16, printed in Strype, *Whitgift*, II. 501. James Montagu gave a not quite identical list in a letter to his mother, printed in Ralph Winwood, *Memorials of Affairs of State*, ed. E. Sawyer (3 vols., 1725), II. 13–14.

[38] Printed in Cardwell, *History of Conferences*, 212–17. It was drafted by Patrick Galloway. The king 'with his own hand mended some things, and eeked other things which I had omitted'.

[39] PRO, SP 14/6/18 (Strype, *Whitgift*, II. 503–5). Toby Matthew's account mentions no change either to Catechism or Articles, Cardwell, *History of Conferences*, 161–6.

[40] Larkin and Hughes (eds.), *Stuart Royal Proclamations*, I. 74–7. Cf. the proclamation of 16 July 1604, ibid., 87–90.

[41] The request hinged on a disputed interpretation of 13 Eliz. c. 12, which required that every minister shall 'subscribe to all the Articles of Religion which only concern the confession of the true Christian Faith and the Doctrine of the Sacraments', which the Puritans construed exclusively of those they held to concern ceremony. Attorney-General Hobart adjudged in 1608 that the intention of the Act was inclusive: 'that clause is rather declaratory, affirming that all the Articles do concern faith and the Sacraments, than the contrary'. Usher, *Reconstruction*, I. 373–4. Professor Elton agrees with Hobart, *Parliament of England*, 212–13, esp. n. 63.

of the 1604 Parliament. When, in April, a committee of the House of Commons asked for a conference with the Lords, at the top of the agenda was the request 'that the Articles only concerning the doctrine of faith and of the sacraments, whereunto the Ministers ought to subscribe by the Statute of the xiii year of the reign of the late Elizabeth, may be explained, perfected, and established, by Parliament. And that no contrary doctrine be taught within the realm . . .', but it was immediately followed by the request that the Lambeth Articles, 'as things proceeding from some of themselves', be added to the Thirty-nine.[42]

By then it was too late. The king had already given licence to Convocation to prepare ecclesiastical canons, and the fifth of those canons, promulgated later in 1604, decreed excommunication upon anyone who should assert that any of the Articles were in any part superstitious or erroneous.[43] The Commons request for revision elicited a letter from James to Bancroft ordering the Convocation to reaffirm the Articles as they had been issued in 1571.[44] In a solemn session on 18 May a copy of the Articles was duly signed by the assembled clergy of the southern province.[45]

As significant in its way as the failure to revise the Articles was the very rapid agreement as to the enlargement of the Prayer Book Catechism. In line with what Reynolds would appear to have said at the conference,[46] the opportunity was taken to add a section on the sacraments. Two sacraments only, those of baptism and the Supper of the Lord, were 'generally necessary to salvation'. The inward and spiritual grace received in baptism was defined as 'a death unto sin, and a new-birth unto Righteousness: for being by nature born in sin, and the children of wrath, we are hereby made the children of Grace'. The addition quickly drew a protest from Stephen Egerton[47] that the wording savoured of 'the popish doctrine, if not of seven sacraments, yet of more than by our Church hath always been acknowledged'. Again, the real rift at Hampton Court was exposed as being that between moderate and radical Puritans. In line with the emphasis immediately after the conference on the minimum of change, the promised 'one, uniform catechism' was quietly forgotten. No doubt any attempt to produce it would have brought into

---

[42] Babbage, *Puritanism and Richard Bancroft*, 237; *Commons Journal*, I. 199–200.

[43] Cardwell, *Synodalia*, I. 167–8, 250.

[44] Usher, *Reconstruction*, I. 345.

[45] Lambeth Palace Library MS 879, transcribed in T. Bennet, *Essay on the Thirty-nine Articles* (1715), 358–65.

[46] According to Harley MS 828 'Dr Reynolds moved that there might be a more perfect Catechism, made for the instruction of all sorts, as well in the mysteries of the Lord's Supper, as of Baptism, and all other things needful, whereunto it was readily yielded.' Usher, *Reconstruction*, III. 345.

[47] Babbage, *Puritanism and Richard Bancroft*, 79.

the open the differences between the outlook of Reynolds and that of Egerton.

It has been suggested, nevertheless, that the Puritans gained much of the substance of their demands when in 1607 a 'semi-official' commentary appeared, written by Thomas Rogers and dedicated to Bancroft, the tone of which, it is claimed, was distinctly Calvinist.[48] The title page, certainly, proclaims the author's conviction that the English Articles, and the propositions he has deduced from them, are 'agreeable both to the written word of God, and to the extant Confessions of all the neighbour Churches, Christianly reformed', but the introduction soon makes clear his hostility to the Puritan programme. The point of appealing to the Confessional Harmony was to demonstrate that the Puritan scruples about subscription to the Articles as they stood were without foundation. Rogers derided the claim of 'these learned and all-seeing brethren' that the Articles were 'but the bishops' decrees . . . and reveal some little truth';[49] and he attacked the framers of the Millenary Petition for having dared to suggest that there were errors and imperfections in the church 'even in points of doctrine (as if she erred in matters of faith) or desired that an uniformity of doctrine might be prescribed (as if the same had not already been done . . .)'.[50] Far from approving the campaign to alter the Articles, Rogers went on to applaud their ratification as they stood in the Convocation of 1604[51] as clinching his claim that the English Church had maintained a consistent uniformity of doctrine from the time of Cranmer and Parker to the accession of James I. The dedication of the book to Bancroft need occasion no surprise, therefore.

Nor can it be claimed that Rogers's exposition of the Articles takes a 'Calvinist' stance on the matters in dispute at Cambridge in the 1590s or at Hampton Court in 1604. The burden of Reynolds's complaint had been the inconsistency between Articles XVI and XVII, and especially the suggestion in Article XVI that grace may be lost. In commenting on that article, Rogers showed no hesitation in spelling out the implication that 'the very regenerate may depart from grace given, and fall into sin, and yet rise again unto newness of life', and he cited the scriptural examples of David, Solomon and Peter.[52] Nevertheless, 'such as do fall from grace, and yet return again unto the Lord by true repentance, are to be received as members of God's church'. Consequently, 'no men utterly are

[48] Tyacke, *Anti-Calvinists*, 25–7.

[49] Thomas Rogers, *The Faith, Doctrine and Religion professed, and protected in the Realm of England, expressed in 39 Articles* (Cambridge, 1607), 16. This is a revised version of his earlier work *The Englishe Creede consenting with the True Auncient, Catholique Apostolique Church.*

[50] Ibid., 21. Rogers's words echo the Oxford reply to the Millenary Petition: see p. 142 above.

[51] Ibid., 22.

[52] Ibid., 137–8.

to be cast off as reprobate which unfeignedly repent', and among other texts to prove that proposition Rogers cited 1 Tim. ii, 4 without any restrictive gloss, and 2 Pet. iii, 9: 'The Lord would have no man to perish, but all men to come to repentance.'[53]

Rogers's exposition of Article XVII[54] reclaimed only a limited portion of the ground thus surrendered. Certainly, there is a predestination of men to life, that predestination is from eternity, and it is 'of the mere will and purpose of God', but nevertheless 'in Christ Jesus', and those thus predestined cannot perish. Bearing in mind Rogers's restriction of predestination to election, we find nothing contentious thus far. Even when he went on to identify as erroneous the doctrine 'that the very elect, totally and finally, may fall from grace, and be damned',[55] he had said nothing from which either Overall or Andrewes would have dissented, though strict Calvinists would not have liked the hint of equivocation in the word 'very'. Similarly erroneous was the doctrine that 'the regenerate may fall from the grace of God; may destroy the temple of God, and be broken off from the vine, Christ Jesus'.[56] That certainly looks like a Calvinist formulation, but Rogers made no attempt to reconcile it with his contradictory explanation of Article XVI.

There was little else that was contentious. Bolsec was condemned for the doctrines that no man more than any other was predestined, and that it is in man's power to be elected, and similarly the papists were in error for their doctrine of salvation by works and their denial that any man may be persuaded that he is predestined to salvation, but these were all easy targets, their choice explained by the author's overriding desire to prove to sceptical Puritans that the Articles as they stood were a more than adequate safeguard against popish error. Rogers's concluding remarks on Article XVII drew out the implications of the injunction that 'we must receive God's promises in such wise as they be generally set forth' by insisting that 'the promises of grace and favour to mankind are universal'.[57] The Gospel must therefore be preached to all, and likewise the sacraments administered to all. Rogers's teaching is unmistakably that the death of Christ is sufficient for all: the inevitable moderate Calvinist gloss (drawn from Peter Lombard), but efficient only for the elect, is significant by its absence. Absent also are any discussions of reprobation

---

[53] Ibid., 139–40.
[54] Ibid., 142–58.
[55] Ibid., 147. The inclusion of the words 'and be damned' suggests that Rogers does not intend to condemn the doctrine of total as distinct from *final* falling from grace. But his whole method sacrifices precision and consistency to comprehensiveness.
[56] Ibid. It was 'one of Glover's errors', and the only way to reconcile it with what Rogers has said on Article XVI is to take it as one, not three.
[57] Ibid., 156.

(let alone absolute and irrespective reprobation), Christian assurance, or the irresistibility of grace.

Rogers's book, therefore, provides no grounds for qualifying the judgment that the Hampton Court Conference was a decisive defeat for any Puritan hope that the formularies of the Church would be pushed further in a Protestant direction. In respect at least of the doctrinal discussions there is no substitute for Barlow's account, and there is no reason to doubt its substantial accuracy. It must remain doubtful whether the king ever seriously contemplated any extensive revision of the Articles. There is no evidence from what took place at Hampton Court to support the contention that either for James I or his bishops the doctrine of predestination was at all central to the Christian faith. On the contrary, both the discussions on the first day and the subsequent reforms show how incomparably more important were issues to do with the doctrine and practice of baptism, and therefore of sacramental grace. Reynolds, it would seem, shared that perception. For all who took part in the conference, though not perhaps for those waiting outside, predestination was a subordinate issue.

The debate on Calvin

Thomas Rogers's book is a good example of the varying uses to which confessional harmonies could be put in the late sixteenth and early seventeenth centuries. Although originally part of the response to Counter-Reformation apologetic which pointed to the doctrinal differences between the Reformed Churches, in England they had been popular with those who wanted to assimilate the church to dogmatic Calvinism,[58] alienating those who preferred to see her as standing midway between Rome and Geneva, and for whom all that mattered was that she was Catholic and Reformed.[59]

The story of Benjamin Carier illustrates that alienation in practice. A fellow of Corpus, Cambridge, in the last two decades of the sixteenth century, he experienced at close quarters the influence of Perkins and Whitaker and the power of their appeal to Calvin and Beza. As a canon of Canterbury, he had signed the Thirty-nine Articles in the Convocation of 1604, but by 1613 he had become a Catholic. He justified his conversion by arguing that current English divinity, as represented by the

---

[58] When an English adaptation of the Geneva *Harmonia confessionum fidei* was printed at Cambridge in 1586, Whitgift indicated his disapproval, and copies were called in. John Morris, 'Restrictive Practices in the Elizabethan Book Trade', *Trans. Cambridge Bibliographical Soc.* 4 (1967), 276–90.

[59] For examples of this double appeal in the early Stuart church, see my 'The *Via Media* in the Early Stuart Church', in K. Fincham (ed.), *The Early Stuart Church* (forthcoming).

most popular preachers, was Calvinist, being grounded upon Calvin's *Institutes*, and implacably predestinarian. He warned the king:

if their principles be received once . . . and digested by your subjects, they will openly maintain that God hath as well predestinated men to be traitors as to be kings, and he has as well predestinated men to be thieves as to be judges, and he hath as well predestinated that men should sin, as that Christ should die for sin, which kind of disputations I know by my experience in the country, that they are ordinary among country Calvinists, that take themselves to be learned in the scriptures, especially when they are met in an alehouse and have found a weaker brother whom they think fit to instruct in these profound mysteries.[60]

Carier argued that this teaching was wholly at odds with the Book of Common Prayer, which contained nothing inconsistent with Christian antiquity, 'except only that it was very defective, and contained not enough'. Adopting the standard categories of Roman polemic in reference to the English Church,[61] Carier divided English churchmen sharply into a majority of doctrinal Puritans and a beleaguered minority of 'temperate Protestants' who 'can endure the Church of England as it is, but could be content it were as it was'.[62] For Carier, it seems, the Anglican *via media* was fast disappearing.

Carier's concern was above all popular preaching, and there is no doubt that in some parishes the teachings of Perkins were propagated with energy, and that there was pressure for Bezan orthodoxy at a local level by tightly knit groups of Cambridge graduates, as in the case of William Williams, the rector of Asgarby in Lincolnshire in the late 1590s.[63] But not all counties were as polarized as, say, Lincolnshire and Lancashire. 'County divinity', like theological debate, was variegated, and there is ample evidence in the early Jacobean period of the importance for some moderate churchmen of the ideal of the Church of England as a middle way between Rome and Geneva.[64] What is important for the present argument, however, is that even those who theologically respected Calvin began a process of delicate but unmistakable disengagement from the harsher constructions erected on his doctrine of predestination, whether by Beza or by Perkins and Whitaker.

George Hakewill's[65] reply to Carier is a case in point. In approving the Prayer Book and yet condemning Calvin, Carier had overlooked the

---

[60] *A Treatise, written by M. Doctour Carier, wherein he layeth down sundry learned and pithy considerations, by which he was moved to forsake the Protestant Congregations* (Liège, 1614).

[61] Ibid., 20–1.

[62] Ibid., 2.

[63] H. Hajzyk, 'The Church in Lincolnshire, c. 1595–c. 1649', Cambridge University Ph.D. thesis, 1980, 225–43.

[64] As I have demonstrated in 'The *Via Media* in the Early Stuart Church'.

[65] G. Hakewill, *An Answere to a Treatise written by Dr Carier . . .* (1616).

Thirty-nine Articles, and ignored the tempered respect in which Calvin had been held not merely by the leading English Reformers, but even by the more sober Roman commentators like Stapleton and Salmeron. Hakewill was able to demonstrate a whole range of doctrines on which the English Articles and Calvin were in harmony, yet opposed to Trent: but he made no attempt to include the doctrine of predestination among them. Instead, he claimed that Calvin's doctrine – and even Beza's – differed not at all from that of St Augustine, the scholastics, and of Bellarmine. On the issue of predestination without any condition of faith, or of persevering without any condition of works, for example, Hakewill resorted to a distinction between predestination 'as considered before the Fall' (unconditional) and 'considered after the Fall', in which he granted that both conditions were required, not as meritorious causes, but 'as marks and effects infallible of our salvation'.[66] In spite of Carier's misrepresentations, that was the doctrine not merely of Calvin, Beza and Zanchi, but also of Catholic theology. Similarly, reprobation of the greatest part of the world without any respect of infidelity, heresy or wickedness was – 'rightly understood' (and Hakewill here invoked the distinction between positive and negative reprobation) – not merely the doctrine of Calvin, and of the other continental Reformers, but of the Church of England, St Augustine, Aquinas and of Bellarmine himself. In conclusion, Hakewill argued, he could do no better than quote King James himself, and he proceeded to put into his mouth Bancroft's words at Hampton Court approving the doctrine of predestination considered *ascendendo*, not *descendendo*, 'the sincerity of our own hearts being as it were the counterpoise of God's eternal decree, locked up in the cabinet of his counsel'. 'The way to assure ourselves that we are in the number of those that are sealed to life, is to call on the name of Christ, in our profession, and to depart from iniquity . . . the one is required in our life, and the other in our belief.'[67]

Hakewill's line, therefore, was to defend Calvin and Beza by a minimizing emphasis upon the inscrutability of the decree of predestination, and to concentrate on the execution of the decree. This was very much a defensive stance, and the same defensiveness is apparent in his claim that if papist apologists like Kellison 'had the charity to interpret the speeches of our men as gently and as favourably as they do their own, there would appear little difference or none at all' between them. The point cannot have been well taken by the followers of Perkins and Whitaker, but Hakewill was by no means alone in making it.[68] Thomas Morton,

[66] Ibid., esp. 137–8, 285–6.
[67] Ibid., 300–1.
[68] Ibid., 101.

Richard Field, John White, and even more explicitly Robert Abbot, all defended Calvin by taking the line that he had not said any more than was accepted as orthodox in the Roman Church. This was not only to disengage from some of the detail of late sixteenth-century Calvinism, but undermined the claim that the papist doctrine of predestination was Pelagian.

Among the authors specifically recommended by Hakewill was his 'late fellow chaplain'. The reference was to John White, whose *The Way to the True Church* was first published in 1608.[69] White prefaced his work by in turn quoting Morton: 'There is no point of our faith, but many learned in their own church hold it with us, and no point of papistry that we have rejected, but some of themselves have misliked it as well as we.'[70] White's purpose was to discuss 'the principal motives persuading to Romanism'. Two things, he thought, drew men to popery: 'the name of being ancient' and 'the reputation of great learning'. It was therefore necessary for him to demonstrate that, notwithstanding the harmony of the Protestant Confessions, the Church of England had not changed its faith. In doing so, he had to admit, 'there are jarrs amongst us', but they did not extend to points of faith; they were only 'quarrels and dissensions of some particular men',[71] of the kind that had troubled the church in all ages. The extent of this implicit disavowal of doctrinal puritanism becomes clear when he discusses salvation, where without equivocation he undertakes to demonstrate that Protestants taught the necessity or 'requisite condition' of good works.[72] Similarly, when discussing predestination, 'the learned of their own side teach it as we do'. The arguments that Luther and Calvin's doctrines made God the author of sin were 'only clamorous and verbal quarrels arising from malice'. Claims that Protestants denied free will were false: they denied it only in part, attributing the impotence of man's will to do good not to 'the bondage of God's predestination' but to Adam's Fall. The counterpart to this minimizing interpretation of Calvin's doctrine was an appeal to the more uncompromising Roman authors. The doctrine of election upon foresight of grace and good works, for example, was not orthodox Romanism, but proceeded 'from the ignorance and rashness of a few . . . who care not what they say, so they may be barking against Calvin'.[73]

[69] John White, *The Way to the True Church, wherein the principal motives persuading to Romanism are familiarly disputed . . . and driven to their issues, where, this day they stick between the Papists and us . . .* (1608).
[70] Ibid, from the preface 'To the reader' (unpaginated).
[71] Ibid., 75.
[72] Ibid., 122.
[73] Ibid., 138, 143. John White, *A Defence of the Way to the True Church against A.D. His Reply* (London, 1614), 133.

Richard Field's *Of the Church*[74] was another reply to Bellarmine's attack on Luther and Calvin. On the central issue of whether Calvin's doctrine made God the author of sin, Field replied that 'Calvin, and we, hold it hellish blasphemy to say God impels, persuades, or inclines the will to evil, before it had any thought of it, or inclination to it.'[75] Denial of grace was another matter. To suggest that man had been denied the grace without which he could not but fall would indeed be tantamount to making God the author of sin. Calvin had not said that. All that he had said (and in saying so he had merely followed St Augustine) was that man had been denied the grace without which God had foreseen he would not continue, though in respect of duty he ought and in respect of ability he might if he would.

Field went on to discuss the origin of sin. God's eternal purpose was to make man a rational and intellectual creature, with the power to choose. That purpose could not be fulfilled without the possibility of an evil choice. God was not without infallible means to keep man from the possibility of falling, and foresaw that if he were created without those means he would finally fall. Notwithstanding that, He saw that it was best to create and leave him so, and that if sin should enter He could take an occasion thereby of the manifestation of greater good than man would otherwise ever know. Therefore, said Field, 'we assert no absolute decree to all sin irrespective of man's will'. All that Calvin, Beza and the rest meant if ever they said that God effectually moved man to sin was that consequent upon his rejection of God, God decreed that man should fall into 'self-love, pride and all evils of that kind'.[76]

But had not Calvin rejected any such connection between the divine decrees and the divine prescience? Not so, replied Field. Invoking the scholastic distinction between foreknowledge *simplicis intelligentiae* (what is possible) and foreknowledge *visionis* (what actually will come to pass), Field argued that Calvin had nowhere said that the divine decree was purposed before all prescience, merely before prescience of what actually would happen. It was a misrepresentation of Calvin to suggest that he had taught 'that simply and absolutely the end wherefore God purposed to make man was the manifestation of the severity of his justice, and the riches of his mercy, or that he might save some, and condemn others'. God's purpose in Creation could not be isolated either from the benefits He thought it good to bestow on man, or from His foreknowledge of what would ensue from the bestowal of those benefits. Bellarmine's charge that

---

[74] Richard Field (1561–1616) had been a chaplain in ordinary to Queen Elizabeth and was Prebendary of Windsor. A friend of Hooker, he was appointed Dean of Gloucester in 1609.
[75] Richard Field, *Of the Church* (5 vols., 1606–10), III, chap. 23, esp. 119.
[76] Ibid., 120–1.

Calvin asserted that God purposed the entrance of sin originally out of His own liking, in order that He might have matter of punishment, was a gross calumny. 'But the end and purpose of bestowing such benefits only, and no other, notwithstanding his foreknowledge of what would fall out, if so he did, was that he might show his mercy and justice in saving and condemning whom he would. And against this, Bellarmine neither doth nor can except.'[77]

Field's defence of Calvin thus came near saying that the divine decrees could not be isolated either from the wholeness of the nature of God or from the presupposed freedom of man, taken together. Like John White, he was prepared to accept that not all Protestants would subscribe to that account, and therefore the implication that there were doctrinal differences among Protestants: but he denied that such differences concerned the essentials of the faith, and claimed that similar differences divided papists.[78]

One further example of Jacobean Calvinists' increasing repudiation of Bezan doctrine may be given. Robert Abbot,[79] usually regarded as a strict Calvinist, lectured against Arminius, Vorstius and Bertius at Oxford in the period 1613–15, and at any rate for the benefit of undergraduates was prepared to indulge in the polemic that Arminians and papists agreed on the doctrine of grace, and to warn his students against reading the schoolmen.[80] He took a very different line, however, when he replied to the papist Bishop's attack on Perkins. On the matter of predestination Abbot was clear that Perkins's doctrine was not that of the early church. Bishop, by ignoring the distinction between damnation and reprobation, had misrepresented Calvinist doctrine: but in spite of what might be said in defence of Beza and his followers,

Yet we for our parts do not therein assent to them nor see in their reasons any such weight as that we should be moved thereby to vary from the common received judgment of the early church. We therefore resolve as most consonant and agreeable to the course of Scripture, that God purposing to do a work for the setting forth of his own glory, did consequently determine the manner thereof in the creation of Angels and men, whom he would leave in the hand of their own counsel, and suffer them, the one in part, the other wholly, to fall from the state of their original. Yet for mankind, he thought it most fit in respect of the end whereat he aimed, to provide a Redeemer and Saviour, and for that end

---

[77] Ibid., 123.
[78] Ibid., 'An Appendix containing a Defence of Such Parts and passages of the former four Books . . .', third part, 2.
[79] Robert Abbot (1560–1617) was appointed Regius Professor at Oxford from 1612, and Bishop of Salisbury from 1615. He was associated with attacks on both Laud and Howson for alleged leanings towards popery.
[80] Thomas Fuller, *Abel Redevivus: or the dead yet speaking*, ed. W. Nichols (2 vols., 1867), II. 290–1.

purposed the Incarnation and death of Jesus Christ his only begotten Son, in whom and for whose sake he elected out of the generations of men a remnant towards whom he would make the riches of his mercy most abundantly to appear and be glorified in them; the rest he deputed to be vessels of his wrath, and instruments of his purposes both for the executing of his judgements, both one upon another, and for the use and benefit of his elect. These counsels and purposes we understand to be without difference of time with him who at one sight beholdeth all things from the beginning to the end, but the natural process and subordination thereof we hold to be in this sort most rightly described, even in the same manner as God hath executed and manifested the same unto us. Neither do we conceive how it can stand good to have this connection framed otherwise, for it is absurd to think that God would decree what to do with man before he had decreed to create man; and how should he elect if they were not first in his purpose out of whom he should elect? . . . How then should God elect men to be vessels of mercy, but that we must first presuppose misery in respect whereof he would shew mercy? In a word, how should we be said to be *elected in Christ* and *accepted in Christ*, if God's purpose of election be by order of causes antecedent to Christ's mediation?[81]

Similarly with reprobation. It presupposed the fall of man, and God might justly have reprobated all mankind. Instead, of mere mercy, he willed to save some. Beza's formulation of the divine decrees was contrary to that of the primitive church, and in Abbot's view attempts to defend it by certain scholars had involved the church in unnecessary conflict — 'not, even now, without scandal and danger'.[82]

This is not an isolated example of Abbot's ability to rise above contemporary polemic, not least his own. Another is told by the distinguished classical scholar and theologian Isaac Casaubon, who came to England in 1610, attracted by the reputation of the English Church for patristic studies and because it offered a *via media* between Rome and Geneva. In 1613 he attended a disputation in Oxford on the relation between faith and works in salvation over which Abbot presided. Although, Casaubon relates, Abbot taught that before justification it is faith alone which saves, 'he commended good works, and taught their necessity, in such a way that nothing seemed to me to be wanting. He cited Luther on chapter v of the Epistle of the Galatians: *sola fides nos servat, sed non sola fides sufficit.*' Abbot had supported his view by going on to distinguish between two senses of the word 'salvation'. The first was salvation at the moment of our calling, necessarily inchoate and incomplete, purely dependent on the grace of God; the second, salvation in the longer term, which invariably required good works for its con-

[81] R. Abbot, *The Third Part of the Defence of the Reformed Catholic Against Dr Bishop's Second Part of the Reformation of a Catholic* (1609), 58–9.
[82] R. Abbot, *In Richardi Thomsoni Anglobelgici Diatribam de amissione et intercisione justificationis et gratiae animadversio brevis* (1618), 83.

firmation. Casaubon, notably allergic to extreme formulations, was delighted.[83]

Robert Abbot was not always so eirenic. He gave quite a different impression to Richard Field, who also heard him at the Oxford Act when he 'first began to read upon these points, which are commonly called the Arminian points', and 'being returned unto his lodging, he was much offended at it, and said unto Dr Bostock, who was then present with him, You are a young man, and may live to see great troubles in the Church of England, occasioned by these disputes.'[84] The two faces of Robert Abbot both represent realities, the one the vitality of theology, the other the force of polemic. It is only the polemic which would justify the model of an English Church divided into Calvinists and Arminians. Precisely the same is true, it will now be argued, of the relations which were developing between the English Church and the Netherlands.

Remonstrants, Contra-Remonstrants and the English Church

The moderation of James I's pronouncements on predestination stands in sharp contrast to his known allusions to Arminius. Although, he confessed, 'it was our hard hap not to hear of this Arminius before he was dead',[85] the king lost no time, as soon as he had been told about him, in warning the Netherlands of the danger of such 'seditious and heretical preachers'.[86] Unfortunately the 'corrupt seed which that enemy of God' had sown amongst them had already divided them into religious factions which now threatened the unity of their state, and would, indeed, 'by little and little bring you to utter ruin, if wisely you do not provide against it, and that in time'.[87]

These comments were all made in connection with the proposed appointment, in 1611, of Conrad Vorstius to succeed Arminius as Professor of Theology at Leiden. To all appearances he was an ideal choice. Already a professor at Steinfurt, he had written a polemic against Bellarmine, and Beza had given a favourable judgment of him fourteen years before. Coming from outside Holland, he would be untainted by the quarrels which had disturbed the University of Leiden. The only problem was whether

[83] Isaac Casaubon, *Ephemerides*, ed. J. Russell (2 vols., Oxford, 1850), II. 982–3. Casaubon was sufficiently impressed to ask Abbot to read over and correct six leaves of his MS *Exercitationes* against Baronius. Ibid.

[84] Nathaniel Field, *Some Short Memorials Concerning the Life of that Reverend Divine Doctor Richard Field*, ed. J. Le Neve (1716–17), 22. It adds piquancy to this story that King James had wanted to give Field the see of Salisbury but was persuaded to give it to Abbot instead.

[85] *His Majesty's Declaration concerning His Proceedings with the States General of the United provinces of the Low Countries in the cause of D. Conradus Vorstius* (1612), 18.

[86] Ibid., 4.

[87] Ibid., 18.

he would accept the post once he had learned the background and had met Gomarus.[88]

Unfortunately for Oldenbarnevelt, the Advocate of Holland ultimately responsible for the appointment, and anxious to get it right, that issue rapidly paled into insignificance as questions began to be raised about the orthodoxy of Vorstius' recent treatise on the nature of God, and he rapidly became the target of Contra-Remonstrant accusations of Socinianism.[89] Such was the horror of that heresy that protests poured in from the States of Friesland, Zeeland and others against the appointment. To those protests was added an enquiry from Caron, the Netherlands' ambassador in England, who had been asked by the Archbishop of Canterbury what steps the States intended to take the prevent the Socinian Vorstius from corrupting the young at Leiden.[90]

Abbot's informant had apparently been Sibrandus Lubbertus, professor at Franeker, and a strong supporter of the Contra-Remonstrants, working in concert with an English schoolmaster, Matthew Slade,[91] who had emigrated in 1595 to join the Brownist congregation at Amsterdam. Slade threw himself into the campaign against Vorstius, sending marked copies of the *Tractate* and subsequent *Apology* to both Abbot and Thomas Holland, the Regius Professor at Oxford; Lubbertus wrote to Thomas Morton, and other leading churchmen were contacted.

Their campaign to get the king involved in Contra-Remonstrant opposition to Vorstius was a resounding success. The fact that the English ambassador sat in the States General gave James legitimate reason for intervention. He denied that his involvement in the affair was the result of vanity or the ambition to encroach on the liberty of another state. It was one of the main duties of a king, he claimed, to extirpate heresy, not merely in his own dominions but in others, and he was motivated only by zeal for God's glory, charity to his neighbours and allies, and the just reason he had to fear the spread of the 'like infection' to his own country.[92]

---

[88] J. den Tex, *Oldenbarnevelt* (2 vols., Cambridge, 1973), II. 522ff.

[89] Faustus Socinus (1539–1604) was associated with the application of reason to the interpretation of Scripture. To claim, however, that 'in common parlance' he 'merely gave a belated name to a particular form of Erasmianism' (Hugh Trevor-Roper, *Catholics, Anglicans and Puritans; Seventeenth Century Essays*, (1987), 95) is to ignore altogether the doctrinal content of Socinianism, which involved a denial of the divine nature of Christ, and therefore of the doctrine of the Trinity. The death of Christ was not a satisfaction for sin, merely an inspiration for man's moral actions, through which alone came justification. It was this last point above all which has rightly been described as the '*damnosissima heresia* of Socinianism'. H. J. McLachlan, *Socinianism in Seventeenth Century England* (Oxford, 1951), 14.

[90] den Tex, *Oldenbarnevelt*, II. 527.

[91] F. Shriver, 'Orthodoxy and Diplomacy: James I and the Vorstius Affair', *English Historical Review* 336 (1970), 452. P. Sellin, *Daniel Heinsius and Stuart England* (1968), 83.

[92] *His Majesty's Declaration*, 46.

The king's condemnation of Vorstius left nothing to be desired by the Contra-Remonstrants. He was not merely a heretic, but an 'Atheist', 'a Viper, who may make a fearful rent, not only in their Ecclesiastical, but also in their politic state'.[93] His books deserved to be burned, and James had given order that this should be done publicly in St Paul's churchyard and also in both universities. They should do the same, and even if they were merciful enough not to burn the author himself, he could not conceive that they would allow him to remain in their dominions.[94]

Oldenbarnevelt was convinced that the violence of the king's response was due to misinformation and prejudice.[95] He believed that it would not be too difficult to win the king over. After all, James had personally told him eight years earlier that he had as much trouble with rebellious Calvinists as Oldenbarnevelt himself, and had described them as Puritans. Some of them were now in close contact with the supporters of Gomarus. The king had seen the Remonstrance, and he had told a Netherlands embassy that the differences at issue did not concern the fundamentals of the faith.[96] Furthermore, the king tended to favour the Remonstrants' stance on church polity, which was strongly Erastian.

James I's objection to Vorstius, however, had little if anything to do with predestinarian doctrine. He condemned Vorstius for heresies against the fundamentals of the faith, and especially as a Socinian. The king had 'read over and over again with our own eyes (not without extreme mislike and horror) both his books',[97] and had found denials of the eternity and omnipotence of God, the suggestion that God had a body, that He was not infinite, but mutable in nature, and limited in knowledge. James's indignation may have been compounded by the circumstance that Becanus had dared to suggest that the king himself, in his writings on the oath of allegiance, was guilty of the same heresies. In attacking Vorstius, therefore, the king was concerned to vindicate his own orthodoxy. He attacked Vorstius, for example, for presuming to criticize the schoolmen: 'in the main ground of Christian religion', they were 'worthy of all commendation'.[98] The *Declaration* quotes no theologian later than Aquinas.[99] Vorstius' offence was that he had left 'the high beaten pathway of the catholic and orthodoxal faith', whereas the 'ancient

---

[93] Ibid., 6.
[94] Ibid., 19–20.
[95] Oldenbarnevelt was not entirely wrong. Slade's letters accused the Arminians not merely of the pernicious errors of popery, but of approving polygamy and even adultery (British Library, Add. MS 22962, ff. 5^r, 24).
[96] den Tex, *Oldenbarnevelt*, II. 527; Shriver, 'Orthodoxy and Diplomacy', 453.
[97] *His Majesty's Declaration*, 18.
[98] Ibid., 62–3.
[99] Shriver, 'Orthodoxy and Diplomacy', 471.

faith needs not to be changed like an old garment, either in substance or in fashion'.[100]

James was actively encouraged in his identification of Vorstius as a Socinian, and hence in his condemnation of Arminius and the Remonstrants, not only by his archbishop but also by his ambassador, Sir Ralph Winwood.[101] It is doubtful whether the king had ever read Arminius, whose works were not published until 1610, for in spite of his theological expertise he showed no enthusiasm for recent authors, and he employed others to do his reading for him.[102] In linking the heresies of Vorstius with the Remonstrants he was, furthermore, encouraged by their joint espousal of liberty of prophesying. It did not help the Remonstrants that their desire for toleration tended to mute their own criticisms of Vorstius. Oldenbarnevelt for his part was reluctant to condemn a man before letting him speak in his own defence, and disinclined to be dictated to by James, still less by James's ambassador.[103]

As to Vorstius himself, a compromise was eventually reached whereby although another professor was appointed, he was allowed to remain in Holland. Hugo Grotius was convinced that his summoning to Leiden was disastrous for the Remonstrant cause.[104] Oldenbarnevelt disagreed. He was confident that on predestination the king could be persuaded to support the Remonstrants. To that end he approved, early in 1613, Caron's suggestion that the five points should be translated into French and a commentary added which the ambassador could take to James, together with the draft of a letter for the king to send back. He hoped by those means to get the seal of royal approval for the States' efforts to suppress the disputes about predestination, to ban controversy and to enjoin mutual toleration until they were able to achieve a final settlement. James not only approved the draft as submitted, but added his own comment that having seen the opinions of both parties, and the reasons on which they were based, he 'found neither the one nor the other so wide of the mark that they could not consist both with the truth of the Christian faith and with the salvation of souls'.[105] In the king's own words, therefore, the points in dispute did not concern the fundamentals of the faith.

Abbot and Winwood thought differently, and moreover resented Caron's direct approach to the king, without their knowledge. Contra-

[100] Ibid., 60.
[101] den Tex, *Oldenbarnevelt*, II. 531. Shriver, 'Orthodoxy and Diplomacy', 456.
[102] The bulk of the writing was the work of the clerk of the council, George Calvert, D. H. Willson, 'King James I and his Literary Assistants', *Huntington Library Quarterly* 8 (1944–5), 55–6.
[103] den Tex, *Oldenbarnevelt*, II. 535; Shriver, 'Orthodoxy and Diplomacy', 473.
[104] den Tex, *Oldenbarnevelt*, II. 536.
[105] Ibid., II. 545; C. Hartsoeker and P. Limborch (eds.), *Praestantium ac Eruditorum Virorum Epistolae Ecclesiasticae et Theologicae* (Amsterdam, 1684), 351.

Remonstrant and Remonstrant rivalry for James I's ear could only threaten the delicate compromises agreed after the controversies of the 1590s. This danger was well illustrated by Oldenbarnevelt's next move in the same direction, the employment of Grotius to explain his policy to the king, and win the support of bishops like Andrewes and Overall. However tempting in the short run, this expedient not only threatened to resurrect predestinarian debate in England, but in the long run proved fatal to Oldenbarnevelt himself.[106]

Abbot and Grotius have left very different accounts of the results of the visit. According to Abbot, Grotius was simply a busybody, and the king was thoroughly bored with his mere tittle-tattle.[107] Grotius for his part shared Oldenbarnevelt's optimism about winning James's support, not only against the Contra-Remonstrants, but for his plans for the re-union of the Christian churches on the basis of a new Confession which would avoid contentious issues and allow for differences in *adiaphora*. He had read the king's *Premonition*[108] and was impressed that in the king's own confession of his faith the controverted points 'beloved by the more rigid' were entirely absent. He had shown himself both reverent of antiquity, and as a vindicator of good order. He therefore hoped that James would preside at a Council to which even the more moderate Romanists should be invited.[109] When Grotius arrived in England, however, he soon had to abandon those ambitious plans and devote all his energies to countering Archbishop Abbot's misrepresentation of the Remonstrants. He told Casaubon:

I wrote to you recently concerning what the archbishop is about . . . With every effort he is seeking . . . to overturn . . . the toleration with us of those who in the matter of Predestination prefer to imitate the moderation of the Fathers, than the audacity of the moderns . . . What would he not dare if Canterbury were Rome? Thus he seeks to damn the opinions of Andrewes and Overall and of so many of the saints in the mouth of the king in respect of our men. They are the quarry through a flank attack on us. For how will the king be able to tolerate in his own church what he condemns in a foreign? Meanwhile I was not without good opportunity of encouraging Ely [Andrewes] that he should use that liberty as it behoved him. I am also asking our ambassador to warn the king how much the plumes of our Cathars will rise if their supporters are successful in that which they are so strongly attempting.[110]

---

[106] den Tex, *Oldenbarnevelt*, II. 548.

[107] Ibid., 547.

[108] *A Premonition to All Most Mighty Monarchs, Kings, Free Princes, and States of Christendom* (1609), printed in C. H. McIlwain (ed.), *The Political Works of James I* (1918), 110–68. The king's confession of his faith excluded any statement of the doctrine of predestination, although in the course of denying the existence of purgatory he professed his belief in 'a Heaven and a Hell, *praemium & poena*, for the Elect and reprobate'.

[109] Grotius to Casaubon, 7 January 1612: P. Molhuysen and B. L. Meulenbroek (eds.), *Briefwisseling van Hugo Grotius* (11 vols., The Hague, 1928–81), I. 192–3.

[110] Grotius to Casaubon, 22 May 1613: ibid., 239.

In a private conversation with the king, Grotius did his best to counter Abbot's prejudices. He claimed that James had agreed that his archbishop 'did not fully understand the issues. I told him that I thought so too: and that because I had praised the king's own advice, I was considered by him to be a heretic. The king smiled.'[111] During the course of their conversations, the king reiterated his view that he did not regard the doctrine of predestination as fundamental, and that he thought the extreme opinions of Calvin and Beza were 'not free from blasphemies'.[112] He favoured a ban on polemical preaching rather than a National Synod, but warned that it would require careful formulation if it were to be acceptable to all parties.[113]

Grotius took that suggestion back to Oldenbarnevelt, and it was agreed that he should work on a draft. The material section of the final version read:

these contentions having been carried on with so much heat, that some divines have been accused of teaching directly, that God has created some men in order to damn them; that he has laid certain men under a necessity of sinning; that he invites some men to salvation to whom he has resolved to deny it; other divines are also charged with believing that men's natural strength or works may operate their salvation . . . wherefore . . . the pastors shall declare unto the people . . . that men are not indebted for the beginning, the progress and the completion of their salvation, and even of faith, to their natural strength or works, but to the sole grace of God in Jesus Christ our Saviour; that we have not merited it; that God has created no man to damn him; that God has not laid us under a necessity of sinning, and that he invites no man to be saved, to whom he has resolved to deny salvation.[114]

Grotius sent a copy of the resolution to Casaubon, who replied that he had discussed it with the king, the archbishop and others, all of whom approved, for it was desirable for the reputation of Protestantism to place a bridle on human curiosity. The edict would effectively keep the people free of the twin dangers of Manicheism and Pelagianism. Their only reservation was that in 'one small matter' the form of words suggested might be vulnerable to criticism,

for among the dangerous doctrines to be avoided, this also is stated: *quosdam a Deo ad salutem invitari, quibus omnino salutem non dare decrevit*, which is repeated a little further on. But if 'many are called, few chosen' (Matt xx, 16) and if, as St Paul many times repeats, *certus est servandorum numerus, quos ab aeterno Deus elegit*: it follows necessarily that not all men are called to salvation by the same purpose, and with the same efficacy. If therefore the authors of the edict wish to deny this, without doubt there are many who will oppose themselves to their opinion.[115]

---

[111] Ibid.
[112] den Tex, *Oldenbarnevelt*, II. 547.
[113] Ibid.
[114] M. de Burigny, *The Life of Hugo Grotius* (1754), 47–8.
[115] Casaubon to Grotius, 30 May 1614; *Briefwisseling van Hugo Grotius*, 316.

The suggestion that public discussion of the finer points of predestinarian controversy should be inhibited came, therefore, from the king himself, and the advice from his court correctly anticipated the difficulty of couching the instruction in terms acceptable to both parties.

The private correspondence which followed Grotius' visit also operated towards a middle way between Remonstrant and Contra-Remonstrant. In May 1613, Grotius submitted an analysis of the doctrine of predestination for Overall's comments. Overall was happy to approve, but he was afraid they would not please Grotius' opponents, 'especially the more rigid followers of Calvin's opinion, if I know them well', prepared to yield little to moderate views.[116] Overall proceeded to offer his own, impromptu, suggestions as to a middle course between the doctrine of an absolute decree (which he rejected as inconsistent with divine goodness and love, contradictory to human nature, and opposed to the revelation of both Old and New Testaments),[117] and predestination from human co-operation foreseen. He granted that philosophical grounds might be found for both, or indeed for any doctrine of predestination, but he preferred to argue first from Scripture, secondly from the ancient Fathers, and only in third place from arguments dependent on the nature of God.[118] On that basis, he was prepared to agree with Grotius that a conditionate decree was none the less a true decree, even of the divine good pleasure; and he was prepared to grant that such a decree was logically prior to the decree to provide the means of salvation.[119] It was better, Overall thought, to conceive God first to have willed absolutely the conditionate means, than that the purposed end was independent of the condition, or absolute. He further agreed that Grotius was right to make the goodness of God the basis of the divine acts, and to take predestination as being of man as sinner.

On that basis, according at any rate to our human conception, an order or series might be suggested:

1. The divine foreknowledge [*praescientia simplicis intelligentiae*] both of what is possible and not contradictory, and of what is future *ex hypothesi*.
2. The propensity of the divine goodness to express itself, and its glory to be illustrated thereby.
3. The decree of God freely to create man in his own image, as a free rational being, to eternal life under the condition of obedience.
4. The foreknowledge [*praescientia visionis*] of the fall of man and of its evil consequences.
5. The mercy of God, and the decree to send His Son in our flesh as Mediator

[116] Overall to Grotius, 26 May 1613; ibid., 241.
[117] Ibid., 244.
[118] Ibid., 242.
[119] Ibid., 241.

and Redeemer, so that by his own merit and satisfaction he might achieve salvation for man, and by his own grace and power apply it.

6. To that decree is linked the conditional decree or promise of the Gospel, namely gratuitious justification through faith to those who believe, and of their remaining in faith and justification until their eternal salvation.

7. Thence follows the decree to call men to salvation, both externally through preaching and internally through the grace and working of the Holy Spirit in the minds of those who hear.[120]

Overall's careful formulation reflected his consciousness of the need to avoid Pelagianism, and in emphasizing that all the power in the human will which co-operated to salvation came from God, he concluded in the words of Tertullian that ultimately those who, with that help, strive to believe are finally compelled to believe. It cannot be the work of man, for the things to be believed are by their nature hidden. It was from thence also, and in a similar way, that the particular decrees to grant perseverance to some were to be understood. 'And this is the opinion which, it seems, most of the ancient Fathers have held concerning predestination to salvation, or at least intended.'[121]

There was, after Augustine, a further development. According to some, there were men to whom grace was granted, not merely that they might, but that they would believe, and believe until final repentance. Overall was prepared to accept that as at least a tolerable addition to his understanding of St Augustine's teaching. Grotius was left in no doubt that he could not expect support from those otherwise favourably disposed towards him in the English Church unless he accepted it too.[122]

The contacts between Remonstrants and English churchmen, therefore, whether at an official or at a private level, operated towards compromise. Grotius appreciated the essential moderation of the English Church,[123] and by the same token the dangers of polarization in that church from Bertius' attempts to claim support in it.[124] He knew that neither Overall nor Andrewes was prepared to countenance any simplistic identification between their stance and that of the Remonstrants.[125] If, on the one hand, the Netherlands disputes were a threat to harmony in the English Church, it is no less true, whether in the influence of Overall and Thomson on the Remonstrants, or later in the contribution of the delegation to the Synod of Dort, that the impact of the Church of England upon the Netherlands was emphatically in favour of moderation.

---

[120] Ibid., 242–3.
[121] Ibid., 243.
[122] Grotius to Casaubon, 13 May 1614, ibid., 312–13.
[123] Ibid., 313.
[124] Bertius to Uitenbogaert, 8 June 1614, ibid., 324–5.
[125] Vossius to Grotius, April 1615, ibid., 379; Grotius to Vossius, February 1616, ibid., 499.

Falling from grace

The suggestion that James I, Andrewes and Overall together represented an Anglican *via media* on the doctrine of predestination would have angered Archbishop Abbot, from whose perspective the king was a consistent guardian of Calvinist orthodoxy, while Andrewes and Overall were tainted with Arminian error. It remains to test Abbot's perception against the contemporary evidence, by reference to the Calvinist doctrine of perseverance.

The claim to James I's Calvinist orthodoxy goes back to accounts of the Hampton Court Conference, although, as has been seen, there is nothing in either Barlow's or the anonymous Puritan account to support it. A third version would even have James offering to change Article XVI to read 'the Elect might often fall from grace and faith'.[126] It was not until later that Thomas Sparke claimed that the king had approved 'the addition of some such words' (he does not say what they were) 'as whereby plainly it might appear that it taught not, that the regenerate or justified, either totally or finally, fall at any time from the same'.[127] By insisting that he excluded the possibility of total falling, and by having him talk of the regenerate or justified rather than of the elect, Sparke was able, whether consciously or not, to bring James within the limits of Calvinist orthodoxy.[128] That was Abbot's view. It may be that the king chose not to disillusion him.

Calvinist orthodoxy, then, taught the indefectibility of justifying faith. The Arminians, said Calvinists, taught that the elect could fall from grace both totally and finally. This allegation is not supported by the evidence. No theologian in the Church of England taught that the elect might fall finally in this period. It is often said that Andrewes did so. The evidence is a letter of Abbot's to Winwood following Grotius' visit in 1613. According to this account, Grotius (addressing the king) had said

I do perceive that your great men do not all agree in those questions now controverted amongst us; for in talking with my Lord of Ely, I perceive that he is of opinion that a man that is truly justified and sanctified, may *excidere a gratia*, although not *finaliter* yet *totaliter*. The King's majesty knowing that my Lord of Ely had heretofore inclined to that opinion, but being told the king's judgment

---

[126] Quoted from the anonymous account 'in favour of the Bishops' (Baker MS Mm.1.45, ff. 155–7) printed in Usher, *Reconstruction*, II. 335–8. Cf. White, 'Debate: The Rise of Arminianism Reconsidered', 223.

[127] Thomas Sparke, *A Brotherly Persuasion to Unitie and Uniformitie Touching the Received and Present Ecclesiasticall Goverment* (1607), 3–5.

[128] It should be noted that the discussion of falling from grace (or from justification, or regeneration) was conducted at Hampton Court in the context of Article XVI, which is about sin after *baptism*, and not of Article XVII, which deals with predestination.

of it had made shew to desist from broaching any such thing (for then it was as well *finaliter* as *totaliter*) did secretly complain to me that my Lord should revive any such thing, and especially make it known to a stranger. Whereupon I moved my Lord in it, and told him what the Doctor had said, and to whom; but thereunto he replied with earnest asseveration, that he had not used any such speech unto him, and was much abused by that report; and thereupon offered by letters sent unto Holland to challenge Grotius for it, as having done him a singular wrong to report so of him to the king. I replied, that I held it fitter to let him alone; not to draw contention upon himself with so busy a man. I would satisfy the king, and so might his Lordship also; but he would do well to be wary how he had to do with any of those parts ill affected; for he had once before been so served by Bertius . . . who vauntingly gave it out that his Lordship and the Bishop of Lincoln were of his opinion.[129]

While there is evidence to confirm Abbot's suggestion that Grotius and Bertius tried to enlist Andrewes's support for the Remonstrant cause, there is no other evidence that Andrewes ever asserted the possibility of the final falling of the elect. Quite the contrary. As he observed in his private judgment of the Lambeth Articles, no theologian had ever asserted *fidem in electis finaliter excidere*.[130] He went even further, and granted that the faith from which apostates fell was never a true and lively (*vera et viva*) faith. Whether the Holy Spirit could be taken away or extinguished for a time was a difficult question. On the one hand there were clear scriptural warnings against it. They had to be taken seriously. Yet he was aware that the impossibility of total falling might be expounded to mean that although all faith could be lost, there nevertheless remained a chance of recovery.[131] At Hampton Court, James I developed precisely that line of thought in order to resolve the controversy over Article XVI.

Andrewes was indignant, therefore, not merely because he had said no such thing, but because he believed no such thing. Perhaps Abbot understood that. His major concern, no doubt, was to defend what he took to be Protestant orthodoxy by inhibiting contacts between the Remonstrants and their likely allies in England. Such was Andrewes's aversion to controversy that the manoeuvre in his case was entirely successful. Grotius thereafter avoided consulting him for fear that his letters would be unwelcome.[132]

A more detailed example of misrepresentation on the question of falling from grace is provided by the story of Richard or 'Dutch' Thomson.

---

[129] Winwood, *Memorials of Affairs of State*, III. 459–60. The important words here are 'a man that is truly justified and sanctified', which in Abbot's mind would have meant specifically the elect. Andrewes would without question have been alert to the inevitable misrepresentation had he so expressed himself.

[130] Andrewes, *Catechistical Doctrine*, 299.

[131] Ibid.

[132] Grotius to Casaubon, April, 1614. *Briefwisseling van Hugo Grotius*, I. 307.

Born in Holland of English parents, Thomson was educated at Clare Hall, Cambridge, where he graduated in 1587. Thomson kept up a correspondence with friends in Holland; apparently he had known Arminius, and in 1608 he wrote to tell Dominic Baudius of the Dutch theologian's growing reputation in Cambridge.[133] Perhaps because of these contacts, Thomson had incurred the strong disfavour of Archbishop Abbot, but he published nothing on predestination before his death in 1613. According to Robert Abbot, that was not for want of trying, for a book had been ready in 1600 which the author had not been able to publish in England;[134] afterwards, however, it had been taken over to Holland and published at Leiden in 1616. According to Abbot, it was a patchwork of papist, Arminian and philosophical error. Prepared only for the corruption of religion, it would not have seen the light of day even in Holland but for the Remonstrants' fatal addiction to the liberty of prophesying. Abbot treated it to a lengthy, systematic and ill-tempered refutation.[135]

It is therefore worth asking what exactly Thomson thought, for in him if in anyone we might expect to find 'Arminianism'.

Thomson's starting point[136] was the nature of justification: how far may grace and justifying faith stand with mortal sin? In essence, his contention was that a man once justified does not necessarily always remain justified. It is possible to fall from grace either altogether or for a time, as for example through grave sins, through heresy or through errors against the fundamentals of the faith, and either to die without repentance or to recover through saving penitence. In the first case, grace was lost; in the latter, it was interrupted. Thomson's discussion, interestingly, does not centre around the distinction between *finaliter* and *totaliter*. On the contrary, he quoted Tertullian, Jerome and Peter Martyr in support of the contention that what is eventually recovered cannot properly be said to have been altogether lost.[137] That would imply the identity of total and final falling: *amissio*.

Thomson did not suggest that grace might be lost by the elect. His argument was rather that the reprobate might attain a state of justification: justification was not special to the elect. In support of this basic contention, he pointed to the double application of the word: justification according to the law, and justification according to the Gospel. The example of Adam was enough to prove that it might be lost according to the law, but of course his main task was to show how he could reconcile

---

[133] Dominicus Baudius, *Epistolarum Centuriae Tres* (Leiden, 1620), III. 730–1.

[134] R. Abbot, *De Gratia et Perseverantia Sanctorum; Exercitationes aliquot* (1618), sig. C4ᵛ.

[135] R. Abbot, *In Richardi Thomsoni . . . Diatribam . . . animadversio brevis.*

[136] R. Thomson, *Diatriba de Amissione et Intercisione Gratiae, et Justificationis* (Leiden, 1616).

[137] Ibid., 5–6.

the idea of falling from justifying grace with the doctrine of predestination.

Thomson's account of predestination[138] began with the involvement of mankind in the curse which attached to the loss through Adam of righteousness according to the law. It proceeded, through the divine unwillingness to contemplate the death of the sinner, to the appointment of Christ as Mediator of the whole human race. Thus far, Thomson emphasized, no means are necessary as far as man is concerned, and therefore the mediation is in respect of all. But then through the merit of Christ God is reconciled, so that He absolves some men from guilt and receives them in grace. It is at this stage that means are necessary, and this therefore has respect only to who turn and believe, who use the means (they are faith, penitence and the sacraments), without which ordinarily no one is saved. That, Thomson suggested, was presumably Calvin's judgment in his commentary on Romans v, 15. As St Augustine had put it, all are redeemed, but not all are taken out of captivity. It was remarkable, Thomson observed, that learned men (he was referring to Perkins) should in some places approve this doctrine and in others treat it as if it were a heresy.[139]

Thomson's account of predestination, therefore, was that God, out of his superabundant mercy, separated some men, to whom He decreed from eternity to give efficacious calling and final perseverance in grace accepted according to His purpose, the rest being passed by: thus the sheep and the goats in the language of our Lord, the vessels of mercy and the vessels of wrath in the language of St Paul, the *praedestinatos* and the *praescitos* in the language of the Fathers. This was the doctrine of Scripture and the Fathers, and the meaning of Romans ix, notwithstanding the arguments of those who had brought in Christian Stoicism.[140]

Thomson then proceeded to argue that true faith and justifying grace might be lost. It was possible for the reprobate to be justified at times.[141] Where in the Bible or in the Fathers, he challenged, is it taught that no reprobate can ever be justified?[142] Did not our Lord Himself say that many are called, few are chosen? St Augustine, Calvin and Beza could all be cited in confirmation.[143] All the biblical references which talk of the

---

[138] Ibid., c. 4, esp. 16.

[139] Calvin's words: 'Et si passus est Christus pro peccatis totius mundi, atque omnibus indifferenter Dei benignitate offertur, non omnes tamen apprehendunt.' The reference to Perkins is *De praedestinatione*, 91 and 151.

[140] Thomson, *Diatriba*, 18.

[141] The reprobate could be 'predestinate' and therefore saved *sensu diviso* (for God acts freely): 'in sensu tamen composito non potest'. Ibid.

[142] Ibid., 19. Thomson took Romans viii, 29–30 to refer only to the elect.

[143] Ibid., 20–1. The references are to St Augustine, *De Corrept. et grat.*, cc. 7 and 9; to Calvin *Instituties*, III.24.8, granting that sometimes special calling is not of 'believers', and may therefore be temporary; and to Beza on Gal. v, 4 granting 'gradus aliquos verae fidei in reprobis'.

elect persevering in true faith unto the end imply that others do not. How can those who do not persevere fall from a faith which they have never had? John xv, 26 is clearly written of the reprobate ('Every branch . . .'), for how can anyone who is in Christ not be in a state of justification, having believed? Texts like 1 Tim. i, 19 ('made shipwreck of the faith') Heb. vi, 4 ('For as touching those who were once enlightened and tasted the heavenly gift, and were made partakers of the Holy Ghost . . . and then fell away, it is impossible to renew them again unto repentance . . .') and Heb. x, 29 could not be explained away. Attempts to suggest that there was some difference in essence between the justifying faith of the elect and that of reprobates failed. 'No one can say Lord Jesus, unless in the Holy Spirit.' 'Whosover shall call upon the name of the Lord shall be saved. How shall they call on him in whom they have not believed?'[144]

This doctrine harmonized with the experience of the church and especially with its doctrine of baptism. All infants who are baptized into the church are also justified, and many at some time fall from grace. To the objection that the justification in baptism is merely an outward profession, Thomson countered with references to the contrary teaching of the Liturgy, of Scripture, supported indeed by Ursinus, Bucer and Luther, and of course by St Augustine.[145] Indeed, Thomson argued, the Christian church had been unanimous in its teaching on the sacrament of baptism until the present age, in which for the first time the doctrine of predestination and reprobation was wrested against it, and the use of any outward signs suggestive of the inward grace of the sacraments, as the sign of the cross in baptism, was resisted.[146]

Furthermore, Thomson argued, the divine command to believe implied a real possibility of believing, prevenient grace preparing the will. How could anyone contend that God commanded what in reprobates was impossible? He could not take seriously the argument that the command was merely to leave reprobates without excuse. As Prosper himself had granted, if anyone suggested that those who do not believe do not believe because they are predestinated not to believe, he was not a Catholic.[147] Finally, the concept of sin against the Holy Spirit could concern only reprobates, and clearly presupposed faith in Christ and the grace of the Holy Spirit. These arguments were all supported by reference to St Augustine.[148]

Thomson turned to *intercisio*: the temporary falling of the elect.[149]

[144] Ibid., 22.
[145] Ibid., 32–5.
[146] Ibid., 36. Thomson argued that the controversy about rebaptizing indicated how far baptism was from being a mere sign, ibid., 39.
[147] Ibid., 40.
[148] Ibid., chap. 8, 41–4.
[149] Ibid., part II, 45ff.

Their final perseverance notwithstanding, Thomson denied that the elect necessarily remained in a state of faith from the moment of their first justification until the time of their glorification. On the contrary, their faith and their state of justification (the two were inextricably linked) were subject to temporary lapses caused, for example, by grave sins and persisting until repentance. For so long they were, as Zanchi had granted in his submissions to the Strasburg Senate, worthy of eternal death. Again, St Augustine's teaching was the same.[150]

The argument turned on the nature of justifying faith, and whether a dead faith was the same in kind as a true and lively faith. Thomson followed Peter Martyr in claiming that it was,[151] and therefore declined to follow those theologians who concluded that because faith cannot be lost finally in the elect, it must therefore always be living and working through love. He supported his stance, as before, partly by appeals to reason, partly by appeals to Scripture, and especially to those texts which talked of the temptations of the world, the flesh and the Devil. His 'adversaries' (the language annoyed Robert Abbot) of course did not deny them, but pointed to the prayers and promises of Christ to the elect. Those promises, Thomson riposted, did not guarantee a continuum of justifying faith, and in any event they were conditional. Even Beza had granted that all sins were common to the elect and reprobate, final impenitence alone excepted.[152] To the argument that the threats attached to warnings against final impenitence were merely hypothetical, he countered by asking whether the promises of final perseverance were not hypothetical too: conditions were attached to both threats and promises.[153]

The truth was, as both Prosper and St Augustine had understood,[154] that divine predestination was, as far as we are concerned in our human state, unknown to us. Who, as St Augustine asked, dare presume himself to be one of the elect? We must all, therefore, apply both promises and threats indifferently to ourselves, each of us seeking to follow and examine himself according to the rule of Holy Scripture. This had indeed been the teaching of the original Articles, until the return of the exiles from Geneva,[155] some of whom had rejected the phrase in the original Article XVII that the decrees of predestination are unknown to us. Nevertheless, the revised article was still explicit that the counsel of God is secret to us. There is no way of knowing whether we are in grace, much less whether

---

[150] Ibid., 47. Thomson appealed to Bucer in support.
[151] Ibid., 49–50, referring to Martyr on Romans vii.
[152] Ibid., 73, citing Beza on John v.
[153] Ibid., 75.
[154] Ibid., 79–80.
[155] Ibid. Thomson dubs the returning exiles 'Allobroges'.

we are among elect, while in this mortal coil.[156] This doctrine accorded best with Scripture and with Christian experience. The Apostles were clear examples of the elect who had lost faith, at least in so far as it was necessary to salvation, for a time. Peter's denial and Thomas's incredulity were both examples of the truth of our Lord's words, 'Only believe: behold the hour comes when all shall be scattered to their own homes.' To deny that Peter's refusal to confess that he was a follower of our Lord amounted to loss of faith, and therefore of justification, was tantamount to impugning the promise of justification to those who repent and believe.[157]

The usual response to such arguments was to say that the state of justification could be lost only by sins which involved the whole will, and to suggest that the elect were incapable of such. For Thomson that argument undermined the true Reformation doctrine of the necessity of good works, and he was able to quote Calvin against the Libertines and Peter Martyr on Romans vii[158] on the dangers of using St Paul's words about the struggle between the will and the flesh as an excuse for every wickedness. At least the old distinction between mortal and venial sins, however corrupted by the scholastics, had the merit of warning us that certain sins (adultery and murder, for example) could not stand with a state of justification, as again both Peter Martyr and Martin Bucer had made clear.[159] It was a papist calumny that Protestants excluded good works, love, hope and all the other fruits of the spirit from the justified, because they taught that we are justified by faith alone. Again, the early Reformers were unanimous in their insistence on the need for repentance in those who fall into sin after their justification: here was a strong wall against that 'fanatical delirium' of those who dream that the sins of the elect have once and for all been remitted on account of the efficacy and dignity of the merits of Christ, 'a doctrine which in one phrase destroys faith, repentance, the sacraments and every provision of the Church'.[160] Again, the Scriptures, St Augustine and the consent of the Protestant Confessions were unanimous against it.

Therein especially lies the interest of Thomson's *Diatriba*. Whatever the links between him and the Dutch, Abbot was quite wrong to suggest that his teaching was derived from papists and Arminians. There is no

[156] Ibid., 81. Thomson argues that although believers can and should be certain that they are in a state of grace, Scripture does not teach that grace is subordinate to election in the sense that once it has been received, salvation itself is securely established.
[157] Ibid., 89 (printed as 53). Thomson argues that Luke xxii, 32 ('And thou, when thou turn again, establish thy brethren') implies a lapse, and therefore an intercision of faith and justification, to be followed by repentance and confirmation.
[158] Ibid., 101 (printed 65), quoting Calvin, *Contra Libertinos*, 18 and Peter Martyr on Romans vii. Thomson is in no doubt that this chapter refers to the regenerate.
[159] Ibid., 121 (printed 85).
[160] Ibid., 136.

evidence at all of direct dependence. There is no obvious dependence on either Melanchthon (referred to occasionally) or Hemmingsen (not quoted at all). It is true that Thomson appealed to reason, and although he made no extensive use of Hooker, he obviously admired him.[161] The authorities he refers to are first and foremost Scripture and the church Fathers. There are several references to Chrysostom, Basil and the other Greek Fathers (Thomson was a noted philologist, and one of the translators of the Authorized Version), but St Augustine is undoubtedly pre-eminent: there is a whole chapter of testimonies from him proving the possibility of *amissio*. Beyond that, Thomson repeatedly and insistently quoted the first-generation Reformers: Bucer, Peter Martyr and Calvin. In spite of his remarks about 'Stoics', 'Cathars' and the return of the 'Allobroges' from exile at the beginning of Elizabeth's reign, he was only in a limited sense an anti-Calvinist. What was provocative, on the contrary, was the frequency with which he cited the authorities beloved by his 'adversaries'. He often appealed to Calvin against the followers of Calvin. Equally provocative must have been his references to the Augsburg, Saxon and Bohemian Confessions.[162] His book is evidence of the very wide range of influences available to counter Cambridge high Calvinism in the late sixteenth and early seventeenth centuries.

[161] Ibid., 136 and 161, where he is called 'flagellum Catharorum'.
[162] Ibid., 153, 'cui Calvinus volens ac lubens art. 11 contra Anabaptistos'.

9   The Synod of Dort

The evolution of royal policy

In January 1616, Sir Dudley Carleton succeeded Winwood as ambassador at The Hague. His sympathies were decidedly with the Contra-Remonstrants, and he chided Oldenbarnevelt for comparing them to the English Puritans. He considered the Arminians to be novelists, favourers of popery, and he blamed them for disturbing the peace of the Dutch Church.[1] Carleton explained to the king that the resolution of 1614 had not settled the dispute, and that both sides were claiming his support, the Remonstrants on the basis of the letter of 6 March 1613, their opponents appealing to his *Declaration* against Vorstius.[2] Carleton and Winwood (now Secretary of State) set out to resolve the ambiguity in the Contra-Remonstrants' favour. It was the more urgent, in that (as Carleton conceded) 'the worst cause had the better men', and (as Winwood admitted) 'I cannot deny but that universal grace is a plausible learning to flesh and blood.'[3] In February 1617, Carleton assured the Dutch that 'his Majesty is of the opinion, that the Contra-Remonstrants, which profess the ancient and received doctrine acknowledged by an unanime consent of all the reformed churches, should not give place to the factious opinions of Vorstius and Arminius'.[4] At the same time, the king was coming round to the view that the dispute ran so deep that it could be resolved only by a synod, and a letter to that effect was despatched on 20 March.[5]

Royal policy towards the conduct of the synod began to be formulated. The king was firmly opposed to any revision of the existing formularies. The Heidelberg Catechism, to which all the Reformed churches consented, expressed the ancient doctrine.[6] James objected, furthermore, to Utrecht

---

[1] Sir Dudley Carleton, *Letters from and to Sir Dudley Carleton*, ed. P. Yorke (1775), 99–100.
[2] Ibid., 58
[3] Ibid., 89, 101.
[4] Ibid., 102.
[5] Ibid., 122–3.
[6] Ibid., 112.

as the place of meeting on the grounds that the Arminians were strongly entrenched there, 'and [he] would like better of a place of more indifferency'.[7] He warned that the proposed resolution that the 'deputies shall only search the word of God' would in all probability make matters worse:

for the Arminians, Vortians and all other heretics, fly unto the word of God . . . and therefore these words should be tempered with this clause following, that they shall diligently search the word of God, and in case they differ upon the interpretation, that they shall have recourse unto the interpretation given thereunto by the general consent of the ancient church and councils, and approved doctors thereof, before the time of the church's defection to popery, joining thereunto the most learned and best divines of our religion.

The Remonstrants attempted, without success, to counter these developments. In 1616 Grotius appealed for toleration on the grounds that 'in England at this very time there are persons of both persuasions in some of the most eminent stations of the Church, without any infingement of ecclesiastical unity'.[8] At the same time he took the opportunity to correct the Contra-Remonstrant version of the Lambeth Articles, emphasizing James I's refusal to countenance their inclusion in the Thirty-nine. In June 1617, Overall wrote to Grotius[9] reassuringly that only recently the king had endorsed moderation on the question of predestination. The Remonstrants overreached themselves, however, with the publication of a bitter attack on Carleton,[10] and with claims by Caron that James had approved both their doctrines and their preference for a provincial rather than a national synod. On 22 December 1617, the king wrote to Carleton with an explicit rebuttal.[11] Caron had 'doubly mistaken us', for he had approved a provincial synod 'only as preparative to the national', and as to the five articles,

it is true, that we told him, that the articles (at least four of them) as they were delivered to us in writing, were perhaps not greatly to be misliked: but we said withal that they were expressed with cunning and art to make a specious shew, but that the doctrine commonly delivered there was not correspondent to these articles: so as the articles served but for a bait to swallow doctrine, which was of more danger than the articles would pretend. This being the truth, you may use it . . . to answer all reports which you shall hear to the contrary.[12]

---

[7] Ibid., 199.

[8] Gerard Brandt, *The History of the Reformation . . . in and about the Low Countries . . . translated from the Low-Dutch* (4 vols., 1720–3), II. 208–14.

[9] *Briefwisseling von Hugo Grotius*, I. 572.

[10] Brandt, *Reformation in the Low Countries*, II. 392; *Letters from and to Sir Dudley Carleton*, 205.

[11] *Letters from and to Sir Dudley Carleton*, 221–2.

[12] It seems that James had consulted his bishops, and that it was the fifth head that was the stumbling block. Caron to Oldenbarneveldt, 30 November 1617, Johan van Olden-

Remonstrant propaganda, therefore, had by 1617 succeeded only in driving the king back into the arms of the Contra-Remonstrants.

It remains to be enquired how far James was being swayed by Abbot and Winwood, and how far he was influenced by any understanding of the theology of Arminius.[13] In November 1617 Edward Simpson, a fellow of Trinity College, Cambridge, preached before the king at Royston. According to John Chamberlain[14]

he fell upon a point of Arminius doctrine touching universality of grace, and so handled it that he was much displeased, and sent to the doctors and heads of houses in Cambridge to convent him and examine his sermon. They returned a favourable censure that this and this may be said, which was so far from satisfying the king that he sent for them all (or the most part) to Newmarket where the question was so narrowly discussed that he was enjoyned to retract what he had said, in the same place at the King's return thither after Christmas.

What had Simpson said? Nothing about the universality of grace.[15] His sermon was preached upon the text John iii, 6: 'That which is born of the Spirit is spirit . . .', and its central thesis was that sin could neither dominate nor dwell in the regenerate. Simpson argued that those who have been baptized, who are under grace, regenerate or born again 'cannot be both spiritual and carnal . . . cannot have Christ and Belial', and that anyone who was conscious of a combat or conflict between his conscience and his concupiscence should conclude that he was not regenerate.

Simpson's sermon was an attack, carried to the extreme, on antinomianism and neglect of good works. 'It is indeed to be feared, there be many which do falsely imagine themselves to be spiritual, when indeed they are carnal.'[16] The world had too many such Libertines, and Simpson charged them with false security. Nevertheless, the implications of his sermon were far from Arminian, or from the universality of grace: here was a highly exclusive restriction of the truly regenerate to those who could truthfully say that they were 'dead to sin'. A major implication was anti-Arminian, for Simpson expounded Proverbs xxiv, 16 ('Septies cadit

---

barneveldt, *Bescheiden Betreffende zijn Staatkundig Beleid en zijn Familie*, ed. S. P. Haak and A. J. Veenendaal (3 vols., The Hague, 1934–67), III. 364–5. The Contra-Remonstrants were reluctant to believe it. Festus Hommius to William Ames, 14 December 1617, PRO, SP 84/81/29. I owe this reference to Dr A. Milton.

[13] For the political pressures, see C. Grayson, 'James I and the Religious Crisis of the United Provinces, 1613–19' in D. Baker (ed.), *Reform and Reformation: England and the Continent, c. 1500–c. 1750*, Studies in Church History: Subsidia 2 (Oxford, 1979), 195–219.

[14] *The Letters of John Chamberlain*, ed. N. E. McClure (2 vols., Philadelphia, 1939), II. 121.

[15] Camb. Univ. Lib., MS Ff.5.25, ff. 80^r–91^v. Did Chamberlain think it was John iii, 16?

[16] Camb. Univ. Lib., MS Ff.5.25, ff. 87^v.

justus') to refer to falling not into sins, but into afflictions or calamity.[17] There was, it is true, a technical agreement with Arminius on the interpretation of Romans vii, which Simpson also took to refer to the unregenerate, but the constructions erected upon that common basis were quite different. Where Arminius had used it to modify the doctrine of depravity after the Fall, Simpson used it to deny the power of sin in the regenerate.

If the king was indeed misled by the common exegesis of Romans vii, that may explain why he confounded Arminianism with Socinianism. Of course Simpson's theology was wrong-headed. The judgment of the Vice-Chancellor and the Heads was a model of good sense and moderation. They believed that a regenerate man, although born again, remained in some sense carnal; sin still dwelt in the regenerate, though it did not dominate; and Simpson was quite mistaken to suppose such a doctrine to be inimical to good works. They all thought that Romans vii could apply to the regenerate (but they did not insist it should be so restricted). The Heads made no reference to Arminianism.[18]

The king had rightly said the preacher's doctrine tended to desperation. But according to Simpson's own account, in almost the same breath he spoke 'bitterly of Arminius and the Remonstrants',[19] and according to Abbot 'the heads were exceedingly lessoned by the king to take care no such seed grow in the University'.[20] Perhaps James was in addition influenced by the Bishop of Winchester, who seems to have taken an initiative in the proceedings, and who had previously told him (apparently without foundation) that Simpson had been dismissed from Sir Moyle Finch's household for 'perverse opinions in theology'.[21] Less than a year before the Synod of Dort, therefore, the Jacobean court was one where the Remonstrants were regarded above all as Socinians, and where faction piled rumour on polemic.

As the synod drew nearer other, more clearly theological influences asserted themselves. One was the distinction between fundamental doctrines necessary to salvation, and those matters of less importance about which conscientious differences of opinion were tolerable. However ill informed James was about Arminius, he regarded the doctrine of

---

[17] Ibid., f. 90ʳ. Cf. Simpson's letter in *Praestantium ac Eruditorum Virorum Epistolae*, 398.

[18] Camb. Univ. Lib., MS Ff.5.25, f. 93.

[19] *Praestantium ac Eruditorum Virorum Epistolae*, 400.

[20] PRO, SP 105/95/16. For further evidence of the king's concern about undergraduate support for the Arminians in 1617, see British Library, Harley MS 7038, f. 91. Early in 1618, Anthony Cade referred to 'the spreading of those opinionate and fanciful younglings, who drawing bad juice from Arminius . . . begin to bud and blossom in our Academy'. Anthony Cade, *St Paul's Agony* (1618), sig. A3ᵛ, quoted in Tyacke, *Anti-Calvinists*, 43.

[21] *Praestantium ac Eruditorum Virorum Epistolae*, 400. Like Thomson, Simpson had links with the Dutch Remonstrants.

predestination among the latter. He was also interested in Pierre du Moulin's proposals for the drawing up of a common Confession, to which all the Reformed churches could subscribe, on the basis of which negotiations would, it was hoped, be opened with the Lutherans for the achievement of Protestant unity. Du Moulin's intention was that James I should play an important part, and the king's own image of himself as peacemaker fitted him for the role. In both the distinction between fundamentals and inessentials, and in respect of ecumenical reunion, the king was aligned with Remonstrant rather than Contra-Remonstrant opinion. Grotius also welcomed du Moulin's proposals.[22]

These contrary pressures were ultimately reflected in the instructions for the English delegates to Dort.[23] They were enjoined to agree among themselves before delivering any opinions on the matters discussed. If, as was no doubt likely, any issues were raised on which they were uncertain, they were to be guided 'by the scriptures and by the doctrine of the Church of England'. Consistent with the distinction between fundamentals and inessentials, and with the king's approval of the Resolution of 1614, was the instruction to advise Netherlands ministers that they 'do not deliver in the pulpit . . . those things for ordinary doctrines which are the highest points of the schools, and not fit for vulgar capacity, but disputable on both sides'. Consistent with the king's opposition to the Remonstrants was the insistence that 'they use no innovation in doctrine, but teach the same things which were taught twenty or thirty years past . . . and especially that which contradicteth not their own confessions so long since published and known to the world', and which conformed to the neighbour Reformed churches. In accordance with the king's image of himself as peacemaker, the delegates were told that 'if there be main opposition between any which are overmuch addicted to their own opinions, your endeavour shall be, that certain positions be moderately laid down, which may tend to the mitigation of heat on both sides'. More detailed advice would if necessary be communicated through the ambassador, 'who is both acquainted with the form of these countries and understandeth well the questions and differences among them'.

The choice of delegates reflected the king's confidence in his ambassador, and their joint concern, while supporting the Prince of Orange, to protect themselves (especially after the charges of partiality against Carleton) against the accusation that they had prejudged the issues in debate. They were chosen above all as learned theologians, fair-minded

---

[22] John Platt, 'Eirenical Anglicans at the Synod of Dort', in D. Baker (ed.), *Reform and Reformation: England and the Continent*, c. 1500–c. 1750, Studies in Church History: Subsidia 2 (Oxford, 1979), 221–43.

[23] Printed in Thomas Fuller, *The Church History of Britain*, ed. J. S. Brewer, (6 vols., Oxford, 1845), V. 462–3.

men, but certainly free of covert sympathy for the Remonstrants. Their leader was George Carleton, a member of Prince Charles's household, and cousin to Sir Dudley, to whom he had in 1617 sent a written 'refutation of Arminius' for the ambassador to show to any learned person 'holding with Arminius', for 'though they be adversaries in this particular, yet would I learn whatsoever I could understand from them'.[24] The second member of the delegation, Joseph Hall, the recently appointed Dean of Worcester, was also known to have reproved the Arminians for disturbing the peace of the church, while yet regarding Arminius himself as 'acute and learned'.[25] The other members of the delegation were two Cambridge theologians: John Davenant, the Lady Margaret Professor, and Samuel Ward, Master of Sidney Sussex College.

The outlook of the English delegates was in marked contrast to that of Archbishop Abbot. They went to obey the king's instructions, to contribute to bringing peace to the Dutch Church, to assist in the formulation of sound theology, and to show that the English Church was free from the same disputes, loyal to the ancient faith. Their interest was in theology, and not in politics. They were opposed to the Remonstrants, but their concern was to convince rather than to condemn. They saw themselves, it will be argued, as representatives of their king and as apologists of the English Church and its formularies, rather than as defenders of 'Calvinist' orthodoxy. They believed that the synod could be the foundation for renewed Protestant unity, and were dismayed when they found themselves as it ended accessories in re-emphasized division.

Preliminaries

On Tuesday 6 November 1618, George Carleton addressed the States General on the need for peace and unity. He appealed to the essential harmony of the Reformed Confessions. What was in them with which the Dutch Church alone now wished to quarrel? His message from King James was to resist innovation, to accept the consent of other churches, and to deliver to posterity the teaching they had received from their forebears. They should take care lest their theologians, leaving the simplicity of the Holy Scriptures, led them into 'abstruse and intimate quirks'. At the very least, they should ensure that their ministers abstained in their sermons 'from those deeper speculations, which pose the Schools themselves, and our sharpest wits, and may with probability on both sides be disputed'.[26]

[24] Platt, 'Eirenical Anglicans', 234.

[25] *The Works of Joseph Hall*, ed. P. Wynter (10 vols., Oxford, 1863), VI. 302.

[26] George Carleton, *An Oration made at the Hague, before the Prince of Orange, and the Assembly of the High and Mighty Lords, the States General, by . . . the Lord Bishop of Llandaff* (1619), 6–8.

The theme of peace was reiterated by Joseph Hall when he preached before the synod.[27] He too distinguished between popular theology and problems like predestination which were a matter for the schools, endless 'like the Mathematical Line, *divisibilis in semper divisibilia*'. It was quite unfitting 'for the vulgar mind to attempt with profane foot to ascend the highest pinnacles of heaven and there to scrutinize with presumptuous eyes the holy places of God . . . to presume to reason concerning the most abstruse doctrine of Predestination!'. The dispute could be resolved if both sides prepared a plain summary of Romans ix. Hall claimed to speak as a man of no party, but as a friendly adviser. John Hales, who was present as the personal representative of the ambassador, thought, however, that to reiterate George Carleton's instructions to keep the Dutch confessions unaltered was itself enough to indicate that the delegation were 'a party against the Remonstrants'.[28]

The claim to impartiality was nevertheless no mere pose. Late in December, Walter Balcanqual arrived as King James's representative from the Scottish Church.[29] 'The king had most strictly charged him, and with greater earnestness than could be imagined, *to exhort the clergy of these Provinces to peace.*'[30] When Joseph Hall was compelled to return home because of sickness, he was replaced not by John Prideaux, as Abbot and Dudley Carleton would have liked, but by Thomas Goad, the nominee of the delegates themselves. When the time came to say farewell to the synod, Goad, it was remembered, 'exhorted them to bring back the strayed sheep with gentleness, and not to use them rigorously, and concluded with a certain Latin verse to that purpose'.[31]

The Remonstrants hoped for a fairer hearing from the foreign delegates, and especially from the English, than from their own countrymen. Their leader Episcopius called upon Bishop Carleton to ask him to use his influence in favour of Grevinchovius, who had been rejected as *persona non grata*. Carleton had to point out that he was powerless to intervene.[32] Hales's letters to the ambassador nevertheless chronicle a growing uneasiness with the way in which the Remonstrants were treated in the early weeks of the synod, and a perceptible reassessment of the merits of their case.[33] As early as 24 November 1618 he was disconcerted by the

---

[27] The Latin text in Hall, *Works*, X. 253–61.
[28] *The Golden Remains of the Ever-Memorable Mr John Hales of Eton College: Letters from the Synod of Dort* (2nd edn, 1673), 12. The references are all to the second pagination sequence.
[29] Balcanqual sat by himself just below the English delegates.
[30] Brandt, *Reformation in the Low Countries*, III. 98; *Golden Remains*, 54.
[31] Brandt, *Reformation in the Low Countries*, III. 306.
[32] *Golden Remains*, 173.
[33] Discussed by Robert Peters, 'John Hales and the Synod of Dort', in G. J. Cuming and D. Baker (eds.), *Councils and Assemblies*, Studies in Church History 7 (Cambridge, 1971), 277–87.

difficulty of discovering exactly what was going on. Because the Remonstrants had not yet appeared, he assumed that nothing of importance had happened. In fact, crucial decisions had already been made.[34] Hales noted that the opinions of the foreign theologians were in most cases sought only after the vote on an issue had been taken. His requests for information on some of these decisions were met with evasion. When he asked, after a ruling that the children of 'ethnic' parents should not be baptized until they reached years of discretion, what would happen if the child's life were in danger, he was shocked to be told that 'want of baptism would not prejudice them with God, except we would determine as the Papists do, that baptism is necessary to salvation'.[35]

Although the British delegation thought the Remonstrants' refusal to give their opinions on the Belgic Confession and Heidelberg Catechism until after the judgment on the Five Articles was perverse,[36] Hales was nevertheless taken aback when it became apparent that the synod had prejudged the doctrinal issues by refusing to admit them except as *citati*.[37] His faith in the synod's authority was shaken by the ease with which it flouted in the evening decrees which it had solemnly passed the same morning.[38] Then, just when the Remonstrants appeared to be becoming more tractable, the foreign divines were dismayed to hear the president Bogerman expel them, in an intemperate speech accusing them of lies, fraud, equivocations and deceit. The foreign delegates were expected to approve the *fait accompli*. Balcanqual wrote to Carleton that if the Remonstrants 'should write that the President produced a sentence not that of the Synod, they should not lie'.[39] Little regard was had to the foreign delegates unless they spoke against the Remonstrants.[40] One of the delegates from Overijssel 'took it evil that we took the Remonstrants' meaning . . . where they spoke best and soundest; but he would have their meaning to be gathered out of all places in their books where they speak most absurdly, which we thought was very far besides the rule of charity'.[41] Hales realized that there was no alternative to accepting the

---

[34] For example, the decisions to provide a new, Contra-Remonstrant, translation of the Bible, and not to baptize the children of 'ethnic' parents. Peters, 'Hales and the Synod of Dort', 281.

[35] *Golden Remains*, 27.

[36] Peters, 'Hales and the Synod of Dort', 283. See also Arthur Lake's reaction to letters from Samuel Ward in Bodl. Lib., MS Tanner 74, 174 and 190: 'I perceive the Remonstrants are refractory, which is so much an argument either of intolerable arrogancy if they think as they pretend or a guilty conscience, if they make this their refuge to continue their credit by declining their trial.'

[37] Hales, *Golden Remains*, 34.

[38] Ibid., 64.

[39] Ibid., 73–4.

[40] Ibid., 78.

[41] The turning point in Hales's theological allegiance was a sermon preached by Martinius of Bremen. Peters, 'Hales and the Synod of Dort', 285.

decisions of the synod, but he was clearly relieved when, early in February 1619, he had to leave Dort, and 'bid John Calvin goodnight'.[42]

The British delegates resisted attempts to use Dort as a means to enforce a narrow Calvinist orthodoxy. Early in December, Pierre du Moulin sent Dudley Carleton proposals that the Reformed churches should draw up a common confession of faith taken from their existing formularies. He hoped that the Lutherans could be invited to a further assembly to be held six months later with a view to exploring the possibility of mutual understanding and tolerance. With the patronage of King James he thought there was a real hope of success.[43] Hales was sceptical from the first.[44] The British delegates, however, were enthusiastic. George Carleton wrote to his cousin that they would draw up a Confession based on the Thirty-nine Articles, and then send it to the Palatine delegation. He anticipated difficulty only on the question of Christ's descent into hell, but wanted to know whether in expounding the Articles they were at liberty to supplement them out of the Scottish Confession and from Jewel's *Apology*, and how to deal with the article enjoining the Homilies, of which no Latin or other foreign translation was available. In spite of these problems, however, he anticipated that if they could reach an understanding with the Palatines, 'all the rest will easily come over: for the Palatine confession is that which carrieth most authority in these Reformed churches'.[45] In the event, the project evaporated: but the episode demonstrates that the British were aware of an ecumenical dimension which in no small measure influenced their contribution to the doctrinal debates at Dort.

Doctrinal definition: the Five Articles

In almost all the general histories of the period, the canons of the Synod of Dort are taken as the pinnacle of an uncompromising predestinarianism, the 'great pentagonal citadel enshrining Calvinist orthodoxy'.[46] The truth, as careful observers have had no difficulty in recognizing from that day to this, is much more complex. In the first place (and leaving aside the question whether the Dutch Arminians, as has been argued, were truer than the Contra-Remonstrants 'to the more liberal spirit of Calvin'),[47]

[42] Hales, *Golden Remains*, 100.
[43] Platt, 'Eirenical Anglicans', 241.
[44] Hales, *Golden Remains*, 66.
[45] *Letters from and to Sir Dudley Carleton*, 331–2. For the wider context of early seventeenth-century ecumenism, see Trevor-Roper, *Catholics, Anglicans and Puritans*, esp. 53–6, 192–9.
[46] The phrase is taken from W. R. Godfrey, 'Tensions within International Calvinism: The Debate on the Atonement at the Synod of Dort, 1618–19', Stanford University Ph.D. thesis, 1974, 265.
[47] For which see Foster, 'Liberal Calvinism: The Remonstrants at the Synod of Dort.'

orthodox Calvinism in 1619 was dynamic and variegated, encompassing a significant theological diversity. The decrees of Dort, while condemning the Remonstrants, took pains to obscure that diversity. In the words of a near contemporary, 'there was a great deal of wash and *Fucus*, of daubing and paintry used, at the drawing up of the Canons touching the several Articles, to make them look of the same complexion'.[48] The accommodation of in some cases bitter differences of opinion in the disinheritance of Arminianism was achieved by the presentation of the decrees of the synod in three distinct parts. A preface condemned Arminius and the Remonstrants in general terms as novelists and schismatics. The doctrine of the synod was then presented in a series of canons under the five heads of the Remonstrance of 1610 with a *Rejectio errorum* appended to each head: the heresies condemned were (by implication rather than by quotation from their writings) supposed to be Remonstrant errors. Finally, there was added the Sentence of the synod against the Remonstrants.[49]

The decrees of the synod cannot, therefore, be assumed accurately to reflect the theology even of any particular Dutch delegation, still less that of any of the foreign contingents. That has to be reconstructed from other material, and in particular from the written submissions required from each delegation. The main evidence for the theology of the British delegation is accordingly not the canons of Dort, but the *Collegiate Suffrage*[50] presented to the synod on 9 March 1619.

The first head: election and reprobation

The general condemnation of the Arminians at Dort has been allowed to obscure the fact that Gomarus' insistence on 'supralapsarian' predestination left him in virtual isolation, supported only by the delegates of South Holland. Gomarus failed in his attempt to have it enshrined in the canons of Dort, which (Canons, I, §7) take fallen man as the object of the divine decree.

The entire British delegation repudiated the Bezan doctrine. The British

---

[48] Laurence Womock, *Arcana Dogmatum Anti-Remonstrantium, or the Calvinists' Cabinet Unlocked, in An Apology for Tilenus against a pretended vindication of the Synod of Dort*, 53.

[49] The canons of Dort are available in Schaff, *Creeds of the Evangelical Protestant Churches*, 550–79 (Latin), and 581–97 (English, but without the preface, the rejections of errors, and the sentence against the Remonstrants).

[50] *The Collegiat Suffrage of the Divines of Great Britaine concerning the Five Articles controverted in the Low Countries* (1629). The original Latin version was published in 1619. For the other Suffrages, and for much else, *Acta Synodi Nationalis . . . Dordrechti habitae anno 1618 et 1619. Accedunt plenissima de quinque articulis theologorum judicia* (Dordrecht, 1620) is indispensable.

Suffrage defined reprobation (or, as they put it, 'not electing') as 'the eternal decree of God . . . not so far to take pity of some persons fallen in Adam, as to rescue them effectually, through Christ, out of the state of misery'.[51] They thought 'the proper act of reprobation, as it is opposed to election . . . to be no other than the denying of the same glory, and the same grace, which are prepared for the sons of God by election'. Rejecting Beza's distinction between the decree and its execution, they insisted that 'God damns none, or destinates to damnation, except in consideration of sin.'[52]

Gomarus attempted to argue that the English Confession left the issue open, quoting merely the phrase 'quosdam ex humano genere' from Article XVII. The claim prompted a notable intervention from George Carleton:[53]

my Lord of Landaff replied, that he himself and the rest of his colleagues could not choose but think themselves by that speech touched for temerity or ignorance; for since they in their judgement had delivered the contrary for *homo lapsus*, it was as much to say as that they had delivered that in the Synod, which was not according to the judgement of the Church of England, but to let the Synod know that they had said nothing in their judgement, which was not the judgement of their church, they desired the Synod to hear the words of their confession; so Dr Goad read publicly the seventeenth Article of the confession, where the words are *quosdam ex humano genere, in exitio & maledicto*, which last words Gomarus had left out . . . The President told Gomarus roundly enough . . . that men ought to be very careful that they do not rashly meddle with the judgements of other Churches.

Carleton took the opportunity to suggest that since all the foreign divines agreed, there was no reason why the Synod, on account of 'the particular opinion of one professor, who in this did disassent from the judgement of all the Reformed Churches', should leave the matter as an open question. That was to go too far. Gomarus appealed to the authority of both Whitaker and Perkins, 'whom he took to be such men as would not disassent from the Confession of the Church of England'.[54] That sufficed to protect his own position, but it could not disguise how far English theology had moved.

Readers approaching the canons of Dort for the first time will be disappointed if they expect to find a detailed exposition of double and absolute predestination. There is much on election, but very little on reprobation. To have discussed reprobation would have exposed differences among the Contra-Remonstrants. All that the canons include, therefore, is a denial

---

[51] Ibid., 30.
[52] Ibid., 38.
[53] Hales, *Golden Remains*, 129.
[54] Ibid., 130.

that the decree makes God the author of sin ('the very thought of which is blasphemy', I, §15). The British *Suffrage*, by contrast, was explicit in repudiating irrespective reprobation. In the synod, they went further, and 'produced a long list of expressions, which they desired might be rejected . . . because both the Remonstrants and the Papists took occasion from thence to slander the Reformed churches', but according to Brandt other delegates objected on the grounds that to do so would tarnish the reputation of some of the best-known Contra-Remonstrants. The British request was met half-way by including a repudiation of some of the more excessive 'slanders' in the conclusion to the canons.[55]

As to election, the canons of Dort assert that it is 'not founded upon foreseen faith, holiness, or any other good quality or disposition in man, as the prerequisite, cause, or condition on which it depended; but men are chosen to faith and to the obedience of faith, holiness etc.' (I, §9). 'The good pleasure of God is the sole cause of this election' (I, §10). 'The elect, in due time, though in various degrees and in different measures, attain the assurance of this their eternal and unchangeable election' (I, §12). The British *Suffrage* asserts the same doctrines, but the final balance is perceptibly different. In the first place, prominence is given to the doctrine that 'Christ is the head and foundation of the elect, so that all saving graces prepared in the decree of election are bestowed upon the elect only for Christ, through Christ and in Christ.'[56] Secondly, the doctrine of assurance is substantially qualified. 'We likewise grant that the assurance of election in the children of God themselves, is not always so constant and continual, but that oftentimes it is shaken with temptation, and for a time suppressed, so that not only the degree of assurance is lessened, but even election itself, in respect of the sense and apprehension of the Elect, seems uncertain and ready to vanish . . . we confess that the Elect justified, when they fall into grievous sins, are not only deprived of the present taste of their Election, but also conceive a great fear of the contrary, namely of God's wrath and revenging justice.'[57] Finally, on the most important issue of all, election *ex praevisa fide*, the *Suffrage* grants 'we do not deny, but that there is such a good pleasure of God by which he hath decreed to choose faith as a condition of conferring election, that is, by which he would have the actual obtaining of salvation (especially of those which are of ripe years) to depend on the condition of foregoing faith. But this is not the very decree of election.'[58] Those words should be carefully weighed. There is nothing so explicit in the Dort canons. At

[55] Ibid., 150; Brandt, *Reformation in the Low Countries*, III. 278–9.
[56] *Collegiat Suffrage*, 5.
[57] Ibid., 23–4.
[58] Ibid., 28.

the same time, the doctrine of election *ex praevisa fide* as the whole truth about predestination was rejected on two grounds, both of which were important to the British delegates: the first was that such a doctrine took all the mystery out of the doctrine of predestination; the second, even more important, was that Remonstrant doctrine was impossible to reconcile with the 'donation of real grace in the baptism of infants'.[59]

The second head: the extent of the Atonement

At perhaps no point were the tensions within international Calvinism more acute than on the extent of the Atonement.[60] These tensions were fully reflected in the British delegation. In the event, a minority within that delegation were able, first to convince the majority in favour of their more liberal views, and subsequently to persuade a largely hostile synod into substantial modification of the canons.

The issue first came into prominence late in January 1619 with a clash between Gomarus and Martinius of Bremen. As Hales explained to Carleton,[61] the quarrel arose out of a discussion on the question 'In what sense may Christ be said to be *Fundamentum electionis*?':

The doctrine generally received by the Contra-Remonstrant in this point is, that God first of all resolved upon the salvation of some singular persons, and in the second place upon Christ as a mean to bring this decree to pass. So that with them God the Father alone is the author of our election, and Christ only the executioner. Others on the contrary teach that Christ is to be so held . . . as that he is not only the executioner of election, but the author and procuror of it.

When Martinius began to defend the latter view, Gomarus threw down his glove and demanded that the synod grant the two of them a duel. Although the session ended with prayers, 'zeal and devotion had not so well allayed Gomarus his choler, but immediately after Prayers he renewed his challenge'.

The theological sympathies of the British delegation were originally with Gomarus. George Carleton did his best to persuade Martinius to change his mind. Then on 1 February, Balcanqual was invited to introduce consideration of the 2nd Article with a treatment of the Remonstrants' claim that 'the will and intention of the Father in giving up the Son to the death of the cross and the intention of the Son in undergoing that

---

[59] The point is worth stressing. The British divines did not develop the argument at Dort, because they knew that neither the Remonstrants nor the Contra-Remonstrants shared their views on baptism. *Collegiat Suffrage*, 104.

[60] This section owes much to an unpublished paper by John Platt, 'The British Delegation and the Framing of the Second Head of Doctrine at the Synod of Dort'. On the whole question see also Godfrey's thesis.

[61] Hales, *Golden Remains*, 86–7.

death was to bring salvation for each and every man both the lost and the saved'. Although Balcanqual's speech followed orthodox Calvinist lines, it avoided polemic, and was well received by the Remonstrants.[62] A week later Balcanqual had to inform the ambassador that both Davenant and Ward agreed with Martinius.[63]

Concerning this second Article I beseech your Lordship give me leave to express my grief, as there is difference touching it in the Synod, so there is much difference about it in our own College . . . the question amongst us is whether the words of the Scripture, which are likewise the words of our Confession (*Christus oblatus est aut mortuus pro toto humano genere, seu pro peccatis totius mundi*) is to be understood of all particular men, or only of the elect who consist of all sorts of men . . . both sides think they are right, and therefore cannot yield unto another with a safe conscience.

The delegation agreed that the question of the interpretation of Article XXXI of the English Confession had never been officially determined, and that 'it is no matter of salvation in which we differ'. They wrote to Archbishop Abbot, from whom Balcanqual expected confirmation of the restrictive view ('the received exposition of the reformed Doctors, confirmed much by my late Lord of Salisbury [Robert Abbot] . . . who was thought to understand the meaning of our confession as well as any man').[64] Samuel Ward, whose support for an unrestrictive view was grounded upon advice he had already received from his friend Arthur Lake,[65] also wrote to John Young, the Dean of Winchester, a cleric close to King James. Balcanqual's subsequent comment is revealing, since the king's approval was claimed for contradictory courses of action:[66]

My Lord his Grace his letter is to have us conform ourselves to the received distinction and restriction with which his grace acquainted his majesty and received approbation from him, but I must needs say that the directions which your lordship hath sent from secretary Naunton do seem to will us to be as favourable to the general propositions as may be, giving as little offence to the Lutherans as we can, which counsel in my poor judgement we have already followed.

In point of fact, however, contrary winds had delayed both letters until after the delivery of the British *Suffrage* to the synod. By 9 March, therefore, the delegation had resolved their differences.

They did so as the result of Davenant's advocacy, as may be demon-

[62] Brandt, *Reformation in the Low Countries*, III. 215. For Balcanqual's speech, see Bodl. Lib., MS Tanner 74, ff. 166–9.
[63] Hales, *Golden Remains*, 101.
[64] Ibid., 103.
[65] For the correspondence between Ward and Lake, see Bodl. Lib., MS Tanner 74, ff. 132–6.
[66] Hales, *Golden Remains*, 135. This letter was written over a week after the Suffrage had been presented to the synod.

strated by comparing the private memorandum he prepared on the 2nd Article with the final version submitted in the British *Suffrage*. Both start by granting, in accordance with the majority in the synod, that 'out of an especial love and intention . . . Christ died for the elect that he might effectually obtain for them and infallibly bestow on them both remission of sins and salvation',[67] and that 'out of the self-same love . . . faith and perseverance are given to the same Elect, yea and all other things by which the condition of the Covenant is fulfilled'. But, Davenant's paper continued,

we also hold these two ensuing propositions, which we have also exhibited, and were in like manner approved by the *Exteri:*

1. *Deus lapsi humani generis miseratus misit Filium suum, qui se-ipsum dedit pretium Redemptionis pro peccatis totius mundi.* Which proposition is equipollent to the express article of the Church of England, set forth by authority Anno 1562 [Article XXXI]. . . which is also delivered *totidem verbis* in the Consecratory prayer before the Receiving of the Holy Eucharist in the Book of Common Prayer.

2. *In hoc merito mortis Christi fundatur universale Promissum Evangelicum, juxta quod omnes in Christum credentes, remissionem peccatorum, & vitam aeternam reipsa consequantur.*

According to these last two propositions, we do hold that our blessed Saviour by God's appointment did offer himself up to the Blessed Trinity for the redemption of mankind, and by this oblation once made, did found, confirm and ratify the Evangelical Covenant, which may and ought seriously to be preached to all mankind without exception. *Quicunque credit salvabitur; si tu crederes, salvaberis.* And moreover we hold this ensuing proposition, which was in like sort approved as the rest.

3. *In Ecclesia uti juxta hoc Promissum Evangelii salus omnibus offertur, ea est administratio gratiae suae quae sufficit ad convincendos omnes impoenitentes, & incredulos, quod sua culpa voluntaria, & vel neglectu, vel contemptu Evangelii perierint, & beneficia oblata amiserint* . . . And consequently we hold, that the whole merit of Christ is not confined to the Elect only, as some here do hold, and was held in the Colloquy of the Hague by the Contra-Remonstrants.

Davenant's paper, which was drafted to justify the delegation's stance to the king,[68] goes on to give 'the reasons which move us to hold these three

---

[67] *Collegiat Suffrage*, 43–4. Davenant's memorandum is printed in Hales, *Golden Remains*, 188–90. The British sent a declaration entitled *Reasons of enlarging Grace beyond Election*, which they all signed, to Abbot on 11 March; printed ibid., 184–6.

[68] So Dr Platt argues on the basis of John Young's letter to Ward, thanking him for a communication of 18 February: 'this day I acquainted his majesty with every particular of them at length. His majesty will cause a letter to be written to his ambassador there to signify his pleasure to the synod as you desire that in their canons they would have a special eye to the definitions of the ancient councils against the Pelagians and the constitution of other reformed churches and likes very well of your media via wishing you to hold to the articles of the Church of England in any case for your parts and to that purpose I showed his majesty these two articles [the 17th and 31st, cited by Davenant] in the book'. Bodl. Lib., MS Tanner 74, f. 196.

latter assertions'. In the first place they were convinced that this was the 'undoubted doctrine of the holy Scriptures, and most consonant to Antiquity, Fathers and Councils, to whom our Church will have all preachers to have special respect in doctrinal points'.[69] They add that the universality of redemption was supported by Articles II, VII and XV of the Thirty-nine, 'and elsewhere in the Communion Book and Homilies'. Secondly, the universality of the promises of the Gospel was taught in Article XVII,

> that we must receive God's promises in such wise, as they be generally set forth in Holy Scripture where our church doth signify that the Promises of the Gospel do appertain *to all generally* to whom they are published, and according to this we hold, that the reason why the promises of the Gospel are not effectual to all to whom they are published, is not through any defect in Christ's death . . . or that this promise pertained not to all . . . but that the *defect is inherent in man, who will not receive that grace,* that is truly and seriously offered on God's part. This doctrine must needs be maintained; otherwise we cannot see what ground God's ministers have seriously to exhort and invite all to repentance, and believe in Christ, according to the mandate and promise of the Gospel.

Davenant's paper went on to urge that none of the Reformed Confessions restricted the benefit of Christ's death only to the elect. Notwithstanding their agreement on the extent of the Atonement, they claimed that they would in all the five articles 'sufficiently define against the Remonstrants', and at the same time avoid the 'absurdities, which by unavoidable consequence will fall upon them which hold the rigid opinion of Piscator and some in these provinces, touching the doctrine of Reprobation . . . which assertions we think no divine can justify'.

The task of persuading George Carleton, Balcanqual and Goad to agree to these propositions cannot have been easy.[70] It can only have been achieved because they were prepared to follow the king's instructions and be guided by the appeal not merely to Scripture, but to the ancient Councils and to the Articles of the Church of England. It is also clear from Davenant's paper that the delegation had very much in mind the views of other bishops and divines of the Church of England. 'We know that sundry of the most learned bishops and others in England do hold the same; and we doubt but if the tenents of sundry of the Contra-Remonstrants here were made known unto them, they would disclaim them.' Davenant had gone to Dort armed with a four-page memorandum

---

[69] Davenant was thinking of the canons of 1571. The same point was often stressed by Overall.

[70] George Carleton had laboured not only with Martinius but also with Davenant, who, as he wrote to tell Abbot on 18 February, 'would rather have his right hand cut off, than change anything'. Carleton still hoped that Abbot would use his private influence with the synod. Hales, *Golden Remains*, 182–3.

headed 'Dr Overall. De Praedestinatione Divina, De Morte Christi'.[71] A comparison with Davenant's own paper makes clear his debt to Overall. In commenting on the first of the Remonstrant articles, Overall argued that the teaching of the Church of England was plain from its 17th Article, in which, he argued, the general promise was to be understood 'to be by virtue of the Gospel covenant'. By that promise 'everyone may safely repose himself by a steadfast faith and, by a certain hope and trust, may "come boldly to the throne of grace", at the same time assuring himself that if he does not trust in God's promises nor obey his commands he must blame himself and not God and own too that it is through his own negligence and not for want of divine grace'. As to the death of Christ, 'the opinion of our Church is so plain and everywhere consistent with itself, that Christ died for all men or for the sins of all men, that it is to be wondered that any of us should ever have ventured to call it in question'. Overall supported that conclusion by reference to precisely those authorities – Articles II, VII, XV and XXXI, together with the Catechism and the prayer of consecration in the sacrament – that Davenant used in his submission to the king. To no small degree, Overall's statement became definitive of where the Church of England stood as a result of the internal debates of the British delegation at Dort.[72]

The Synod as a whole could hardly be expected to respond to the same arguments. Nevertheless, the British delegation were not wholly unsuccessful in urging other considerations in their efforts to influence the canons under the second head. Chief among these were exhortations not to deviate from the Confessions of the other Reformed churches, the requirement not to prejudice relations with the Lutherans, and the aim of avoiding over-precise definition. As a result of these efforts (and, no doubt, of Martinius of Bremen), the final canons balanced an insistence that God actually applies the salvation accomplished in Christ only to the elect (II, §§8 and 9) by an acknowledgement in II, §3 of the infinite value of Christ's death and in II, §5 'of the evangelical promise that whoever believes in Christ crucified shall

---

[71] Exeter College, Oxford, MS 48. I am indebted to Dr Platt's paper for this important point.

[72] Overall's influence on Davenant and Ward would have appalled Archbishop Abbot, had he known about it. Aware of his contacts with Grotius, he had written to tell Dudley Carleton: 'I do easily perceive that from some few private men but especially from one bishop who is more learned than judicious those Arminian tricks have been fomented out of England' and how at Cambridge after succeeding Whitaker 'he did infect as many as he could till by sharp rebuke and reproofs he was beaten from the public avowing those fancies. But certainly today being in a higher place he doth retain that leaven ... [and] doth smother those conceits among us but is content to send beyond the sea all the encouragement he can. And he maketh no bones as I fear to deliver doubtful things for true and feigned things for certain.' PRO, SP 105/95/9ᵛ.

not perish but have everlasting life' and of the consequent need to preach the Gospel to all men.

There were limits to what could be achieved. Both Ward and Davenant had been prepared to go some way towards meeting the Remonstrants by accepting their distinction between the *impetratio* (appropriation) and the *applicatio* of Christ's death, and Ward entered into lengthy correspondence with the president of the synod on that issue.[73] In spite of his advocacy, the *Rejectio Errorum* condemned the distinction as Pelagian.[74] Similarly, Davenant's efforts to strengthen the third canon further with the words 'that the promise of Christ should be applied to all who believe' were unsuccessful.[75] Finally, the British would have liked the death of Christ to have been set down in the fifth canon as the reason *why* the Gospel should be preached to all men.[76] Their failure to obtain that addition, which would have destroyed the compromise achieved in the canons under the second head, and committed the provinces to an unrestrictive doctrine of the Atonement, was surely inevitable.

The third and fourth heads: free will and conversion

By comparison with the debates on the second head, the discussion of Articles III and IV was uneventful. There was no internal disagreement in the British delegation, and George Carleton's address to the synod was accorded general approbation.[77] It was easy, after all, to achieve at least an appearance of unanimity by a general condemnation of Pelagianism. It would, however, be quite wrong to conclude that even here the British delegation's perspective was the same as that of the majority of the provincials at Dort. A comparison of the *Suffrage* with the official canons justifies Balcanqual's claim that the British judgment 'was most just and equal, condemning the rigidity of some of the Contra-Remonstrants' opinions, though not by that name, as well as the errors of the Pelagians, the Semi-Pelagians, and Remonstrants'.[78]

Where the Dort canons begin with a statement of uncompromising Reformed orthodoxy as to the state of man after the Fall ('blindness . . . horrible darkness, vanity, and perverseness of judgment . . . wicked, rebellious and obdurate in heart and will, and impure in all his affections' (III/IV, §1)) and subsequently temper it with qualifications, the British

---

[73] Lake, 'Calvinism and the English Church', 57.
[74] 'Nam isti, dum simulant se distinctionem hanc sano sensu proponere, populo perniciosum Pelagianismi venenum conantur propinare' looks like an oblique reference to Ward!
[75] Evidence in the Dutch archives cited in Dr Platt's paper.
[76] Godfrey, 'Tensions', 263–4.
[77] Hales, *Golden Remains*, 117.
[78] Ibid., 133.

Suffrage from the first attempts a mediate position: 'The will of man being fallen, is deprived of the supernatural and saving graces with which it was endowed in the state of innocency, and therefore to the performing of any spiritual actions it is able to do nothing without the assistance of grace.'[79] While prepared to grant that there is not merely the possibility of sinning but also 'an headlong inclination to sin', they readily grant that it is entirely within the scope of free will, prior to regeneration, for a man to decide whether or not he will go to church, or whether, once there, he will listen to the preacher or stop his ears.[80] 'Inward effects', such as a sense of sin, prior to regeneration, are of course dependent on the Holy Spirit working through the preaching of the Gospel, but everyone who hears the word is seriously invited to faith and conversion. There is no feigning in God's promises. 'If God should not seriously invite all, whom he vouchsafes this gift of his word and Spirit, to a serious conversion, surely both God should deceive many whom he calls in his Son's name, and the messengers of the Evangelical promises might be accused of false witness, and those, who being called to conversion do neglect to obey, might be more excusable.'[81]

The *Suffrage* goes on to speak cautiously of the operation of prevenient or 'exciting' grace. It was surely with the Contra-Remonstrants in mind that they asserted 'never in the Scriptures is there the least mention that God is wont, or is willing, at any time, without some fault of man going before, to take away from any man the aid of his exciting grace . . . Thus the orthodox Fathers who had to do with the Pelagians ever taught.'[82] Far from being irresistible, the inward effects prior to conversion were often 'stifled and utterly extinguished by the fault of our rebellious will'. Even in the 'very elect', it could happen that they were resisted, and the grace of God thereby 'repelled' and 'choked', 'yet God doth urge them again and again, nor doth he cease to stir them forward, till he have thoroughly subdued them to his grace, and set them in a state of regenerate sons'.[83]

An equal balance is shown in the treatment of conversion. Regeneration presupposed a mind moved by the Spirit through the instrument of the word, 'which must be observed, lest anyone should idly and slothfully expect an Enthusiastical regeneration, that is to say wrought by a sudden rapture without any foregoing action either of God, the word or himself'. They go on to stress the work of the spirit of regeneration in removing

[79] *Collegiat Suffrage*, 64–5.
[80] Ibid., 68–9; cf. the Dort canons, III/IV, §4.
[81] *Collegiat Suffrage*, 72.
[82] Ibid., 73–4.
[83] Ibid., 74–6.

sinful inclinations, and in the performance of 'spiritual actions leading to salvation', quoting Prosper: 'grace creates good in us'.[84]

The Dort canons speak unambiguously of faith as the gift of God. It is God who produces 'both the will to believe and the act of believing also'.[85] The British *Suffrage* by contrast distinguishes what is to be ascribed wholly to God from 'our actual conversion, wherein out of our reformed will God himself draweth forth the very act of believing, and converting; and this our will being first moved by God, doth itself also work by turning unto God, and believing, that is by executing withall its own proper lively act'.[86]

In their *Rejectio errorum* under this head, the British delegation balanced their repudiation of the Remonstrant concept of grace operating only by a 'gentle or moral suasion' by including a strong disavowal of the Contra-Remonstrant teaching that 'a man cannot do any more good than he doth or omit any more evil than he doth omit'. Although they did not name them, Piscator and Maccovius were both associated with that doctrine.[87] The British did not mince words in condemning it as 'false and absurd'. To accept it would be doubly harmful, for not only would all punishments be thereby 'without cause menaced', but sins whether of omission or of commission would be impossible, and the prayer 'Forgive us our trespasses' become redundant.[88]

The British delegation tried hard but without success to persuade the synod to repudiate both that doctrine, and the associated teaching that 'God moved the tongues of men to blaspheme him.'[89] Bogerman's answer was to deny that the Netherlands churches were responsible for such harsh modes of expression; it was the English, the French and the Germans, he alleged. When the British insisted that the Remonstrants had given chapter and verse, that as a result the Reformed churches were brought into disrepute, and that after all no reproach would be cast on any of the leaders of the Reformation, 'it being only what was started but yesterday, as it were, there being scarce seven years elapsed since the birth of it', the synod remained unrepentant, 'especially since it appeared that even the Holy Ghost himself had made use of some of the same ways of speaking'.[90] The only concession was the inclusion of unspecified 'many other things of a like nature' in the slanders repudiated by the synod, so that if the delegation were reproached, they could at least reassure their

---

[84] Ibid., 80–1.
[85] III/IV, §14.
[86] *Collegiat Suffrage*, 83.
[87] Womock, *Arcana Dogmatum Anti-Remonstrantium*, 39–40.
[88] *Collegiat Suffrage*, 98–101.
[89] Hales, *Golden Remains*, 150.
[90] Brandt, *Reformation in the Low Countries*, III. 279.

critics that the doctrines complained of had been rejected by a general formula. It was not satisfactory.

The fifth head: perseverance

Where the Dort canons are content to assert the doctrine of the perseverance of the saints in five pages, the British *Suffrage* combines a delicately enunciated exposition with a careful discussion of controverted issues.

The *Suffrage* asks first whether those who are not elect 'may ever come to a state of justification and sanctification and so be among the saints'.[91] Unlike many in the synod, the British were prepared to grant that some of the non-elect are able to yield an unfeigned assent to scriptural truth, and (a sure sign that they were treading on Contra-Remonstrant toes) they quoted Calvin in support. There were some at least who were punished 'not because they feigned the faith they never had, but because they forsook the faith they had'.[92] The British delegation did not scruple to attribute not merely knowledge and faith, but even some degree of consequent amendment of life, to some at least of the reprobate. Their phraseology was careful: 'upon those good beginnings, testified by the external works of obedience, they are reputed, and by a charitable construction ought to be taken for believers, justified, and sanctified men'.[93]

Subsequently, of course, some of the ground thus given was retaken. In reality, 'they never attain unto the state of adoption and justification, and therefore by the apostasy of these men, the apostasy of the saints is very erroneously concluded'.[94] A '*lively* faith which justifies a sinner and worketh through love' is peculiar to the elect, and apostasy is 'only of those who never reached home to true justification . . . either therefore the apostasy of the true sons of God ought to have been proved by evident places of Scripture, or else that offensive name and title . . . should have been foreborne'.[95]

A similar delicacy of tread marked the treatment of perseverance. On the one hand, it was plain according to Scripture that 'God giveth to all the elect a certain continued connexion of spiritual benefits', and that their state of justification was never interrupted. No sooner was the assertion made, however, than it was qualified. 'These . . . regenerated and justified

---

[91] *Collegiat Suffrage*, 104.
[92] Ibid., 106. They quote St Augustine, *De Corrept. et Grat.* c. 9: 'they were not sons when they were in the profession and had the name of sons, not because they feigned their righteousness, but because they remained not in that righteousness'.
[93] *Collegiat Suffrage*, 111.
[94] Ibid., 112.
[95] Ibid., 115–17. The reference is to Peter Bertius' *De Apostasia Sanctorum* of 1613.

do sometimes through their own default fall into heinous sins, and thereby do incur the fatherly anger of God, they draw upon themselves a damnable guiltiness and lose their present fitness to the kingdom of heaven.'[96] In that state, the elect 'neither ought nor can persuade themselves otherwise than that they are subject to eternal death'. God who has ordained the end has also ordained the means: those means are 'a renewed performance of faith and repentance'. The *Suffrage* hastened to dissociate itself from antinomianism. 'They are deceived therefore that think the elect wallowing in such crimes, and so dying must notwithstanding needs be saved through the force of election.'[97] The salvation of the elect is sure, but sure only through the way of faith, repentance and holiness. 'In the mean time, between the guilt of the grievous sin, and the renewed act of faith and repentance, such an offender stands by his own desert to be condemned; by Christ's merit and God's decree to be acquitted; but actually absolved he is not, until he hath obtained pardon by renewed faith and repentance.'[98] Yet 'the seed of regeneration' was said to remain, and the 'right to justification' was not lost, though 'the effect of justification' was for a time suspended. It was difficult territory.

Standing on that ground, the presentation of the doctrine of assurance was necessarily muted. The faithful 'may or can have within themselves' a 'persuasion' that they will persevere, but they are not always actually so persuaded.[99] The persuasion of faith 'cannot come into act and vigour, without the endeavour of holiness'. It can and should be fostered 'by watching, fasting, prayer, and mortifying the flesh, and other means appointed by God'. Even then, it 'hath not that degree of certitude, that can always shut out all fear of the contrary'.[100] It is of a lower order than the certainty of dogmatical faith, and dogmatical faith itself is less certain than mathematical demonstration. It is vulnerable to temptation, and liable to assault by our own concupiscence and by the Devil. Nevertheless, 'when a faithful man, after much struggling, has got the upper hand of these temptations, that act, by which he doth apprehend the fatherly mercy of God towards him, and eternal life to be conferred without fail upon him, is not an act of floating opinion, or of conjectural hope . . . but it is an act of a true and lively faith, stirred up and sealed in his heart by way of adoption'.[101]

By itself this part of the British *Suffrage* would be remarkable enough. It amounts to a tacit disengagement from the doctrine of assurance

[96] Ibid., 121.
[97] Ibid., 124.
[98] Ibid., 126–7.
[99] Ibid., 140–1.
[100] Ibid., 145–8.
[101] Ibid., 153.

defended by Whitaker and the Cambridge Heads in the 1590s and an effective repudiation of the practical syllogism. There is, however, additional evidence to demonstrate that it understates the differences between the British delegation and the majority in the synod. In the papers which Samuel Ward brought back from Dort there is a record[102] of the changes the delegation wished to be made under the fifth head of doctrine and their reasons for them.

It is clear from this evidence that they were able in material respects to influence the final version of the canons. (1) They persuaded the provincials to add the words 'according to his purpose' to canon V, §1, and would have preferred a similar qualification to have been added to V, §4: the effect was to suggest that perhaps there are some who are called, and (in respect of iv) some who believe, perhaps even some who are justified *not* according to purpose. (2) The final form of V, §5 was influenced by the British: 'By such enormous sins, however, they [i.e., the elect] . . .' was their suggestion to replace 'By such sins God is enormously offended . . .' In the same canon, the admission that by such sins the elect 'incur a deadly guilt' was also added to the draft at the request of the British. They asked for the wording to be even stronger, and to include 'nor are they judged worthy of entering the kingdom of heaven, until through the exercise of faith and repentance they return into the right way, and are absolved from this guilt', but the final version remained weak with 'very grievously wound their consciences, and sometimes lose the sense of God's favour'. (3) In V, §6 the British asked that the assertion that the elect do not lose the grace of adoption or forfeit the state of justification be qualified by the addition of the word 'altogether' (*prorsus*) and the admission that they may fall into grievous sins and contract the guilt thereof. This was not granted. (4) In V, §8 they successfully asked for the word 'efforts' (*studiis*) to be omitted from the assertion that 'it is not in consequence of their own merits or strength or efforts, but of God's free mercy' that the elect are preserved from total falling from grace. They argued that far from excluding human efforts, the canons ought to be inculcating them, and that teaching did not at all impugn the doctrine of God's free mercy independent of all human merits. (5) In commenting on V, §9 (concerning assurance) the British cautioned against teaching a degree of assurance that in fact 'no one or at any rate few of the faithful in reality experience'. The certitude of the doctrine itself was one thing; our persuasion of it quite another. Although Scripture taught clearly enough the perseverance of the elect, there was nothing in it to justify any particular

---

[102] Sidney Sussex College, Cambridge, Samuel Ward MS L2, entitled 'A Theologis Ecclesiae Anglicanae de canonibus formandis aliisque in Synodo Dordacena proposita.' These MSS have been calendared by Margo Todd.

individual concluding that he was truly faithful or that he would necessarily persevere until the end; that was only an inference derived from the act of faith and its effects of holiness, both of which wavered and were obscured on account of the weakness of the flesh and our subjection to sin. In spite of this long excursus, no formula was suggested, and there is no evidence of any alteration to the canon. (6) The British suggested that V, §13 should be extended to include, among the means designated by God towards the kindling and arousing of perseverance, 'exhortations, warnings, promises, and threatenings'. This would appear to have been granted by adding an extra canon 14.

Even more striking are the British comments on the *rejectio errorum* under this head. By far the most important was their successful request to exclude from condemnation those who taught that true believers and regenerate ('vere credentes et regenitos') were able to fall from the faith of justification. The reasons which they gave merit attention:

We ourselves think that this doctrine is contrary to Holy Scripture, but whether it is expedient to condemn it in these our canons needs great deliberation. On the contrary, it would appear

1. That Augustine, Prosper and the other Fathers who propounded the doctrine of absolute predestination and who opposed the Pelagians, seem to have conceded that certain of those who are not predestinated can attain the state of regeneration and justification. Indeed, they use this very argument as an illustration of the deep mystery of predestination; which cannot be unknown to those who have even a modest acquaintance with their writings [!].

2. That we ought not without grave cause to give offence to the Lutheran churches, who in this matter, it is clear, think differently.

3. That (which is of greater significance) in the Reformed churches themselves, many learned and saintly men who are at one with us in defending absolute predestination, nevertheless think that certain of those who are truly regenerated and justified, are able to fall from that state and to perish and that this happens eventually to all those, whom God has not ordained in the decree of election infallibly to eternal life. Finally we cannot deny that there are some places in Scripture which apparently support this opinion, and which have persuaded learned and pious men, not without great probability.

Those powerful arguments were effective, and the canon was dropped. As a corollary, the British also asked for the doctrine that temporary faith differed from justifying and saving faith only in duration not to be rejected by the synod. Although they did not themselves agree, they recognized that there were many in the Reformed churches who were of the opinion that temporary faith could also be justifying faith, but who nevertheless acknowledged that it differed not merely in duration, but also in degree from the faith of the elect. They would have preferred the question to be left undetermined. The synod nevertheless retained that canon.

The significance of this hitherto unnoticed evidence will hardly escape the reader. It implies a readiness by the British delegation not indeed to agree with Overall under this head of doctrine, but to accept that his understanding of it was perfectly legitimate within the Reformed tradition.[103] Similarly, and again without actually agreeing with him, they were in effect conceding the force of much that Richard Thomson had written. They were prepared to acknowledge that Overall was supported by a substantial body of opinion within the English and other Reformed churches, and by the Lutherans. They did their best to persuade the provinces not to isolate themselves from that tradition.

The closing sessions

As the synod drew towards its close, Balcanqual oscillated between dismay and optimism. Towards the end of March 1619 he wrote to complain that the president made canons without consultation, and that an amicable conclusion to any synod of which Lubbertus and Gomarus were members was inconceivable.[104] The Palatines, who 'think everything they speak should be taken for text', had attacked Samuel Ward,[105] and then Lubbertus 'flew out, but with such raving and fierceness of countenance, such unheard bitterness against our College'.[106] Davenant had wanted to reply, but had been restrained by the president. Unless the ambassador intervened,

we are like to make the synod a thing to be laughed at in after ages. The president and his provincials have no care of the credit of strangers, nor of that account which we must yield at our return unto all the men that shall be pleased to call for it; their canons they would have them so full charged with catechetical speculations, as they will be ready to burst; and I perceive it plainly that there is never a Contra-Remonstrant minister in the synod, that hath delivered any doctrine which hath been excepted against by the Remonstrants, but they would have it in by head and shoulders in some canon, that so they might have something to show for that which they have said.[107]

Carleton may well have used his influence, for early in April Balcanqual could write that the deputies had 'taken pains I must needs confess to give our college all satisfaction'. Apart from the changes to the second head,

---

[103] Again, it is necessary to grant that Archbishop Abbot would have vehemently disagreed. He still refused to accept that there was a problem, or to distinguish between regeneration, justification and sanctification, as in his letter to Dudley Carleton, PRO, SP 105/95/48^v–9^r, quoted by Lake, 'Calvinism and the English Church', 53–4.
[104] Hales, *Golden Remains*, 140.
[105] Ibid., 135.
[106] Ibid., 140.
[107] Ibid., 141.

they had omitted a reference to infants being damned for sins both actual and original 'so I know now of no matter of disagreement among us worthy the speaking of'.[108] Only five days later, however, he had to report the synod 'so full of trouble about things altogether unnecessary, they are so eager to kill the Remonstrants, that they would make their words have that sense which no grammar can find in them'. The delegates had been confronted with extra canons 'which we never heard of till that hour' implying Remonstrant heresy on the absolute power of God and even Socinianism. A whole session was spent in which the British in isolation protested against the inclusion of the last heterodox, which the provinces would retain 'only to make the Remonstrants odious, though they find the very contrary of that they would father upon them in their words'.[109] Eventually it was dropped, and on 25 April Balcanqual wrote:

Now at last we have made an end of the business of the five articles; what trouble we have had in these last sessions none can conceive but those who were present at them; and what strange carriage there hath been in them, especially on the president his part, it is too palpable, he hath deceived all men's hopes of him very far.

The development which inspired that letter was the personal censure of the Remonstrants which took the British entirely by surprise:

we were never made acquainted with it before the very instant in which it came to be read, and because the delegates must not be stayed from their going to the Hague, therefore all the synod must say Amen to it; between the forenoon and the afternoon session, there was strange labouring with the *Exteri* for getting their consent to it; yet we meddled not with it; all I can say is, me thinketh it is hard, that every man should be deposed from his ministry, who will not hold every particular canon; never did any church of old, nor any Reformed Church, propose so many articles to be held *sub poena excommunicationis* . . . None of us have the Canons yet, neither shall till the Estates have approved them.[110]

Even when the words 'perturbatione patriae et reipublicae' were dropped from the censure, the British refused to sign it. They said they neither approved nor disapproved: it was a matter for the provinces.[111]

The British delegation did sign the canons. In one important respect, their approval was obtained on a false pretence. They were unhappy about the words 'This doctrine the Synod judges . . . to be agreeable to the confessions of the Reformed Churches', and signed on the understanding that they would be changed to 'our Reformed Churches'.[112] They gave two reasons. In the first place, they argued, the British included the Lutherans

---

[108] Ibid., 143.
[109] Ibid., 144–5.
[110] Ibid., 145–6.
[111] Ibid., 155.
[112] Ibid., 152–3. Brandt, *Reformation in the Low Countries*, III. 282.

among the Reformed churches, and they had been instructed to do nothing to prejudice relationships with them.[113] Secondly, the British themselves had attended the synod as representatives of the king, and not of the Church of England, and there were many doctrines to which they had given their assent at Dort which were not covered by the English Confession. When the canons were published, however, the word 'our' had not been substituted. Bogerman was suspected of omitting it on his own authority.[114]

The British delegation were similarly embarrassed when they were asked to approve the Belgic Confession. They gave a general assent to the doctrinal articles, but covered themselves carefully: 'they think nothing of substance to be contained in it which is repugnant to Scripture, though they notice certain small matters liable to dispute which could easily be corrected in the next edition from the collated copies'.[115] Their assent did not include the articles on church government,[116] on which they professed themselves to have no opinion, but meanwhile maintained that the polity of their own churches was of apostolical institution. George Carleton, indeed, took occasion publicly to blame all the doctrinal troubles of the Netherlands Church on their lack of bishops and any respect for authority, so that 'everybody in that country wrote and spoke as he pleased'.[117] In the end, harmony was restored when both provincials and foreigners joined in the condemnation of Vorstius. Further emphasis was given to the independent stance of the British when they reserved the right to interpret the descent of Christ into hell differently from the other Reformed churches, and by their parting admonition to the local magistrates of the grave offence which had been caused them by the neglect of Sunday observance tolerated in Dort.[118]

The role of the British delegation has attracted contrasting judgments. Then and since, some were convinced that they had subscribed themselves, and committed their church, to extreme Calvinism.[119] The extreme Calvinists themselves did not think so; on the contrary, they were liable to accuse them of being 'more than half Remonstrants'.[120] Such

---

[113] Ibid., 155–6.
[114] Brandt, *Reformation in the Low Countries*, III. 282.
[115] Ibid., 288; Hales, *Golden Remains*, 160–1.
[116] Articles XXX–XXXII.
[117] Hales, *Golden Remains*, 161; Brandt, *Reformation in the Low Countries*, III. 288.
[118] Hales, *Golden Remains*, 162.
[119] For example, De Dominis wrote to Joseph Hall: 'I call you, O Hall! and your colleagues . . . to witness concerning what you there agreed to in the name of the Church of England; which certainly was not what the said church prescribes by her articles to be believed, but pure Calvinistical doctrines.' Quoted by Brandt, *Reformation in the Low Countries*, III. 308.
[120] Ward to Ussher, 26 May 1619, *The Works of James Ussher*, ed. C. R. Elrington (17 vols., Dublin, 1847–64), XV. 144–5.

judgments, whether of the delegation as a whole or of individuals, are inevitably superficial. The doctrinal issues discussed at Dort are simply not susceptible to easy classification.

This book does, however, suggest some important modifications to traditional assumptions. What is striking in the first place is the extent to which the king's instructions, even where they involve inconsistencies, provide the key to the role of the British delegation. There was an inconsistency between the assumption that the delegation would support the Contra-Remonstrants (especially in the persons of Gomarus and Lubbertus) and that they would act as peacemakers. There was a deeper, theological, inconsistency (of which the delegates themselves may not have been fully aware) between the condemnation of Remonstrant doctrines and the recognition that the Lutherans should be conciliated. There were in addition the problems caused by the genuine differences of opinion among the British, and the fact that they were called upon to face doctrinal issues of which no determination had been made in the Church of England. The evidence reviewed here demonstrates that they were determined to do justice not only to their own views, but to those of others in the English Church. As the debates unfolded, it became clear how far English theology had moved since the last decade of the sixteenth century. As a result of the debates, the interpretation of the Thirty-nine Articles was established definitively on the extent of the Atonement, and on other issues a permissive latitude was defended. It is not unreasonable to claim that as a result the thrust of English theology was confirmed as a middle way, a way that concentrated on fundamentals and avoided extremes, but nevertheless was comprehensive and eirenic.

10 Policy and polemic, 1619–1623

The decade after 1619 is commonly seen as a decisive watershed in the doctrinal evolution of the Church of England. Just as the Synod of Dort, with which it began, is taken as confirmation and summit of the allegiance of that church to international Calvinism, so the Declaration prefixed to the Thirty-nine Articles, which marked its end, is regarded as the final step by which that same Calvinism was effectively outlawed.[1] In the years between, the publication of the controversial works of Richard Montagu and the failure to condemn them at the York House Conference, coupled with the episcopal changes of 1626–8 and above all the appointment of Montagu himself to the see of Chichester are taken to be the major steps whereby a previously dominant Calvinist theology was replaced by Arminianism and its hierarchy swamped by adherents of the new doctrine. This was the decade, in short, which saw 'the rise of English Arminianism'.

That picture, it will be argued, is conceptually flawed and at odds with much of the evidence, which demands a much more subtle colouring than any simplistic 'Calvinist' and 'Arminian' polarity is capable of accommodating. While it will not be denied that there was at one stage strong support for the Remonstrants, hitherto unused evidence will be adduced to show that it antedated rather than followed the appearance of the *New Gagg*. An attempt will be made to relate it to other developments, ecclesiastical and political, that were more or less coincident with it. The evolution of Richard Montagu's theology will thereafter be reviewed, and its orientation in its contemporary setting assessed; it will be suggested that the concerns of Durham House were substantially independent of support for the Remonstrants in the English Church. The Protestant responses to the *New Gagg* and the *Appello Caesarem* will thereafter be considered, in order to demonstrate the full range of the underlying anxieties raised by the Montagu case. Finally, the role of the court, first under James, and then under Charles, will be re-examined in order to show that both monarchs were hostile to Arminianism, and that royal policy was

[1] Tyacke, 'Debate: The Rise of Arminianism Reconsidered', 211; *Anti-Calvinists*, 8, 50–1. The Declaration is indexed only under 'Arminianism'.

intended to suppress it. The Declaration of 1628, it will be argued, far from inaugurating an Arminian regime, was substantially successful in preventing further controversy.

From the perspective of Archbishop Abbot and those who thought like him, the importance of the Synod of Dort had been much more than merely theological. They had wanted it to confirm the position of the Church of England as an integral member of the Reformed church, and of its head as leader in the struggle against the papal Antichrist. They were unable to accept that the synod had not been the great theological-political conference which they had hoped for.[2] The outbreak of the Thirty Years War was decisive in exposing their illusion, for had they been right, James would have entered the war against Spain to secure the *dénouement* their apocalyptic theology taught them to expect. Instead, they had to stomach the opening of negotiations for a Spanish marriage for Prince Charles and before long the employment of English resources against foreign Protestants. For some the only explanation of this unpalatable political reality was a papist conspiracy at the heart of the government,[3] and the only compensation the cultivation of a theological myth as to what Dort had really meant before James I became a victim of that conspiracy.

For both theological and political reasons, therefore, there was in the aftermath of the synod, and in spite of the mediating role played by the British delegation, a sharpening of theological polarities in the English Church. On the one hand, extreme anti-Arminian stances were adopted in traditional strongholds of Calvinist orthodoxy. They are evident in some of the sermons preached at Paul's Cross, a large number of which attacked Arminianism in the years immediately following the synod.[4] They are apparent also in some of the Oxford Act theses of 1618 and 1619.[5] This Calvinist assertion was not limited to theology. A sermon at Oxford preached in April 1622 by a young divine named William Knight,[6] which defended Pareus' doctrine that an inferior magistrate might take up arms against his sovereign in defence of religion, provoked, as we shall see, a massive outburst of anti-Calvinism in both universities, as the strident assertion of extreme positions on one side provoked counter-assertions on the other. At the Cambridge Commencement of 1622

---

[2] S. Adams, 'The Protestant Cause: Religious Alliance with the West European Calvinist Communities as a Political Issue in England, 1585–1630', Oxford D. Phil. thesis, 1973, 275.

[3] Prynne began his *Hidden Works of Darkness* with the marriage project; John Rushworth's *Historical Collections* (7 vols., 1659–1701), written to explain the origins of the Civil War, starts by pointing out its 'mighty influence upon the Universal state of Christendom'.

[4] Tyacke, *Anti-Calvinists*, 257–62. Of the 27 Paul's Cross sermons identified as dealing with predestination during James's reign, 10 were preached between 1617 and 1622.

[5] Ibid., 74–5.

[6] Fincham and Lake, 'Ecclesiastical Policy of King James I', 199.

William Lucy, a chaplain to the Duke of Buckingham, preached a sermon which was said to have been 'totally for Arminianism, wonderfully bold and peremptorily, styling some passages of the contrary by the name of blasphemy'.[7] In the following January it was paralleled by a similar sermon at Oxford, preached by Gabriel Bridges. Unlike Lucy, he was summoned before the Vice-Chancellor and ordered to read a public submission.[8]

It would indeed be very surprising, particularly in the light of the treatment of the Remonstrants at Dort, if academic and clerical opinion in the English Church had not become polarized. The resulting alignments nevertheless require careful assessment. In 1619, Grotius wrote to Andrewes from prison,[9] but no reply by Andrewes has survived. In 1621, however, Andrewes received a visit from the Dutchman Georg Doublet, who was duly entertained to dinner in Farnham Castle. In a revealing letter, Doublet told of Andrewes's refusal to eat without drinking the health of Grotius, Vossius and Erpenius, whose names he kept repeating with the comment that in his house at least they could be heard.[10] Andrewes bitterly deplored the prejudice against Grotius which made it impossible to contemplate his presence in England. In the same year Grotius heard from John Cosin of Overall's death two years earlier,[11] and in 1622 Christopher Wren, who was chaplain to Andrewes, wrote mentioning Laud,[12] but there are no other letters from English clergy to Grotius even after Laud became Archbishop of Canterbury. Occasional expressions of friendship and good-will passed through third parties, like Francis Junius[13] (who became librarian to the Earl of Arundel in 1621) and later through Meric Casaubon.[14] They reflect above all the mutual admiration of men of learning. Before leaping to the conclusion that they prove at any rate Andrewes's 'Arminianism', we should also register the letter he received in September 1619 from Pierre du Moulin, enclosing a copy of his book against the Arminians. It was an argument full of thorns, said du Moulin, in which it was impossible to satisfy human judgment,

---

[7] T. Birch (ed.), *The Court and Times of James I* (2 vols., 1849), II. 319–20. The text of Lucy's sermon is not extant. He proceeded to a BD degree and then a DD the next year, in spite of considerable opposition. He received no preferments under Laud, but became Bishop of St David's at the Restoration.

[8] Tyacke, *Anti-Calvinists*, 74–5.

[9] *Briefwisseling van Hugo Grotius*, II. 24–6; letter dated 19 November 1619.

[10] G. J. Vossius, *Epistolae,* ed. P. Colomesius (2 vols. in 1, 1690), II. 29; letter of 3 September 1621.

[11] *Briefwisseling van Hugo Grotius*, II. 99–101; letter of 30 June 1621.

[12] Ibid., 246–7; letter of 27 September 1622.

[13] Ibid., 240–1. Junius wrote to tell Grotius of Andrewes's, Laud's and Harsnett's good-will towards him.

[14] For the correspondence with Meric Casaubon, see *Briefwisseling van Hugo Grotius*, VII. 307–8, 423–4, 456.

but he would prefer to be admonished by Andrewes than praised by anyone else.[15]

The Dutch thinker who did begin to make an impact in England in the aftermath of the Synod of Dort was the regent of the States College at Leiden, Gerard Vossius. He was brother-in-law to Junius, and had been a close friend of Grotius since 1613. Unlike Grotius, he preferred to remain on the sidelines in the theological disputes – he chided a former pupil who in a letter to his father used the word 'Gomarist'[16] – and he pressed both parties to peace and tolerance. Vossius shared Grotius' admiration for the English Church, and he had been shocked by Matthew Slade's attack on Erasmus, which he described as 'a disgusting piece of writing', but his first direct contacts with English clergy had been with the English delegates to Dort, with whom he had dinner on a visit to the synod, and whom he admired for their respect for ecclesiastical antiquity and for a church order in agreement with his ideas. That admiration, as will be shown, was mutual. It is a mistake to assume that Vossius' English friends were exclusively the clergy of Durham House, bound to him by 'Arminianism'.[17]

Vossius had been drawn by Grotius into a more active role in the Dutch disputes, and as a result published a History of Pelagianism.[18] Characteristically, it offered a basis of compromise between Remonstrant and Contra-Remonstrant positions. Grotius was anxious to assure Andrewes that it represented his own views as well. Unlike the Remonstrants, Vossius was absolutely opposed to changing the Belgic Confession. He argued that the Confessional Harmony published at Geneva was in accord with the church of antiquity in teaching the intention of the Son of God from the beginning of the world that all mankind should be saved.[19] Yet Vossius was far from teaching either election *ex praevisa fide* or universal grace. There could be no question that to a great part of mankind the truth of the Gospel was hidden, and we can only with St Paul refer this to the inscrutable judgment and impenetrable abyss of the divine wisdom.[20] But to go further than St Paul, and with St Augustine attribute it to an absolute decree, was not warranted by Scripture. Vossius similarly denied that the perseverance of some, and the lack of perseverance of others, were to be attributed to an absolute

---

[15] Petrus Molinaeus to Andrewes, September 1619, British Library, Sloane MS 118, f. 23^r.

[16] C. S. M. Rademaker, *The Life and Work of Gerardus Joannes Vossius, 1577–1649* (The Netherlands, 1981), 89.

[17] Ibid., 127–8.

[18] G. J. Vossius, *Historiae de Controversiis quas Pelagius eiusque reliquiae moverunt* Libri septem (Leiden, 1618).

[19] Ibid., sig. a2.

[20] Ibid., 548.

decree.[21] He claimed that neither Augustine nor Prosper denied that justifying faith and regenerating grace could be lost.[22] He did not, however, question that there are some who are granted the assurance that they cannot fall: but this assurance was not granted to all the elect.[23] There are degrees of faith. On reprobation, all Vossius would say, on the evidence of Scripture, was that the reprobate are genuinely called. He suggested three theses: that those whose infidelity or lack of perseverance is foreseen suffer eternal punishment; that the reprobate have deserted God before he deserts them; and that we do not know why God grants saving grace to one more than to another when both are equally unworthy: it is the hidden judgment of God.[24]

In the aftermath of the synod, Vossius' neutrality and friendship with Grotius inevitably made his position difficult, and he was obliged to resign as regent. He was asked to clarify some suspect passages in his Pelagian History. Yet notwithstanding his published views, his refusal to sign the Dort canons (he also declined to endorse the Remonstrant Articles), and his repeated failure to publish a statement confirming his adherence to what St Augustine had taught at the end of his life, he remained on the academic staff at Leiden, on condition that he refrained from writing or teaching against the determinations of Dort.[25] In 1622 he was appointed to a professorial chair, and in 1624 cleared from unorthodoxy by a synod at The Hague. His History of Pelagianism proved acceptable to the vast majority of his Dutch co-religionists, and he personally remained throughout on good terms with Gomarus. His reputation as a distinguished scholar who was not prepared to be identified with either the Remonstrants or the Contra-Remonstrants but who nevertheless liked to be on friendly terms with both was well understood on both sides of the Channel.

In August 1622, Doublet, who had once been Vossius' pupil, wrote to tell him of the situation in England.[26] He told the story of Knight's sermon, and how it had come to the ears of the king, and of the rash young man, bound in chains, being brought in front of the monarch:

no one doubting that he would pay with his head for his licence in speaking so rashly; but when the hearing of his case began, the young man . . . claimed that he believed this to be the common opinion of all the reformers, and so taught by all the learned among them, citing Pareus in his commentary on the epistle to the Romans, Bucanus in his Commonplaces, and . . . the book *Vindiciae*

---

[21] Ibid., 549.
[22] Ibid.
[23] Ibid., 571–2.
[24] Ibid., 789–90.
[25] Rademaker, *Vossius*, 144–50.
[26] *Vossius, Epistolae*, ed. Colomesius, II. 30–1.

contra Tyrannos[27] [The king] made this small excuse for this young man, that he was a beginner in theology; he did not forgive him for his understanding of more than the authorities had said, and the hypotheses he had drawn from them. And so with Knight detained in prison, the censure of the Universities was passed on the aforesaid authorities. Oxford University condemned certain selected theses as erroneous, false and impious, and voted Pareus' commentary on Romans to be consigned to a public burning, which was accordingly done, as many copies as could be found in booksellers' shops and scholars' libraries being searched for. Cambridge University consigned Bucanus' Commonplaces and [the] *Vindiciae* also to a public burning; and the authors themselves (if the Senate confirmed the proposals put forward, but it was not yet approved when I was in Cambridge) were branded with perpetual infamy. I would have written this before, when it was all new, but I would not have been able to send, along with the Oxford decree I enclose herewith, a copy of the Cambridge one, much more elegant in form, and framed in considerably more bitter language . . . I thought there was in the Cambridge Senate rather more bile directed against those rigid professors of the reformation at Geneva, whether on account of the fact that they hold everything that can be called Puritan in hatred; or because many there are very closely committed to the opinions of the Remonstrants. I was there at the time of the Commencement, at a most splendid public feast, at which more than thirty doctors of Theology, and other knights and nobility were present, where there were the most bitter disputations about predestination, free will, and the other heads of doctrine so greatly controverted among yourselves, some of the company resolutely defending the opinions of the Remonstrants, against Doctor Balcanqual, long since known to you from the time of the Synod of Dort, and others; on which matter, when I expressed astonishment, one or two of the doctors (to whom the Bishop of Winchester had recommended me by letter) told me that they could not tell me which party, the Remonstrants or the Contra-Remonstrants, had more followers in the university. This I afterwards discovered in private conversations to be true in very many particulars. He indeed who is now Vice-Chancellor of the University[28] (a position of great authority here) is extreme in favour of the Remonstrants, as is the man who at his request drew up (certainly most elegantly) the proposal for the Senate,[29] and who was already in close touch with me, gave it to me to read privately, asking me not to make a written copy before he had published it, or to communicate it to anyone, because it was still uncertain whether it would ever be published in such plain language.

[27] Doublet named 'Stephen Junius Brutus' as the probable author, but the book is now attributed to Philippe du Plessis Mornay (1549–1623).

[28] The Vice-Chancellor was Leonard Mawe. In 1623 he was chosen, along with Matthew Wren, to accompany Prince Charles and Buckingham to Spain, and in 1626 took the lead in the campaign to secure Buckingham's election as Chancellor of the university. He was appointed Bishop of Bath and Wells in 1628, but died in 1629. Fuller described him as 'a good scholar, a grave preacher, a mild man, and one of gentle deportment'.

[29] It has not been possible to identify the author of the draft, but according to Harley MS 7038, p. 93, the doctors of theology 'circum circa astantibus' when Pareus' book was publicly burned were (in addition to Mawe), Thomas Comber, Thomas Bainbridge and Elias Travers. It may have been Comber: a fellow of Trinity since 1597, he was skilled in languages, had lived abroad with du Moulin for three years, and followed Mawe as Master of Trinity. He was Vice-Chancellor in 1631 and again in 1636.

Since he asked this as a sincere friend I am unable to reveal anything more about it to you. I cannot conceal . . . that many men are most affectionate towards the name Vossius; as also Balcanqual the Scot, who was at the synod [of Dort], but especially Dr Jerome Beale, the Master of Pembroke, a most learned man, who did me many favours, and wished also, when opportunity offered, that I would convey his affection towards you.

Doublet's account commands conviction, but at the same time implies some significant adjustments to the balance of theological forces previously assumed to have obtained in the two universities in 1622–3. In the first place, very significant support for the Remonstrants can hardly be denied. The sermons of Lucy at Cambridge and Bridges at Oxford, it would appear, represented opinions much more widespread than has usually been supposed. At the same time, predestinarian dispute was only one dimension of a many-faceted polarity, embracing on the one side hostility to Puritanism in all its forms, and to Calvinism in some; and on the other including suspicions of popery, Jesuits,[30] and of the king's foreign policy. Thirdly there were on both sides moderates looking for a middle way; the reality was a spectrum and not merely polarities. It was the moderates above all who looked to Vossius, and it was they whom Doublet mentioned by name. He would appear to have been particularly well informed in linking Jerome Beale and Balcanqual among them, for Beale's election to the mastership of Pembroke had followed a royal message that the fellows should avoid anyone suspected of either 'Arminianism or Puritanism', and Balcanqual had been among Beale's supporters.[31] As theological tensions mounted, it was the moderates who continued to look to Vossius. There had been rumours following the end of the Synod of Dort that James I would offer him a position in England, and in 1624 he was recommended, not by any English 'Arminian' but by William Boswell and Dudley Carleton, for the professorship in history and political science created by Lord Brooke in the University of Cambridge.[32]

Theological polarity was exacerbated by political circumstances. Knight's sermon had been provoked by the negotiations for the Spanish Match. A number of Calvinists found themselves in prison for preaching against

---

[30] Mead, writing about Lucy's sermon, reported the rumour that there were a dozen or fourteen Jesuits at the 1622 Commencement. Birch, *Court and Times of James I*, II. 320.

[31] Beale's candidature had been supported by Lancelot Andrewes, and the royal message came after Beale had been accused of Arminianism by Ralph Brownrigg. Tyacke, *Anti-Calvinists*, 45. I cannot agree with Dr Tyacke that Beale's *private* letters to Samuel Ward in 1629, from 'your ingenuous and true loving friend', amounted to putting Ward 'in the dock'! (ibid., 50–1). On the content of the letters, see below, p. 234 n. 107.

[32] Rademaker, *Vossius*, 226–7. Tyacke makes no reference at all to Vossius' influence in England; Trevor-Roper, who stresses it, describes him simply as an 'Arminian'.

it.[33] The negotiations brutally exposed the shallowness of the king's glib readiness immediately after Dort to exploit militant Protestant polemic.[34] Following Knight's sermon, injunctions were sent to Oxford University on 24 April that students in divinity 'should apply themselves in the first place to the reading of the scriptures, next the councils and ancient fathers, and then the schoolmen, excluding those neoterics, both Jesuits and puritans, who are known to be meddlers in matters of state and monarchy; that thereby they may be the better enabled only to preach Christ crucified, which ought to be the end of their studies'.[35] Matters were made even worse, however, by the release of many popish recusants from prison in order to assist the marriage negotiations. The king sugared the pill by expressing his hopes for a reciprocal release of Protestants in foreign gaols,[36] but his denials that he favoured 'the Romish religion' failed to carry conviction, and further steps were needed to restrain hostile preaching. The preamble to the Directions to Preachers,[37] issued on the king's authority in 1622, claimed that extravagant preaching had always been subject to governmental control, and that of late 'divers young students by reading of late writers and ungrounded divines, do broach many times unprofitable, unsound, seditious and dangerous doctrines, to the scandal of this church, and disquieting of the state and present government'. Preachers under the rank of bishop or dean were told to restrict themselves to the scope of the Articles of Religion and the Homilies; those of afternoon sermons to some part of the Catechism, or a text from the Creed, Ten Commandments or Lord's Prayer. The best course for children was to exercise them in the Catechism, 'which is the most ancient and laudable custom of teaching in the Church of England'. No preacher other than bishops or deans were to 'presume to Preach in any popular auditory the deep points of Predestination, Election, Reprobation, or of the Universality, Efficacy, Resistibility, or Irresistibility of God's Grace; but leave those themes rather to be handled by Learned men, and that Moderately and Modestly by way of Use and Application, rather than by way of Positive Doctrines, being fitter for the schools and univerities than for simple auditories'. Preachers of all ranks were to avoid 'bitter invectives and undecent railing

---

[33] Birch, *Court and Times of James I*, II.10, 256–7. For saying that 'if the king should change the religion he would be the first one to cut his majesty's throat', a 'poor silly fellow' was executed at Winchester in March 1621. Ibid., 233. Andrew Willett was confined for distributing a treatise against the Spanish match. Carleton, *Letters*, II. 140.

[34] CSPD, 1619–23, 49. Letter of George Carleton to Dudley Carleton, 30 May 1619.

[35] The instructions were also sent to Cambridge, but in the Privy Council letter the reference to the schoolmen was quietly dropped, perhaps on the initiative of Archbishop Abbot. A. Milton, 'The Laudians and the Church of Rome, c. 1625–1640', Cambridge University Ph.D. thesis, 1989, 216 n. 109.

[36] Cardwell, *Documentary Annals*, II. 147.

[37] Lambeth Palace Library, MS 943, f. 81.

speeches against the persons of either Papists or Puritans', but were expected 'to free both the doctrine and discipline of the Church of England from the aspersions of either Adversary, especially where the Auditory is suspected to be tainted with the one or the other infection'.[38]

Abbot received the Directions early in August, and issued them to diocesan bishops with a brief covering letter on 12 August. They were ill received[39] as a restraint on preaching, and in a further letter of 4 September the archbishop was obliged to explain the king's reasons for issuing them. Too many defections to popery and Anabaptism were the result, it was claimed, of the addiction of preachers

to a soaring up in points of divinity, too deep for the capacity of the people, or a mustering up of much reading, or a displaying of their own wit, or an ignorant meddling with civil matters . . . or a venting of their own distates, or a smoothing up of those idle fancies which in this blessed time of a long peace do boil in the brains of unadvised people; or lastly, a rude or undecent railing, not against the doctrines, (which when the text shall occasion the same, is not only approved but much commended by his royal majesty) but against the persons of papists and puritans.

The best weapon against both popery and Anabaptism, the king claimed, was the doctrine contained in the Articles of Religion, the two books of Homilies, the lesser and the greater Catechism. That was the 'whole scope' of the doctrine which the Church of England had used to drive out these two enemies in the time of her first reformation. Far from intending to diminish preaching, he hoped the number of sermons would increase, with a better grounding in fundamentals, which were 'more diligently observed in foreign Reformed Churches than in England'.[40]

No one who knew him, certainly none of his diocesan bishops, can have had the slightest doubt of Abbot's distaste for the instructions to preachers, and his inner dissent from the apology he was now obliged to make for them. In a widely circulated but undelivered letter[41] of which he was assumed to be the author he accused the king of betraying the Protestant religion:

By your act you labour to set up that damnable and heretical doctrine of the Church of Rome, the whore of Babylon. How hateful will it be to God, and grievous unto your good subjects, the true professors of the Gospel, that your Majesty, who

[38] Cardwell, *Documentary Annals*, II. 201–2.

[39] Ibid., 203.

[40] Ibid., 204. For John Donne's response, see G. R. Potter and E. M. Simpson (eds.), *Sermons* (10 vols., Berkeley and Los Angeles, 1953–62), IV. 200–1.

[41] Lambeth MS 943, f. 79. Although Abbot assured the king that he was not the author, he never publicly disclaimed the letter, which certainly represented his views. Kenneth Fincham, 'Prelacy and Politics: Archbishop Abbot's Defence of Protestant Orthodoxy', *Historical Research* 61 (February 1988), 59.

hath often disputed and learnedly written against those wicked heresies should now show yourself a patron of those doctrines which your pen has told the world and your conscience tells yourself are superstitious, idolatrous, and detestable. And hereunto what you have done in sending the prince into Spain, without the consent of your Council, the privity and approbation of your people . . . Besides this toleration which you endeavour to set up by your Proclamation, it cannot be done without a Parliament, unless your Majesty will let your subjects see, that you will take unto yourself a liberty to throw down the laws of the land at your pleasure . . . I beseech your Majesty to consider . . . lest . . . your Majesty do not draw upon the kingdom in general, and yourself in particular, God's heavy wrath and indignation.

By contrast, clergy who did not share the archbishop's perspective saw the opportunity of exploiting the changed climate in the interests of their own churchmanship. Harsnett was one. Translated to Norwich in 1619, he was able, with the king's approval, to act against factious preaching among lecturers, and in visitation articles without parallel among Jacobean bishops, he asked whether any lecturers maintained doctrines contrary to the Articles of Religion.[42]

The decline in the political influence of Calvinist clergy was compounded by changes on the episcopal bench in the last years of James's reign. The promotion of John Howson was a snub to the archbishop.[43] The death in particular of James Montagu of Winchester in 1618 (he was succeeded by Andrewes, translated from Ely) removed a powerful Calvinist influence at court.[44] In 1621 John King of London died, to be succeeded by George Mountaigne, and in the same year James was finally persuaded to approve Laud's elevation to St David's. Abbot's loss of political influence dates from 1621, and almost certainly resulted from his diplomatic intrigues in support of Bohemia against the wishes of James I.[45]

Both Rushworth and Heylyn took the Directions to Preachers as a sign of James's conversion to Arminianism.[46] Heylyn even suggests that Laud was their principal architect.[47] More recently, Andrewes has been seen as another influence pushing the king in an 'Arminian' direction.[48] In

---

[42] P. Collinson, *Godly People: Essays on English Protestantism and Puritanism* (1983), 488–9.

[43] Howson was promised the reversion of the bishopric of Oxford in 1617. James I, it seems, had not talked to him before 1615, when he appeared at Greenwich to answer accusations levelled at him by Archbishop Abbot, the failure of which 'landed a bishopric for his opponent'. N. Cranfield and K. Fincham, 'John Howson's Answers to Archbishop Abbot's Accusations at his "Trial" before James I at Greenwich, 10 June, 1615', in Camden Miscellany 29 (1987), 327.

[44] Heylyn, *Cyprianus Anglicus*, 63–4.

[45] Fincham, 'Prelacy and Politics', 52–3.

[46] Rushworth, *Historical Collections*, I. 64–6.

[47] Heylyn, *Cyprianus Anglicus*, 97–9.

[48] Tyacke, *Anti-Calvinists*, 103.

reality, however, James remained as hostile to Arminianism as he had always been. His dislike of the finer points of predestination being aired in popular preaching had been evident at Hampton Court and in his instructions to the British delegation to Dort. Laud had nothing to do with the Directions to Preachers; he was away in Wales, and at this stage had little influence at court.[49] As to Andrewes, the evidence cited is a sermon preached at court in April 1621 in which Andrewes remarked:

I pray God he be well pleased with this licentious touching, nay tossing his decrees of late, this sounding the depths of his judgements with our line and lead, too much presumed upon by some in these days of ours . . . God's secret decrees they have them at their fingers' ends, and can tell you the number and order of them just with 1, 2, 3, 4, 5.[50]

This, we are told, demonstrates Andrewes's anti-Calvinism, on the grounds that he was attacking the 'five articles of Dort'.[51] In fact, of course, the Five Articles were associated with the *Remonstrants*, but Andrewes was referring neither to those articles nor to the Contra-Remonstrant canons of Dort (numbering far more than five though presented, following the Remonstrants' articles, under five general heads). His protest was directed against anyone who presumed to number the divine *decrees*: and that must include Arminius as well as Beza. The mistake, furthermore, misreads Andrewes's temperament; it continued to be 'contrary to his disposition and course to meddle with controversies'.[52] Like James I, he had always disapproved of preaching about predestination; and he refused altogether to speculate about it. They were agreed in wanting to silence Remonstrants and Contra-Remonstrants alike.

The Directions were in fact drawn up by the Lord Keeper, Williams, but their content according to Hacket[53] was 'his Majesty's command', after the Synod of Dort had 'awakened the opposition of divers scholars in our kingdom, who lay still before'. Dismayed that contentions about predestination were disturbing pulpits 'every Sunday', the king had first, says Hacket, tried to reconcile the conflicting parties, but when this failed had 'commanded silence to both sides, or such a moderation as was next to silence'.

It would appear, therefore, that even before Richard Montagu's *New Gagg* had been published, there were powerful forces threatening to tear the English Church apart. Militant Calvinists, neglecting both the

[49] On Laud's whereabouts, see W. Scott and J. Bliss (eds.), *The Works of William Laud*, Anglo-Catholic Library (7 vols., Oxford, 1847–60), III. 139–40.
[50] Andrewes, *Works*, III. 32.
[51] Tyacke, *Anti-Calvinists*, 103.
[52] Carleton, *Letters*, I. 264.
[53] J. Hacket, *Scrinia Reserata: A Memorial offer'd to the Great Deservings of J. Williams . . . Archbishop of York* (1693), I. 89–90.

theological and the political reality, took British attendance at Dort as the signal for a vigorous but what was to prove a decidedly rearguard action. In Cambridge, and probably also in Oxford, the long-standing dislike of many for any kind of Puritanism was reinforced by a powerful reaction in favour of the Remonstrants.[54] To that extent, English 'Arminianism' was already mature by 1622. In the face of those polarities, there can be no question that a number of influential thinkers, Dutch and English, were urging the defusing of controversy and theological reconciliation. Relatively independent issues made their task more difficult. The thrust of James I's foreign policy after the outbreak of the Thirty Years War involved the alienation and isolation of many of his leading churchmen, from Archbishop Abbot down. They detected a fundamental change in the orientation of the court, but their underlying anxiety was far from being limited to the doctrine of predestination, however central that remained for them: it was nothing less than the future of Protestantism as they saw it. Concern about Arminianism was part of a wider concern about popery, and it seemed to offer a promising leverage in a court which had been notable for its hostility to the Remonstrants. The charge could be used by those whose acquaintance with the theology of Arminius or his followers was at best cursory, and there is ample evidence that from early in the 1620s on it was so used, especially by laymen, with those wider connotations very much in mind. Accusations of 'Arminianism', the latest form of 'doctrinal popery', would bring counter-accusations of 'doctrinal puritanism'. New labels sharpened old polarities. Richard Montagu became the focus of the polemical dichotomy.

[54] Doublet's letter to Vossius is compelling evidence of the strength of the reaction in favour of the Remonstrants inside the universities. In so far as there was a 'rise of English Arminianism', this is it! It was not so much a school of theology, or even a clerical 'party', as a phase of the anti-Puritan tradition in the English Church, a relatively short-term but none the less powerful response to a particular combination of circumstances. For other examples of the same phenomenon, typical of seventeenth-century society, see the discussion by Jonathan Scott of the successive phases of mid-century radicalism in *Historical Journal* 31 (1988), 455.

11 A gag for the Gospel?
Richard Montagu and Protestant orthodoxy

ı The *New Gagg*

When Richard Montagu published the *New Gagg*[1] in 1624, he was just short of his fiftieth birthday. He had been at Cambridge in the last decade of the sixteenth century, and the key influence in his theological training was Overall, 'that . . . most accomplished divine, whose memory shall ever be precious with all good and learned men'.[2] From Overall, Montagu had learned to study Scripture with the aid of the Fathers. 'The course of my studies was never addressed to the modern epitomisers; but from my first entrance to the study of divinity, I balked the ordinary and accustomed bypaths . . . and betook myself to *Scripture*, the rule of *Faith*, interpreted by *Antiquity*, the best expositor of Faith and applier of that Rule; holding it a point of discretion to draw water as near as I could, to the well-head, and to spare labour in vain in running further off to cisterns and lakes.'[3]

Just as some of his contemporaries refused to believe that the author of the *New Gagg* had never read a word of Arminius, recent scholars convinced of the novelty of his opinions have suggested Baro, Hemmingsen or Hooker as possible influences.[4] Montagu's Commonplace

---

[1] R. Montagu. *A Gagg for the New Gospell? No. A New Gagg for an Old Goose: or, An Answer to a Late Abridger of Controversies* (1624).

[2] R. Montagu, *Appello Caesarem: A Just Appeal from Two Unjust Informers* (1625), 31.

[3] Ibid., 11f. See also 45f. In his Declaration justifying the approbation of the *Appello Caesarem*, Francis White wrote: 'I have always esteemed . . . that the common tenet of antiquity is the approved doctrine of the Church of England . . . and . . . that in matters dubious and [of] probable opinion, it is [a] safer and better means to preserve unity in religion to adhere to the ancients, where their judgment is uniform or their reasons probable, than to modern and novel divines, who being distracted in opinions, do multiply questions and by subtle and curious disputations make many things of very good use generally before these times established dubious and uncertain, and lay new ground, which sectaries work upon, and wean out of them errors of dangerous consequence.' Bodl. Lib., MS Rawlinson C 573, ff. 23ᵛ–24ʳ.

[4] E.g., Tyacke, 'Debate: The Rise of Arminianism Reconsidered', 207: 'Montagu was just old enough to have picked up some of his theological ideas from other Continental sources during the late 1590s.'

Books,[5] however, makes no references to any of them. The vast majority of the authorities cited are patristic. Pride of place is held by St John Chrysostom, with Gregory of Nazianzus and Basil also prominent; but there are also many appeals to St Augustine's anti-Pelagian writings. The appeal to the church Fathers was not a polemical device, but a first principle of Montagu's theological method. Typically, therefore, in commenting on Romans vii, 18 he mentioned the view of Cassian that the 'beginning of grace is from ourselves', which he then refuted by reference to Prosper's exegesis that Paul here refers to man under the dispensation of grace. Similarly, in his comments on 1 Tim. ii, 4 he noted the interpretation of Chrysostom, and contrasted it with that of St Augustine, and on 2 Thessalonians ii, 3 he noted the view of Basil that the son of perdition is the Devil rather than Antichrist.

Montagu's interest in patristics was reflected both in his circle of friends and in his early career. He had a high regard for Lancelot Andrewes, 'our Gamaliel', as he described him in letters to John Cosin.[6] After Cambridge he moved into the circle of the bibliophile Sir Henry Savile, the Provost of Eton, where he became involved in the project to transform the college into a centre for patristic research and publication to rival Leiden and Paris.[7] Other protégés of Savile were John Hales and Richard Thomson. Montagu's task was to work on Gregory of Nazianzus and St Basil the Great, and the first fruit of his endeavours was an edition of the Invectives of Gregory of Nazianzus against Julian which appeared in 1610.[8] Subsequently, like many of James I's clergy, he became involved in the refutation of papal apologists, first overseeing the publication of Casaubon's answer to Baronius, and then working on a further reply of his own which appeared in 1622.[9]

Montagu had gifts which fitted him to be a polemicist. He was widely read. He had a natural wit and a ready pen. 'Such was the equability of the sharpness of his style he was unpartial therein, be he ancient or modern writer, Papist or Protestant, that stood in his way, they should

---

[5] Montagu's Commonplace Books are in Archbishop Marsh's Library, Dublin. The *Liber Mixtae Theologiae* is shelfmarked Z4:2:10 and the *Notes on the Epistles of St Paul* Z3:1:8. They both have the signature 'R. Montague' on the inside upper cover and on internal evidence appear to have been completed over a long period. Although it is impossible to be certain that all the entries are in Montagu's handwriting, their contents are entirely consistent with the outlook of the *New Gagg*.

[6] *Correspondence of John Cosin*, ed. G. Ornsby, Surtees Society, vols. 52 and 55 (Durham, 1869–72), I. 70.

[7] J. S. Macauley, 'Richard Montague, Caroline Bishop, 1575–1641', Cambridge University Ph.D. thesis, 1964.

[8] R. Montagu, *Sancti Gregorii Nazienzeni in Julianum invectivae duae* (STC 12346, 1610).

[9] Sheila Lambert, 'Richard Montagu, Arminianism and Censorship', *Past and Present* 124 (1989), 43.

all equally taste thereof.'[10] His works were the works of a polemicist, consisting of strings of assertions and counter-arguments, rather than systematic expositions.[11] In spite of his admiration for Overall, Montagu lacked the subtlety and the capacity for logical rigour of an academic theologian. 'To be too wise *in Divinis* often proveth stark folly.'[12] He tended to rely instead on his own compound of pastoral insight and common sense.

Montagu's preoccupation with the defence of the Church of England against Rome meant that he became well read in the controversial writings of the Roman apologists, especially Bellarmine and Becanus. For polemical purposes, he could accept their accounts of what 'Calvinists' or 'Lutherans' believed without being overly concerned with their accuracy or fairness. From the Roman standpoint, too, the existence in England of 'Puritan' doctrines was a commonplace.[13] Montagu readily agreed. He was happy to dissociate the doctrines of the Church of England from those of both 'Calvinists' and 'Puritans'. In his Commonplace Books he noted where the 'Calvinist' interpretation of key New Testament texts was at variance with that of Chrysostom, and under the heading 'Hypocrisy' reflected on a passage of Gregory of Nazianzus which afforded a perfect description of the Puritans.[14]

In 1615 Montagu had become a royal chaplain, and began to move into the circle of clergy surrounding the king. He hoped that by distinguishing himself in the defence of the Church of England against Rome he might win preferment. His first loyalty was to that church, and he referred to the king as 'Nutritius Ecclesiae', 'the sum of our happiness'. It was the king who personally instructed him, after the death of Casaubon, to work on a reply to Baronius.[15] Montagu and the king had much in common as theologians: a strong sense of the appeal to antiquity; a contempt for those who were too much addicted to modern commentators; an impatience with theological niceties; a tendency to cut through complexities with a sturdy common sense; a ready acknowledgement of the fundamentals which Rome and the Church of England had in common; even, it must be said, an inclination to scurrilous asides about Puritans.

---

[10] Fuller, *Church History*, V. 15–16.
[11] V. E. Raymer, 'Durham House and the Emergence of Laudian Piety', Harvard University Ph.D. thesis, 1981, 234–5.
[12] *Correspondence of John Cosin*, I. 34.
[13] 'The world knoweth, there are three kinds of subjects in the realm, the Protestant, the Puritan, and the Catholicly affected . . . Puritanism differing from Protestantism in 32 Articles of doctrine (as their own books and writings bear witness)'. *A Supplication to the King's Most Excellent Majesty: A Plea for Toleration for Catholics* (1604) 3, 46.
[14] *Notes on the Epistles* Ephesians i, and I Tim. ii, 4; *Liber Mixtae Theologiae*, s.v. 'Hypocritia'.
[15] *Correspondence of John Cosin*, I. 21. Macauley, 'Richard Montague', 73.

As Francis White was later able to demonstrate,[16] both the general thrust of Montagu's theology and many of his detailed arguments had been anticipated in the writings of the king himself and in those of theologians known to have his approval. In assuming that Montagu's claim for the king's approval of the *New Gagg* must be false, his opponents were guilty of a serious error of judgment.[17]

Where Montagu's opponents were still obsessed by the supposed political threat from Rome, he and many others were preoccupied by the theological and pastoral threats. The preface to the *New Gagg* described the tactics of papist 'limitors' who frightened Montagu's parishioners at Stanford Rivers with cries of *'Damned Heretics, out of the Church. No Service: no Sacraments: no Ministry: no Faith: no Christ: no Salvation'* — 'terrible shawefowls', Montagu called them, designed to 'scare poor souls that have not the faculty of discovering cheese from chalk'.[18] His anxiety has to be taken seriously. If the Church of England was to succeed in her efforts to win over church papists, and perhaps even more importantly to arrest the trickle of converts to Rome, then she had to find an answer to Roman apologetic on each of those sensitive issues. She had, furthermore, to counter the continuing appeal of ancient patterns of piety, to respond (as Laud, especially, contended) to a widely felt need for order and reverence in the externals of church worship, and to restore (as Laud again believed) the church's dignity as an institution in society at large. This, and not doctrinal innovation, was what gave identity and coherence to the clergy of Durham House.

The *New Gagg* was provoked by John Heigham's *The Gag of the Reformed Gospel*.[19] Heigham had listed no fewer than fifty-two doctrines proclaimed, he alleged, by the Church of England which he undertook to refute 'by express texts from their own approved English Bible'. A few examples will convey the flavour of the whole. 'In matters of faith, we must not rely on the judgment of the Church and of her pastors, but only upon the written word.' 'Apostolical traditions, and ancient customs of the Church (and not found in the written word), are not to be received.' 'That Antichrist shall be a particular man; and that the Pope is Antichrist'. 'That only faith justifieth, and that good works are not absolutely necessary to salvation'. 'That the bread of the Supper, is but a figure or

---

[16] Bodl. Lib., MS Rawlinson C 573. White cited the king's *Apology*, Casaubon's *Letter to Peron*; Bilson's *Perpetual Government of the Church*; Andrewes's *Tortura Torti* and *Responsio ad Apologiam Cardinalis Bellarmini*; and de Dominis' *Ostensio Errorum Francisci Suarez*.

[17] For Montagu's well-justified confidence in the king, see Lambert, 'Richard Montagu, Arminianism and Censorship', 43.

[18] Montagu, *New Gagg*, 'To the Reader' (unpaginated).

[19] John Heigham was the real author of Matthew Kellison, *The Gag of the Reformed Gospel* (Douai, 1623).

remembrance of the body of Christ received by faith, and not his true and very body'. 'That Jesus Christ descended not into hell, nor delivered thence the souls of the Fathers'. 'That the blessing or signing with the sign of the Cross is not founded in Holy Scripture'. 'That it is both superfluous and superstitious to repeat one and the same prayer sundry times'.

The reader will recognize many of these doctrines from what has already been said about *A Christian Letter* and the Hampton Court Conference. Montagu's reply insisted on the moderation of the Church of England on one disputed doctrine after another. Heigham's account of English doctrine was 'raked together out of the lay stalls of deepest Puritanism, as much opposing the Church of England as the Church of Rome'.[20] His account reflected, naturally, Catholic rather than Protestant priorities: the role of the saints merited six chapters; predestination and perseverance only one each. Montagu's reply mirrored those priorities. If Arminianism involved a preoccupation with predestination, then the *New Gagg* was certainly not Arminian. What he did have to say on predestination was nevertheless soon subjected to the closest scrutiny.

Heigham had raised the question of perseverance. According to the Church of England, he claimed, 'faith once had cannot be lost'. Montagu denied it. Opinions varied. He granted that 'some' restricted justifying faith to the elect, but it was not the doctrine of the Church of England, or of all Protestants. The question was in any event 'fitter for the schools than for popular discourses'.

That faith once had . . . cannot be lost, may be interpreted, and is, more ways than one. Whether not lost at all, whether totally or finally lost. Men are divided in this tenent. Some suppose neither totally nor finally; some totally but not finally; some both totally and finally; which is indeed the assertion of Antiquity and your school . . . I determine nothing in this question positively, which the Church of England leaveth at liberty unto us, though the learned in the Church of England assent unto antiquity.[21]

Even Calvinists were divided on the matter, Montagu claimed, and total and final falling the 'Protestants of Germany maintain at this day'.

He took a similar line on the question of the divine decrees. Accurately, but unpalatably, he pointed to the disputes on the doctrine among papists as well as Protestants. All of them acknowledged that the decrees were eternal, and therefore inevitable. The point of dispute, which Heigham had failed to identify, was whether they were *irrespective*.

Some Protestants, and no more but some, have considered God, for this effect of his will, in reference to Peter and Judas, thus; that Peter was saved,

[20] Montagu, *New Gagg*, 'To the Reader', sig. 2ᵛ.
[21] Ibid., 157–8.

because that God would have him saved absolutely; and resolved to save him necessarily, because he would so, and no further; that Judas was damned as necessarily, because that God, as absolute to decree, as omnipotent to effect, did primarily so resolve concerning him, and so determine touching him, without respect of anything but his own will; insomuch that Peter could not perish, though he would; nor Judas be saved, do what he could. This is not the doctrine of Protestants: the Lutherans in Germany detest and abhor it. It is the private fancy of some men I grant . . . The Church of England hath not taught it, doth not believe it, hath opposed it; wisely contenting herself with this qualification and limitation Art. 17. *We must receive God's promises as they be generally set forth unto us in Holy Scripture*; and not presuming to determine of when, how, wherefore or whom; secrets reserved to God alone.[22]

A broader issue, but related to predestination, was the question of free will. Heigham had accused the Church of England of teaching that as a result of the Fall man had lost free will altogether. Montagu answered that this question too was one 'of obscurity', like predestination itself a matter of debate within the papist schools as among Protestants.

In conclusion, the condition of man since the fall of Adam is such that he cannot turn, nor prepare himself to God, by or through his own natural or human power and strength. This is the doctrine of the Church of England. Prevented by grace, and assisted therewith, he then putteth his hand to procure augmentation of that grace, and continuance to the end. No man cometh unto God, but he is drawn. Drawn, he runneth or walketh, as his assistance is, and his own agility and disposition to the end . . . And the wisdom of the Church hath not ventured far, to put a tie of obedience upon men's belief, in points of inextricable obscurity almost, of concordance in working of Grace, and Predestination, and Free-will.[23]

Heigham would have done better to omit the question, the differences of opinion 'hanging on such niceties'.

Among the chapters on predestination, it was Montagu's remarks on the doctrine of perseverance that aroused most hostility. His disclaimer of any definite views was widely regarded as a mere evasion.[24] Nevertheless, the doctrine he defended (that justifying faith was not confined to the elect) had been accepted by the British delegates to Dort as that held by many of the 'learned' within the Reformed churches. Of course some Calvinists were offended by his assertion that the Church of England left the question open, but in this he was surely correct, and the British delegates to Dort had admitted as much. It was going much too far,

---

[22] Ibid., 179.
[23] Ibid., 110.
[24] 'He said indeed he suspended his determination of the question; but to what purpose, when he said it was the assertion of Antiquity to which he everywhere subscribed?' Huntington Library, Ellesmere MS 6878 35 B/14. I am indebted to Dr Kevin Sharpe for letting me have a photocopy of this manuscript, which is an examination of the Information against Montagu, and of his defence, signed J.A.(?). It has so far not been possible to identify the writer.

however, to deny that the interpretation of antiquity, and especially of St Augustine, was disputed: there were many 'learned' in the Church of England – more learned, indeed, than Montagu – who held differently.[25]

There was less to object to in his treatment of the divine decrees. Certainly, he believed that the primary divine purpose was the communication of His own goodness.[26] The Fall of man in Adam was the result of his own free will, having been created as changeably good in the image of God.[27] Predestination to life was the work of God to draw out of misery those who will take hold of His mercy. The charge of Arminianism depended on the inference that because both the Lutherans and the Church of England rejected an irrespective decree, they agreed in holding election to be conditional on faith foreseen.[28] But that is not what Montagu says.[29] On the contrary, he stressed that the Church of England (in Article XVII) holds the decree to be *secret*. His purpose, like that of Andrewes, was not to offer an alternative theory of election, but to discourage what he regarded as illegitimate speculation upon it.[30] The distinction between inevitability (which preserved God's foreknowledge and omnipotence) and necessity (with its implication of a fatalistic annihilation of the will) was widely accepted, even among 'Calvinists'. Finally, it must be repeated, few mainstream Calvinists now insisted on irrespective predestination:[31] they far more commonly said that it was a mere anti-Calvinist calumny, and went on to argue that God appoints means to the fulfilment of the decree. Montagu can also be defended on the question of free will, where his treatment was provocative only to those who liked to think that all papists were Pelagians, and for whom any commendation of the Council of Trent was a sign of heresy.

---

[25] In the *Appello Caesarem*, Montagu spoke more circumspectly.

[26] Ibid., 62; see also Commonplace Book, s.v. 'Praedestinatio'.

[27] Ibid., 62–3; see also Commonplace Book s.v. 'Lapsus Adami'.

[28] As J. A. pointed out, it was the 'pseudo-Lutherans' rather than the Lutherans who so held. Ellesmere MS 6878 35 B/14.

[29] 'Herein Mr Mount. will not contend that the Church of England consents with the Lutherans; although he doth say both reject the irrespective decree . . . the Informers were too rash to deduce out of Mr Mount a consent in the point; though he had said that both disclaim the doctrine of the Calvinists.' Ellesmere MS 6878 35 B 14. 'As for consent with the Lutherans, I do nowhere declare it', Montagu, *Appello Caesarem*, 47.

[30] Buckeridge made the same point in his funeral sermon preached after the accession of Charles I. Raymer, 'Durham House', 154.

[31] White cited Robert Abbot's comment ('perilous, pernicious, truculent, novel, to be abhorred, repugnant to wholesome verity, the seminary of direful contention') and the Suffrage of the British delegation to Dort. 'Wherefore I am persuaded Mr M hath not exceeded in defacing this dangerous opinion of absolute reprobation, and I heartily desire our holy Mother the Church of England not to suffer such pestilent weeds either apertly or covertly to spring up in the Lord's harvest.' Bodl. Lib., MS Rawlinson C 573, ff. 31ᵛ–35ʳ.

Of course there were wider issues. Although Montagu was ready to distinguish between 'sound Calvinist doctrines' and 'mere opinions, or Genevan chaff' (and he blamed the 'unlettered dolt' Heigham for his failure to do so),[32] he took the teaching of Calvin to be irrelevant to the Church of England. His recognition of the differences amongst Protestants and cavalier dismissal of all extreme positions as 'Puritan' were unpalatable to those who liked to see their faith as homogeneous with that of the continental Reformed churches. His very moderation on the doctrinal issue of predestination[33] was provocative to those who piety involved, in the tradition represented above all by William Perkins, an intense speculation on the psychology even more than on the theology of election. The general orientation of his theology reflected fundamental differences of outlook between him and his opponents. His letters to his friend John Cosin demonstrate, even when allowance is made for the indiscretions of a private correspondence, a highly polarized churchmanship and a hostility to Puritanism which turned to paranoia as the public attack on the *New Gagg* gathered pace. Prideaux at Oxford, together with the archbishop's chaplains Featley and Goad, figure prominently among his *bêtes noires*. As his opponents drove to one extreme, he fled to the other. They feared an influx of Arminians to replace vacancies among the bishops; he was terrified that the church was about to be 'swallowed up with a Puritan Bishopriqry'. They threatened that he would be forced to recant; he told Cosin that 'before God it will never be well till we have our Inquisition', and wished that the king could be persuaded 'to take strict order that these Allobrogical doormice should not so much as peep out in corners or by owl-light'.[34]

Montagu had been the target of political hostility since 1621, when he had been 'threatened' in Parliament over his reply to Selden's history of tithes.[35] His enemies were given further ammunition by the publication early in 1624 of a reply to de Dominis on the invocation of Saints.[36] The Parliament of 1624 met early in February, just as Montagu was instructing Cosin to correct the errors in the printer's copy of the *New Gagg* that was to go to the king. The parliamentary attack on Montagu came late

[32] Macauley, 'Richard Montague', 192.
[33] For Montagu's resolve not to depart from the 'middle way', see *Correspondence of John Cosin*, I. 39, 56 ('I . . . will neither favour Arm[inianism], nor patronise Calv[inism] . . .') and 125. Cf. *Appello Caesarem*, 104–5: 'truth is ever in the midst betwixt two extremes'.
[34] *Correspondence of John Cosin*, I. 22, 50. For a wider consideration of Montagu's churchmanship, see Raymer, 'Durham House', 89–109, 234–68.
[35] Lambert, 'Richard Montagu, Arminianism and Censorship', 45.
[36] R. Montagu, *Immediate Address unto God alone: First delivered in a Sermon before his Maiestie at Windsor, since Revised and Inlarged to a Just Treatise of Invocations of Saints* (1624).

in April when a petition was submitted to the House of Commons, emanating from John Yates and Nathaniel Ward, supported by an 'information' of twenty-one articles listing Montagu's doctrinal errors.[37]

Although in the Commons it was claimed that Lindsell and Cosin had licensed the *New Gagg*, the truth (however unpalatable to Montagu's enemies) was that James I had endorsed the book from the start.[38] It is equally clear that the parliamentary campaign against him was orchestrated by Archbishop Abbot.[39] When summoned by the archbishop, Montagu went only on the king's command, and it was the king who then undermined Abbot's attempt[40] to persuade Montagu to produce a revised edition from which all that gave offence had been removed.[41] Instead, he wrote the provocative but appropriately entitled *Appello Caesarem*. 'I were too ungrateful if I did not adventure *extremum potentiae* for the Church, having such encouragement at my Sovereign's hand.'[42] In the original manuscript there was much naming of names so that the king should know the full extent of the Puritan mafia bent on Montagu's destruction.[43] Montagu left it to Cosin to decide what to omit, and also if anything should be added: and the printed version includes several passages which refer to Montagu in the third person for which Cosin is almost certainly responsible.[44] Although Prynne blamed Laud for the appearance of the *Appello*,[45] he was markedly cool to Montagu;[46] Andrewes also failed to 'open his mouth and speak out';[47] even Neile, 'the only true and real friend the Church hath of your rank', appeared reluctant to enter the lists.[48] Buckeridge uncharacteristically on this occasion seems to have applied a spur,[49] but he was the only bishop who did. It was, however,

---

[37] Tyacke, *Anti-Calvinists*, chap. 6, esp. 147–8. See also Gardiner's account in *History of England*, vi.

[38] *Debates in the House of Commons, 1625*, ed. S. R. Gardiner, Camden Society, NS 6 (1873), 46; Lambert, 'Richard Montagu, Arminianism and Censorship', 43–6; for varying degrees of reluctance to accept the evidence, see n. 25.

[39] Lambert, 'Richard Montagu, Arminianism and Censorship', 46.

[40] The king had told him 'that he needed not to review it unless he would', and then later, when Montagu was accused of popery, had sworn 'By God, if this be Popery I am a Papist'. Gardiner, *Debates in the House of Commons, 1625*, 46, 35.

[41] Montagu had been prepared at that stage for Morton to review it. *Correspondence of John Cosin*, I. 35.

[42] Ibid., 21.

[43] Ibid., 34, 27f.

[44] Ibid., introduction, ccxiii, and 43, 66.

[45] Prynne, *Canterburies Doome*, 157; cf. Heylyn, *Cyprianus Anglicus*, 125f. Laud 'countenanced it not'. Laud, *Works*, iv. 289.

[46] As Montagu recognized, *Correspondence of John Cosin*, I. 24: 'I hope to see him one day where he will both do and say for the Church. Interim if someways he concede I blame him not. *Dulce est desipere in loco.*'

[47] Ibid., 70, 74.

[48] Ibid., 33, 46, 84.

[49] Ibid., 76.

the king himself who decided that it should be published, and a reluctant Francis White was instructed to look it over and affix his approbation to the book.[50] On the advice of that 'timorsome Dean', as Montagu described him, passages were added from Perkins and others.[51] If White hoped to disarm Montagu's opponents, the effects of the quotations were spoilt by the author's own additions: 'thus your own dictators', 'thus Calvin, the founder of your fancies'.[52] Unfortunately for Montagu, James died before the book was published, and it was Charles who was left to salvage what he could of peace in his church.

The York House Conference

Pressure from Montagu's opponents, and especially from the Earl of Warwick and Lord Saye, persuaded Buckingham to allow the case against him to be debated at York House early in 1626. Thomas Morton, Bishop of Coventry and Lichfield, and John Preston[53] were engaged to present it. Montagu himself was represented by Buckeridge, Francis White and John Cosin. The discussion was conducted in the presence of a number of lay lords, notable among whom were the Lord Chamberlain, the Earl of Pembroke, and James Hay, the Earl of Carlisle.

The conference began without either Montagu himself or Preston present. To judge by the account of the first session compiled afterwards by White and Cosin,[54] Morton made a poor showing. In part this was the result of the extreme charges he attempted to prove. Montagu was guilty of 'heresies and blasphemies', he had abused authority, uttered treason, 'rejected and vilified' various writings of King James, opposed the articles and religion of the Church of England, overthrown 'the whole Gospel of Jesus Christ', and finally 'opened a great gap for popery to be brought in'. Morton made no mention of Arminianism.[55]

On one issue after another Morton found himself defending positions which, if they had not been altogether repudiated, at least no longer represented mainstream English Protestantism. The first charge concerned the doctrine of Antichrist. Buckeridge pointed out that the Church of England had not pronounced upon the issue, and Morton was reluctantly obliged to drop it.[56] The importance he attached to it was in truth

---

[50] Montagu, *Appello Caesarem*, sig. A4ᵛ, dated 15 February 1625.
[51] *Correspondence of John Cosin*, I. 51, 54.
[52] Montagu, *Appello Caesarem*, 51.
[53] Thomas Ball, *The Life of the renowned Dr Preston . . . writ in the year 1628*, ed. E. W. Harcourt (Oxford, 1885), 118–19.
[54] Not, however, published until it appeared in *The Works of John Cosin*, ed. J. Sansom, Anglo-Catholic Library (5 vols., Oxford, 1843–55), II. 1–81.
[55] Ibid., 21.
[56] Ibid., 23.

beginning to look outdated. Although the French had recently asserted it,[57] the doctrine no longer loomed so large as it had in the Elizabethan period:[58] James I himself had granted that it was 'not a matter of faith',[59] and the British delegates to Dort had urged that it should not be incorporated in the synodical canons.

Similarly, in attempting to demonstrate Montagu's departure from Article XXI of the Thirty-nine in arguing that 'a true and lawful General Council never did err', Morton found himself obliged to defend a significantly wider conception of fundamental doctrine than proved acceptable to his hearers. Montagu's underlying assertion, that there was no difference between the Church of Rome and that of England in 'fundamentals', was one with which James I concurred.[60] Montagu had in any event made it clear that he acknowledged only the four 'true and lawful' Councils accepted as binding by both Elizabethan statute and by James I.[61]

Morton then turned to the doctrine of justification, and claimed that Montagu's explanation of it was contrary to the 11th Article, tending to the popish doctrine of good works. White and Cosin had no difficulty in exposing the weakness of the charge. Montagu's exposition was unimpeachable by Lutheran standards, or even by Robert Abbot's. The words Morton complained of were from the *New Gagg*:[62]

In the first signification then of justification we acknowledge instrumentally faith alone and causally God alone; in the second and third, besides God and faith, we yield to hope and holiness and sanctification, and the fruits of the Spirit in good works. But both these are not justification, rather fruits and consequences, and effects or appendants of justification, than justification, which is a solitary act.

Montagu had gone on to argue, along standard Protestant lines, that in justification in the larger sense *fides* was *sola* but not *solitaria* and that St Paul did not deny works to the regenerate or St James deny the act

---

[57] Ibid., 80.
[58] Even under Elizabeth, formal assent to the doctrine concealed fundamental disagreement on its importance. P. Lake, 'The Significance of the Elizabethan Identification of the Pope as Antichrist', *Journal of Ecclesiastical History* 31/2 (1980), 161–78. Montagu appealed to Jewel in support of his opinion.
[59] John Williams, Lady Margaret Professor of Divinity at Oxford from 1594 until his death in 1613, had long before denied publicly that the Pope was Antichrist, and when in the course of Howson's 'trial' of 1615 George Abbot had adduced this to demonstrate his popish affections, James responded 'that is no point of popery'. PRO, SP 14/80/113, f. 120. In 1582, John Prince, of New College, Oxford, entered *Prima Demonstratio quod Papa non sit Antichristus ille insignis* at the Stationers' Company, but STC has no corresponding entry. *A Transcript of the Registers of the Company of Stationers, 1554–1640*, ed. E. Arber (5 vols., 1875–94), II. 191.
[60] Ibid., 78.
[61] Ibid., 27–8.
[62] Montagu, *New Gagg*, 148.

of faith, and had concluded his exposition by reference to the 12th Article with the words '*justus factus* through the grace of Christ is *justus declaratus* by his holy life and conversation'. This was all so routine that Morton can scarcely have hoped to demonstrate otherwise. As Carlisle commented, 'If this be not good divinity, why do you preach good life?'[63]

Morton tried again by accusing Montagu of having taught that we get to heaven by our own deservings. Montagu had explicitly repudiated that doctrine.[64] At this point Pembroke began to display his impatience with the bishop. What had given offence was the passage 'The good go to the enjoying of happiness without end, the wicked to enduring of torments everlasting. Thus is their state diversified to their deserving.'[65] With the sole exception of Saye ('the word deserving is very offensive unto a right believer and a sound Protestant'),[66] the peers agreed that the words were the very words of Scripture. There was all the difference in the world between *per opera* and *propter opera*. Pembroke concluded that the objection was a very poor one: 'My lord bishop, you stretch and wrest a well-meaning man's words too far.'[67] Extreme solifidianism had never been part of the Protestant mainstream, and it is hard to believe that Morton can have had any real confidence in his own espousal of Saye's doctrinal puritanism.

A similar result followed when Morton alleged that Montagu had written that the Church of Rome 'hath continued in the right doctrine of the sacraments'. In fact, as White pointed out, this omitted the crucial words 'instituted by God'. According to Morton, the Church of Rome acknowledged seven, the Church of England only two. But Cosin knew his Catechism better. 'Two only, as generally necessary to salvation', he quoted.[68] In a wider sense the Church of England recognized others, as he was able to demonstrate, to Morton's embarrassment, from other places in the Prayer Book.[69] At this point it was agreed that Montagu himself ought to be heard, but Pembroke was clearly unimpressed with the case against him, and as far as Buckingham was concerned the session was at an end. 'If these be the greatest matters you be grieved with, I can see no reason but Mr Montagu should be defended.'[70]

---

[63] *The Works of John Cosin*, II. 31.
[64] Montagu, *Appello Caesarem*, 206.
[65] Ibid., 233.
[66] *The Works of John Cosin*, II. 31.
[67] Ibid., 52.
[68] Ibid., 34.
[69] Ibid., 55. The Informers had objected that Montagu had acknowledged ordination to be a sacrament. 'J.A.' commented; '[They] do but trifle here out of prejudice; and they are too straight-laced. For we may, with Mr Montague, call it a Sacrament Improper, and less necessary to salvation.' Ellesmere MS 6878 35 B/14.
[70] *The Works of John Cosin*, II. 35.

It was not until then that the matter of predestination was raised. Saye interjected that they had not discussed the 'chiefest matter of all', namely falling from grace, and the definitions of the Synod of Dort against the Arminians. White tried to pre-empt further argument by suggesting that Montagu had not resolved the question either way, but in the discussion that followed[71] it was Morton's doctrine that was made, paradoxically, to look the more popish. When White asked whether a man who is justified and who remained unrepentant after committing a foul sin remained still in a state of justification, Morton at first denied that he was ever justified, but granting the hypothesis (as in the case of David), his answer was 'yes'. Under pressure from Buckeridge, he tried to distinguish between justification and remission of sins, so that 'a man may be justified, though he be not actually justified'. As White pointed out, the Protestant doctrine was that there was no justification which was not actual, habitual justification being a popish error. Morton corrected himself. What he really meant was that the man was justified on the part of God, but not for his own part. That was scarcely an improvement. Again, it was Protestant (indeed Calvinist) doctrine that there was no justification which was not applied. Morton persisted. 'He was justified in the sight of God, by the grace of predestination and election.' But that, said Buckeridge, was tantamount to saying that God could not see any sin in the elect, and White added that if God's predestination always made man in a state of justification, then 'St Paul was a justified man when he was knocking out St Stephen's brains.' God's predestination was His eternal purpose that things should be done in time, and what was done in time could have no temporal existence until it was done. And what good would follow from a doctrine that taught men that once they had been in a state of grace and justification, they could assure themselves of remaining in that state by the operation of a grace of predestination conceived always to remain in them? 'Teach you this divinity?' Buckingham asked Morton, 'God defend us from following it', and Pembroke and Carlisle added that as far as they could see it was 'a most pernicious doctrine, and unfit for any people to hear'.[72]

Only at this stage did Preston, who had arrived late, offer to 'make the matter as clear and evident as it might be'.[73] Such sins did indeed, he conceded, make 'a forfeiture of their interest into the hands of God, and he might take the seizure if he pleased', but once a son, always a son. He denied the imputation of antinomianism: the 'seed of God' remained

---

[71] Ibid., 35f., 57–8.
[72] Ibid., 59.
[73] Ibid. Bodl. Lib., MS Tanner 303 has a rival account of the exchanges which followed Preston's belated arrival 'related by him, or one of his own partisans'.

in sinning sons, 'as in water there remains a principle of cold even when it boils over'. Otherwise, we would be perpetually in and out of sonship, and could have 'neither certainty or comfort in our estate'.[74] The warnings in the New Testament about having no inheritance in the kingdom of God were meant of those 'who never were sons', however much they might seem to be.[75]

What, then, of the Catechism, according to which in baptism we are 'made sons of God, and the heirs of everlasting life'? 'That's but the judgment of charity', said Saye; 'and we say so, because we know nothing to the contrary', added Morton.[76] Baptism, he claimed, was a sign not of a present, but of what it was hoped would be a future event.[77] Cosin reminded him of the words in the Prayer Book order of baptism: 'Doubt ye not, therefore, but earnestly believe that He hath received this present infant, and that he hath made him a partaker of his everlasting kingdom.' It was the Catholic faith, White reminded him, that all infants baptized were regenerated and received remission of original sin.[78] Carlisle told Morton that 'he had much disparaged his own ministry, and did not only dishonour the Church of England, but also debase the Sacrament'.[79]

A week later there was a further meeting.[80] This time Montagu himself attended. While Morton now steered altogether clear of predestinarian doctrine, Preston talked of little else. His record is of considerable interest in demonstrating how far he had been left behind by the adjustments made to the moderate English Calvinist position evident at Dort. Yet paradoxically, of the three parties to the discussion he seems to have known most about Arminianism; and judging by his version, Montagu certainly knew least. Acknowledging that White was not vulnerable on the issue, Preston attempted to demonstrate that Montagu had taught election *ex praevisa fide*.[81] His evidence was the passage in the *New Gagg* which denied that the doctrine of irrespective predestination was taught by the Church of England, together with Montagu's attempt to explain himself in the *Appello Caesarem:*

---

[74] Ball, *Life of Preston*, 119–22.
[75] Cosin, *Works*, II. 37, 61.
[76] Ibid., 61; cf. 37.
[77] Morton's doctrine was not that of William Whitaker, who insisted 'infants are baptized, not to make them the children of Abraham, but because they are the children of Abraham'. G. W. Bromiley, *Baptism and the Anglican Reformers* (1953), 203.
[78] Cosin, *Works*, II. 37.
[79] Ibid., 62.
[80] Cosin provides only a summary of this second meeting. *Works of Cosin*, II. 73–4, Ball's version in his *Life of Preston*, 123–41, based on British Library, Harley MS 6866, and Burney MS 362.
[81] Harley MS 6866, fo. 77^{r-v}.

There must needs first be a disproportion, before there can be conceived election or dereliction; unto which we are now come in the mass of perdition, as they call it wherein all alike being plunged actually, God passeth by, looketh on, considereth intuitively, once, at once, *singulos generum, genera singulorum*, in that very woeful plight, and out of his mercy, in his love, *motu mero* not otherwise stretched out to them deliverance in a Mediator, the man Jesus Christ, and drew them out that took hold of mercy, leaving them there that would none of him; there, whither they had fallen of *themselves*; not whereinto He had thrown them headlong, out of his mere irrespective will, because he would; through his absolute power, because he could; with the irresistible necessity of an inevitable decree, creating them to perish everlastingly. This is enough absolutely, to free and acquit God from being Author of Sin, which he so detesteth, or Author of Death, which he made not, to which he is an enemy, being Life, and from being Author of destruction, which is merely of ourselves; he being *Pater misericordiarum*, and wholly, freely, and desiredly, giving, procuring, effecting our salvation day by day. If this be Arminianism, *esto*. I must profess it.[82]

In the discussion which followed, White challenged Preston to assert irrespective reprobation, and Preston countered by charging Montagu with the assertion of conditional election. According to Preston, White at this point left Montagu to answer for himself, and a nonplussed Montagu beat a hasty retreat.[83] He was obliged to admit that he had gone too far in asserting that the Church of England had determined against irrespective election. He is said to have confessed:

indeed he had not considered some things set down by him in these points of Arminianism whom he had not read. Neither did he think that this book which he had written somewhat negligently against an adversary should be brought to so strict an examination by friends, and that he would write a book to the contrary to explain himself better, and that he would do it with butter and honey. To which one of the lords replied, 'it is indeed better so, than to write in gall and vinegar as you have done the former'.

[82] Montagu, *Appello Caesarem*, 64–5. Preston cited the *New Gagg*, 179 as evidence 'that he holds election out of foresight, or to be a respective conditional decree', and *Appello Caesarem*, 58, which denied 'that absolute irrespective decree of God's to save Peter infallibly, without any consideration had to his faith, obedience and repentance'. In his memorandum for Andrewes, White defended Montagu's account by making the distinction between 'election to grace', which was irrespective of faith and obedience, and 'election to glory', for which they were both necessary. 'But even if in treating predestination to glory [he] has not satisfied all men, and if other divines can make the point more clear, he entreateth them not to be over-rigid in censuring him . . . and if they reject absolute predestination both in word and consequence he intendeth not to be contentious in the other passage which concerneth the order of election.' Bodl. Lib., MS Rawlinson C 573, f. 36r–v. 'J.A.', by contrast, thought that Montagu had made clear his rejection of election *ex praevisa fide* by his reference to the use of means. 'The Informers were too rash to deduce . . . a consent in the point.' Ellesmere MS 6878 35 B/14 on the basis of *Appello Caesarem*, 74.

[83] British Library, Harley MS 6866, f. 78r–v. Cf. Ball, *Life of Preston*, 130.

As to Arminianism, therefore (as one of the lords promptly observed), 'Dr White disclaimed it, and Mr Montagu retracted it.'[84]

Yet it was not quite game, set and match to Preston. When 'one of the lords' repeated that many desired to see the decisions of Dort brought in, and White opposed it, Preston offered to defend any of its canons White chose to attack. He was immediately challenged on the extent of the Atonement. Preston's response was in turn to ask White[85] if he placed the decree to offer Christ to all before the decrees of election and reprobation or after them. When White answered 'Before', Preston turned to the lords for confirmation that to hold the doctrine of universal redemption was tantamount to Pelagianism.[86] He himself made clear his contrary view of the order of the decrees. He denied any intention to save reprobates; the most he would concede was to make them '*salvabiles* in regard to the sufficiency of Christ's death, though they be not *salvabiles* in regard to their inability to apprehend it'.[87] It was a merely cosmetic adjustment to the doctrine of limited Atonement. Preston's doctrine was no longer typical of English Calvinism.

There was no one present at York House to play the role of James I at Hampton Court, and to offer theological bridges between the polarized stances on display. A notable example is the discussion on falling from grace, which repeats the argument at Hampton Court without anyone interposing to remind the company that they were all agreed on the need for repentance. There was no cleric of the subtlety of Davenant to state a moderate Calvinist position. Of the laymen present, it is clear that only Coke and Saye took the charge of Arminianism seriously, and their final references to Dort cut no ice with either Pembroke or Carlisle: 'in England we have a rule of our own'.[88] If the historian wishes to identify the lay English Protestant mainstream, Pembroke is undoubtedly a better model than Saye.

The defence of 'orthodoxy'

The extensive publications of 1626 provoked by the *Appello Caesarem* confirm the evidence of York House that for many Protestants the concern about Montagu far transcended the issue of predestination. Anthony Wotton[89] listed eighteen points of popery as opposed to two points of

[84] Harley MS 6866, f. 78[v].
[85] Ibid. In the margin is written 'for this is the touchstone to know whether it be Arminius's opinion or no as they know who are acquainted with these controversies'.
[86] Harley MS 6866, f. 79[v].
[87] Ibid., f. 80[v].
[88] Cosin, *Works*, II. 38, 64.
[89] A. Wotton, *A Dangerous Plot Discovered . . . wherein is proved that R. Mountague . . . laboureth to bring in the Faith of Rome and Arminius* (1626).

Arminianism. Matthew Sutcliffe similarly described the book as a 'mountain of Popish heresy' and compared Montagu to de Dominis in his efforts 'to lessen controversies and compose matters between the Pope and us'.[90] George Carleton was another who saw Rome as the real issue: as he wrote to his cousin, he was sure 'that either England must fall or Rome must fall in the end . . . In diverse places the doctrine of general grace is published in such confidence as if it were the doctrine of the Church of England.' Carleton wanted the Dort canons, together with the Lambeth Articles, adopted as official formularies.[91] In his published reply to Montagu[92] he was nevertheless prepared to be magnanimous. 'I think the author of the Appeal is a young scholar of the Arminian school and did not well foresee these consequences, but from the grounds that he hath laid, these things must follow . . . He follows the same course as the Pelagians whether wittingly or as I rather think unwittingly.'[93]

Another writer who accepted the equation between Arminianism and Pelagianism was Daniel Featley. He published a table of Pelagian and semi-Pelagian errors,[94] but charged Montagu only with 'demi-Pelagianism', based upon 'his slight and dilute purgation from the aspersions of Arminianism', his alleged defence of Arminius, 'his casting a blur upon the Synod of Dort that blasted them', and his disparaging of the Lambeth Articles.[95] Montagu's errors were more of omission than of commission, but Featley doubted whether Montagu was telling the truth when he asserted that he had not read Arminius; perhaps he 'may have heard all Arminius read over to him'. In any event Montagu's errors were popish as well as Arminian, and to some extent a mixture of the two. Featley took the oppor-

---

[90] M. Sutcliffe, *A Brief Censure upon an Appeal to Caesar* (1626) (STC 18032). British Library copy, p. 9. All surviving copies are imperfect. The attribution to Sutcliffe rests on the *Diary of John Rous*, ed. M. A. E. Green, Camden Society, 66 (1856), 5. The editor wrongly identifies it as the *Unmasking of a Mass-monger, or a vindication of St Augustine's Confessions from the calumnies of a late Apostate*. Featley also made the comparison with de Dominis. *A Second Parallel, together with a writ of Error sued against the Appealer* (1626).

[91] PRO, SP 14/16/9, in a letter to Dudley Carleton of May 1624. Seven years earlier, before going to Dort, he had written to ask the truth of a report that as Arminius was writing a book, 'his right hand rotted, and so he died'. CSPD., 1611–18, 489.

[92] G. Carleton, *An Examination of those Things wherein the author of the Late Appeale holdeth the Doctrines of the Pelagians and Arminians to be the Doctrines of the Church of England* (1626).

[93] Ibid., esp. 2–3, 14–15, 50–1.

[94] D. Featley, *Pelagius Redivivus, or Pelagius raked out of the ashes of Arminius and his schollers* (1626). Also in Latin.

[95] D. Featley, *A Second Parallel*. In *A Parallel of New-Old Pelagiarminian Error* (1626), part of the original *Pelagius Redivivus*, demi-Pelagianism was identified as consisting of the doctrines that election is from foreseen faith; the number of the elect uncertain (Grevinchovius is quoted); the universality of grace and calling; works of preparation; the will's freedom in conversion; and impugning perseverance.

tunity to deny that James I had ever turned Arminian, and asserted that a month before his death, when he had first seen a book by Arminius, he soon 'discovered it to be no better than a half-faced groat of the Semi-pelagian alloy . . . and forthwith stabbed it through with his royal pen'.[96]

The theology of James I was also a preoccupation of Francis Rous.[97] Rous's emphasis, however, was not on the king's Calvinism but on his true Catholicity. He quoted the schoolmen as well as the Reformers; Francis White alongside Thomas Rogers; and Cassander and Corro in addition to the Declaration against Vorstius, in his highly eclectic and, on the whole, moderate exposition of the doctrine of predestination. He even spoke approvingly of Overall and Hooker. His attack on Montagu was only by implication, and he made no effort to confront difficult issues like the relationship between election, justification, regeneration and sanctification, which were at the heart of the theological debate. In a polemical appendix, however, Rous voiced his concern that clergy and papists were secretly fomenting religious division by bringing in 'Arminianism'. He offered no doctrinal analysis. It was called 'a kind of twilight and a double-faced thing that looks to two religions at once'. It was 'like a flying fish'. The religious division it caused 'almost forfeited the Low Countries to the Spaniard'. The danger was that England will 'lose religion, land and all'.[98] It is hard to resist the conclusion that both Featley's and Rous's writings were designed primarily to support the parliamentary campaign against Montagu: for success, moderate opinion needed theological reassurance, and hostile opinion a diet of anti-popish and anti-Pelagian prejudice.

Of course, these writers had to allay suspicions of their own 'doctrinal puritanism'. Montagu's addiction to the concept rankled. Carleton spoke for many in his reluctance to accept that there were doctrinal differences among English Protestants:

This is the first time that ever I heard of a Puritan doctrine in points dogmatical, and I have lived longer in the church than he hath done. I thought that Puritans were only such as were factious against the bishops in the point of pretended discipline; and so I am sure it hath been understood hitherto in our Church. *A Puritan doctrine* is a strange thing because it hath been identified on both sides, that Protestants and Puritans have the same doctrines without variance

---

[96] Featley, *Pelagius Redivivus*, sig. A3^v.

[97] F. Rous, *Testis Veritatis: The Doctrine of King James . . . Of the Church of England of the Catholicke Church, Shewed to bee One in the Points of Predestination, Free-Will, Certaintie of Salvation* (1626).

[98] F. Rous, *A discovery of the Grounds both Natural and Politick of Arminianisme*. See also Rous's well-known speech in the 1629 Parliament, in which Arminianism was described as a Trojan horse, with men inside ready to 'open the gates to Romish tyranny and Spanish monarchy. For An Arminian is the spawn of a Papist; and if there come warmth of favour upon him, yet shall see him turn into one of those frogs that rise out of the bottomless pit.'

. . . according to the harmony of the several confessions of these Churches.[99]

He challenged Montagu's account of the Hampton Court Conference: for him it was, like the Lambeth Articles, a demonstration of the Calvinist unanimity of the Church of England, of which both Reynolds and Overall were representative. Carleton tried to play down Reynolds's comments on Article XVI: he had not, he claimed, said it was unsound; he had only asked that the phrase 'yet neither totally nor finally' be added to it. On the contrary tack, he glossed over Overall's refusal to countenance a strictly 'Calvinist' doctrine of perseverance, and denied that he had ever said that the justified could fall either totally or finally.[100] The theological isolation of Montagu could be achieved only by means of such distortion.

Significantly, there were more appeals to the teaching of Overall in the replies to Montagu than there were citations of Calvin. Even John Yates, whose exposition of predestinarian doctrine was undilutedly 'Calvinistic',[101] praised Overall for having a mind 'ever known to be sound in all divinity'. Conversely, appeals to the determinations of Dort were distinctly muted.[102] An English translation of the canons had appeared in 1619, but it was not reprinted, although the opportunity was taken to reprint, and to translate, the *Suffrage* of the British delegation.[103] The nearest that the English reader could get to the teaching of the Remonstrants was through Pierre du Moulin's hostile *Anatomy of Arminianism*,[104] but du Moulin's defence of the Dort decrees was emphatically 'sublapsarian'.

In the *Appello Caesarem*, Montagu had asserted that the Synod of Dort had in some points condemned the discipline of the Church of England. It was a sensitive point, and in republishing their *Suffrage* the British delegates took the opportunity to set the record straight.[105] They assumed that the charge rested on their approbation of the Belgic Confession, of which Articles XXXI and XXXII asserted parity of ministers. Montagu had, however, overlooked the fact that in deference to the *exteri*, those articles had not been subject to discussion. They revealed that

---

[99] Carleton, *An Examination*, 121.

[100] Ibid., 190–2.

[101] John Yates, *Ibis ad Caesarem, or A Submissive Appearance before Caesar* (1626), 66.

[102] Henry Burton was an exception. 'Of all other passages in the Appealer's Appeal I muse at none more, than this elevating and slighting of the Synod of Dort. What? so to disrepute the Synod of Dort? O spare it! either speak not at all of it, or reverently and honourably.' H. Burton, *A Plea to an Appeale: traversed dialoguewise* (1626), 88–9.

[103] STC 7067.

[104] Pierre du Moulin, *Anatomy of Arminianism* (1626).

[105] For Montagu's tart comments on the Synod of Dort, mentioned only in passing in the *New Gagg*, see *Appello Caesarem*, 69–71. For the response of the British delegation, see W. Balcanqual, *A Joynt Attestation, avowing that the discipline of the Church of England was not impeached by the Synode of Dort* (1626).

through their leader Carleton they had declared their 'utter dissent' from the two articles. They had been criticized for not putting down their position in writing, but the procedures had given them no opportunity to do so. They pointed out that their signatures had not been appended to the Confession, but they clearly felt that the official record would have done them more justice had it drawn attention to their known dissent from the articles in question. They had throughout the synod taken care to guide their judgments by 'that sound doctrine we had received from the Church of England'. The last thing they wanted was to force any of the synodical decrees on their fellow members of that church;[106] nevertheless, they claimed, there was nothing either in those decrees or in their own *Suffrage* which was inconsistent with Scripture, or with the doctrine of their church.

The effect of the controversy, therefore, was on the whole to force the delegates to Dort on to the defensive. This did not necessarily make their theological stance more flexible. On the eve of the York House Conference, Samuel Ward delivered a notable Cambridge sermon which extolled the university as a bastion of resistance to Pelagianism and Arminianism.[107] Like John Davenant, he was driven to a much narrower conception of orthodoxy than they had jointly been prepared to defend at Dort.[108] The one delegate who did attempt to reach a balanced verdict on the theological questions at issue was Joseph Hall.[109] It grieved him to see the Church of England threatened with the divisions which had afflicted the Netherlands as a result of Montagu's 'tart and vehement observations', but he diagnosed the problem as more 'mis-taking' than 'mis-believing'. It seemed to him that Montagu had meant to express 'not Arminius, but Bishop Overall, a more moderate and safe author',[110] and he therefore set down, as an introduction to a project of pacification, a series of quotations on each of the five points, firstly from Overall, and secondly from the British delegation's *Suffrage*, to demonstrate the common ground

---

[106] Ibid., But cf. George Carleton's letter of May 1624, quoted in the text above, p. 231.

[107] Samuel Ward, *Gratia Discriminans: Concio ad Clerum habita Cantabrigiae* (1626). Jerome Beale wrote to remonstrate, sending Ward page references from Corvinus to demonstrate that he 'agrees with St Augustine . . . embracing that with both arms which you quote'. Their difference of opinion about the Thirty-nine Articles, as Beale saw it, was whether grace was always irresistible: Beale was happy to agree that it overcame all resistance *in those who believe*, but not necessarily in all those in whom it began to work; and he contended this to be the teaching of the Articles. They differed in their reading of St Augustine on perseverance, Beale following the line taken shared by Thomson and Overall. Bodl. Lib., MS Tanner 72.314 and MS 80.143.

[108] Bodl. Lib., MS Tanner 290.81, Davenant to Ward 10 October 1625. For Davenant's verdict on Montagu's errors, see MS Tanner 279.297.

[109] *Via Media: The Way of Peace, in the Five Busy Articles, commonly known by the Name of Arminius,* printed in Hall, *Works*, IX. 489–516.

[110] Ibid., I, introduction, xliv.

between them. He hoped that his analysis would make further controversy unnecessary.

Hall's treatment is conspicuous both for its theological grasp and for its fairness to those who followed 'the acute Arminius'. Both sides, he pointed out, granted that the only motive of predestination was the will and good pleasure of God: the difference was that the Remonstrants looked at faith and infidelity as conditions in those who were to be chosen or rejected. Provided that they were sincere in granting faith to be the gift of God, he could see no grounds for quarrel. After all, St Augustine had admitted that God in our election 'had an eye to our qualification with that faith which he would give us.'[111]

As to the proper definition of man as object of the divine decree (and Hall's understanding of this aspect of the debate is unmatched in English theology), there were no fewer than six possible opinions. He could see no reason why the harsh consequences implicit in any of the four supralapsarian definitions (man indefinitely and commonly considered; man uncreated; man as creable, fallible, savable; man as created, but in pure naturals) should be passed over in silence, while the infralapsarian alternatives (man fallen, 'which is the most common tenet', and man as believing or disobeying the will of God, 'the Arminian tenet') were paraded with so much hostility. Provided that faith was acknowledged to be the gift of God, Hall could see no danger in the Arminian definition, since all agreed that faith was necessary to salvation. He took a similar line on the order of the divine decrees. Whether one preferred the Arminian sequence of four or the Calvinist version, provided that all were acknowledged to be of mere grace according to the divine good pleasure, eternal and unchangeable (as, Hall pointed out, the Remonstrants had conceded at the Colloquy of The Hague), and yet not alleged to be irrespective (and this, he reminded his readers, had been granted by the Contra-Remonstrants), the matters of dispute could be confined to the schools, and there was no need for 'the souls of quiet Christians to be racked with subtle questions'.[112] As far as the Church of England was concerned, Overall's middle way offered an admirable compromise. There was no reason, he thought, to gib at the concept of a 'general conditionate decree': Zanchi himself had used exactly the same language,[113] and had cited testimonies from Luther, Bucer and others in support. Even the notion of an antecedent and a consequent will of God had been defended, Hall pointed out, by appeal both to Zanchi and Polanus.[114]

---

[111] Ibid., IX. 500 n. 1, quoting *De dono Perseverantiae*, c. 14, as both Hutton and Andrewes had.
[112] Ibid., IX. 503–4. Hall did not use the words 'supralapsarian' and 'infralapsarian'.
[113] Ibid., 506–7, quoting Zanchi, *de Praedestinatione Sanctorum*, Explicatio, Thesis II.
[114] Ibid., 508.

Hall's treatment of the remaining points of controversy was along the same lines: the Church of England, with the benefit of Overall's guidance, had no need to trouble itself with the scruples of foreign divines. This was especially true on the question of perseverance, where his moderation was 'worthy to be written in letters of gold'. If each side was consistent in charitably interpreting the opinions of the other, the remaining points of controversy would be seen to be 'little other than verbal'.[115] Hall showed his manuscript to Montagu, who was prepared to accept the suggested compromise.[116] Although Hall's book was not published,[117] it remains important evidence that the pursuit of a theological *via media* was not entirely dead as the new king entered upon his inheritance.

[115] Ibid., 513.
[116] Ibid., I, introduction, xliv.
[117] Ibid. See also Lambert, 'Richard Montagu, Arminianism and Censorship', 59–60.

GReat King protect vs with thy gratious hand,
    Or elſe *Armenius* will o're ſpred this Land :
For if in *England* th'enemy doth appeare,
This is the ſhape of him we need to feare.
He raiſeth Factions, and that brings in iarres,
Which broacheth Errors, and vpholds the wars :
The *Netherlands* ruine, he ſought to bring,
In *England* now he doth the ſelfe ſame thing.
To rayle, to write, to publiſh bitter gall,
To change Religion, and ſubuert vs all.
His Squint-ey'd lookes & *Lanſa-Wolſa* gowne,
Shewes how Religion he wil ſoone throw down.
His grynding pate with weather-Cocks turn'd
Seeketh the *Churches* tenets for to ſtaine : (braine,
The Chriſtal ſtreams of truth he ſhuns moſt pure,
The tryall of *Gods* word he'le not endure :
But vnto *Error* caſt his blinking eye,
Preſuming *Truth* doth not the ſame eſpie.
Hereſie vpon a ſtately *Beaſt* doth ſtand,
Armenius bids him welcome, holds his hand.

Truth by her brightneſſe, and her ſincere heart,
Shewes that with *Hereſie* ſhee takes no par.
Treades on their *Mountebanke* & *Cozning* tricks,
Blowne in his eares, by *Pelagius* and *Ieſuites.*
Which makes his *Wind-mil* for promotions grace
Publiſh his Bookes abroad in euery place :
And begs protection for his workes of wonder,
Which againſt *Truth* he bellowes forth like thun-
Thus doth *Armenius* to preferment riſe, (der.
By Equiuocating and his Cheuerill lyes :
And *Truth* to all appeales to open view,
Bidding all Hereſies for ere adew   (heart
Deſiring our great C H A R L E S to take to
And by the Parlament make *Armenius* ſmart.
Which being done *England* ſhall euer bleſſe
The *King,* the *State,* the *Churches* happineſſe,
And if for telling truth, I burne or frye;
What then deſerues he that tels a lye?
        FINIS.   1 6 2 8.

Figure 2 A broadsheet of anti-Arminian polemic, catalogued as 'Arminianism: verses addressed to Charles I in 1628'. Arminius is depicted rejecting Truth and taking Heresy by the hand, while a Jesuit whispers heretical notions into one ear and Pelagius blows into the other. Reproduced by permission of the Bodleian Library, Oxford. The verses are printed on page 236.

12   Arminianism and the court, 1625–1629

Accounts of the reign of Charles I are all but unanimous that 1625 was a turning point. A major reason for the change, it is agreed, was the new court's commitment to 'Arminianism'. That commitment has, indeed, been made to bear an increasing weight of interpretation by 'revisionist' historians. Stressing the relative weakness of early Stuart Parliaments, they have denied that they were set on an inevitable collision course with the monarchy, and have argued that Charles and Buckingham both did all that could have reasonably been expected in trying to work with them. The breakdown of 1629 was therefore not necessary but contingent: the result not of intractable differences of political ideology dividing the court, but of the strains of war on an antiquated political machine, together with the 'rise of Arminianism'.[1] Even those unconvinced by the revisionists' arguments have not questioned the Arminian orientation of the court: they have tended, rather, to emphasize its political implications by claiming that the court clergy who were committed to it also encouraged the king in his inclinations to absolutism and in his hostility to Parliaments.[2] The contribution of this chapter to that debate will be to re-examine the evidence for what most historians take for granted: that Charles I and his court were ideologically committed to 'Arminianism'.

It was already evident that the new king inherited a deeply divided court, and that the tensions were political as well as religious. The alienation of Archbishop Abbot over the Spanish match went to the heart of that primate's conception of Protestant orthodoxy, but it also embraced con-

---

[1] See above all C. Russell, 'Parliamentary History in Perspective', in *History* 61 (1976) and more fully in *Parliaments and English Politics, 1621–1629* (Oxford, 1979). Among revisionists, Kevin Sharpe is an exception in declining to emphasize Arminianism.

[2] See, especially, R. Cust, *The Forced Loan and English Politics, 1626–1628* (Oxford, 1987); R. Cust and Ann Hughes (eds.), *Conflict in Early Stuart England: Studies in Religion and Politics, 1603–1642* (1989), especially the introduction and C. Thompson's chapter 'Court Politics and Parliamentary Conflict in 1625'; J. P. Sommerville, *Politics and Ideology in England, 1603–1640* (1986); and Trevor-Roper, *Catholics, Anglicans and Puritans*, esp. 'Laudianism and Political Power'.

stitutional issues.[3] The story of Richard Montagu illustrates all these themes: Protestant orthodoxy affronted by the contents of the *New Gagg*, but also the deplorable spectacle of king and archbishop using the hapless author as a counter in their oblique campaign against each other, with Durham House clerics engaged on one side, and parliamentary Puritans on the other.

In one sense, at least, the accession of Charles might be expected to have reduced the ideological tension. He came to the throne committed to playing a full part in the European struggle against Spain and to secure the restoration of his brother-in-law, the Elector Frederick, to his dominions in the Palatinate. That foreign policy was obviously welcome to Calvinist sentiment. The prominence at court of John Preston, the Puritan for whom Buckingham had secured election as Master of Emmanuel College, Cambridge, was a symbol of what was confidently expected to be a new direction in English policy. Understandably, therefore, it was said that on the death of James 'the bishops generally, and Dr Preston's enemies . . . were crestfallen'.[4] Undoubtedly one of the keys to understanding what happened in 1625–6 is the disillusionment and then outrage of committed Protestants as their hopes were dashed. The first stage in that process was the opening of negotiations for the marriage of Charles to the French princess Henrietta Maria, and the diplomatic pressure that followed for a relaxation of the recusancy laws. All Buckingham could do was lamely to tell Preston that there were no Protestants to be had; that marrying a subject had always been 'unlucky and fatal to kings of England'; and that the French were less rigid in religion. The underlying truth, of course, was that for Charles and Buckingham the Spanish war was not 'confessional'.[5]

The apprehension of the bishops early in 1625 was shared by Montagu. The dedication of the *Appello Caesarem* to Charles I reflected the considerable apprehension with which he waited to see how the new king would react. Charles and Buckingham were cautious and anxious if possible to defuse controversy.[6] Buckingham had close links not only with Preston, but also with Laud. There was every reason, especially with a Parliament in prospect, to see if the Montagu case could be resolved without alienating either group of his supporters. Among the steps taken by the new court to brief itself on the issues involved was the request to Laud, as early as

---

[3] See above, pp. 204, 211–12, 214.
[4] Ball, *Life of Preston*, 111.
[5] Ibid., 108.
[6] Buckingham's latest biographer agrees that he was seeking a balance between the two sides. R. Lockyer, *Buckingham: The Life and Political Career of George Villiers, First Duke of Buckingham, 1592–1628* (1981), 258.

December 1624, to provide a short summary of 'doctrinal puritanism',[7] and subsequently a schedule of clergy marked 'O[rthodox]' and 'P[uritan]' (the categories were suggested by Buckingham) for submission to the king.[8] That Charles decided to consult Andrewes 'and learn from him what he would have done in the cause of the Church, and bring back his answer, especially in the matter of the Five Articles' should not be taken as a sign of partiality.[9] Andrewes's age, wisdom and experience (he had after all been consulted by Whitgift on just the same issues in 1595!) made such consultation entirely appropriate, and the king's respect for his judgment was shared by Dudley Carleton.[10] Andrewes was of course not the only bishop consulted: Davenant too was asked for his opinions. So was John Preston.[11]

The hostility between the rival factions who had links with Buckingham is another of the key elements in 1625–6. They were playing for much higher stakes than Montagu. In 1624, Preston had suggested to Buckingham that the lands of cathedral chapters should be sold to pay the king's debts and to finance the campaign to recover the Palatinate:[12] a confessional war might yet have provided the opportunity for further reformation! Against that threat, Laud's militance in proclaiming the identity of church and state, and clerical support for the Forced Loan, are easy to understand. It was common sense that the court should seek to retain the support of both factions, or if that was impossible, not altogether to alienate either. The balance swung from one side to the other during Charles's first Parliament, which met in June 1625. Montagu was charged with encouraging popery, disrespect to King James (by disparaging the Synod of Dort and by denying the Pope to be Antichrist), and contempt of the Commons (by publishing the *Appello Caesarem*).[13] In July he was judged guilty of contempt, summoned to kneel at the bar of the Commons, and required to give a bond of £2,000 for his reappearance

---

[7] Laud, *Works*, III. 155–6. The list is not extant, and we have only Heylyn's unreliable word for it that five of the ten points referred to the canons of Dort. Laud gave a list of 'Brownist' opinions, also of ten points, in his 'Answer to Lord Say's Speech touching the Liturgy.' *Works*, VI. 130–4.

[8] Ibid., III. 159.

[9] Ibid., 160. Cf. Tyacke, *Anti-Calvinists*, 167.

[10] Dudley Carleton sent George Carleton's speech at Dort on perseverance to John Chamberlain with the comment 'to my capacity it will satisfy the best judgements, of which you may make trial, by showing it to my Lord of Winchester'. Letter of 26 March 1619, in Birch, *Court and Times of James I*, II. 148.

[11] Ball, *Life of Preston*, 114; for Davenant's, see Bodl. Lib., MS Tanner 279.297. Ellesmere MS 6878 35 B/14 may well be the result of another approach.

[12] Hacket, *Scrinia Reserata*, I. 204.

[13] *Debates in the House of Commons, 1625*, 48–9. Pym's report of April had more boldly listed the three charges as doctrine contrary to the formularies, sedition, and the encouragement of popery. Ibid., 179–84.

in August when he would be punished after consultation with the Lords. But in spite of disclaimers, the Commons had claimed the right to judge doctrine. Ever sensitive to encroachments on his own authority, Charles informed the House that 'what had there been said and resolved, without consulting him, in Montagu's cause, was not pleasing to him'.[14] Two days later, Parliament was prorogued. But Montagu himself did not believe that this implied Charles's approval of his books.[15]

Passions on all sides were high when Parliament reassembled at Oxford in August. On the one hand were those who had backed the Commons attack on Montagu, and whose primary concern was the protection of Protestant orthodoxy. Twenty years later, in the course of his funeral sermon for Daniel Featley, William Loe recalled how, in the lower House of Convocation, 'five and forty of us, whereof he was the chief, made a solemn covenant among ourselves to oppose everything that did but savour or scent never so little of Pelagianism or Semi-Pelagianism'. After Loe 'had made protestation (an occasion being offered) in these terms *Atque odi ego Arminianismum ac Bellarminianismum*', Featley had put his arms round him with the words 'Well said good brother, I protest and will swear the like.'[16]

On the other side were the clergy of Durham House, who believed that the right of Convocation, licensed under the great seal, to judge of doctrine was under threat. They were right in thinking that their argument would have a powerful appeal to the king. It is above all that concern which lay behind the letter of Howson, Buckeridge and Laud to Buckingham dated 2 August 1625, the second day of the Parliament.[17] 'The Church has never submitted to any other judge, nor could she without departing from the ordinance of Christ and inviting further dangerous consequences for herself.' To support that primary concern the bishops arrayed a battery of supporting arguments, stressing the relative doctrinal latitude of the Church of England compared with Rome and the fact that King James had seen and approved all the opinions in Montagu's book. While not committing themselves to supporting everything Montagu had written, they distinguished between fundamentals, and those 'such as are fit only for the Schools, and to be left at more liberty for learned men to abound in their own sense, so they keep themselves peaceable and disturb not the Church'. Finally, they turned to the offensive. Describing some (but not all) of the opinions opposed to those of Montagu

---

[14] Laud, *Works*, III. 167.
[15] Ibid., 167–8.
[16] William Loe, *A Sermon preached at . . . the Funeral of . . . Daniel Featley* (Oxford, 1645), 25.
[17] Laud, *Works*, VI. 244–6.

as 'fatal' (i.e., fatalistic), they proceeded to echo Burleigh's verdict at the time of the Lambeth Articles by asserting 'how little they agreed with the practice of piety, and obedience to all government', and to recall how Elizabeth had then suppressed them 'and so they have continued ever since, till of late some of them have received countenance at the Synod of Dort'. There were no grounds for granting that synod any authority in the English Church. 'Our hope is, that the Church of England will be well advised, and more than once over, before she admit a foreign synod, especially of such a church as condemneth her discipline and manner of government, to say no more.'

It is going too far to suggest that this letter amounted to an 'approbation of Montagu's public views', to say nothing of the attempt to adduce it as the main evidence of Laud's 'Arminianism',[18] but it may be granted that in their efforts to persuade Charles and Buckingham to resist the determination of doctrinal issues in Parliament, the signatories had resorted to anti-Calvinist polemic. The reference to the Lambeth Articles was no doubt intended to encourage Charles to follow Elizabeth and James I in refusing altogether to countenance them. A further anxiety (and, it may be granted, a shrewd polemical point) was plainly the writers' conviction of the implied danger to episcopacy if the determinations of Dort were granted authority in England. The signatories could of course rely on the king to support his own authority, national independence and episcopacy: but in spite of his agreement to protect Montagu from further parliamentary proceedings, there is still no evidence that Charles approved of his books.

The Remonstrants had traditionally supported peace between the Dutch and Spain, which would have undermined Charles's own foreign policy. In his efforts to build up international support, the new king made his hostility to the Remonstrants clear, and in October 1625 wrote in strong terms to the States General of the dangers of 'sects and factions of religion, brought in by the truce and liquourishness after the trade with Spain and hope of entertaining of either the Arminian or Roman religion'.[19] Charles would no doubt have been reluctant to admit that his own church was also riven with faction, but if Montagu's opponents could have convicted him of attempting to introduce similar errors into the English

---

[18] Tyacke, *Anti-Calvinists*, 268–8. It is not certain that they thought the Lambeth Articles were more objectionable than the canons of Dort. Dort was a much more recent, and therefore more delicate issue than the Lambeth Articles, and the remark that 'some of them have received countenance' may well have been designed to avoid giving unnecessary offence to the British delegates to the synod.

[19] PRO, SP 84/129/189ᵛ, 'Instructions for Buckingham and Holland for mission to the States General', 17 October 1625. Confirmed by Conway to Carleton, 4 October 1626, SP 84/132/90ʳ.

Church, there is no reason to doubt that Charles would have had little hesitation in condemning him.

If Montagu's books were considered to require examination, then Convocation was from the clergy's point of view the appropriate forum. Laud was naive enough to favour that course, while Andrewes was opposed to it.[20] Eventually, they agreed instead to recommend a pardon for Montagu combined with an inhibition of further discussion.[21] The king did not immediately accept that advice. The news that the case would be debated at York House filled Laud with dismay.[22] The initiative, as has been seen, had come from the Earl of Warwick and Lord Saye and Sele. Confident that there would be no difficulty in proving Montagu's unorthodoxy, they hoped that Buckingham would thereafter be forced to abandon him, together with his clerical backers. Neither Buckingham nor Preston welcomed the confrontation. 'The Dr and the Duke were both unwilling to an open breach, loved to temporize and wait upon events.'[23] Preston's performance at the conference undoubtedly disappointed his parliamentary friends, but its outcome was much less decisive than Cosin and Thomas Ball pretended.[24] Buckingham had no reason to abandon any of his Calvinist supporters: Sir John Coke, who had spoken up for Dort, remained Secretary of State. Of course the duke had not paid the price required for the support of the group associated with Warwick and Saye and Sele, but, given the verdict of uncommitted laymen like Pembroke, it is difficult to see how he could reasonably have done so. As to Preston, it was not so much the commitment to Montagu as the use of ships against the Huguenots of La Rochelle that made him doubt 'the saintship of the duke of Buckingham, whom otherwise he loved very much'.[25]

On the other side Cosin, it is true, boasted of Charles's commitment 'to our cause', but his confidence was not shared by Montagu himself,

---

[20] J. P. Lawson, *The Life of William Laud* (2 vols., 1829), I. 269.

[21] Laud, *Works*, VI. 249. This letter, signed by Mountaigne, Neile, Andrewes, Buckeridge and Laud, limited its approval of Montagu to saying 'we have met and considered, and for our particulars do think that [he], in his book, hath not affirmed anything to be the doctrine of the Church of England, but that which in our opinions is the doctrine of the Church of England, or agreeable thereto'.

[22] 'I understood what D.B. had collected concerning the cause, book and opinions of Richard Montague, and what R.C. had determined with himself therein. Methinks I see a cloud arising and threatening the Church of England. God of his mercy dissipate it.' Laud, *Works*, III. 179–80.

[23] Ball, *Life of Preston*, 118.

[24] Cosin summed up the York House Conference: 'the king . . . swears his eternal patronage of our cause' (Cosin, *Works*, II. 74), and Ball wrote that 'the Duke and Doctor Preston were not so great friends as before, but that the Duke sticked to the Prelates, and would, in the issue, leave Dr Preston and the Puritans.' Ball, *Life of Preston*, 141–2.

[25] Ibid., 109.

who felt only two months afterwards that 'The king and God favour us never so little.'[26] The strength of the opposition to Montagu still weighed with the king. There were reports prior to the assembling of the Parliament of 1626 that he would be left to the Commons 'to stand or fall according to the justice of his cause'[27] and that Charles would support the Puritan party because it was strongest in the state. John Williams was reported to have heard this from the king's own mouth.[28] When Parliament met, Buckingham through his agents 'disavowed' Montagu and his books,[29] and on 20 April the king himself 'signified his dislike of Mr Montagu his writings'.[30] He then reassured the Commons that he would refer the doctrinal issues to Convocation, but that meanwhile he would 'have his or any other book in that argument to be perused before it go to the press and so well allowed that it shall give no such scandal'.[31]

It was only when clergy of all shades of opinion began to urge him to inhibit further doctrinal debate that Charles changed his mind. In addition to the Durham House clergy, Joseph Hall had strongly recommended it. Pointing out that the Dutch quarrels had only gone to extremes after the conference at The Hague, and therefore advising against any debate in Convocation, he advocated a 'severe edict of restraint to charm all tongues and pens upon the sharpest punishment from passing those bounds which the church of England, guided by the scriptures, hath expressly set. If any man complains of an unjust servitude, let him be taught the difference between matters of faith and scholastical disquisitions.'[32] The debate was between those who advocated that both sides should be silenced, and those who argued that 'Arminianism' alone should be suppressed. In a court sermon of June 1626, James Ussher discussed the alternatives. Denying that he spoke 'as being hired on any side', he supported the latter course, but with remarkably qualified arguments. He was prepared to admit that the Arminians might have truth on their side, but even if they did, it was not a truth that concerned the foundation of the Christian faith. They should be silenced because they threatened the peace of the church, and because their opponents were in the majority. He was prepared to swear that if he were an Arminian, he would in those circumstances hold his peace. 'Perhaps this is not so wise counsel as some do give, who advise that both sides should be silent: but do you think it so easy a matter to silence all those who have moved the troubles?'[33]

[26] Correspondence of John Cosin, I. 90.
[27] Fuller, Church History, VI. 25.
[28] Heylyn, Cyprianus Anglicus, 172. Hacket, Scrinia Reserata, II. 80, 111.
[29] The Correspondence of John Cosin, I. 88–9.
[30] Commons Journals, I. 847.
[31] PRO, SP 16/4/18, misdated July 1625. Macauley, 'Richard Montague', 320.
[32] Hall, Works, IX. 498.
[33] Ussher, Works, XV. 348–9, 351. Samuel Ward, agreeing that only the Arminians should be silenced, wrote: 'God's blessing be upon you for this good service so opportunely performed. I pray God his Majesty may have a true apprehension of the ensuing danger.'

The surviving records of the drafting of the proclamation 'for peace and quiet in the Church of England' demonstrate that the tactical debate continued until the moment of publication. The first draft, which appears to have been prepared in the Privy Council, reflected the policy Ussher asked for. The preamble was unambiguous in 'finding that of late some questions and opinions have been broached by Richard Montagu and others'. It granted that offence had been given 'partly by the public expounding of them and partly by the sharp and indiscreet handling and maintaining of them', but the result was nevertheless a 'danger of men being drawn to Arminianism and Popery'.[34] This draft carries the endorsement that it was to be seen by a committee of bishops, under the chairmanship of Abbot, to include at least seven of Mountaigne, Neile, Andrewes, Harsnett, Buckeridge, Felton, Davenant, Field and Laud. The king's personal involvement is reflected in alterations in his own hand. In the proclamation as published, the reference to Montagu by name was dropped, and one or two concessions were made to the case for his defence. That the charges against him had not been proved was suggested by the additional 'seem to have been broached'; and it was conceded that his book had at first been 'meant against the Papists'. It was granted, furthermore, that 'some of either parts have given much offence'; and the 'late written books of both sides' had raised the hopes of the papists. The explicit use of the word 'Arminianism' was dropped, and the final version spoke imprecisely of the danger of 'schism and Popery'.[35]

The process of drafting, therefore, reflected modifications to an originally explicit anti-Arminian policy. Montagu nevertheless took the proclamation as a sign that he was to be abandoned, and he was by no means alone in that view.[36] In fact Abbot honoured his part of the implied bargain

[34] For *A Proclamation for the establishing of the Peace and Quiet of the Church of England*, see Larkin and Hughes (eds.), *Stuart Royal Proclamations*, II. 90–1. The draft is PRO, SP 16/29/79.

[35] PRO, SP 16/540/404 is another draft of the first paragraph in the handwriting of Laud, which may have contributed to the final version. Laud's wording (if his it be) still blames Montagu, the material passage reading 'some questions and opinions seem to have been broached or raised in matters of doctrine and the tenets of religion established, which at first were meant against the Papists only, but afterwards in the opinion of many produced other effects, and such as are like to breed great trouble and disquiet in the government of both Church and State'. The perspective, characteristically, is that of an ecclesiastical statesman rather than a theologian.

[36] *The Correspondence of John Cosin*, I. 95: letter of 28 June 1626: 'For else, why was the Proclamation so carried? Why are not the opponent writers questioned? Why write they still, as I hear, even since the Proclamation, *impune*? and I must hold my peace, sit down possess my soul in patience'. Again, 'now that the Proclamation is held to be against me . . .', Ibid. See also 103, 'Thinking more seriously upon these times, I have wondered at my Lord of St David's passage with me, as if His Majesty were not resolved against the side.' For other perceptions that the Proclamation was directed against Arminianism, see Russell, *Parliaments and English Politics*, 298 n. 4; Historical Manuscripts Commission, *Eleventh Report, Appendix I (The Manuscripts of Henry Duncan Skrine)* (1887), 76 ('This is meant to extinguish Arminianism which has lately been spreading in this country'); and the House of Commons Remonstrance of March 1628.

by presiding in High Commission to instruct printers and booksellers to withdraw the books which had been written against Montagu.[37] Davenant,[38] by contrast, was concerned that Durham House clergy would exploit the proclamation. If he meant by that the propagation of Arminianism, they made no attempt to do so. It is true that immediately after it Neile wrote to the Cambridge Vice-Chancellor to ensure that predestination was not debated, as had been proposed, at the forthcoming Commencement,[39] but that was surely according both to its spirit and its letter. Cosin, it seems, was active in making sure that Featley's *Pelagius Redivivus* was suppressed, although according to Featley's printer his efforts were counter-productive.[40]

Of course militant Protestants complained. Henry Burton wrote in the preface of an exposition of the Book of Revelation that

whereas upon a Proclamation published in your Highness's name . . . expressly forbidding any printing or preaching of such doctrines as were repugnant to the doctrine of the Church of England established, we all hoped that all Arminian and Popish doctrines would be hushed and silenced, we by experience find it quite contrary: for all the Arminians shamelessly alleging that all their doctrines are according to the Church of England, under this pretence they would suppress all truth as forbidden by your Royal proclamation, which if it were true, it should not be lawful any more to preach the Gospel, than to print books in defence of it. So that some are neither afraid nor ashamed to say, in plain terms, that they must license no books against Arminius. Good God, what pitiful times we live in, and how different from former, as I was bold to tell my Lord of London.[41]

More provocatively, Samuel Fell launched an inflammatory attack on the whole policy behind the proclamation a few months later in an address

---

[37] British Library, Harley MS 390, f. 83ʳ: 'Yesterday afternoon also the High Commissioners at Lambeth being the Archbishop himself, Dr Balcanqual, Dr Goad, Sir Henry Martin, the King's Advocate etc all of a contrary opinion to Montague, yet called the stationers and Printers before them whom it concerned, and charged them neither to print nor sell any of those 7 or 8 books which during the Parliament had been published against Montague' – Letter of Joseph Mead to Sir Martin Stuteville. On this evidence alone Tyacke writes (*Anti-Calvinists*, 157): 'Calvinism was proscribed, on the basis of the 1626 proclamation, and Arminianism established as the highway to ecclesiastical preferment.'

[38] Bodl. Lib., MS Tanner 72.135. See also Ussher, *Works*, XIII.351 and XV.404.

[39] Cambridge University Archives, Lett 12 (1625–44), no. 6 (26 June 1626).

[40] A note in some copies of Featley's *Cygnea Cantio* (sig. G) signed by the printer Robert Mylbourne says that Cosin (as chaplain to Mountaigne, Bishop of London) procured *Pelagius Redivivus* to be called in and 'utterly suppressed', and that 300 copies were taken from him. 'But herein he was not his craftsmaster, but was cousened himself: for though a great number of the copies of that work were taken from me, upon his clamour, and delivered to the Bishop of London that then was, yet they were all given back to me again: and by the stir he made about them, they were much more inquired after, and sold the better, being called for even from the remotest parts of Scotland.'

[41] Henry Burton, *The Seven Vials or A Brief and Plain Exposition upon the 15: and 16: chapters of the Revelation* (1628).

delivered at Oxford. 'To say peace, peace, where there is no peace is the voice of Jacob but the hand of Esau . . . A middle way between God and Baal was always pernicious.' His opponents were 'reformed Bolsecs', 'rabid [*fevardentios*] Anglicans', 'spiritu Ignatiano debacchantes in sacros Calvini manes', who were able neither to preach, speak, write or joke (and they valued jocularity above all else) without tearing Calvin to pieces, or labelling him a Puritan. The contention was not wrangling about trifles, or about the boundaries of the faith: it was about idolatry, about the tyranny of Antichrist, about counterfeit money changers in the temple of God. 'Nemo inter vos et familia mollium istorum Lutheranorum, nemo Proteus Theologus, aut chameleon literatus.'[42] It is sometimes said that all parties to the theological debates of this period used the language of moderation, that everybody claimed truth to be a middle way between extremes. That was not true of Fell, nor is it true of many others, as Joseph Hall found when he reported that his project of pacification, the *Via Media, The Way of Peace in the Five . . . Articles* was 'cried down for the very title's sake'.[43] Militant Protestants conceived of their orthodoxy not as a middle way, but as a Gospel diametrically opposed to the teachings of Antichrist, and if they were honest and consistent, like Fell, they said so.

There is little evidence that 'Arminianism', whether narrowly defined as a doctrine of predestination or more widely as a 'bridge to Popery', played a significant role in the year and a half which elapsed before the next Parliament. The dominant issues were the continued progress of the war, the Forced Loan by which it was financed, and the political dominance of Buckingham. It was those issues, and not doctrinal matters, which completed the political eclipse of Archbishop Abbot.[44] He had for some time before absented himself from meetings of the Privy Council, blaming his gout. His sequestration followed his refusal to license Sibthorp's sermon in favour of the Forced Loan.[45] He complained that he was excluded from the administration of church patronage. 'With bishoprics and Deaneries, or other Church places, I was no more acquainted, than if I had dwelt at Venice, and understood of them by some

---

[42] Samuel Fell, *Primitiae, sive Oratio habita Oxoniae Nono Novembris et Concio Latina ad Baccalaureos Die Cinerum* (Oxford, 1627), 9–16. He had recently been appointed Lady Margaret Professor.

[43] Hall, *Works*, I, introduction, xliv.

[44] Cust, *The Forced Loan and English Politics*, 35–71; Russell, *Parliaments and English Politics*, 323–40.

[45] Neile, Buckeridge, Mountaigne, Howson and Laud were appointed to exercise Abbot's jurisdiction. 'In July 1627 Charles sequestered the Calvinist Archbishop Abbot from his ecclesiastical jurisdiction, which was then vested in a commission composed of Arminian bishops', writes Tyacke, *Anti-Calvinists*, 167.

Gazette.'[46] But if Abbot was excluded from the court, other 'Calvinists' were not. Buckingham's entourage still included staunch Calvinists.[47] In August 1627, Henry Lesley, one of the royal chaplains, preached on the doctrine of predestination in a court sermon, which was then published at the request of Pembroke's brother, the Earl of Montgomery, and in October John Preston preached a prophetic sermon on the eve of the disaster at Rhé.[48] A sequence of deaths on the episcopal bench in 1626[49] prompted intense speculation, but most of the sees were kept vacant: and the two appointments of the period, Francis White to Carlisle in 1626 and Joseph Hall to Exeter in 1627 (he had earlier been offered Gloucester),[50] were both of men generally recognised to be moderates.[51]

'Arminianism' did become an issue in the Parliament of 1628, certainly in the perspective of John Pym, but this was only after its definition had been further widened to include not merely 'popery', but also 'a plot to introduce arbitrary government'.[52] It is a matter of debate whether Pym's major preoccupation was religious or constitutional.[53] Yet in spite of the Commons' notorious susceptibility to anti-papal rhetoric, there proved to be little mileage in accusations of Arminianism. Only four clergy (in addition to Montagu) were named. Sibthorp and Mainwaring figured on account of their sermons for the Forced Loan: theology was not an issue. Cosin was named on account of his *Private Devotions*: the issue was popery. The only cleric against whom charges of doctrinal Arminianism might have carried weight was Thomas Jackson, but after Sir Edward Coke had vouched that he was 'learned and honest', little more was heard against him.[54]

---

[46] Rushworth, *Historical Collections*, I. 434–56. Abbot pictured Laud as being closeted for hours with Buckingham 'and feeding his humour with malice and spite'. Neile and Laud were made Privy Councillors for their confutations of Abbot's objections to Sibthorp's sermon.

[47] Cust, *The Forced Loan and English Politics*, 53.

[48] Ibid., 74.

[49] Senhouse, Felton, Lake, Andrewes and Cary all died in 1626. 'To have the power of disposing so many chief bishoprics together is a matter of moment, either to build or pull down that faction in the church, which the present state or chief statesman like not.' Meddus to Mead, 7 October 1626. T. Birch (ed.), *The Court and Times of Charles I* (2 vols., 1849), I.155.

[50] ''Tis known I preferred Bishop Hall to Exeter', said Laud, *Works*, IV. 297.

[51] Notwithstanding the placard: 'Is an Arminian now made bishop?' at White's consecration. Birch (ed.), *Court and Times of Charles I*, I.179. Cosin preached a characteristically pugnacious consecration sermon. Cosin, *Works*, I. 97.

[52] H. Schwartz, 'Arminianism and the English Parliament, 1624–1629', *Journal of British Studies* 112/2 (1973).

[53] Sommerville, *Politics and Ideology in England*, 222. Cf. C. Russell, 'The Parliamentary Career of John Pym, 1621–9', in P. Clark *et al.* (eds.), *The English Commonwealth 1547–1640* (Leicester, 1979).

[54] Sommerville, *Politics and Ideology*, 222.

Outside the Commons, it is doubtful if 'Arminianism' loomed nearly as large. Perhaps the best comment on Pym's perspective comes from a paper written for the Privy Council by Sir Robert Cotton prior to the summoning of the third Parliament. He anticipated that 'religion is a matter that they [the Commons] lay nearest to their conscience', but his analysis of the 'jealousy' which led them 'to doubt some practice against it' centred on the secrecy still surrounding the diplomatic agreement with the French over the recusancy laws, coupled with the fact that not only Buckingham's mother but 'many of his ministers in near employment about him . . . talk much of his advancing men papistically devoted . . . and that the recusants have got these late years by his power more of courage (than assurance) than before'. Cotton advised appropriate action to 'clear these doubts (which perhaps are worse in fancy than in truth)' against 'the squeamish humours that have more a violent passion than a settled judgement, and are not the least of the opposite number of the Commonwealth'. The issues of the French marriage, of popery and of the enforcement of the recusancy laws were real grievances, of course, but they were traditional: Cotton made no reference to 'Arminianism'.[55]

Royal policy in 1628 reflected above all the king's hopes for an amicable relationship with his third Parliament. Before his assassination Buckingham attempted to conciliate those who had opposed him, and was prepared to follow new counsels to that end.[56] The king throughout remained outspokenly hostile to Arminianism, and Laud and Neile were obliged humiliatingly to renounce it in the Council, which they did, we are told, with tears in their eyes; only after this was Charles persuaded to appoint Laud Bishop of London.[57] Richard Montagu's appointment to Chichester on the death of George Carleton, which even Heylyn thought injudicious, should not be allowed to obscure the thrust of policy.[58] Montagu's elevation, which seems to have been the work of Buckingham and perhaps also of Dudley Carleton,[59] may have been part of a much

[55] Robert Cotton, *The Danger wherein the Kingdome now standeth, & the Remedie* (1628). On Pym's role, see Russell, 'The Parliamentary Career of John Pym'.

[56] PRO, SP 16/114/17, a letter of Carleton to Elizabeth of Bohemia dated 27 August 1628: 'he [Buckingham] having a firm resolution . . . to walk new ways but upon old grounds both of Religion and policy, finding his own judgment to have been misled by errors of youth and persuasions of some persons he began better to know'.

[57] 'The king did utterly dislike these novellers; then were these two bishops, with tears in their eyes, present and protested they hated those opinions and the questions, and they renounced them upon their knees.' W. Notestein and F. H. Relf (eds.), *Commons Debates for 1629* (Minneapolis, 1921), 35, 122.

[58] Heylyn, *Cyprianus Anglicus*, 185. Prynne without foundation claimed that it was the work of Laud. *Canterburies Doome* (1646), 157. Cf. Laud, *Works*, IV. 273; House of Lords MSS XI.431.

[59] According to Prynne's account, Laud claimed Dudley Carleton's influence, which is not impossible, for they had worked together under Sir Henry Savile, and were old friends.

wider agreement to let bygones be bygones which involved also Abbot's restoration to his jurisdiction. The appointment of the Earl of Holland to succeed Buckingham as Chancellor of Cambridge University was another sign of the king's endeavour to heal polemical divisions. Pembroke, reconciled to Buckingham early in 1628, remained a close friend of the king. At the end of 1628 Dudley Carleton, now Earl of Dorchester, was appointed Secretary of State. There was even a rumour that Saye and Bedford were to be made councillors.[60] At the same time, perhaps through the mediation of Attorney-General Heath,[61] Montagu wrote to Abbot renouncing any intention of upholding Arminianism. Although, unfortunately, his letter does not seem to have survived, its existence was widely reported,[62] and in view of what had earlier passed between Montagu and both Preston and Joseph Hall, it is far from incredible. Early in 1629, a proclamation called in the *Appello Caesarem*, on the grounds that 'it was the first cause of those disputes and differences, which have sithence much troubled the quiet of the Church'.[63]

The Declaration prefixed to the Thirty-nine Articles in 1628, which reinforced the 1626 Proclamation, it has recently been said, 'abandoned the neutrality of the proclamation' and by ordering that 'these disputes be shut up in God's promises, as they be *generally* set forth to us in the holy scriptures . . . Charles I glossed the Thirty-nine Articles in favour of the Arminians and their doctrine of universal grace.'[64] In fact, the king had made clear in June that he was committed to suppressing Arminianism,[65] and confirmation that he was determined to satisfy those who were hostile

---

[60] L. J. Reeve, *Charles I and the Road to Personal Rule* (Cambridge, 1989), 60.

[61] Heath wrote a conciliatory letter to Montagu. PRO, SP 16/118/33.

[62] References to Montagu's letter to Abbot are Pory's to Mead of 12 December 1628 reporting 'he did not only subscribe to the Council of Dort, but also did reject the five tenets of Arminianism' (Birch (ed.), *Court and Times of Charles I*, I. 449) and Beaulieu's to Puckering of 24 December (Birch, II.3.) See also *Historical Manuscripts Commission, Seventh Report, Appendix I* 544, Thomas Barrington to Lady Johanna Barrington, 6 December 1628. In *Historical Manuscripts Commission, Twelfth Report*, Appendix, Part I, 373 is printed a paper of Sir John Coke's asking Abbot for a copy of Montagu's letter 'importing a recantation or desertion of those opinions wherewith he hath been charged. Of this letter his Majesty desireth to have sight.'

[63] Larkin and Hughes (eds.), *Stuart Royal Proclamations*, II. 218–19. Charles reminded the Commons, in his *Declaration Showing the Causes of the Late Dissolution* of March 1629, that 'because it did open the way to those schisms and divisions which have since ensued in the Church, we did, for remedy and redress thereof, and for the satisfaction of the consciences of our good people, call in that book, which ministered matter of offence'.

[64] Tyacke, *Anti-Calvinists*, 50.

[65] Sir Humphrey May reported from the king 'that his heart is as firm to religion as any, and that he will take all occasion to suppress all Popery and Arminianism'. Sir John Maynard added 'And for Arminianism I have heard him protest against it'. *Historical Manuscripts Commission, Thirteenth Report*, Appendix, Part VII (Manuscripts of the Earl of Lonsdale), 45.

to it comes from a letter written late in November 1628 by John Pory to Joseph Mead:[66]

Yesterday, also, after dinner, his majesty was pleased to declare himself at the Council board, how he would make preparation for a good proceeding in parliament. He knew the Commons would first begin with religion. Two sects there were which they would stumble at, the papists and Arminians. For papists he would have them all turned out of office, and out of commission, unless they would conform. And for the Arminians, he would have the bishops about the town compare their opinions with the book of Articles, and to condemn such tenets as were not agreeable thereto.

It was this royal resolve that resulted in the Declaration prefixed to the Thirty-nine Articles. A group of bishops met at Lambeth under Archbishop Abbot to give effect to the king's desire.[67] Although there is little other evidence of the drafting of the 1628 Declaration, the king would appear to have sought a wide consensus through discussions in the Council,[68] and the policy adopted would certainly have been approved by Dorchester.[69] The Declaration[70] begins by stating the king's duty as supreme governor to preserve unity of religion:

We have therefore, upon mature deliberation, and upon the advice of so many of our bishops as might conveniently be called together, thought fit to make this Declaration following: – That the Articles of the Church of England, which have been allowed and authorised heretofore, and which our Clergy generally have subscribed unto, do contain the true doctrine of the Church of England agreeable to God's Word: which we do therefore ratify and confirm; requiring all our loving subjects to continue in the uniform profession thereof, and prohibiting the least difference from the said Articles; which to that end we command to be new printed, and this our Declaration to be published therewith.

The Declaration then proceeded to deal with the differences which had arisen over the doctrine of predestination:

That for the present, though some differences have been ill-raised, yet We take comfort in this, that all clergymen within our realm have always most willingly subscribed to the Articles established; which is an argument to us that they all agree in the true, usual, literal meaning of the said Articles; and that even in those curious points in which the present differences lie, men of all sorts take the Articles of the Church of England to be for them; which is an argument

---

[66] Birch (ed.), *Court and Times of Charles I*, I. 439.

[67] Ibid., 451, and II. 3. The only evidence to suggest that the Declaration was the work of Laud is a letter from Robert Baron of 1634 (PRO, SP 16/266/3) quoted by Prynne, *Canterburies Doome*, 160–1.

[68] CSP, Venetian, 1628–9, 432. In spite of Abbot's continued absence, 'Calvinism' was still well represented on the Council in 1629. Reeve, *Charles I and the Road to Personal Rule*, 189.

[69] For Carleton's impatience with predestinarian arguments, see his letter to James Montagu, PRO, SP 105/95/20ᵛ.

[70] Printed as STC 10051, and thereafter used to preface the Thirty-nine Articles as reprinted in the Book of Common Prayer.

again that none of them intend any desertion of the Articles established:
That therefore in these both curious and unhappy differences, which have for so many hundred years, in different times and places, exercised the Church of Christ, we will that all further curious search be laid aside, and these disputes shut up in God's promises as they be generally set forth to us in the Holy Scriptures,[71] and the general meaning of the Articles of the Church of England according to them; and that no man hereafter shall either print or preach to draw the Articles aside any way, but shall submit to it in the plain and full meaning thereof, and shall not put his own sense or comment to be the meaning of the Article, but shall take it in the literal and grammatical sense:
That if any public reader in either of our Universities, or any head or master of a college, or any other person respectively in either of them, shall affix any new sense to any Articles, or shall publicly read, determine, or hold any public disputation, or suffer any such to be held either way, in either of the Universities or colleges respectively, or if any divine in the Universities shall preach or print anything either way, other than is already established in Convocation with our Royal assent; he or they the offenders shall be liable to our displeasure, and the Church's censure in our Commission ecclesiastical, as well as any other; and we will see there shall be due execution upon them.[72]

In Dorchester's judgment, the king had every reason to hope that he had settled 'all things . . . as well in church as commonwealth' to secure 'a fair and loving meeting with his people'.[73] But the king's commitment to the existing formularies was not enough to satisfy the House of Commons, who in January 1629 showed that it was they rather than Charles who were not content to accept them as they stood. The intermittent campaign to add the Lambeth Articles to the Thirty-nine, which went back to the Hampton Court Conference, was resuscitated, with the canons of Dort now added for good measure. Under the leadership of Pym and Rich, the Commons protested[74] that they 'do claim profess and avow for truth the sense of the Articles of Religion which were established in Parliament in the 13th year of Queen Elizabeth which by the public acts of the Church of England and the general and current exposition of the writers of our church have been delivered unto us; and we reject the sense of the Jesuits,

---

[71] Far from being a gloss, these words are a direct quotation from Article XVII.

[72] At the same time, the canons of 1604 were also reprinted. A riposte was the reprinting by 'R.Y. for T. Downs, to be sold at the great north door of St Paul's' of the Irish Articles of 1615 with the royal arms on the reverse of the title page (STC 1426) 'entered by order of the Irish stock'.

[73] Reeve, *Charles I and the Road to Personal Rule*, 60.

[74] Notestein and Relf (eds.), *Commons Debates for 1629*, 23. As Laud noted, there were no such 'public acts' and asked (himself) 'Must we reject *all* the sense of the Jesuits and Arminians?' *Works of William Laud*, VI. 11.

Arminians and all others wherein they do differ from us'. A reply drafted in Charles's own handwriting,[75] but apparently never delivered, nevertheless demonstrates that as far as he was concerned the policy difference concerned not the end but the efficacy of the means:

His M[ajesty] hath taken notice of your declaration concerning Religion, which he mislikes not, because he sees not that therein you take to yourselves the inter-pretation of Articles of Religion (the deciding of which in doctrinal points only appertains to the clergy in Convocation). Nevertheless because His Majesty hath lately made a publication to keep the true Religion of the Church of England without alteration and in unity, which being made with great deliberation and hav-ing the advices and consents both of his Council and the Bishops, does wonder, that since as he conceives ye concur in one end, ye should not be satisfied with his said Publication or at least shew his M[ajesty] where it is too weak to perform the wished end. Wherefore he as Supreme Governor under God of the Church of England requires that ye either rest content with his Publication or proceed no further in this business until ye shew clearly to him in what the publication comes short in maintaining without alteration those articles you mention.

After the session had ended, Sir Thomas Roe wrote that had the Com-mons 'sweetened' the king with the grant of supply, 'they might have done what they pleased in the establishing of religion'. Whether or not he was right, that judgment is not consistent with a court perceived by 'Calvinists' as committed to Arminianism. Roe considered the king's declaration of the reasons for the dissolution 'true for matter of fact and satisfactory to all those that seek satisfaction'.[76] The advice submitted by Attorney-General Heath, probably of similar date, points to the same conclusion.[77] Like Cotton before him, he thought religious peace could be secured if the legal proceedings against recusants were resumed. In addition, he sug-gested that 'if his Majesty be pleased, by some public examples, as occa-sion shall be offered, to discountenance new fangled opinions and advance the sober and orthodoxal divines', that would 'drawe a reverence to our church and a stabilitie in religion'. That is all he said on the subject, and he thought it would be enough to restore good relationships between the king and his people. It is reasonable to claim that Heath's advice, far from being a recipe which Charles fatally ignored,[78] reflected a prescription already being implemented. Together with other evidence that the king

---

[75] PRO, SP 16/540/404.
[76] PRO, SP 16/139/21, transcribed in L. J. Reeve, 'Sir Thomas Roe's Prophecy of 1629', *Bulletin of Historical Research* 56 (1983), 115–25.
[77] PRO, SP 16/178/3 and 4.
[78] L. J., Reeve, 'Sir Robert Heath's Advice for Charles I in 1629', *Bulletin of the Institute of Historical Research* 59/140 (1986), 215–25.

was perceived to be hostile to Arminianism,[79] and that ecclesiastical patronage was exercised without discrimination against Calvinists,[80] it demands a reassessment both of the thrust and the success of royal policy.

That policy was demonstrably more principled and more even-handed, though less superficially adroit, than James I's had been. Nor should the failure of Charles's third Parliament be allowed to obscure the success of the Declaration prefixed. The fact that Laud as Bishop of London and Abbot as archbishop shared responsibility for censorship ensured that the understanding of 1628 was not merely cosmetic,[81] and the king remained vigilant in requiring his archbishop to keep him informed as to its implementation. Dorchester, as Secretary of State, sent Abbot formal instructions that he was to ensure the bishops 'give charge in their triennial visitation and all other convenient times both by themselves and the archdeacons, that the declaration for the settling all questions in difference be chiefly observed by all parties',[82] and for the next four years the archbishop submitted an annual return to that effect,[83] as in due course Laud was required to do after him. In the long run the Declaration was definitive in putting an end to predestinarian controversy in the Church of England. In accepting the sincerity of conscientious convictions on both sides, in standing by existing formularies, in avoiding the condemnation or enunciation of specific doctrines and in its judicious agnosticism, the settlement it offered was wise and generous. In the short run, to be sure, there would be minor skirmishes; in the medium term, it was to be swept away by the Civil War and superseded by the Westminster Confession; but ultimately, when the Prayer Book and the Thirty-nine Articles were restored, the Declaration was restored with them. The countless surviving copies of Articles and Declaration signed by incumbents after the Restoration bear witness to its wide acceptance as a settlement of predestinarian controversy in the history of the English Church.

The evidence reconsidered in this chapter prompts some final observa-

---

[79] For Calvinist claims that Charles was hostile to Arminianism, see William Twisse, *A Discovery of D. Jackson's Vanitie* (Amsterdam, 1631), 3; and *Anti Montacutum: An appeale or remonstrance against R. Mountagu* (1629), 3. In one of the British Library copies of I. R. *The Spy, Discovering the Danger of Arminian Heresy and Spanish Treachery* (Amsterdam? 1628), there is a rare plate depicting the realm under siege by the forces of popery and Arminianism, in which the king is shown defending the 'castella della verita' built with blocks carrying the names of the books of Old and New Testaments, the church Fathers and the sixteenth-century Reformers, topped out by one labelled 'William Perkins'.

[80] The Calvinist Barnaby Potter was appointed bishop in 1629. Nicholas Cranfield has defended the integrity of ecclesiastical patronage under Charles I in an unpublished paper, 'Chaplains in Ordinary at the Stuart Court'.

[81] C. Thompson, 'The Divided Leadership of the House of Commons in 1629', in K. Sharpe (ed.), *Faction and Parliament: Essays on Early Stuart History* (Oxford, 1978), 284.

[82] PRO, SP 16/153/40; STC 10404.7. Cf. Laud, *Works,* V.307–9. In 1632 Abbot certified that 'of Arminian points there is no dispute'.

[83] Laud, *Works,* V. 311–14.

tions on the debate with which it began. That the tensions were both religious and constitutional seems evident, but it can be argued that 1625 was less decisive than 1618. What changed with the accession of Charles I was not the ideology of the court but the personality of the king and the thrust of foreign policy. Abbot's loss of political influence dates from the beginning of the decade, but it became a total eclipse as a result of the Forced Loan. The religious concerns emphasized by sober-minded and thoughtful contemporaries related primarily to the French marriage and the enforcement of the penal legislation against Catholics. These were traditional anxieties, surfacing now, as previously, in consequence of political circumstances. 'Arminianism' was the preoccupation of a minority, a preoccupation which has much less support in the contemporary records than is generally recognized.[84] There were indeed two different conceptions of Protestant orthodoxy ranged against each other in 1625–9, but they were well established, many-faceted, and related essentially to perceptions of Rome.

[84] Two examples: the editor of the *Letters of John Holles, 1587–1637* (Thoroton Society Record Series, vols. xxxi, xxxv and xxxvi) remarks (vol. xxxi, introduction, lxiv) that 'For a man of his strict Puritan piety and sobriety, the letters have surprisingly little comment on the growth of Arminian influence which so worried the Commons.' The CSPD for 1628–9 has but three entries indexed under 'Arminianism'.

13 Thomas Jackson

If contemporary fears of Arminianism were focussed on Montagu rather than on the court, they were not limited to him. The name most often coupled with his was that of Thomas Jackson. The author of an unsigned manuscript dating from *c.* 1630 entitled 'Reasons for the suppressing of Arminianism in the Church of England'[1] was shaken by Montagu's elevation to Chichester, but took comfort from King Charles's friendly reception of Carleton's book against him, from the Declaration prefixed, but most of all from the proclamation suppressing the *Appello Caesarem*. He nevertheless considered the publication in 1628 of Thomas Jackson's *A Treatise of the Divine Essence and Attributes* more dangerous than anything of either Montagu or Arminius.

The title of Jackson's book was reminiscent of the notorious volume of Vorstius condemned by King James. Unlike Montagu, however, Jackson was well known, even Prynne granted, as 'a man of great abilities, and of a plausible, affable, courteous deportment'.[2] He was 'no way a friend to the Church of Rome'.[3] The combination of plausibility and profundity, it was feared, would 'entangle many, who cannot so easily get out of his nets again'.[4] Jackson had dared to state publicly, in his dedication to the Earl of Pembroke,[5] that he knew he would be taken for an Arminian.[6] In the highly charged atmosphere of 1628, that was a self-fulfilling prophecy.

[1] Bodl. Lib., MS Rawlinson D 1347.114, copied from Eng Hist b 2: 'Reasons for the suppressing of Arminianism in the Church of England in the present controversy of Predestination and the dependents thereupon, drawn partly from Divinity, partly from Equity and Conveniency'. See also Bodl. Lib., MS Eng poet e 57, 'Notes on Arminianism in the flyleaf of a student's book', which also links Jackson with Montagu.

[2] Prynne, *Anti-Arminianisme*, 270.

[3] Bodl. Lib., MS Rawlinson D 1347.29ᵛ.

[4] Bodl. Lib., MS Eng poet e 57.

[5] The author of MS Rawlinson D 1347 had 'heard that [it] was distasted by the noble lord'.

[6] In his dedication, dated November 1627, Jackson wrote: 'It is not so unusual, nor so much for me to be censured for an *Arminian*, as it will be for your Lordship to be thought to patronize Arminianism. To give your lordship that satisfaction therefore in this point, which I am not bound to give unto others: if the man which most mislikes the *Arminian*

What makes Jackson deserve more than a passing mention is that, in spite of his undoubted links with Durham House, in personality and outlook he was quite different from Neile himself and from other members of his circle. In Jackson, for example, there was nothing of Richard Montagu's evident enjoyment of polemic, place-hunting and ecclesiastical intrigue. There was little of his conscious appeal to the church Fathers against the first- and second-generation Reformers; on the contrary, there is some evidence of Lutheran and Reformed influences. His approach to the doctrine of predestination was different. As William Twisse observed, whereas others 'under a show of modesty and simplicity hold off themselves and others from admitting so high points; as not willing to believe that which is above their comprehension', Jackson approached the matter in 'a clean contrary way, and would bear the world in hand, that the failings of our divines in this doctrine, come from shallowness, and want of profound knowledge, in metaphysical speculations'.[7] Twisse claimed that he was a 'ringleader', but for the student of the early seventeenth century, Jackson's philosophical theology is interesting and important because it seems to have been unique.

Jackson was born in 1579 into a Newcastle family with merchant connections.[8] His academic abilities attracted the attention of Lord Eure, and he was sent to Oxford in 1595 to pursue theological studies at The Queen's College under the care of Eure's friend Richard Crakanthorpe. Two years later he was admitted as a scholar of Corpus Christi, where he became a probationary fellow in 1606. He lectured in divinity both at Corpus and at Pembroke, and was several times elected Vice-President of his college. In 1613 he published his first book, *The Eternal Truth of Scriptures;* dedicated to Lord Eure, it was the first volume of a projected commentary on the Apostles' Creed. Further instalments followed: *How Far the Ministry of Man is Necessary* in 1613, *Blasphemous Positions of Jesuits* in 1614 and *Justifying Faith* in 1615. Although he was summoned from Oxford to be instituted vicar of St Nicholas, Newcastle (it was only then that he came to the notice of Richard Neile), Jackson continued to write. A volume of sermons dedicated to Neile, *Christ's Answer unto*

---

or *Lutheran* doctrine in the points most controverted through the Reformed Churches, will but agree with me in these two, that the Almighty Creator hath a true freedom in doing good; and Adam's offspring a true freedom in doing evil, I shall not dissent from him in the other points controverted, unless it be in this, that there needs be no other controversy between the Arminians and their opposites in point of God's Providence and Predestination.' Thomas Jackson, *A Treatise of the Divine Essence and Attributes* (1628) preface, sig. *3.

[7] Twisse, *Discovery of D. Jackson's Vanitie*, Printer's preface.

[8] I owe the biographical information which follows to M. E. Van der Schaaf, 'The Theology of Thomas Jackson (1579–1640): An Anglican Alternative to Roman Catholicism, Puritanism and Calvinism', University of Iowa Ph.D. thesis, 1979.

John's Question, appeared in 1625, *The Original of Unbelief* in 1625 and *The Holy Catholic Faith and Church* in 1627. In 1631 he returned to Corpus as President. His tenure was marked by peace in his college, and by the publication of further volumes of his commentary, all of which were Christological,[9] and which in the dedication to King Charles he described as 'the best fruits of my best and flourishing years'. A royal chaplain from 1631, he was appointed Dean of Peterborough a year or so before his death in September 1640. A number of his works still awaited publication. Barnabas Oley edited some of them in a three-volume collection of 1653–7; a second collection, which included all the known surviving works, followed much later in 1673.

The effect of Crakanthorpe's teaching, whether by action or reaction, upon the young Jackson can only be guessed. Although Prynne refused to believe that he could have learned any of his 'poisonous doctrines' from Oxford, his early transfer to the college of Jewel and of Hooker may well be the key to his theological development. According to a tradition originating with Anthony Wood it was not until his sojourn in Newcastle that he was converted from the 'rigid Calvinism'[10] of his youth, but in the disputes which disturbed Corpus Christi College after the death of John Reynolds in 1607, Jackson was identified with those who supported Walter Browne against the faction led by Daniel Featley. Browne, whose library included five works by Arminius, was accused of being a 'Papist' by his opponents.[11] If, as seems likely, Jackson was the translator of Gabriel Powell's *De Adiaphoris* into English in 1606, he was then already identified with the defence of the church's polity and of its right to ordain rites and ceremonies.[12] As to predestination, Jackson's published works provide no evidence that he was ever a 'rigid Calvinist'. In a treatise on Romans ix, 18–24, entitled *God's Just Hardening of Pharaoh*, which was written in 1612[13] but not published by Jackson in his own lifetime,[14] he adopted substantially the position he took later in *The Divine Essence and Attributes*. Furthermore, as early as 1612 he had linked matters of polity with doctrinal commitment, characterizing English divines who had become overwrought by controversies in foreign Reformed churches as

---

[9] Notably, *The Knowledge of Christ Jesus*, 1634; *The Humiliation of the Son of God*, 1635; *The Consecration of the Son of God*, 1638.

[10] Van der Schaaf, 'Thomas Jackson', 31–5.

[11] Tyacke, *Anti-Calvinists*, 65–6.

[12] Van der Schaaf, 'Thomas Jackson', 39–42.

[13] *The Consecration of the Son of God*, in Thomas Jackson, *Works* (12 vols., Oxford, 1844), VIII, 256n.

[14] An edition was, however, 'published by another without my consent or knowledge' according to Jackson, *Works*, IX. 972. It appeared as the second of three treatises in William Milbourne's *Sapientia Clamitans* (1638). *Correspondence of John Cosin*, I. 222.

'the crazed and ill-tempered presbytery (I mean zealous adherents to rigid tenents of reprobation)'.[15]

All the indications are, therefore, that Jackson's theological stance was from an early date integrated with a readiness to defend both the polity and the liturgy of the church as by law established. He was widely read in both the Fathers and the Reformers, but his works are sparing in appeals to authorities other than Scripture. They are distinguished, on the contrary, by their application of reason to the problems of theology. In so doing, Jackson's originality lay in his extraordinary independence of mind, especially of the dominant scholasticism of his day. He believed that man was endowed by his Creator with the gift of knowing things truly.[16] Provided that the understanding was properly used, theology was a 'science', or body of knowledge capable of being deduced from a given set of first principles. 'The principles of divinity being once known . . . the establishment of orthodoxal conclusions may be made as certain and perspicuous by logic, as the like can be in any other science.'[17]

In the course of explaining the right use of the understanding, Jackson evolved an epistemological *via media* between the 'enthusiast's'[18] demand for appeal to holy writ and the Roman Church's elevation of institutional authority. The separatist or enthusiast used the Scriptures to excess, or mingled them 'with the secret inspirations of their private spirits, or wrest them to their own fancies'.[19] In so doing, they abandoned the understanding, and abused the Scriptures more than those who rejected them altogether. The mistake of the Romanist, by contrast, was to place his church above Scripture. That was equally irrational, for the believer was required to abandon the conclusions of his own understanding and accept uncritically the voice of the Pope.[20]

Jackson's exposition of specific doctrines was also marked by an independence of mind in seeking to avoid erroneous extremes. In the

---

[15] *God's Just Hardening of Pharaoh*, in Jackson, *Works*, IX, 506; see also *The Original of Unbelief*, Ibid., IV. 395.

[16] Van der Schaaf, 'Thomas Jackson', 48; Jackson, *Works*, IV. 88.

[17] Van der Schaaf, 'Thomas Jackson', 90–1.

[18] Jackson does not use the word 'Puritan'.

[19] Van der Schaaf, 'Thomas Jackson', 73. Although the plain words of Scripture must be believed absolutely, the Holy Ghost had never undertaken to teach 'what propositions be negative or affirmative, universal, particular or singular; or how any or all of these be convertible, whether absolutely, by accident, or by contraposition; or how to frame a perfect syllogism out of them . . . we might easily discern all or most of those unhappy controversies which have set the Christian world for these late years in combustion, to have been hatched, maintained and nourished by such pretended favourites of the Spirit, as either never had faithfully learned any true logic, philosophy or ingenuous arts, or else had utterly forgotten the rules which they had learned or heard'. *Christ's Exercising his Everlasting Priesthood*, in Jackson, *Works*, IX. 19–20.

[20] Van der Schaaf, 'Thomas Jackson', 82; Jackson, *Works*, II. 173–7.

doctrine of justification, for example, he sought a middle way between the Tridentine error of inherent righteousness, which was bound to lead to 'final doubting or despair', and the opposite errors of 'some Protestants', which might 'minister occasion of carelessness or presumption'.[21] The former error rested upon a mistaken understanding of the Fall as merely the privation of original righteousness, which made Christ's satisfaction for sin superfluous, and destroyed the need for unmerited grace.[22] Jackson praised the Lutheran theologian Matthias Flacius Illyricus, and also Calvin and Peter Martyr, all of whom understood that it was real, a rebellion and not merely a privation.[23]

On the other hand, a 'jealousy of coming too near the papists' by admitting more justifications than one[24] had led some Protestants into saying that it was a once-for-all event, distinguishing too sharply between justification and sanctification. Jackson suggested instead a threefold justification.[25] The first was 'radical or fundamental', and was the infusion of 'habitual grace' or faith; the second 'actual' by which he understood 'actual supplications made in faith' for the remission of sins committed, whether before or after the infusion of faith; the third 'virtual', which consisted in the performance of precepts such as 'Watch and pray continually.'[26] Underlying these distinctions was Jackson's concern to reconcile faith and works, and a reluctance to accept that works were required for sanctification but not for justification. The same reluctance influenced his treatment of faith. He offered variations on the theme that although we are justified by faith *only*, that faith is not *alone*. For example, although faith and repentance are indeed distinct, they are in practice always conjoined, so that 'faith always moves to repentance, and repentance restores faith to its proper throne'.[27] Elsewhere, Jackson came near to equating faith and obedience:

Surely if in all those places of the Old and New Testaments wherein salvation is ascribed to *faith*, or unto *faith alone*, the apostles or prophets had substituted obedience instead of faith, there could have been no dangerous misnomer; for as the faith is, such is the obedience, and *e contra*. Both terms equally imply two (the same) things necessary to salvation: first, a submission of our wills to God's will, or a readiness to do his will revealed; secondly, when we have done as well as we can, to deny ourselves, and renounce all confidence in our best works, whether of faith or of obedience.[28]

[21] Jackson, *Works*, XI. 320.
[22] Van der Schaaf, 'Thomas Jackson', 92–7.
[23] Jackson, *Works*, IX. 64; Van der Schaaf, 'Thomas Jackson', 213.
[24] Jackson, *Works*, III. 357.
[25] Elsewhere Jackson talks of justification more generally as final absolution. See the discussion in C. F. Allison, *The Rise of Moralism* (1966), 48–56.
[26] Jackson, *Works*, III. 357.
[27] Ibid., 358–9.
[28] *The Consecration of the Son of God*, in Jackson, *Works*, VIII. 216.

It was in the context of this discussion of justification (and not of predestination) that Jackson offered his thoughts on perseverance:

> though faith or grace at their first infusion may assure us our sins are remitted; yet we may not take these or other pledges of God's love as a full discharge or final acquittance of all reckonings between him and us, but rather as a stock bestowed upon us to begin the new world with, for which, with the increase, we must still think ourselves accountable. Though it be a truth, (not unquestionable) that a man once actually justified, or truly sanctified, cannot finally use God's graces amiss; yet it is very doubtful, whether one may not either abuse, or not use, such gifts of God, as, rightly used, or employed to his glory, might have been means infallible of justification . . . the immediate qualification for remission of sins is not the habit or inherence, but the right use of grace, or perseverance in prayers conceived by that faith which unites us unto Christ.[29]

If virtual justification is interrupted, either by negligence or contrary acts, past sins recover their weight, and incline the mind 'to distrust of God's favour or our sure estate in grace'.

> I dare boldly say, that not the least sin against the law of God, committed after regeneration, but (were it possible for the regenerate to give indulgence to it) would (at the least) exclude them from life eternal. Nor doth this argue, as some captious reader will perhaps imagine, that a man may fall either finally or totally from the state of grace; but rather, that all impossibility he hath of not so falling, essentially depends on a like impossibility of not continuing his indulgence to known offences, or negligence in repenting or bewailing secret sins. Even after the infusion of faith most perfect, faithful repentance is as absolutely necessary to salvation as the first infusion was . . . it is but the next step to hypocrisy, a mere perverting of the use of grace, thus to infer − I have true faith, therefore I shall always use it aright: a wise man would rather argue thus − I have the right use and exercise of grace, therefore my faith is true, and such as will justify.[30]

There was nothing there which would have offended James I, but in order to honour the Declaration prefixed, Jackson omitted the whole discussion when his book was reissued in 1631.

Justifying Faith seems to have occasioned no controversy on its first appearance. *The Divine Essence and Attributes*, by contrast, has been described as a 'theological bombshell'.[31] Fundamental was Jackson's conviction that it is possible for man to conceive of God as He is. It was, he granted, necessary to eliminate extraneous causes of error, such as contention (even in defence of the truth), because contention aroused the passions.[32] It was important to listen to the conscience and to live

[29] *Justifying Faith*, in Jackson, *Works*, III. 368.
[30] Ibid., 356.
[31] Van der Schaaf, 'Thomas Jackson', 8.
[32] Jackson, *Works*, IV. 376.

obediently thereto. Prayer was vital.[33] Provided those conditions were met, God could be conceived by analogical reasoning. The goodness of God, especially, could be known by analogy with the moral law in the human conscience. That by itself was shocking to those who, like William Twisse, believed that the Fall had destroyed man's reason and left a void between God and man bridgeable only by special revelation.[34] Jackson compounded the offence by explaining other attributes in ways that seemed to threaten the divine transcendence.[35] He admitted, for example, that God's power was infinite: but His wisdom placed restraints upon His exercise of it.[36] He explained the divine omnipresence by invoking the model of a sphere whose centre is everywhere and whose circumference is nowhere.[37] '[God] is in every centre of bodily or material substances, in every point imaginable of this visible universe, as an essential root, whence all and every part of what is besides him spring, without waste or diffusion of his substance, without nutriment or sustentation from any other root or element.'[38]

Even more provocatively, Jackson explained the notion of eternity along Neoplatonist lines[39] as that from which each temporal moment is continually replenished as a stream is replenished by a fountain. He then applied the concept to explain the possibility of divine foreknowledge of future contingencies:[40]

The correct notion of eternity is a point which we must believe, if we rightly believe God to be eternal, or know what eternity is; a point which would to God they had seriously considered, which have had God's eternal decree and the awards of it most frequently in their mouths and pens. As he is no Christian that would deny whatsoever is by God decreed was so decreed before all worlds; so he is no Christian philosopher, much less a true Christian divine, that shall refer or retract the tenor of this speech *before all worlds* to that only which is past before the world began.

It was a fallacy that God has necessarily decreed everything that is, and that therefore all that is comes to pass of necessity. God had not 'set the course of nature a-going with an irresistible and unretractable swinge, and since only looks upon it with an awful eye, as masters sometimes watch their servants whether they go the way they are commanded'.[41]

---

[33] Ibid., XI. 213–14; Van der Schaaf, 'Thomas Jackson', 62.
[34] Van der Schaaf, 'Thomas Jackson', 183ff.
[35] Ibid., 173.
[36] Jackson, *Works*, V. 81.
[37] Ibid., 54.
[38] Ibid., 48.
[39] Jackson admired Plotinus' thought (*Works*, IV. 404; V. 60–2).
[40] Ibid., V. 73.
[41] Ibid., 111.

Contingency may be decreed as well as necessity. The error that the divine foreknowledge rests upon the immutability of the divine decree overlooked the truth that every wise decree presupposed wisdom,[42] and contingency may be the object of infinite wisdom. Far from freedom of choice being incompatible with the immutability of God's will, without it we cannot conceive God to be as infinitely wise as His decree is immutable.[43] The words 'should' and 'might' 'are as infallible signs in divinity as in grammar of a potential';[44] what we should have done or might have done was possible for us to have done. God's foreknowledge extends to these contingents, and 'in the Divine Essence all real effects, all events possible, whether necessary, casual, or contingent, are eminently contained, the perfect knowledge of his own essence necessarily includes the perfect knowledge, not only of all things that have been, are or shall be, but of all things that might have been or possibly may be'.[45] To conceive the decree as a past act would prejudice God's absolute and eternal power of jurisdiction. 'What grant or promise soever he make cannot bind the exercise of his everlasting liberty for a moment of time; they last no longer than *durante bene placito*; seeing gracious equity, and only it, is his everlasting pleasure. He ever was, ever is, free to recompense every man according to his present ways.' We must therefore think of it as the axis upon which every successive or contingent act revolves.[46]

The Divine Essence and Attributes provoked William Twisse into writing a refutation,[47] followed by a treatise[48] in recognition of which he was offered a professorship at the University of Franeker.[49] He thought Jackson's heresy was the result of deserting St Paul, St Augustine and Calvin for Plato, Pelagius and Servetus.[50] Twisse rejected Jackson's epistemology as a desertion of Aristotle; he was 'more foul than Arminius himself' because 'more void of scholastical argument'. Theologically, Twisse reasserted an unrepentant supralapsarianism.[51] Although he

---

[42] Ibid., 88–9.
[43] Ibid., 93.
[44] Ibid., 94.
[45] Ibid., 100.
[46] Ibid., 114–15.
[47] Twisse, *Discovery of D. Jackson's Vanitie*.
[48] William Twisse, *Vindiciae Gratiae, Potestatis ac Providentiae Dei* (Amsterdam, 1632).
[49] Van der Schaaf, 'Thomas Jackson', 17.
[50] S. Hutton, 'Thomas Jackson, Oxford Platonist and William Twisse, Aristotelian', *Journal of the History of Ideas* 39 (1978), 635–52.
[51] Ussher to Samuel Ward, 'Dr Twisse I see (as you feared) hath followed the rigid part.' R. Parr, *Life of Ussher* (1686), 399. See also John Davenant to Samuel Ward, 22 May 1632, Bodl. Lib., Tanner MS 71.140: 'Methinks he bestows too much pains in arguing against ye received opinion, which presupposeth man's fall.' Davenant also disagreed with Twisse's exclusion of the non-elect altogether from *gratia Christi*.

granted that man can normally know what is good,[52] and that the divine will is exercised in a good manner, he denied that man can extrapolate from the moral law in reasoning about the divine nature, and he 'came close to making the blanket assertion that God is utterly unbounded by human expectations of right and wrong'.[53] His answer to Jackson's claim that supporters of irrespective predestination made God's will the rule of His goodness was to reply that God had an infinite lawful power which extended to everything not logically contradictory.[54] Any power actuated by God must be just. He rejected Jackson's notion of eternity, and reaffirmed God to be utterly transcendent. Where Jackson had argued that God's power for good was subject to the contingency of free will, Twisse affirmed that every particular event came about as the result of the divine decree.[55]

As Barnabas Oley put it, in the face of Twisse's criticisms Jackson 'never answered, but in the language of the Lamb dumb before the shearer, silence and sufferance'.[56] Similarly, he published no defence against the accusations of Arminianism made by Henry Burton.[57] He was, however, sufficiently provoked to preach on the text Jude, 4,[58] 'Who are the men that trouble the church?' They were those

that bring railing accusations against their betters, against all of what rank or place soever in the church, which dissent from them in opinions concerning election and reprobation, or the tenor of God's decree, being points which they understand not; and yet speak evil of them which seek to rectify their error. But in things that are plain and easy to be understood, which the very heathen knew by the light of nature, as in points of obedience to their lawful prince, or such as are in authority under him, in these (shall I say as our apostle says?) *like brute beasts they corrupt themselves* . . . Another special branch of these men's ungodliness was the *turning of grace into wantonness*; and what do they else, that trouble themselves and their neighbours with intricate disputes how the grace of God doth co-operate with man in his conversion . . . and yet in the mean time violate the bond of peace and charity by their uncivil rude behaviour and scurrilous manner of speech and writing.

Although this sermon remained unpublished, as did a much longer answer to Burton,[59] it is necessary to make reference both to it and to other

---

[52] Twisse, *Discovery of D. Jackson's Vanitie*, 466–8. For Twisse's response to Jackson, see Van der Schaaf, 'Thomas Jackson', 182–200.

[53] Van der Schaaf, 'Thomas Jackson', 185; Twisse, *Discovery of D. Jackson's Vanitie*, 365, 417.

[54] Twisse, *Discovery of D. Jackson's Vanitie*, 453.

[55] Ibid., 288.

[56] Van der Schaaf, 'Thomas Jackson', 18.

[57] Henry Burton, *Israel's Fast* (1628).

[58] 'A Sermon preached on St Simon and St Jude's Day, 1629', in Jackson, *Works*, IX. 340–1.

[59] 'Dr Jackson's Vindication of himself', ibid., IX. 354–84.

unpublished material in order to explain Jackson's theology of predestination in detail.

Burton had misrepresented Jackson by attributing to him the view that there was an objective goodness in man independent of God's will.[60] All he had said was that to create man in God's image was necessarily to create him good. 'God's will declared in the moral law, and working in us both the will and the deed . . . is the cause by which we are made conformable to the divine nature.'[61] He believed that the doctrine of irrespective reprobation, held by all or almost all of those who had protested against *The Divine Essence and Attributes*, undermined that moral law by making the same act no sin in one man, and sin in another. Such doctrines as 'If God did absolutely decree that the sins of the elect should be remitted, then he did absolutely decree that they should be committed' were[62]

not muttered in corners, but maintained as part of that holy doctrine which hath been delivered unto us by the masters of Israel, approved by the best writers in the Reformed churches. These and the like doctrines are held in so precious esteem, that if the lawful pastor seek to root them out where they have been planted by others, he shall be traduced for an Arminian, and, as they hope, be so censured by the high court of Parliament.

Jackson recalled how, when he had taken up his pastoral charge at Newcastle, he had challenged the view of 'a great rabbi in some private conventicles in and about that town' who had distributed papers claiming that 'whosoever was elected from eternity was never the child of wrath, save only in the esteem of men'. Jackson's opposition had led to the charge that he 'went about to refute the doctrine of all Reformed Churches concerning election and reprobation', although, as he pointed out, even the Synod of Dort had expressly repudiated the doctrine that 'the sins of the elect were remitted before they were committed'.[63] The revealed will of God is that He will reward every man according to his ways. God has therefore decreed from eternity to reward the ungodly for their wicked works according to the rule of His justice; and to reward penitent sinners 'not for their works, but according to their works; and so to reward them, not by the rule of his justice, but out of his mere mercy'.[64]

If to maintain these conclusions be Arminianism, I profess myself not to know (in these particulars) wherein the Arminians differ from the orthodox and ancient church. But if Arminius and his followers have taught or maintained any other conclusions, by which the least tittle may be derogated from God's free

---

[60] Ibid., 357.
[61] Ibid., 361.
[62] Ibid., 369.
[63] Ibid., 371.
[64] Ibid., 372.

mercy and grace, by which any thing besides death and non-deserts may be ascribed to man's works or free-will, I no way partake with them in those and the like errors.[65]

Jackson did not expect to convince Burton of his error, reflecting ironically that it was presumably as impossible for anyone who thought himself to be in the immutable state of election to suspect, much less to recant, any sin or error until he had renounced that immature persuasion of his own estate in grace. That was why 'the sage and reverend reformers of the church' had rightly counselled that the deep points of election and predestination 'are to be warily thought upon, they are no fit themes for every man's private meditations, much less seeds fit to be promiscuously sown in every congregation by any seedsman'.[66]

But from men misled with wild zeal unto the doctrine of absolute election and reprobation, as it hath of late years been taught by some, and from men jealous of others (as if they were Arminians) that in this point dissent from them, I can expect no voluntary satisfaction, but rather continuance of the like, unless I could dissuade them from their doctrinal error. For whilst this veil is spread over their hearts, envious or malicious slander, whilst it exonerates itself upon such as they suspect for Achans and Arminians, will be interpreted zeal; violent passions will be taken for the power of the Spirit; such nasty solecisms or rude scurrility as would seem loathsome to heathen artists, will go current with themselves and their associates for sanctified eloquence; and so will ignorance in philosophy or school divinity be applauded for holy simplicity.

The real 'Popish plot', in his view, was not Arminianism, but the doctrine of irrespective reprobation, which Satan had set the Jesuits to spread,[67]

And the Jesuits, as they have long used our pulpits and print-houses, so they attempt to use some in our parliaments as their podders, to drive us into it, if they can . . . put a necessity of this hard choice upon us − Whether [it] were better to live in obedience to a church which adores wicked and naughty men, devils incarnate (for such some of their popes have been) as gods on earth; or to hold communion with that church and society of men, which makes the God of heaven, the Almighty creator of all things . . . much worse than an incarnate devil, yea than any wicked spirit, or than the devil himself, can without slander be conceived to be?

Jackson would have denied that he was being anti-Calvinist, since 'the best is, that of such who at this day do not disclaim the name of Calvinists, the most and best dislike the opinion of absolute reprobation, and so I hope, in good time will every faithful pastor in the church of England,

---

[65] Ibid., 373.
[66] Ibid., 376.
[67] Ibid., 383.

and every elder in this our Israel'. The Lutherans had protested against the same doctrines before the name 'Arminian' had ever been thought of.[68] The problem of predestination had troubled the church in all ages. Instead of blaming Calvin or Beza, still less Perkins or Whitaker, Jackson usually associated 'foreign rigid tenets' with Zwingli, who had derived them 'at the first from some ancient Romish schoolmen'.[69] He deplored the bitter recriminations about it in the Reformed Churches:[70]

Charity binds me to impute the harsh expressions of some good writers and well-deserving of all Reformed Churches, yea the errors of the Dominicans, or other schoolmen (which were more faulty than Zwinglius or his followers in this point) rather unto incogitancy, or want of skill in good arts, than unto malice, or such malignancy as the Lutheran long ago had furiously charged upon the Calvinist, as if they had chosen the Devil, not the Father of Lights, maker of heaven and earth, to be their God.

He had been so shocked as originally not to credit the report that any Protestant had dared to say that he preferred Bellarmine's exposition of the doctrine of predestination to Calvin's, until he had seen it confirmed in Pareus.

But were it part of my present task, I could easily make it appear . . . that cardinal Bellarmine, and many of Aquinas's followers, do make God to be author of sin, by as clear infallible consequence as either Zwinglius or Piscator have done. And he that would diligently peruse Aquinas's writings . . . may find him as straightlaced as Calvin was . . . The best apology that can be made for either must be taken from the Roman satirist's charity, *Opere in longo fas est obrepere somnum*. Calvin and Aquinas were . . . somewhat more than authors of long works.[71]

He could pardon learned men for the inevitable occasional slips, but he could see no defence for those who made what in Calvin's case had merely been an error into a fundamental point of faith,[72] or for those who, without theological training and with other occupations 'do busy their brains and abuse their auditors or readers with idle and frivolous apologies for those slips or errors of worthy writers which stand more in need of ingenuous censure, or mild interpretation or correction, than a justifiable defence.[73]

More there have not been, as I hope, nor more peccant in this kind in any of the Reformed Churches, than in this church of England, though not of it. Some

---

[68] Ibid., 381.
[69] *The Primeval Estate* (*Christ Exercising his Everlasting Priesthood*), in Jackson, *Works*, IX. 536.
[70] Ibid., 22–3.
[71] Jackson cites Pareus, *Act. Swalbacen*, part 1, col. 2, *de Autore Peccati*.
[72] *Christ's Session at the Right Hand of God*, in Jackson, *Works*, XI. 209.
[73] *The Primeval Estate*, ibid., IX. 24.

treatises I have read and heard for justifying the escapes or ill expressions of Calvin or Beza, by improving their words into a worse and more dangerous sense than they themselves meant them in, or their followers in the churches where they lived did interpret them.

Had they been called to account, it might have prompted a new question for debate in the schools, namely 'Whether to attribute such acts or decrees unto God as they do, and yet withal to deny that they concludently make him the Author of sin, doth not argue as great a measure of artificial foppery, or (which is more to be feared in some) of supernatural infatuation, as it would do of impiety, to resolve dogmatically *in terminis terminantibus* that God is the author of sin?'[74]

In his own explanation of the decrees of election and reprobation,[75] Jackson used the analogy of founders of colleges appointing specific penalties for certain offences, and ordaining formal proceedings for sentencing guilty parties. The divine decree represented the rule of law, which was to reward every man according to his works. Although everyone who is reprobated is reprobated from eternity (by that rule of law), no man baptized is born a reprobate. The division of mankind from birth into elect and reprobate would, he claimed, make the work of priests, either for easing troubled consciences or for preventing presumption, a futility. Instead, he proposed that there were four estates. The first, common to us all at birth, is that of sons of wrath. The second follows baptism, in which we are made sons of God by adoption. Thirdly, there is the estate of reprobates; and finally, that of the elect, or the completely regenerate.[76] All reprobates are sons of wrath, but not all sons of wrath are reprobates. The estate of reprobation presupposed 'a greater degree of Satan's working than in sons of wrath'; and 'only unto this work, not unto men's persons or individual natures, is the irrevocable sentence of reprobation awarded'.[77] Judas became an absolute reprobate by resolving to betray the Son of God; he did not betray the Son of God because he was an absolute reprobate from eternity, or from birth.[78] Similarly, in every elect person there must be 'a greater work of God, a greater measure of regeneration or of new birth than that by which he is first made a son of God'.[79] It is this measure of righteousness or of regeneration which was the formal object of the eternal decree. The Church of England taught that as many as are baptized become by their baptism sons of God as are no longer sons of wrath; but she did not teach that their estate

[74] Ibid., 24–5.
[75] 'A Sermon preached on St Simon and St Jude's Day, 1629', Ibid., 340–1.
[76] *The Primeval Estate*, ibid., 314.
[77] Ibid.
[78] Ibid., 320.
[79] Ibid., 315.

is therefore the estate of absolute election.[80] It is only by continuance and growth in that estate that we may arrive at the immutable state of absolute election. Jackson concluded that between the extremes of reprobation and election, the greater part of those who have been baptized are in neither the one state nor the other.[81]

It followed that particular full assurance was not of the essence of faith.[82] Jackson felt that the doctrine was the more to be disliked because it wounded the conscience of the humble, and that it could nurse a presumption which was far worse than doubt or distrust of salvation. Here again, Jackson deplored the contentions about it in the Reformed churches, which he considered to have done more damage than any of the wounds inflicted by the papists. He reflected ironically that if the grace from which it was held impossible to fall included the spirit of wisdom and understanding, then one could only conclude that many who contended most earnestly had either never had it or else had totally fallen from it.[83] The Church of England, he argued, held a golden mean between extremes. As the Homilies taught, we must all firmly believe that the Son of God has paid the price of our redemption. No man can have that full assurance unless he believes that Christ died for all men, meaning the 'whole world, that is to say, Adam, and all that should come after him', in the words of the homily upon the Death and Passion of our Saviour.[84] Upon this foundation of assurance, our persuasions of our assured estate in grace grow together with the purification of our hearts (1 John iii, 3), and only to the extent that they do so grow are they persuasions of faith rather than presumptions.[85] We are told to make our election sure, but is there any man, asked Jackson, who dare say that he is already in an immutable estate of grace?[86] Our preoccupation ought to be the duty of mortification; to be obsessed with strong persuasions of our immutable estate of election independently of performing that duty 'is the readiest and most compendious way that Satan yet hath found to cast men into a reprobate sense, that is to make them without sense or feeling of their sins'.[87]

The accusation of Arminianism, Jackson noted, was in most cases 'an indefinite and confused suspicion' in which no specific charges were made. Typical were Burton's charges that he was a neutralizer, a popish Arminian

---

[80] Ibid., 321.
[81] Ibid., 350.
[82] *Christ's Session*, in Jackson, *Works*, XI. 192ff.
[83] Ibid., 199.
[84] Ibid., 201.
[85] Ibid., 203.
[86] *Primeval Estate*, in Jackson, *Works*, IX, 329.
[87] Ibid., 330.

and an Arminian papist. Barnabas Oley dismissed it as 'a mere noise'.
Jackson himself thought that there were only two genuine issues ('the rest
are but word-bates, or verbal quarrels, arising from ambiguous or
unscholastic expressions')[88] between the Arminians and their opponents.
One was whether men in this life ordinarily do or may attain to an
immutable estate of grace, which Jackson himself believed, but took the
Arminians to deny. The other was the rejection of a necessitating decree.
'If the Arminians would yield to the Church of England in the former,
I think no true member of the Church of England would much dissent
from them in the latter.' The assertion of an irrespective decree deprived
Christ of His office both as priest and judge, and made Him merely a
'doomsman' whose role was just to read a sentence determined long before.
'My exhortation . . . shall be that of the learned and pious Hemmingius
– "That we seek not our assurance of faith or hope in *Parcarum tabulis*
[tablets of the Fates], which were irreversibly written before any part of
the world was made" (if we may believe some heathen poets or stoics,)
but in God's promises made to Abraham, and to be performed by Jesus
Christ, as he is now our High Priest and King, and as the supreme Judge
of quick and dead.'[89]

Jackson's ideas on predestination, like those of Arminius, were
developed in reaction to what they both regarded as an untenably rigid
formulation. Common to both was a confidence in the verdict of the
human reason, a philosophical insistence on divine foreknowledge of contingents, and a theological insistence on the death of Christ for all. There
is no evidence, however, that Jackson was at all well acquainted with
Remonstrant and Contra-Remonstrant literature, and to call him an 'Arminian' is to overlook some fundamental differences. His insistence on the
death of Christ for all was grounded conservatively on Scripture as interpreted by the Prayer Book, the Catechism and the Homilies. His defence of
contingency, by contrast, grew out of an underlying Neoplatonism and led
him to a far more radical position – though an equally careful avoidance
of Pelagianism – than anything in Arminius. Unlike Arminius, he rejected
all concepts of personal predestination, and for that reason was not led to
speculate on the logical order of the divine decrees. Far more radically than
any other English divine in the period, he emptied the doctrine of content and
mystery. It became little more than the promulgation of the moral law, sanc-
tioned by the application of ultimate succour or final penalty. Yet
Neoplatonism aside, even in this respect his thought was not without prece-
dent in the Reformed tradition. Theodore Bibliander, Zwingli's successor
at Zurich, had been driven to much the same conclusions.

[88] Ibid., 316.
[89] Ibid., 536–7.

As has been stressed, Jackson's theology of predestination was not fully elaborated in his published works, although it was substantially implicit in *The Divine Essence and Attributes*. Those who sensed that he represented a threat to conventional Protestantism were right, but there were good reasons apart from restraints on publication why he faded from the limelight. In the first place, his undisguised hostility to Rome and the absence of any animus against the Reformers offered little scope to popular misrepresentation by Prynne and Burton. The appeal of his philosophical theology was moreover necessarily limited to the educated elite. Even within that elite it is unlikely that he would have become the leader of a school. In spite of his insistence on logical clarity, his own use of language lacked the rigour and consistency essential to a convincing synthesis. More importantly, his independence of mind, both in concept and in method, represented far too radical a challenge to conventional thinking. The contrast with the way Laud's mind worked could hardly have been greater.

14   Neile and Laud on predestination

In replying to Burton, Jackson had mentioned that he expected to be charged in Parliament. There, above all, where what Arminianism meant was uncertain, the charge might gain credence. Only by a deliberate strategy of widening its connotations had Pym been able to make it a major issue.[1] After the king's unsatisfactory first answer to the Petition of Right, for example, he claimed that 'Arminian' alteration in religion was linked with a plan to alter the government,[2] and Laud and Neile were named in the Commons' Remonstrance under the heading of innovation in religion. Laud noted in his diary: 'one in the house stood up and said: Now we have named these persons, let us think of some causes why we did it. Sir Edward Coke answered, Have we not named my Lord of Buckingham without showing a cause, and may we not be as bold with them?'[3] The charge of 'Arminianism' carried weight only if it was exploited for its political as well as its polemical connotations.

Neile prepared a formal reply to the Commons accusations.[4] To blacken a man's name with 'imaginary crimes supposed not proved' and to expose him to obloquy as an enemy of church and state could hardly stand 'with charity, Christianity or justice,' but at least it gave him an opportunity to clear his name. 'I pray that credit shall be given to what I shall say for I will speak nothing but truth as I shall answer to God the best judge of truth and the best avenger of falsehood.'[5]

In Parliament, undoubtedly, accusations of Arminianism were subsidiary to charges of popery, and Neile's reply reflected that priority. He took particular pride that he had been born and baptized in the same year as the Thirty-nine Articles had appeared. 'In the profession of that faith I have ever lived, and in it by the power of God I will live and die in professed opposition of Pope and Popery.' He granted the Church of

---

[1] Russell, *Parliaments and English Politics*, 298, 345.
[2] Ibid., 379.
[3] Laud, *Works*, III. 208.
[4] Durham Dean and Chapter Library, Hunter MS 67/14.
[5] Ibid.

Rome 'to be a corrupt adulterated church literally professing the Catholic faith, but in sundry particulars destroying the truth thereof', and he would rather lose his life than join it. The Pope's usurped power he regarded as 'Antichristian tyranny'; papal infallibility he held for no less than blasphemy. He acknowledged only two sacraments 'properly so called'. He described the popish Mass as 'a mere Idol and the celebration to be an action fitter for a stage than for God's church'. Transubstantiation was a 'carnal conceit', and communion in one kind 'execrable sacrilege'. The prohibition of the Scriptures in the vernacular was contrary to St Paul's doctrine. Adoration of images and the invocation of saints were both idolatrous. 'Their phantasy of Purgatory I hold for no better than an old wife's dream.' Indulgences were 'gross pickpurse cosonages of the world, and betraying of men's senses to destruction'. Neile 'utterly disclaimed' merit of works. 'When we have done all that we can do or is commanded us we must acknowledge ourselves to be but unprofitable servants.' He granted confession to be of great use, but he did not hold it to be absolutely necessary, and in the Church of Rome it was altogether abused. Neile indicated his profound distaste for the enumeration of all sins, by which 'they squish out the secrets of men's actions and thoughts, and secrets of States, by advantage whereof they turn the pretext of Spiritual Counsels, and seal of Confession into a school and cloak of villany, perfidiousness, and treason'.[6]

Neile pointed out that neither Burleigh nor Robert Cecil would have tolerated him as chaplain had they suspected him of popery. Both at Paul's Cross and at court he had as often as anyone preached against it, and during his twenty-two years' attendance on King James he had never been suspected of it. His book against de Dominis[7] was evidence of his hostility to it. His treatment of recusants in Durham diocese bore witness to his efforts in bringing many to conformity and in proceeding against those who refused the Oath of Allegiance. The king himself knew of his endeavours to prevent those who were not of the French ambassador's family from flocking to Mass while he was staying at Durham House. Only on the sensitive issue of the stone communion table in Durham Cathedral did he appear on the defensive. He claimed that it was set up without his knowledge. 'I confess I did not greatly allow of it when I first saw it, but I thought it not worthy of adventuring the jarr that might have ensued upon my taking it away when the Dean had set it up', especially as according to the Elizabethan Injunctions it was a thing indifferent.

Neile then turned to the charge of Arminianism.[8] His reply is worth reproducing at length:

[6] Ibid., ff. 1–12.
[7] Richard Neile, *Marcus Antonius de Dominis . . . his Shiftings in Religion* (1624).
[8] Durham Dean and Chapter Library, Hunter MS 67/14, ff. 13–15.

But that I have lived long enough to learn to wonder at nothing, I should wonder how I should come to be suspected of unsound opinions in point of Arminianism, the usherer in of Popery.

I am no gentleman usher . . . I do not know that I ever read three lines of Arminius's writings. Neither do I know that I have a page of any book of his in my study, but by what I have heard of him, take him out of the question of Predestination and Reprobation, he is held to be in all other points a rigid Calvinist.

I have ever carefully avoided . . . these questions, which I confess I am not able to master . . . I will not take upon me to open the mouth of the clay to dispute with the potter[9] why hast thou made me thus, or to enter into the secrets of God's unrevealed counsels, further than in fear and reverence to apply the comfort of God's goodness, and general promises of mercy to all penitent sinners laying hold thereof by faith in Christ Jesus.

I am very confident that no man will or can charge me that either disputing, preaching or writing I ever meddled in those questions; but once, about thirty-five years ago, which was . . . when those questions were first agitated in Cambridge, Dr Baro the Frenchman, being called to account by some of the heads for his opinion wrote a discourse to my Master Wm Burghley the Chancellor . . . to justify himself. I then waiting on him [as] his domestic chaplain, my lord gave me that discourse, willed me to read it and give me my opinion of it. I read it and finding him to be of the opinion that God did elect *propter praevisam fidem* I wrote about the quantity of a sheet of paper against that opinion, and maintained this that *Qui destinavit finem disposuit de omnibus mediis ad finem coaducentibus*, and that faith, repentance, obedience and whatsoever else were *effectus* not *causae electionis*; upon these grounds of Scripture. It is God that worketh in us both will and deed of his mere mercy . . .[10]

If any require a further account of my faith and conscience in the point of Predestination, I pray him to read the 17th article, of our Articles of religion, of Predestination and Election.

I ascribe the whole work of our salvation solely to God, and the powerful operation of the holy Spirit of grace. I yield nothing to man, or man's will. *Homo se habet mere passive in conversione ad Deum. Qui operatur in nobis et velle et perficere ex mera misericordia.* The will of man is altogether averse & perverse till it be informed, reformed and conformed by the holy Spirit, and indued with the grace of obedience to the good motions of the holy Spirit to follow when the holy Spirit leadeth and move when the holy Spirit draweth it. In which sense the holy Spirit may be truly said to work *irresistibiliter* yet not as upon stocks and stones coactive to some men whether they will or not. But *obedientialiter*, giving grace to obey the good motions of that grace which hath disposed of as the means, as well as of the end of salvation. So as it may be said, in the words of the divines of Dort, *Non tollitur voluntas, sed a Deo informatur, dirigitur agitur, et a Deo acta ipsa agit.* And again *Executio decreti electionis pendet a conditionato usu mediorum, de quibus disposuit Deus. Nemo venit ad me nisi Pater traherit eum.*[11]

Of the extent of the salvation wrought by Christ no man shall be offended if I say in the words of the divines of Dort I read *sufficientium* λύτρου, *et meriti*

[9] Rom. ix, 21.
[10] Phil. ii, 13.
[11] John vi, 44.

sui Christus pro omnibus et singulis et mortuus est, et mori voluit. And again, no man's case is so forlorn but that he may assure himself of his part of the salvation wrought by Christ if by faith he can lay hold thereof.

Of perseverance this is what I say. The counsels of God are without repentance. And there is no condemnation to them that are in Christ Jesus. For the foundation of God standeth immovable with this seal, *the Lord knoweth who are his.*[12]

I never yet took upon me to determine of falling either finally or totally. The elect of God may fall grievously, as holy David and St Peter did, and the seed of grace in them may lie for a time as a spark raked up in the ashes. I dare not make any suppositions had David had Peter died in impenitency save I am sure they both were restored by faith, and repentance; and so shall all God's elect, though through human infirmity they fall most dangerously.

Of Reprobation I learn by our Articles to be silent other than with St. Augustine *Non eligere, hoc est reprobare*, the reward of sin is death, *Et perditio tua ex te Israel.*[13] I do ever *praesupponere lapsum* and consider all men *in massa corrupta*. Where I dare not dispute with God, *Quare hunc non illum* and when I am brought to God's decree *non miserendi*, or *praeteritionis* I adore God's wisdom & Justice, and sit down with St Paul's *O altitudo.*[14]

This amounts to a carefully prepared and systematic series of statements on each of the controverted issues. Neile went further than he need have done in insisting that man's will was merely passive in conversion, and that in some sense the work of the Spirit was irresistible. In approving the judgment of the divines of Dort, as for example in distinguishing between the end and the means of predestination, and between the decree and the execution of the decree, he employed Bezan rather than Calvinist terminology. On the extent of the Atonement, he did not claim that it was intended for all, as he might have done; merely that it was sufficient for all. On perseverance he answered with a series of biblical references, and then on the much-discussed test cases of David and Peter his answer was orthodox 'Calvinism' without any saving clauses – he did not suggest that the state of justification might be forfeited through mortal sins, as Overall, with James I's approval, had maintained at Hampton Court. The only point on which his answers were inconsistent with Perkins or Beza was in his view of reprobation, which he took to be non-election, or a passing over (preterition), and he justified that stance by reference to St Augustine and to Article XVII.

If this speech proves Neile's Arminianism,[15] then he was incompetent enough to betray it in the very process of rebutting what as far as he was concerned was an implausible calumny. In reality it demonstrates that he, unlike his accusers, had a clear understanding of the five points

[12] Rom. xi, 29; viii, 1; 2 Tim. ii, 19.
[13] Hos. xiii, 9.
[14] Rom. xi, 33.
[15] A. Foster, 'A Biography of Archbishop Richard Neile, 1562–1640', Oxford University D.Phil. thesis, 1978, esp. 192–206; Tyacke, *Anti-Calvinists*, 111–13.

controverted by the Remonstrants. On every one of them he explained his own position by reference to authorities of unimpeachable authority to English Calvinists, namely, St Paul, St Augustine, and the determinations of the Synod of Dort. It is impossible therefore to accept that he was being deliberately evasive and firm only on non-controversial issues.[16] When Neile said that he was reluctant 'to open the mouth of the clay to dispute with the potter' and that he could be confident only of God's general promises to all penitent sinners, he was signalling his orthodoxy and unwillingness, in the very words of St Paul and of Article XVII, to question the mystery of reprobation or the depths of divine justice, which in his view Baro and Arminius had attempted to do. He was deliberately distancing himself from the Remonstrants.[17] He made no attempt to argue that Arminianism was not a term of obloquy, and he was ready 'if I cannot fairly and truly clear myself let me have the shame and reproach cast upon me'.[18]

Attempts to use other evidence to prove Neile's 'Arminianism', or to suggest a fundamental change of doctrinal allegiance, fail to convince. If on the one hand it was possible for him, like Whitgift and Hutton, to dissent from Baro on election *ex praevisa fide*, that is hardly enough to identify him with 'Cambridge Calvinism'. There is therefore no reason to suppose that he then 'severed his connexions' with it by 1606 just because he was prepared to license two sermons by Richard Meredith, teaching that Christians might pray for remission of sins, grace, perseverance and glory without any limitation, still less to agree that 'such teaching remained only just within the bounds of the doctrinally permissible at this date'.[19] Similarly, the fact that Oldenbarnevelt would have preferred Neile, together with Overall and Buckeridge, to have constituted the British delegation to Dort, cannot be claimed as 'confirmation of Neile's own Arminian views',[20] without implicit subscription to Archbishop Abbot's highly polarized conception of Protestant orthodoxy, an outlook that neither Whitgift, nor Burleigh, nor James I had ever shared.

Laud, like Neile, had long been a target for accusations of popery. The issues which marked him out were his insistence on the necessity of baptism, *iure divino* episcopacy, and especially the visibility of the church, for he was accused both of using arguments derived from Bellarmine and of importing a division between the English and continental churches. None of Laud's assertions was in the least new: but they were enough to

---

[16] Foster, 'Richard Neile', 206.
[17] Cf. ibid., 204; Tyacke, *Anti-Calvinists*, 113.
[18] Durham Dean and Chapter Library, Hunter MS 67/14, f. 2.
[19] Tyacke, *Anti-Calvinists*, 112.
[20] Ibid., 120.

make him a target for accusations of popery in the Oxford divinity school. Like Howson, he was accused by Robert Abbot of betraying it by not preaching against it. 'If they do, at any time, speak anything against the Papists, they do but beat a little about the bush, and that softly too, for fear of waking and disquieting the birds that are in it.'[21] Abbot claimed that 'in the points of *Free Will, Justification, Concupiscence being a sin after Baptism, Inherent Righteousness, and certainty of Salvation,* the Papists beyond the sea can say they are wholly theirs'. No evidence survives of Laud's 'hearing' before King James except an unsigned and undated letter in Neile's handwriting[22] which records that both the Abbot brothers ultimately withdrew their accusation, and promised that it would not be repeated. The king's indignation at the attack on Laud is said to have been one reason for the instructions sent to Oxford in 1616 that divinity students should be encouraged to study the Fathers and Councils, 'and not to insist too long on compendiums and abbreviators'.[23]

The remarkable lack of interest in Laud's theology among writers who are none the less content to label him 'Arminian' is reflected in the neglect of his private notes on Bellarmine.[24] Bellarmine's principal targets were Luther, Calvin and Beza. Laud's notes are therefore invaluable guides to his thinking on the doctrinal issues controverted between Catholic and Protestant apologists. They demonstrate his wide-ranging knowledge of

[21] Heylyn, *Cyprianus Anglicus,* 65–7. The archbishop echoed his brother's view during his sequestration. 'His life in Oxford was to pick quarrels in the lectures of the public readers, and to advertise them to the then Bishop of Durham [Neile], that he might fill the ears of king James with discontents against the honest men that took pains in their places, and *settled the truth* (which he called *Puritanism*) in their auditors. He made it his work to see what books were in the press, and to look over epistles dedicatory, and prefaces to the reader, to see what faults were to be found. It was an observation, what a *sweet man* this was like to be.' Rushworth, *Historical Collections,* I. 440.

[22] PRO SP 14/80/124, endorsed by Laud 'What his Majesty said concerning Dr Abbot's sermon about me'. Neile wrote: 'My good Lord. I moved his Majesty this day touching Dr Laud's return to Oxford. To which his Majesty answered yes, for that there is no cause that he should stay. I have made a full and quiet end to all those matters, I was bold to say "Then Dr Laud shall have peace and be no more troubled in that matter?" "No" said his Majesty, "my Lord's Grace himself acknowledged his brother's error in it, and Dr Abbot himself asked pardon for it, excusing himself that he was put to it, for that all the University did understand that Dr Laud's passage was upon him." '

[23] Prideaux's response in Exeter College was to cause eighteen questions against Arminianism to be publicly disputed, beginning with the interpretation of Romans vii and ending with the condemnation of Arminianism as semi-Pelagianism. A. Wood, *The History and Antiquities of the University of Oxford,* ed. John Gutch (2 vols., 1792–6), II. 328; Lawson, *Life of Laud,* I. 162.

[24] These are contained in volumes held in Archbishop Marsh's Library, Dublin, but printed in the *Works of William Laud,* VI. 607–708. The comments on predestination are datable on internal evidence to the period after 1618. They amount to less than a systematic exposition, but there can be no doubt of their value, when studied alongside Bellarmine's text, as a guide to Laud's thinking on the questions agitated between Roman and Reformed theologians.

patristic and scholastic authorities, and his keen eye for the inconsistencies in Bellarmine's exposition. Laud appears throughout as an uncompromising defender of the Reformers. Even on the doctrine of predestination, he was prepared to defend Beza against Bellarmine.

The evidence for what to most readers will be a surprising claim arises out of Bellarmine's discussion of the first cause of sin in *De Amissione Gratiae*, in which Beza's argument that God is not the author, and that the vessels of wrath become so only as a result of the Fall of Adam, is said to be undermined by his own account of the Colloquy of Montbéliard,[25] in which the decrees of election and reprobation are unambiguously stated to have preceded all prevision of guilt, and indeed any cause whatsoever; and in which God is said to have ordained the Fall as a means to the execution of His decree. A long note by Laud[26] – the longest of all his notes on Bellarmine – defended Beza by asserting that the matter from which Adam was created was not damned, but at worst indifferent, and not such as would by its wickedness have necessarily drawn him to evil. The damnation of the human race was consequent on Adam's sin. Certainly, Laud says, both foreknowledge and the decree to create mankind pre-existed not only Adam's sin but also his creation, but their actual and real creation (*productio*) followed in time and was effected from the damned mass. Perhaps that is what Beza meant. Or perhaps, if Beza was thinking about the actions of God before time began, he meant that God created men from a mass which He foreknew would be damned by the sin of Adam.[27] If Laud had been an 'anti-Calvinist', he would surely have betrayed it by appealing here to the Lutheran arguments used against Beza at Montbéliard.[28] He makes no references whatever to them.

As Bellarmine proceeded to his own, sufficiently uncompromising, exposition of St Augustine, Laud followed him without flinching. When Bellarmine contends that the elect are elected not merely to efficacious grace, but to glory, Laud does not dissent that this is without violence to the will. When, following St Augustine, Bellarmine grants the reprobation of the greater part of mankind because of sin, Laud registers no dissent. Similarly, that in one sense reprobation was to be referred to the will of God, in another to the foresight of sin, was common ground. At one point, indeed, Laud's own doctrine was more uncompromising, for

---

[25] See p. 98 above; and for Beza's account of the proceedings, *Ad Acta Colloquii Montisbelgartensis* (Geneva, 1587).

[26] Laud, *Works*, VI. 696.

[27] The reader of this note will understand why Laud concluded that the problem of predestination was 'unmasterable in this life'.

[28] Laud could scarcely have resisted quoting the *Acta Colloquii Montis Belligartensis* (Tübingen, 1587), had he been theologically 'anti-Calvinist'.

when Bellarmine argued that John vi, 70 ('I have chosen you twelve') referred not to predestination but to the effect of predestination, Laud objected
'Did not the effect of predestination include Judas?'[29] Bellarmine then
discussed St Augustine's conclusion that the failure of God to grant the gift
of perseverance to all the justified must remain a mystery: we cannot say that
it is a punishment for sin, because the justified do not deserve punishment.
Laud's note suggests, but only as a question, that it is perhaps because they
fall from the grace of justification when they were able not to fall. When
Bellarmine defends positive reprobation *ex praevisis operibus*, Laud
merely notes 'He could not damn without just guilt. Who therefore is without
guilt, into which man falls *ineluctabiliter*?[30]

Bellarmine turned to the predestination of angels. He suggested that
in this case, the will of God to save infallibly was prior to the prevision
of good works, on the ground that what is necessary is prior to what is
contingent. Laud's notes take the argument and invert it. He suggests that
(angels being angels) good works are a necessary and not a contingent
effect of grace; but God is free to give that grace. Perhaps, therefore, in
the case of angels predestination does follow prevision of good works.
There was a similar disagreement about the reprobation of angels, where
Bellarmine denied that negative reprobation was consequent on the prevision of sin, because (he claimed) God foresaw that they would infallibly
perish without more grace than that which He willed to bestow on
them. Laud characteristically preferred to think that it might rather
be because they failed to put to good use the sufficient grace they were
given.[31]

This speculation was valuable, Bellarmine suggested, for its relevance
to the predestination of men. Let us imagine, he suggested, that a king
proposes to offer a prize to be won by a race. By divine revelation, he
foresees that if it is run on horses, so and so will be fittest for the prize;
if on chariots, so and so; if on foot, others; if in ships, still others. Then
he decides that it will be contested by chariots, and to all who assemble
for the contest he grants the most appropriate (*aptissimos*) chariots. Surely
the contest would be just, those who were defeated would be justly denied
the prize, and those who succeeded justly awarded it. Laud's only, but
typical comment, was to ask whether he offers the fittest chariots to those
whom he reprobates. Finally, to Bellarmine's conclusion that in the election and reprobation of angels there are greater depths of mercy and justice
than in the predestination of men, Laud corrects him with the comment

[29] Laud, *Works*, VI. 699.
[30] Ibid., 700.
[31] Ibid. Negative reprobation corresponded to Beza's decree to reprobate; positive to his
execution of the decree.

that in the election of men there is more mercy, so less justice; but in their reprobation, more justice, so less mercy.[32]

Other comments afford scattered but suggestive insights. Laud continued to defend Beza and Calvin, pointing out that the Bezan Confession granted the infinite value of Christ's death demanded by God's justice as a propitiation for sin, and that Bellarmine's account of Calvin is repeatedly in error.[33] Similarly, he defended Calvin's exposition of St Augustine on the relationship between grace and free will.[34] In one particularly significant comment, Laud denied that Calvin had taught that the justified cannot commit sin after Baptism. What he did say[35] was that those who are born both of water and of the Spirit cannot fall through final impenitence. *Hoc verum est*, Laud added. Far from dissenting from Calvin's doctrine of perseverance, he signalled his emphatic agreement with it.

The notes on Bellarmine show Laud to be a redoubtable defender of the Reformers. His public utterances provide no reason to change that verdict. His uncompromising hostility to Rome is obvious enough in his major work of Protestant apologetic, the record of his conversations with Fisher the Jesuit.[36] He confessed that he had resolved 'in handling matters of religion, to leave all gall out of my ink', but he was able to appeal to the authority of Calvin in treating the Roman Church with respect.[37] Predestination was mentioned only in passing, when Laud alluded to Bellarmine's accusation that Protestants could not agree whether a man might be certain of his salvation: he pointed out that the Roman Church was also divided on the issue, the Dominican Soto and the Franciscan Vega representing opposite views at the Council of Trent.[38] Predestination for Laud was not so much an issue between Protestants and Catholics, as a problem that had troubled the church in all ages. That was one reason why he was against any attempt to extend the fundamentals of Christian belief beyond the undoubted word of Scripture.[39] He accepted the Creed

---

[32] For Bellarmine's analogy, see *De Gratia et Libero Arbitrio*, III. xvii. For Laud's comments, see Laud, *Works*, VI. 700.

[33] Laud's defence of Beza's Confession, see ibid., 703.

[34] See especially Laud's defence of Calvin's interpretation of St Augustine in *Institutes*, II.3.7. Laud, *Works*, VI. 698 commenting on Bellarmine, *De Gratia et Libero Arbitrio*, I. 12.

[35] Laud's defence of Calvin, ibid., 704, citing *Institutes*, III. 2.11–12.

[36] William Laud, *A Relation of the Conference between W. Laud and Mr Fisher the Jesuit* (London, 1639) was an extended version of an earlier account published anonymously in 1624, and is reprinted as vol. II of *The Works of William Laud*. Widely regarded in Laud's own day as second only to Hooker's *Ecclesiastical Polity* as a vindication of the Church of England, it is largely ignored in modern studies of its author.

[37] Laud, *Works*, II. 150.

[38] Ibid., 57. See also IV. 272–3.

[39] Laud, *Works*, II. 113.

as 'fundamental', because it was founded on that infallible rule. It followed that he was prepared to grant only a limited role either to reason or to tradition. 'If the Church will not err, it must not ravel curiously into unnecessary truths, which are out of the promise, or follow any other guide than the doctrine which Christ has left behind him to govern it.'[40] God had not promised the church that He would reveal the truth in all things. The function of confessional formularies like the Thirty-nine Articles was 'to bind to peace and external obedience where there is not express letter agreed on': they could not make anything fundamental which was not fundamental already,[41] and Laud was prepared to accept a large degree of liberty of conscience outside those fundamentals in the interests of peace and comprehensiveness. If an article was capable of bearing more than one interpretation, then it was 'lawful for any man to choose what sense his judgement directs him to: so that it be a sense, *secundum analogiam fidei*, and that he holds it peaceably, without distracting the church. And the wisdom of the Church hath been, in all ages, or in most, to require consent to articles, *in general*, as much as may be. And the Church, in high points, requiring assent to particulars, hath been rent.'[42] He compared the Church of England favourably with the Roman Church for not having an index of prohibited books. 'Nor will I ever take upon me to express that tenet or opinion, the denial of the foundation only excepted, which may shut any Christian, even the meanest, out of heaven.'[43]

Laud made two other public utterances with respect to predestination. On 5 July 1626, the king asked him to preach on the occasion of a public fast, ordained partly on account of the plague, partly on account of the dangers arising from the war. Laud's warning against 'security', therefore,[44] was deliberately topical. Similarly, current adversities were the background to his warning against questioning the works of providence, which 'many men, yea, and sometimes the best, are a great deal too busy with'.[45] There followed, no doubt with the recent proclamation silencing controversy very much in mind, a reference to those who 'would fain know all the secrets of predestination'. Like Neile, Laud used the text of 2 Tim. ii, 19 to make the point that predestination was 'one of God's foundations', whose secrets were known to Him alone, with the seal 'let every man that calls on the name of Christ, depart from iniquity'. Matthew Hutton for one had used the same text (for the same

---

[40] Ibid., 183–4.
[41] Ibid., 175.
[42] Laud, *Works*, IV. 12.
[43] Laud, *Works*, III. 59–60, 387; W. H. Hutton. *William Laud* (1895), 152.
[44] Laud, *Works*, I. 128.
[45] Ibid., 130–1.

purpose) in his exposition of predestinarian doctrine in the 1590s: it was a commonplace.[46]

Equally central to mainstream Protestantism was Laud's other pronouncement on predestination, delivered in the course of his answer to Saye's speech on the liturgy. He listed a number of 'Brownist', or Separatist errors in which he included William Prynne's notorious assertion that any 'true saint of God' dying unrepentant in a known sin 'shall as surely be saved as if he had lived to repent of it'.[47] In saying that the doctrine was contrary to the whole current of Scripture, that it 'tore up the foundations of religion' and 'induceth all manner of profaneness into the world', Laud was saying nothing that James I, who at Hampton Court had declared his 'utter dislike' of the same doctrine, would not heartily have endorsed. Similarly, in his declaration that 'my very soul abominates' the reprobation from eternity of 'by far the greater part of mankind to eternal fire, without any eye at all to their sin', which was taught by almost all the separatists, Laud's indignation is reminiscent of Whitgift's outrage when confronted with Barrett's recantation.[48]

Laud's contacts with Vossius and Grotius have been adduced to demonstrate his doctrinal commitments, but to suggest that they prove his 'Arminianism' involves little less than a reckless distortion of the evidence.[49] The correspondence with Vossius began only after Vossius had decided, in consultation with Dudley Carleton, to dedicate his study of the Latin-writing historians to Buckingham.[50] In recognition of the offer of a professorship, Vossius sent copies to Cambridge University, and to a number of individual friends and acquaintances, who included George Carleton, Samuel Ward and John Rous as well as Neile and Laud. Laud's letter of acknowledgement appears to be his first direct contact with Vossius. 'Andrewes and Erpenius are dead, let us now join hands', he wrote; 'meanwhile I remain your servant in Christ, and if the name pleases, friend'. Laud took the opportunity to say how much he admired his Pelagian History, but asked Vossius 'noli me in lineis hisce turbatis quaerere, alibi habito, rerum non verborum servus'.[51]

Early fruits of Laud's (and others') good offices were a Cambridge fellowship for Vossius' eldest son, the publication of the *Theses Theologicae* at Oxford in 1628, and the appointment of Vossius himself

---

[46] Ibid. Cf. M. Hutton, *Brevis et delucida explicatio*, 25–6.

[47] Laud, *Works*, VI, 132. The argument comes from W. Prynne, *Perpetuitie of a Regenerate Man's Estate*, 431.

[48] For James I, see p. 146 above. For the same reason Matthew Hutton resisted Puritan pressure for the removal of the prayer against sudden death from the Litany. Strype, *Whitgift*, III. 400–1. For Whitgift, see above, p. 104.

[49] Trevor-Roper, *Catholics, Anglicans and Puritans*, esp. 62, 97–8, 195, 287.

[50] Rademaker, *Vossius*, 228–9.

[51] Laud, *Works*, VI. 250–1.

to a canonry at Canterbury in 1629. In November 1629 Vossius arrived in England, to have an audience with the king, make visits to Oxford and Cambridge and to be entertained by Laud, by George Abbot (Vossius wrote that he 'conversed amiably'), and by Arundel and Pembroke. As a result of the visit, there were renewed hopes that he might settle in England. James Ussher wanted him to be Dean of Armagh.[52]

It is clear, therefore, that Vossius continued to be admired by men representing a broad spectrum of theological opinion. As Thomas Crosfield noted, 'Vossius in the States they do repute not factious or too zealous in dispute, no wrangler or seditious violent man, like to the subtle-close Arminian.'[53] That Laud's admiration for the Pelagian History cannot be adduced to prove his Arminianism is surely put beyond further argument by the fact that it was shared by that decided anti-Pelagian John Richardson, the Dean of Derry, who in 1630 became involved in a sharp exchange with William Bedell over differing interpretations of St Augustine's doctrine of grace. Bedell concluded his reply to Richardson by writing:[54]

You conclude with a large passage of Vossius who setteth down as you say the sum of all, with whom herein you fully content yourself. I do join with you in Vossius's determination in every letter and syllable . . . And for Pelagianism, Semipelagianism and Arminianism (to all which I say Anathema) if in your own judgment, you do absolve me from such not only worthless but wicked opinions, do not I beseech you by accumulating testimonies against them, raise a suspicion . . . that my lips speak wickedness, and my tongue utters deceit: that secretly at least I nourish such monsters, to the quelling whereof your labour is intended.

The main preoccupation of Laud's own letters to Vossius was to encourage him to proceed with his refutation of Baronius. He wanted him to demonstrate 'with insoluble arguments' the respects in which Rome had departed from the early church.[55] When Vossius wrote asking why Laud had not spoken publicly on the controverted questions, he answered:[56]

I have spared no pains to prevent these dangerous and intricate questions from being handled before the people: lest, under the colour of truth, we should violate godliness and charity. I have always been for moderate counsels; lest men of hot tempers, with whom religion is not the main object, should throw all things into confusion. This course may not, perhaps, have given satisfaction. Nevertheless I have kept in mind how solemnly our Saviour recommended charity to his followers; and with what caution and patience his apostle wishes us to treat the

---

[52] Rademaker, *Vossius*, 232–5.
[53] *The Diary of Thomas Crosfield*, ed. F. S. Boas (Oxford, 1935), 25.
[54] E. S. Shuckbrugh (ed.), *Two Biographies of William Bedell* (Cambridge, 1902), 396.
[55] Laud, *Works*, VI. 253. See also 260, 277, among many other references.
[56] From the important letter of 14 July 1629, ibid., 263–6. I have used the translation in C. W. Le Bas, *The Life of Archbishop Laud* (1836), 24–5.

weak. If I should perish by using arts like these, my recompense will be with me: and except in God, I will seek no consolation beyond myself . . . With the blessing of God, I will endeavour that truth and peace may embrace each other. If, for our sins, God should deny us this blessing, my own hope will be for the peace which is eternal.

Again, in January 1629, he wrote 'So God may love me, I know not what can be done, especially by myself, in these festering times.'[57]

The 'festering' times required Laud himself to be circumspect. In 1631 he told Vossius that Francis Junius had brought back letters from Grotius. He was most grateful (he had always known that he was a very learned man), but he had not had leisure to reply. 'You know that I will do for you and for Grotius and his cause what I can.'[58] Emphatically, that did not include the offer of employment in England: 'as things now are with us, it is not even to be contemplated . . . you say that this is a schismatic age, and I don't dare to deny it. Meanwhile it is necessary to bear it, because you are unable to avoid it or to correct it.'[59] In 1636, Laud expressed his pleasure to hear of Grotius' appointment as ambassador from Sweden to the court of France: 'Not so when it was spread abroad that he was called back to Britain. But it was the trumpet of envy which sounded, and as soon as I heard it was a lying report, happiness returned. He has honoured me with his letters from France, for so I feel concerning so learned a man, for whom I wish the best.'[60]

The private exchange of opinions with learned friends was another matter, but even here the initiative and the ideas came from Vossius. In 1632, he wrote to tell Laud[61] that he had received from Ussher a copy of his vindication of Gottschalk. Vossius could not agree that Gottschalk's condemnation by the church had been an error, even though he was prepared to accept St Augustine 'as long as he is not at odds either with himself or with those Fathers he himself cited in part against Pelagius'. Laud replied that he too had been sent a copy of Ussher's book, for which he had thanked him, 'for indeed the Bishop is dear to me on account of his manifold learning'. He had time only to give it a hasty inspection, but he agreed that there was much in it that was not so pleasing, especially the 'more rigid sense of St Augustine, which allowed that venerable Father to stand neither with the more ancient Fathers in the Church, nor with

[57] Letter of February 1630 in Laud, *Works*, VI. 292–4. This is not the letter of a cleric who thinks his faction has just triumphed.

[58] Ibid., 297.

[59] Ibid., 299–300. 'I confess that I always thought his return to his own country barely credible, whoever else was persuaded of it; nor are reasons lacking, though not here and now fit to be stated.'

[60] Ibid., 446.

[61] For Vossius' letter, see Vossius, *Epistolae*, 189–90.

himself'. He would be grateful, purely for his private use, for a fuller account of Vossius' views.[62]

Vossius' long reply[63] listed five major schools of thought on the doctrine of grace and predestination. Apart from the opinion of the early church, which was also that of St Augustine before his confrontation with Pelagius, there were two extreme views, two moderate. At the two extremes were the Pelagians, who denied the necessity of grace, and the 'Predestinatists', who so elevated it that they annihilated free will, and left no place for warning and punishment. Less extreme on the one side were the Semi-Pelagians, who denied only prevenient grace; and on the other St Augustine's later position, asserted against Pelagius, not merely that grace was necessary (here he was in accord with the early church) but that it derived from an absolute decree. This was the teaching that had divided St Augustine's contemporaries. Some had condemned it as false and dangerous. Others had thought it highly questionable but preferred not to condemn it, even to leave it as a matter for scholarly debate. Some (like Prosper) had accepted it, but only as long as it did not conflict with free will. Finally there were those like Gottschalk who had adopted it with enthusiasm. Vossius could not see how he could be absolved from a fatalistic annihilation of the will, and in spite of Ussher's piety and learning he could not accept his attempted vindication. Obviously, he admitted, he and Ussher did not agree in their interpretation of St Augustine. The scholarly difference of opinion was real, but it did nothing to prevent amicable relationships, and the two scholars continued to cooperate with each other, especially in their work on the early Confessions, Vossius sending manuscripts to Ussher, and Ussher dedicating his published work of 1647 to Vossius.[64]

It is impossible to say how far Laud would have endorsed Vossius' analysis in detail. He would have applauded his objections to fatalism and to irrespective reprobation, but as far as he was concerned these were gross distortions of Christian truth, and there is no sign that he saddled either Calvin or Beza with them. He certainly shared Vossius' preference for a middle way, for he had always believed that the truth lay between extremes.[65] Although at Laud's trial the issue of Arminianism was hardly mentioned, his references to it are far from suggesting any covert commitment. He would not have agreed that to preach that Christ died for all men was sufficient to prove the charge, for that doctrine was 'the

---

[62] Laud, *Works*, VI. 299.
[63] Vossius, *Epistolae*, 208–9.
[64] Rademaker, *Vossius*, 287–8.
[65] Laud, *Works*, VI. 85: 'Well, if I do suffer, 'tis but because truth usually lies between two sides, and is beaten on both sides, (as the poor Church of England is at this day by these factions).'

universal and constant doctrine of the Catholic Church in all ages', confirmed by the 'express words of Scripture itself' and allowed orthodox by the Synod of Dort.[66] Laud said that he wished with all his heart 'that this had been the greatest error of Arminius', and although he did not spell out the errors, he was convinced that their advocacy of *libertas prophetandi* had occasioned much 'mischief'.[67] Laud realized none the less that 'Arminianism' was on occasions merely a 'bugbear': a phantom or scarecrow employed for factional purposes.[68] It was better to remain silent for the sake of peace. The price was to leave the accusations against both himself and Neile unanswered. At the bar of history, it seems, that price is still being paid.

[66] Laud, *Works*, II. 305.
[67] Ibid., IV. 263.
[68] Ibid., VII. 275.

15 The personal rule, 1629–1640

Royal policy throughout 1628 had been influenced by Charles's hopes for his third Parliament. The collapse of those hopes, the dissolution of the second session in March 1629 and the decision thereafter to rule without Parliament removed constraints on the court. This final chapter will review the licensing of books and the control of preaching in order to ascertain the thrust of policy during the personal rule.

Licensing policy

Until 1633, Abbot and Laud shared the responsibility for censorship, but most authorizations in that period were the work of Jeffrey, Buckner and Austen, all chaplains to Abbot.[1] An early incident which demonstrates how far the results of licensing policy were from 'suppressing Calvinism' is the story of J.A.'s *A Historical Narration*,[2] told at length, with considerable pride at his own part in it, by William Prynne.[3] According to Prynne the author was John Ailward, 'not long before a Popish priest',[4] whose intention was 'to prove the martyrs and first reformers of the Church to be Arminians, and Arminianism the established doctrine of our Church'. It was, he claimed, 'the greatest affront and imposture ever offered to or put upon the Church of England . . . of the first discovery whereof God made him the only instrument'.

---

[1] P. M. Olander, 'Changes in the Mechanism and Procedure for Control of the London Press 1625–1637', Oxford University B.Litt. thesis, 1976, 69.

[2] STC 4; the sheets were reissued in 1645 with an extra title page as Wing A 804. The British Library copy has this MS note by Thomason: 'This Historicall Narration following was printed in Anno 1631 as you may perceive, and called Inn: by George Abbot Bp: of Canterbury because in it was contained divers dangerous opinions both of Pelagianisme and Arminianisme. It was licensed by Edw: Martine then chaplain to Wm Laud who was then Bp of London, but now Canterbury and condemned by the House of Commons now sitting to loose his head for crimen leze maiestat; to which sentence the House of Lords have not yet fully agreed. This shall serve for ye Instruction of the reder that shall see this new title printed 10 Decemb. 1644.'

[3] Prynne, *Canterburies Doome*, 167.

[4] Prynne, *A Quench Coale* (1637), 2.

In reality, the book was almost entirely a republication of an early Elizabethan tract[5] written to clear the unknown author from accusations of Pelagianism. Prynne claimed that it was the work of John Champneys; that it had been answered by both John Veron[6] and Robert Crowley;[7] and that the republication had been licensed by Laud's chaplain Edward Martin, 'a professed Arminian'.[8] Prynne had been shown a copy by Sir Humphrey Lynde, and to that gentleman's considerable astonishment had not only identified it but shown him copies of Veron's and Crowley's replies. Prynne had then informed Abbot, who duly called in the book, telling Prynne that 'bishop Laud had since been with him . . . who confessed that his chaplain had licensed this Narration in which he had done very ill, but he [Laud] had given him such a rattling for his pains, that he would warrant his Grace he should never meddle with Arminian books or opinions more'.[9]

Abbot had suppressed a volume consisting very largely of quotations from Cranmer, Hooper and Latimer. Prynne, meanwhile, had recently published a whole series of unlicensed attacks on Montagu.[10] But there are plenty of examples of Calvinist works properly licensed after 1629, notwithstanding Henry Burton's complaint that 'MS are now the best help people have to vindicate the truth, printing being nowadays prohibited to them, especially if their writings have any the least tincture of opposition to Arminianism, yea even to Popery itself.'[11] As is generally agreed, there was no restriction on the reprinting of books already licensed until the Star Chamber decree of 1637. In 1635 the Cambridge press reissued the whole of Perkins's works together with his and Beza's tables of the order of predestination.[12] Similarly, Norton's translation of Calvin's

---

[5] STC 5742. 10 *A Copy of an Answer unto a Certain Letter* (The Netherlands(?), 1563(?)).

[6] John Veron died in 1563; Prynne must be wrong, for the John Champneys Veron mentioned had attacked his own writings, which STC 5742.10 does not.

[7] *An Apology or Defence of the English Writers and Preachers, with Cerberus the three-headed dog of Hell* (1566(?)). Robert Crowley was in 1566 vicar of St Giles without Cripplegate, but was deprived and imprisoned by Parker for creating a disturbance about the wearing of the surplice by some singing men in his church. He died in 1588.

[8] Prynne, *Canterburies Doome*, 167.

[9] Prynne told Abbot that Martin had only the previous afternoon at Paul's Cross 'publicly broached, maintained, universal grace and redemption, with all the Arminian errors contained in this book, and condemned in the Synod of Dort, to the great offence of the auditors, as his own chaplains Dr Buckner, Master Austen and Dr Featley could at large inform him'. He urged Abbot to take action, 'but by this bishop's power there was nothing more done'. Ibid.

[10] Prynne's *Old Antithesis* (1629) and *Anti-Arminianisme* (1630). (The Lambeth Palace Library copy has Archbishop Abbot's arms embossed on the front cover!) Several editions of *God, No Impostor*: STC 20459.3 1629; 20459.7 1629; 20460, 1629; 20461, 1630. Prynne's *Perpetuitie* (1626) was licensed by Daniel Featley. Olander, 'Changes in the London Press', 67.

[11] Boas (ed.), *Diary of Thomas Crosfield*, 89.

[12] Perkins, *Works* (Cambridge, 1635) (STC 19653).

Institutes, of which there had been no reprint under Abbot, was reissued in London in 1634.[13] Other republications included Pierre du Moulin's *Anatomy of Arminianism*, Ursinus' *The Summe of the Christian Religion* and William Ames's *Medulla Theologiae* (previously printed at Amsterdam, and now for the first time in London); there was also a new issue of the *Collegiate Suffrage*.[14] Publications from the Oxford press tell the same story. Although Prideaux complained of restrictions in 1628,[15] William Pemble's *Vindiciae Gratiae, A Plea for Grace*, first published in 1627, was republished in 1629, and issued again in 1635 with a preface by Richard Capel; his *Vindiciae Fidei*, first published in 1625, was also reissued in 1629.[16] On a different level, William Gouge's Catechism was reprinted several times during the personal rule. Unusually, this is a Catechism which begins with predestination, and its view was uncompromising.[17] Similarly, Paul Baynes's *Commentary on Ephesians I*, originally entered in 1618, was published in 1632, with an editorial note by Richard Sibbes attacking Arminianism.[18] It expounded the epistle in a supralapsarian sense: to say that man as fallen was the object of the divine decree 'took away the unsearchable mystery of election and reprobation' and made God mutable.[19]

There were also, despite a general impression to the contrary, original publications. Perhaps the most notable were the ten volumes of the sermons of John Preston which appeared between July 1629 and January 1633. Preston had died in July 1628, and by prior arrangement Richard Sibbes and John Davenport published the London sermons, Thomas Ball and Thomas Goodwin the Cambridge ones.[20] *Sermons Preached before his Majesty* first appeared in 1630 and was reprinted four times by 1637: among the sermons, 'The Pillar and Ground of Truth' attacked Rome, and asserted against Montagu that general councils might err on fundamentals. Only the mystical church, the body of the elect, could not err in matters fundamental. 'A Sensible Demonstration of the Deity' exhorted believers to make their calling and election sure. *Life Eternal*, or

---

[13] STC 4425; previous edition, 1611; prior to that, 1599.
[14] Du Moulin's *Anatomy of Arminianisme*, republished 1626 (STC 7309); 1635 (STC 7310). Ursinus' *The Summe of the Christian Religion* (1633) (STC 24539); Ames's *Medulla Theologiae* (1629) (STC 556.5); a new issue of the *Collegiat Suffrage*(1633) (STC 7069).
[15] Parr, *Life of Ussher*, 399.
[16] William Pemble, *Vindiciae Gratiae, A Plea for Grace, more especially the Grace of Faith, or Certain Lectures as touching the nature and properties of Grace and Faith, wherein, amongst other matters of great use, the main sinews of Arminius's doctrine are cut asunder* (Oxford, 1627; 2nd edn, 1629; 3rd edn, 1635); *Vindiciae Fidei* (Oxford, 1625; 2nd edn, 1629).
[17] William Gouge, *A Short Catechism, wherein are briefly laid down the fundamental principles of the Christian religion*, first published 1615, 7th edn, 1635 (STC 12130).
[18] Paul Baynes, *A Commentary on the first Chapter of the Ephesians* (1632).
[19] Ibid., 86.
[20] Kendall, *Calvin and English Calvinism to 1649*, 118, nn. 3, 4, 5.

A Treatise of the Divine Essence and Attributes, delivered in xviii sermons, dedicated to Lord Saye and Sele, went through five editions by 1634; the thirteenth sermon stressed the immutability of the divine decree.[21] There is, it has been suggested, more 'experimental' than 'credal' predestinarianism in Preston's sermons:[22] in the tradition of Perkins, they were preoccupied with the problems of assurance and how to distinguish between the regenerate and unregenerate, but they provide an eloquent demonstration of the survival of that tradition into the 1630s.

The sermons of Richard Sibbes are further evidence.[23] *The Bruised Reed* first appeared in July 1630, and went through many editions during the personal rule. *The Soul's Conflict* appeared in 1632, and *The Privileges of the Faithful* posthumously in 1637. Sibbes also edited editions of sermons by Henry Scudder, Ezekiel Culverwell, John Smith, John Ball and Richard Capel. He was Master of Catherine Hall, Cambridge from 1626, and in 1627 (in spite of Buckingham's election as Chancellor) refused an offer from Ussher to be Provost of Trinity College Dublin. In 1633 he was presented with the vicarage of Holy Trinity, Cambridge by Charles I. Sibbes was a sublapsarian, but was firm that God does not intend to save all. 'We must let God do what he will.'[24] As with Preston, however, there was a relative lack of interest in the doctrine, not on account of Laudian censorship, but because of a pastoral concern that led him 'almost [to] prefer that men forget about the decrees of predestination'.[25]

The sermons of Thomas Taylor reflect the same outlook. *The Practice of Repentance*[26] attacked the doctrine that Christ died for all. *The Progress of the Saints to Full Holiness* incorporated an exposition of the golden chain – Taylor's links were election, justification, sanctification and vocation – as 'degrees of grace'. The first two were 'wholly of God'; whereas a man may fall wholly from his vocation and from a great measure of sanctification, 'some care is preserved in the heart of the elect, by the Lord, so as all sound grace is not quenched'. Taylor included an old-fashioned attack on the papists and the Lutherans (i.e., Arminians), who taught that God has elected all to salvation and that Christ has died for all, and explicitly repudiated predestination from foreseen faith as making God's

---

[21] John Preston, *Life Eternal, or, a treatise of the divine essense and attributes*, ed. T. Goodwin and T. Ball (1631), 92.

[22] Kendall, *Calvin and English Calvinism to 1649*, 123, suggests that the experimental tradition is so strongly developed in Preston that doctrinal predestinarianism has become 'virtually pointless, a mere theory'.

[23] Ibid., 102–9.

[24] Ibid., 105.

[25] Ibid., 103.

[26] Thomas Taylor, *The Practice of Repentance, laid down in sundry directions* (1628), STC 23845; 2nd edn, 1629; 3rd edn, 1632; 4th edn, 1635.

election 'frustrate', dependent on the will of man to 'overrule God's will'. Furthermore, the doctrine of falling from grace undermined God's glory: 'what an uncomfortable doctrine'.[27] This is Calvinism by any definition. In 1634 there appeared a reprinted third edition of *The Parable of the Sower and the Seed* which included a substained attack on the Arminian denial that election is any cause or foundation of perseverance, with an extended discussion of Thomson's *Diatriba*.[28] Yet Taylor's works are marked by a heavy emphasis on sanctification: to stress good works was not a sign of Arminian novelty.

Another example of Calvinist publication under Laud was the appearance of John Prideaux's sermons, published both individually and in a collected edition at Oxford in 1636. Some had been published much earlier, but others were more recent and now appeared in print for the first time. In *Hezekiah's Sickness*, a court sermon originally published in 1621, Prideaux defended the doctrine of immutable predestination. 'I had not dwelt so long upon this, but the unsettled wavering of divers learned men amongst us had given just cause', and Prideaux went on to attack the 'Arminian' doctrine of two distinct wills in God.[29] In *Perez Uzzah*, preached and first published in 1624, he attacked 'our new Pelagians (somewhat worse than old Arians) who begin to incorporate themselves with old Socinians'.[30] Sermons previously unpublished included *A Plot for Preferment*, in which Prideaux complained of the alleged inhibition of naming Reformed writers 'except it be to their disgrace', and *The Patronage of Angels* (preached at Charles's court), in which he recalled with approval King James's attack on Vorstius and Arminius, but he granted that the issues were better dealt with in the schools, 'where both sides may be fully heard, in sifting all particulars', and he echoed King Charles's own views in saying that preaching called for application, 'to the amendment of our lives'.[31]

A few other examples, far from exhaustive, that Calvinism flourished under the personal rule may be added. Catechisms by both Whitaker and Cartwright were published in the 1630s.[32] Arthur Hildersham's *Lectures on Psalm LI*, delivered from 1625–31 and published in 1635, included a 'Calvinist' defence of the doctrine of predestination.[33] Phineas Fletcher

---

[27] Thomas Taylor, *The Progress of Saints to Full Holiness, described in sundry apostolical aphorisms or short precepts tending to sanctification* (1630), STC 23850; see esp. 99, 109.

[28] Thomas Taylor, *The Parable of the Sower and the Seed . . . To which is added, A Mappe of Rome, in five Sermons* (3rd edn, 1634), STC 23842; see esp. 329–53.

[29] John Prideaux, *Hezekiah's Sickness* (1636), 17–18, 20–1. Publication details in F. Madan, *Oxford Books* (2 vols., Oxford, 1895), I. 199–200.

[30] John Prideaux, *Perez Uzzah* (1636), 15, 22.

[31] John Prideaux, *A Plot for Preferment* (1636), 9; *The Patronage of Angels* (1636), 25–6.

[32] I owe this information to Dr Ian Green.

[33] A. Hildersham, *Lectures on Psalm LI* (1635), 248–9.

published *The Way to Blessedness: A Treatise or Commentary on the First Psalm* in 1632: it taught perseverance, and attacked those who failed to make use of the doctrine of predestination. 'Some are so impudent, that they would wholly silence this truth. Some even devilishly blaspheme it as a dangerous and desperate doctrine . . . Others eschew it as a rock, and dare not touch or meddle with it.'[34] John Ball's *A Treatise of Faith*,[35] published in 1631, argued that election is manifested by faith as its effect. It is common to all, and peculiar to those only, who are called according to the purpose of God. Belief in Christ for remission of sins is stronger and more necessary than particular assurance of our salvation. God has made many promises of perseverance, which we must believe: had it not mattered, our Lord would not have mentioned it. This was clearly 'Calvinist' and anti-Arminian, but pastoral and edificatory.

There is no evidence that works like these were the target of the Star Chamber decree of 1637, a principal purpose of which, it is now established, was to protect the monopoly of the Stationers' Company[36] and to settle the disputes between the master printers and their employees.[37] In so far as it was also used to improve government controls over licensing and the suppression of unlicensed books, it was aimed at works like those of Prynne, who had succeeded in getting ten works published in 1636–7 in spite of being confined in the Tower for the seditious libel *Histriomastix*.[38] Predestinarian works were licensed after 1637. One of Laud's chaplains licensed *The Happiness of the Saints in Glory*,[39] which asserts the doctrine of perseverance: 'Of those which thou has given me I have not lost one.' Juxon's chaplain licensed William Sclater the elder's *Sermons Experimental on Psalms cxvi* and *cxvii*, dedicated to Joseph Hall and edited by William Sclater the younger,[40] in which the golden chain was asserted – election, calling, justification and adoption, then sanctification, and certainty of salvation defended. Yet Sclater was acutely conscious of the dangers of presumption, sins 'committed out of persuasion of graciousness', and talked of abuses of Christian liberty: 'I would it were not amongst some professing best minds, that because there is no

---

[34] Phineas Fletcher, *The Way to Blessedness: A Treatise or Commentary on the First Psalm* (1632), 259.

[35] John Ball, *A Treatise of Faith* (1631). esp. 92, 149, 288–97.

[36] S. Lambert, 'The Printers and the Government, 1604–1637', in Robin Myers and Michael Harris (eds.), *Aspects of Printing from 1600* (Oxford, 1987).

[37] Olander, 'Changes in the London Press', 159ff., sheds much light on the Star Chamber decree.

[38] Ibid., 104.

[39] Thomas Goodwin, *The Happiness of the Saints in Glory* (1638), 91. The chaplain was John Oliver.

[40] William Sclater the elder, *Sermons experimental: on psalmes cxvi & cxvii, published by his son W. Sclater* (1638), STC 21844.

condemnation in Christ, therefore they take liberty to sin.' At the same time, predestination was applied in the distinction between the knowledge of doctrine which is propounded to all men, and experimental teaching (he meant his own sermons) in things that concern life and godliness, which was the privilege of the elect.[41] The book is an excellent example of experimental predestinarianism after the Star Chamber decree.

It is easy to find others. They included Richard Sibbes's *The Riches of Mercy in Two Treatises*,[42] his *Two Sermons*[43] and *The Christians End, being the substance of Five Sermons*[44] on the theme, in the best Perkins tradition, of how we may know we are Christ's. In *Light from Heaven*,[45] assurance was preached as no enemy to good works. In *The Returning Backslider*[46] Sibbes discoursed on how to be rooted in grace, and showed 'the large extent of God's free mercy, even unto the most miserable forlorn and wretched sinners that may be, upon their humiliation and repentance'. In the same vein were Henry Ramsden's *A Gleaning in God's Harvest*,[47] and Preston's *The Doctrine of the Saints Infirmities*.[48] Credal predestinarianism was expounded in Richard Rogers, *A Garden of Spiritual Flowers*.[49] It included a discussion of the order of the divine decrees. It was hesitant on perseverance: there were 'Twelve Steps which a man may stride towards Heaven . . . yet except he stride thirteen he shall miss Heaven gate and fall into the fire of Hell forever'. Θρηνοικος, *The House of Mourning, 17 Sermons preached at the funerals of divers faithful servants of Christ*, contained sermons by Featley, Martin Day, Sibbes, Taylor and others in which predestinarian concepts, including 'vessels of wrath', election and reprobation through the secret counsel and purpose of God, abound.[50]

None of this should be taken to imply that censorship under Laud was no different from censorship under Abbot. Featley, as chaplain to Abbot, had exercised particular vigilance to exclude any work which in his judgment might give comfort to papists. Laud, like Abbot, left licensing

---

[41] Ibid., 6, 179, 154.

[42] R. Sibbes, *The Riches of Mercy in Two Treatises*, STC 22501, licensed 11 May 1638.

[43] R. Sibbes, *Two Sermons,* STC 22519, licensed 12 April 1638.

[44] R. Sibbes, *The Christian's end. Or, the sweet soveraignty of Christ over his members. Being the substance of Five Sermons* (1639), STC 224985.

[45] R. Sibbes, *Light from Heaven, discovering the fountaine opened . . . In four treatises,* (1639), STC 22498.

[46] R. Sibbes, *The Returning Backslider, or a commentary upon the whole xiiii chapter of Hosea* (1639, STC 22500).

[47] Henry Ramsden, *A Gleaning in God's Harvest: Four choice handfulls* (1639, STC 20660).

[48] John Preston, *The Doctrine of the Saints Infirmities*, first published 1636; 1638 edn licensed by Thomas Wykes.

[49] *A Garden of Spiritual Flowers* (first published 1609 and much reprinted; 1638 edn, STC 20221, 191).

[50] See esp. pp. 17, 322, 403.

to his chaplains, and it was now Featley's turn to have his books censored. He figured largely in the complaints made against Laud's chaplains at the archbishop's trial.[51] The difference in outlook is well caught in a story told by Sir John Hungerford. When he tried to get some books of Sir Anthony Hungerford licensed, Bray replied that some of it was too harsh. 'Now we are in a winning way to gain papists.' Laud would not interfere.[52] The difference in atmosphere, in outlook and in churchmanship was real, profound and important. It is therefore all the more important to assess its doctrinal character as precisely as possible.

It has been claimed, not merely that Calvinist teaching was subject to a growing censorship, but that there was 'a series of Arminian works', of which at least nine appeared in 1635.[53] Had Laud presided over any systematic attempt to license Arminian publications, or even to give official backing to 'Arminian' glosses of existing formularies, he would have had to answer for it at his trial. Of the nine books cited, only two were then complained of. One was *Five Pious and Learned Discourses* by Robert Shelford, but the complaint did not relate to predestination. It rested on Shelford's refusal to agree that the Pope was Antichrist.[54] Far from being evidence of 'religious questions which only came to the fore during the 1630s' and of an 'overlap with Dutch Arminianism',[55] Shelford's divinity is Jacobean as opposed to Caroline (he died in 1626), indigenous, and recognizably rooted in his education at Peterhouse in the 1580s. The authorities to which he appealed were all conventional: Scripture, the Fathers, the Homilies and the Book of Common Prayer. Many of his concerns may be paralleled in James I's *Meditation upon the Lord's Prayer*, for James too liked decency and ceremony;[56] stressed the importance of receiving the sacrament;[57] deplored the neglect of prayer in favour of preaching;[58] believed that salvation was conditional;[59] was concerned to emphasize the duty of obedience to

---

[51] *Historical Manuscripts Commission*, House of Lords MSS XI, Addenda, 1514–1714, 433–5, 440.
[52] Laud, *Works*, IV. 277–8.
[53] Tyacke, *Anti-Calvinists*, 184–5.
[54] House of Lords MSS XI, 448. A few other books were cited, notably Francis Sales's *An Introduction to the Holy Life*, Pocklington's *Altare Christianum* and Anthony Stafford's *Female Glory*. They concerned auricular confession, purgatory, and the approbation of the Council of Trent. The only book complained of where 'Arminianism' if mentioned at all was not a mere adjunct to popery was *A Historical Narration*.
[55] Tyacke, *Anti-Calvinists*, 54–5.
[56] James I, *A Meditation upon the Lord's Prayer* (1619), 12–13.
[57] The dedication to Buckingham praised him 'in special, in so often receiving the Sacrament'.
[58] Ibid., 4–5.
[59] Ibid., 68.

Christ's precepts;[60] and warned of the danger of 'security'.[61] Shelford's stress on the danger both of extreme solifidianism and of 'naked imputation'[62] represented a return to problems at the heart of the Protestant Reformation. He was far from denying the doctrine of predestination. He appealed to it,[63] and he was clear that only the elect received grace both habitual and effectual. It is true that in dealing with the divine attributes in his fourth discourse, he tilted at 'men which attribute all to fate and necessity', but in defending contingency as the work of divine providence,[64] he was doing no more than echo a Cambridge Commencement thesis of 1602.[65] The posthumous publication of his book may well have been the work of Wren, but Shelford was quite unknown to Laud, who was unaware as late as 1643 even whether he was alive or dead.[66]

What, then, of the other alleged 'Arminian' publications? The misconception underlying Andrewes's inclusion has already been demonstrated.[67] Similarly, in attacking the 'preposterous presumption' of those who set forth systems of the divine decrees, Thomas Jackson was well aware that Arminius was as vulnerable as Beza, and saying nothing with which John Davenant did not agree.[68] Merely to identify with Laud's churchmanship, or to express approval of the Declaration of 1628, is no proof of Arminianism.[69] When Thomas Laurence criticized those who 'presumed upon a fatality of their election and would needs have Heaven promised without the condition of works', he was saying exactly what Bancroft had said in his celebrated outburst at Hampton Court.[70]

[60] Ibid., 73–5, 'It is blasphemy to say that any of Christ's precepts are impossible to be performed', cited by Shelford, *Five Pious and Learned Discourses* (Cambridge, 1635), 147. Shelford did not deny concupiscence in the regenerate, citing Romans vii in support: Dr Tyacke is mistaken to suggest that he applies this chapter to the unregenerate, as is clear from pp. 132, 134–6, 144, 150.

[61] Ibid., 103. 'No man ought to be so secure of himself, as not to be afraid to be corrupted . . . *Qui stat, videat ne cadat.*'

[62] Shelford, *Five Pious and Learned Discourses* (Cambridge, 1635), 71, 124.

[63] Ibid., citing Romans viii, 28.

[64] Ibid., 193, 204–9.

[65] British Library, Harley MS 7038, f. 84, 'Divina providentia non tollit contingentiam'. Cf. f. 88 (1610), 'Dei Decretum non tollit libertatem voluntatis'.

[66] Trevor-Roper, *Catholics, Anglicans and Puritans*, 83, 107.

[67] Above, p. 213.

[68] Jackson, *Works*, VII. 416; Tyacke, *Anti-Calvinists*, 185. Cf. John Davenant, *Animadversions upon a Treatise entitled God's Love to Mankind* (Cambridge, 1641), 17: 'The marshalling of the eternal immanent acts of the Divine understanding or will into First, Second, Third, Fourth, is a weak imagination of man's brain, and so uncertain that amongst twenty who give you such delineations of God's eternal decrees, you shall not find two who agree between themselves in numbering them and ordering them, but where one maketh four, another maketh five, six or seven, &c., . . . and in brief every man ordereth them *secundum suum modum imaginandi*.'

[69] When Christopher Potter praised the policy behind the Declaration in a sermon of 1629, he was congratulated by Morton, Winniffe and Goad.

[70] Cf. Tyacke, *Anti-Calvinists*, 83.

Similarly, Edward Boughen's quotation of Article XVII and of the king's Declaration (in criticizing those who 'made Christ the saviour of but a little flock' and who could not 'endure to receive God's promises in such wise as they be generally set forth') is cited as evidence that he 'aired his Arminian sympathies in print'.[71] Even more tendentiously, James Conyers's sermon against self-righteousness, every whit as orthodox as the parable of the publican and the sinner it echoes, is adduced as yet another example of 'religious change'.[72]

Three works remain. In editing a collection of 'excerpts from various authors', Thomas Chown claimed that they did not go beyond the literal and grammatical sense of the Articles, and his book was licensed by Laud's chaplain, William Haywood.[73] He did include a short section on election and reprobation, but its criticism of fatalists was balanced by other criticisms, including those who sought the reason for the divine decree in nature rather than in grace. The thrust of Chown's comments was to condemn all attempted philosophical explanations as otiose, to emphasize the divine promises set forth in the Scriptures, and the means to salvation therein revealed. Not even Burton or Prynne could scent Arminianism in it, for although the book was briefly mentioned at Laud's trial, that was because it taught (as did Calvin) that the Roman Church was a true church, not differing from the Protestants in fundamentals.[74]

Edmund Reeve's *Communion Book Catechism* is said to have incorporated 'the whole gamut of Arminian doctrine'.[75] Reeve, it is true, admired Overall, Buckeridge and Thomas Jackson ('the most greatly learned doctor of our Church'), but his chief mentor seems to have been Robert Wright, the Bishop of Coventry and Lichfield, who had encouraged him to write an earlier book, *The Christian Divinity out of the Divine Service*, in 1631. Reeve's inspiration was the Prayer Book and the Book of Homilies, and they govern his interpretation of the biblical text. He strongly praised King James's Proclamation of 1604, in respect of ceremonies and due reverence in worship.[76] He defended both the Declaration prefixed of 1628, and the Declaration of Sports.[77] He argued that 'absolute reprobation' was at odds with Ps. lxvii, 12, with Ezekiel xviii, and with the Homily on Falling from God.[78] He argued on the basis of

[71] Ibid., 184.
[72] Ibid., 184–5.
[73] Thomas Chouneus, *Collectiones Theologicarum ex diversis authorum sententiis excerptae* (1635), 15–17.
[74] Laud, *Works*, IV. 335–6.
[75] Tyacke, *Anti-Calvinists*, 185.
[76] Edmund Reeve, *The Communion Book Catechism Expounded* (1636), *passim*.
[77] Ibid., title page, 65–6.
[78] Ibid., 47–8.

1 Cor. xv, 22 that Christ died for the sins of the whole world.[79] He defined the elect as 'all such whom God doth choose out of mankind for himself': he believed that any infant dying after baptism was numbered among the elect; and he argued that the words of administration implied that all who receive Communion are elect. In the thanksgiving after Communion 'the Church declareth in most plain manner who are God's chosen or elect'.[80] Reeve taught that we must pray for God's grace to continue in that estate; and, on the basis of Gospel texts such as John xv, 9–10, that it was possible to fall from grace 'if due heed be not taken'. He denied that any of this conflicted with Article XVII, and asked how a priest could say 'The body of our Lord which was given for thee . . .' to every particular professed member of the church of England in every parish 'if so be that any of them were absolutely reprobated, that is, from eternity unconditionally decreed to be damned in hell fire everlastingly?'.[81] Reeve's churchmanship is unmistakable, and his Catechism is unusual in being deliberately controversial:[82] but there is nothing in either of his books that any communicant would not have heard countless times in his parish church at any time since the accession of Elizabeth.

One indisputably anti-Calvinist work published during the personal rule was Samuel Hoard's *God's Love to Mankind*.[83] With a wealth of documentation from both the Fathers and modern divines, the author[84] attacked both supralapsarian and sublapsarian versions of the doctrine of absolute reprobation. Calvin and Beza were charged with theological novelty, unwillingness to allow their views to be debated, responsibility for bringing Protestantism into disrepute, and complicity with Stoic and Manichaean error. Their attempts to rebut objections that they made God the author of sin were 'a mere fig leaf to cover the foulness of their opinion'.[85] As far as Hoard was concerned, the sublapsarian doctrine as endorsed at Dort and by the British divines who attended the synod was riddled with inconsistencies and was pastorally disastrous.[86] As Davenant for one complained, Hoard failed to provide any reasoned account of the doctrine of election beyond the bald statement that there was 'no decree of damning or saving but what is built upon God's foreknowledge of the

---

[79] Ibid., 60.
[80] Ibid., 62–3.
[81] Ibid., 65–6.
[82] I owe this verdict to Dr Ian Green, whose forthcoming *Religious Instruction in Early Modern England* will shed much light on the whole question of Catechisms during the Personal Rule.
[83] S. Hoard. *God's Love to Mankind, manifested by disprooving his Absolute Decree for their Damnation* (1633).
[84] According to William Twisse, much of the book was the work of Henry Mason.
[85] Hoard, *God's Love to Mankind*, 66–7.
[86] Ibid., 10–11.

evil and good actions of men'.[87] Hoard admitted that he had once subscribed to the doctrines he now condemned. He had no connection with Laud, and his book was published without licence. Its appearance does nevertheless demonstrate that it was relatively easy to evade the licensing laws. To persuade or deceive a printer into producing a book without licence was only one of a number of options. Francis Rous, for example, was able to republish his *Testis Veritatis* by giving it a new title and title page, but otherwise leaving it unaltered.[88] Another device was to publish abroad, as did William Twisse[89] and of course William Ames, whose *Fresh Suit against Human ceremonies* was shipped in reams of blank paper and so 'never looked into or let pass by negligence or falsehood of customs men'.[90]

Such instances illustrate the difficulties of a rigorous enforcement of censorship. It may be readily granted that Laud wanted to suppress books 'contrary to the doctrine and discipline of the Church of England',[91] but in interpreting the Declaration prefixed that did not mean, either for him or for the king, that even moderate views were acceptable. When Charles was presented with a defence of his own Declaration expressing gratitude for the tranquillity it had brought to the church, and arguing that there had always been legitimate differences of opinion on the finer points of predestinarian doctrine, he did not agree that it should be published.[92] In December 1630 Laud received a letter from Samuel Brooke, Master of Trinity College, Cambridge, saying that he had finished his tract on predestination. Fifteen years before he had thought the problem was unmasterable, but since then 'I think I have found an issue out of that wood and wilderness in which we have been lost all this while.' He intended to send it to a few of his friends, confident that they would commend it as 'so indifferently written as might content Arminius

---

[87] Davenant, *Animadversions upon a Treatise*, 131, 149. Hoard's work was also refuted by the anti-Bezan French Protestant Moyse Amyraut in his *Defensio doctrinae J Calvini de absoluto reprobationis decreto* (Saumur, 1641). Armstrong, *Calvinism and the Amyraut Heresy*, 99, esp. for the parallels between Davenant and Amyraut.

[88] STC 21347.7, [Anon.] *The Truth of Three Things, viz. The doctrine of predestination, free will and certainty of salvation* (1633).

[89] William Twisse, *The Doctrine of the Synod of Dort and Arles reduced to the practice* was published at Amsterdam (successors of G. Thorp) in 1631. It is an answer to Tilenus, though it makes reference to Montagu and Jackson as 'our English Arminians'. Other Amsterdam productions were *A Discovery of D. Jackson's Vanitie, or A Perspective Glass, whereby the admirers of D Jackson's profound discourses, may see the vanity and weakness of them, in sundry passages, and especially so far as they tend to the undermining of the doctrine hitherto received*, and *Vindiciae Gratiae*.

[90] Olander, 'Changes in the London Press', 99.

[91] Article 26 of the Star Chamber Decree. Ibid., 176.

[92] Bodl. Lib., MS Rawlinson C 106, 'A Defence of His Majesty's Declaration'. It was written by 'your Majesty's most Dutiful Subjects of Dorchester in Dorset'.

and Gomar, and not a new way so much as the making of the old even
and clean against stumbling hereafter'.[93] Laud's reply, not hitherto
printed in full, is a fitting summary of the thrust of policy:[94]

But for your other Tract I must needs say thus much. Fifteen years study cannot
but beat out something. And I like it well that you mean to have the judgment
of so many and such men upon it. And if God give me leisure, and ye Tract be
not too long, I shall be glad to read it too. And the making even of the old way
will to most men seem better than a new. Nevertheless I am yet where I was, that
somewhat about these controversies is unmasterable in this life. Neither can I think
any expression can be so happy as to settle all their difficulties, neither can I be
of other belief till I am convinced. And howsoever I do much doubt whether the
king will take any man's judgment so far as to have these controversies any further stirred, which now God be thanked begin to be more at peace. And the rather
because should that which you call the smoothing of the old way raise any new
doubt in opposite judgments it would make more noise than ever. And for the
several copies which you mention to send to those friends you name, it shall be
wisdom for you to take heed that none be stolen out privately to the press before
you are aware, which should it happen might breed a great deal of trouble to
yourself and the church. This is all I can say to you in this particular, and sure
I am the safest way is, after your friends have seen it, and objected what they
can, to let it lie by you, and weigh it again: for that I think the argument may
very well bear, and the times too. So in haste.

As archbishop, Laud did not change his attitude. In 1634, when sent a
copy of a bitter anti-Calvinist speech by the Lutheran Matthias Hoe, he
advised Thomas Roe against writing an answer to it, 'for I cannot persuade myself that such a fiery spirit will be quenched by any answer; and
then we shall have reply upon reply, till at last moderate men themselves
be overheated, and all hopes lost'.[95] The cause of peace was best served
by silence.

The regulation of doctrine

A court incident

Inevitably from time to time the underlying tensions resurfaced. They
are evident in an incident of which John Davenant was the victim. In what
became a celebrated court sermon, Davenant briefly alluded to the doctrine of election. Hoping, as Thomas Fuller put it,[96] 'to make him fall
totally and finally from the king's favour', Harsnett seized the opportunity
to manoeuvre the king into asserting his authority. Davenant was

---

[93] CSPD, 1630, 396.
[94] PRO, SP 16/176/46. Cf. Laud, *Works*, VI. 292.
[95] Laud, *Works*, VII. 87–8.
[96] Fuller, *Church History,* VI. 75.

summoned before the Council, where Harsnett accused him of defying the Declaration prefixed. Davenant, with some reason, replied that he had said nothing that was not in accordance with the articles to which the Declaration bound him, but that if he had misinterpreted it, he would in future 'humbly yield obedience thereto'. The orthodoxy of what he had said was granted. He was told that 'the doctrine was not gainsaid, but his Highness had given command that these questions should not be debated'. Davenant asked if he might kiss the king's hand, which was arranged, and the king said that he 'would not have this high point meddled withall or debated, either one way or the other, because it was too high for the people's understanding, and other points which concern reformation and newness of life were more need-ful and profitable'.[97] Heylyn, predictably, had no sympathy, and hoped that 'the lower clergy will not say hereafter as some did of old, that laws are like the spiders' cobwebs which suffer the great flies to break through, and lay hold only upon those of the smaller size'.[98] Davenant complained that the king's declaration 'was abused to the stopping their mouths who defend the truth yet never urged against those who broach contrary errors',[99] but that was only an initial reaction, and the eventual outcome of his appearance before the Council was nevertheless thought by his friends to have been highly satisfactory.[100] Davenant continued to preach at court.

Popular preaching

Outside the highly charged atmosphere of the court, there is less evidence of tension. Until 1633, Laud and Abbot sat together on the High Com-mission, and the records provide several examples of popular distortion of predestinarian doctrine, in the condemnation of which they were at one. Samuel Pretty, a minister of St Michael Paternoster Royal in Lon-don, appeared in 1631 charged with preaching that Christians could not be too secure, 'nay, they ought to sing all care away', that they did not need to be sorry for their sins, for the effects of sin were taken away in believers, and that justification and sanctification were the same.[101] Abbot and Morton were quite as indignant as Laud and Buckeridge, Abbot concluding the proceedings 'briefly but sharply reproving him for

---

[97] Bodl. Lib., MS Tanner 290.86.
[98] Heylyn, *Cyprianus Anglicus*, 214.
[99] MS Tanner 71.109.
[100] Ibid. Bedell to Samuel Ward, MS Tanner 290. 89ᵛ (14 November 1630): 'I am sorry that Arminianism finds such favour in the Low Countries and amongst ourselves, and glad that my L of Sarum (whom I truly love and honour) came off so well in the business touching his sermon.'
[101] S. R. Gardiner (ed.), *Reports of Cases in the Courts of Star Chamber and High Com-mission*, Camden Society, NS 39 (1886), 181–6.

his phrase of singing all care away . . . to what purpose then are all those rules of mortification and growing in sanctification?' That Thomas Townes, John Eaton and John Etsall were all dealt with for teaching that God sees no sin in the elect demonstrates that antinomian distortions of predestinarian doctrine had to be taken seriously; similarly, in 1632 three Essex defendants had to answer charges of teaching that justified persons could not displease God, and that David, when he committed adultery, pleased God as well as when he danced before the ark.[102]

These records make clear why both Laud and Abbot were opposed to the Arminian principle of *libertas prophetandi*.[103] As Bishop of London Laud had, therefore, good reason for devoting so much energy to bringing lecturers under control. Abbot personally approved of the regulations under which he took action.[104] Eventually, as Abbot reported to the king, Laud had been 'forced to deprive two or three men whom no time can tame, nor instruction conquer'.[105] One of them was John Archer, whose offence was not catechizing according to the Prayer Book. Archer had compiled his own Catechism instead. Among many other errors, he had taught that God's hatred was not for evil, but was the cause of all evil in the creature. Men were not reprobated because they were sinful, but sinful because they were reprobated; sin came into the world because God hates reprobates. No man can know that he is hated by God before he dies (or sins against the Holy Ghost). The reason why God conceals his hatred, but reveals his election, is to make us hope. Reprobates may think they are loved, and may even enjoy the means of grace, and by the abundance thereof be lifted up with Capernaum to heaven, but it is only so that God may cast them lower into hell. 'Yea, God may move them by his spirit, but it is to further their damnation.'[106] Laud had every reason to be horrified. His target was not Calvinism, but ignorance and error. In the few other cases where predestination was involved, it usually represented one issue among many.[107]

On that issue, Laud had the full co-operation of 'Calvinist' bishops after Abbot's death, as is illustrated by a letter from Joseph Hall in 1634 which

---

[102] Ibid., 313–14, 316–21.
[103] White, 'Rise of Arminianism Reconsidered', 41; for Laud's comments, Laud, *Works*, IV. 263.
[104] PRO, SP 16/153/40.
[105] Laud, *Works*, V. 310.
[106] PRO, SP 16/176/93 and 16/187/17.
[107] Only Daniel Votier was cited for breach of the Declaration alone. Laud argued with him for an hour and then dismissed him without censure. J. E. Davies, 'The Growth and Implementation of Laudianism with special reference to the Southern Province', Oxford University D.Phil. thesis, 1987, 120. See PRO, SP 16/186/41, 16/186/75 and 16/186/76 for the errors of Meredith Madey, the withdrawal of whose licence to preach was occasioned by Trinitarian, not predestinarian, heresy. Cf. Tyacke, *Anti-Calvinists*, 183.

told him of a 'strange puritanical monster' in Barnstaple, John Cole, who was a 'fellow of very mean condition, yet among the simple sort, especially women, had got an opinion in skill in matter of religion. Having drawn to his house certain maidservants, under pretence to hear repetition of his sermons, he wrought them to his lust, and has for two or three years made use of them at his pleasure, persuading them that these acts might stand with grace.'[108] Small wonder that for practical purposes, Hall thought 'we ought so to regulate our lives and work out our salvation as though there were no secret decree of God respecting us'.[109]

Visitation articles of the 1630s do not suggest that predestination was a major issue. Bishops who made any reference at all to it did so in unexceptionable terms. Laud himself did no more than ask whether there had been any preaching contrary to the Articles of 1563,[110] and his example seems to have been followed by the vast majority. As Bishop of Chichester, Montagu asked 'Doth your minister preach or teach anything contrary to his Majesty's late injunctions, about predestination, falling from grace, etc., to trouble men's minds with those deep and dark points, which of late have so distracted and engarboyled the world?'[111] Duppa, who succeeded him, asked whether the clergy 'preach Christ and him crucified, abstaining from those high points of speculation which have in several ages raised combustion in Christian churches; and therefore to preserve peace among us?'.[112] At Norwich, Montagu asked whether the minister 'in his popular sermon, fall upon those much disputed and little understood doctrines, of God's eternal predestination, of election antecedaneous, of reprobation irrespective without sin foreseen, of free-will, of perseverance, and not-falling from grace; points obscure, unfoldable [i.e., inexplicable], unfordable, untraceable, at which that great apostle stood at gaze with *Oh the height and depth of the riches both of his wisdom and knowledge of God! How unsearchable are his judgments, and his ways past finding out?* Rom xi, 33'.[113] Like Laud's, his concern was with gross misrepresentations of predestinarian doctrine. There is no evidence that any

---

[108] CSPD, 1634–5, 371–2.

[109] From a letter written when Hall was Bishop of Exeter to Ludovic Crocius, professor at Bremen. Hall, *Works* X. 246–7.

[110] Laud, *Works*, V. 431, 444. Laud's enquiry was made of all parishioners. The only question asked about ministers was whether they had delivered 'such doctrine as tends to obedience and the edifying of their auditory in faith and religion, without intermeddling with matters of state, not fit to be handled in the pulpit'. Ibid., 427.

[111] Richard Montagu, *Articles to be enquired of throughout the whole diocese of Chichester* (1631), sig. A4ᵛ.

[112] Brian Duppa, *Articles to be enquired of throughout the diocese of Chichester* (1638), sig. B2ᵛ.

[113] Richard Montagu, *Articles of Enquiry and Direction for the diocese of Norwich* (Cambridge, 1638), sig. B2.

bishop did other than he was conscientiously required to do by the
Declaration of 1628.[114]

The universities

The universities represented the greatest challenge to the policy of silencing controversy. Given the presence of Prideaux and Fell in Oxford, it
is no surprise that the Declaration prefixed was ignored at the Divinity
Act under Pembroke's chancellorship. As late as 1631 Thomas Mason was
able to deny that anyone could entirely fall from faith.[115] There were
those on both sides who were prepared to test the mettle of the new
Chancellor. On the first Sunday of Laud's chancellorship, John Tooker
of Oriel College preached a sermon in which he was 'not content only
to justify the five articles commonly called Arminianism, but he would
needs lay an aspersion upon the synod of Dort'.[116] In writing to the Vice-
Chancellor's deputy, Laud reminded him of the king's order 'prohibiting
all men of all sorts for a time to preach either way concerning them; that
so those unhappy differences, likely to rend this Church as well as others,
might sleep first and die after'.[117] On the other side, Prideaux would
appear to have incited Thomas Hill to preach against the king's orders,
'disparaging the whole order of bishops in point of learning and religion',
and claiming that 'foul and erroneous opinions [were] the readiest steps
to preferment', with a reference to 'Popish darts whet on a Dutch grind-
stone'.[118] Similarly, William Hodges, who later married Prideaux's
daughter Sarah, preached on the forbidden topics and made 'erroneous
and heretical opinions the way to preferment'.[119] In August 1632, Robert
Rainsford[120] of Wadham College was dealt with for maintaining universal grace and election to life from faith foreseen; and William Hobbs[121]
'did unadvisedly handle and insist upon the point of falling from grace'.
In July 1634 the Vice-Chancellor was accused of partiality towards some

---

[114] Price of Brigstock appeared before the High Commission after preaching for four hours
on the theme that God 'had created the greater part of the world in order to damn them'.
Piers of Bath and Wells acted over ministers 'particularising' (naming parishioners as
elect or reprobate) in the pulpit. Davies, 'Growth and Implementation of Laudianism',
122, 124.

[115] Oxford University Archives, Reg. P., f. 275.

[116] Laud, *Works*, V. 15.

[117] PRO, SP 16/166/79. He was examined by the Pro-Vice-Chancellor, Prideaux and Bancroft and convinced them that he had no intention of 'abetting those differences which
had so much disturbed the peace of the church'.

[118] Laud, *Works*, V. 68.

[119] Oxford University Archives, Reg. R., f. 35; see Laud, *Works*, V. 87–90 for Prideaux's
role.

[120] Wood, *The History and Antiquities of the University of Oxford*, II. 1. 382.

[121] Oxford University Archives, Reg. R., f. 54.

of those who had violated the king's edicts, but there was then peace for three and a half years. In 1638 three more cases had to be dealt with.[122] Given the previous extent of factious preaching in Oxford, seven indictments in eight years may be considered something of an achievement, even if it is too much to claim that 'Laud succeeded in putting an end to theological disputes.'[123]

Act questions did become less contentious. In 1634 Calvinism was indirectly defended when Edmund Staunton denied that Protestant apologetics implied that God was the author of sin.[124] The change to a more eirenic tone is illustrated by Arthur Wingham's thesis of 1634, which maintained that those called Lutherans and the Calvinians could unite (*coalescere*) in one church, and by Edmund Diggle's of 1640 that 'in iis, quae non sunt de fide, modesta dissentiendi libertas sit concedenda'.[125] Yet throughout the 1630s there continued to be theses opposing errors of papist doctrine like merit of condignity, sacramental grace *ex opere operato*, adoration of the saints or prayers for the dead, the doctrine of purgatory, of the distinction between mortal and venial sins, and more generally any possibility of reconciliation with the Church of Rome. There were none asserting even by implication any of the Arminian points.[126]

There were limits to what Laud could achieve. Oxford colleges were in many respects autonomous. When Laud discovered, as late as 1635, that the undergraduates at New College spent their first two years studying little but Calvin's *Institutes*, all he could do was to ask the Bishop of Winchester to use tactful influence with the Warden, to broaden their education.[127] Early in 1640 Laud received a complaint that *LXX disputationes theologicae*, by Festus Hommius, had been published at Oxford. Dedicated to Heinsius, the book included an uncompromisingly 'Calvinist' denial of election from prevision of faith, coupled with an assertion of assurance and perseverance which would have delighted Prideaux. Laud's concern, however, was not predestination but Presbyterianism, of which Hommius was known to be a supporter: 'in these broken times' he was not prepared that the university should appear to 'allow and approve' of that doctrine. He could only threaten to suppress the printers if the like

---

[122] Richard Kilby of Lincoln and Jasper Maine of Christ Church were admonished for violating the king's instructions. Laud, *Works*, V. 191. John Johnson recanted: 'I did unadvisedly throughout my sermon insist upon proof of universal redemption and universal grace, not without some bitterness against contrary opinions.' Ibid., 288.

[123] A. D. Hewlett, 'The University of Oxford and the Church of England in the time of William Laud', Oxford University B.Litt. thesis, 1934, 179.

[124] Oxford University Archives, Reg. P., f. 419.

[125] Ibid.

[126] The only 'novel doctrine' specified by Dr Tyacke (*Anti-Calvinists*, 84) is the thesis that it was legitimate to worship God by bowing towards the altar, a position defended by Jewel in his reply to Harding (art. 3, div. 29) and practised by both Elizabeth and James I.

[127] Laud, *Works*, V. 116–17.

happened again.[128] As to the Declaration prefixed, he instructed the Vice-Chancellor as late as May 1640 that 'no man should presume . . . to print there any thing which might break the rule . . . one way or the other'.[129]

At Cambridge his influence was even more limited. The Vice-Chancellor, Holland, was not by any stretch of the imagination a 'Laudian', but royal control of some colleges was on occasions exercised in favour of Laud's chaplains.[130] Nevertheless, according to its latest historian, there were 'no sudden swings in the university's religious attitudes'.[131] Puritanism and popery, both of them susceptible to what may be described as a polemical elasticity of definition, remained the issues over which opinion was polarized. The preoccupations of those hostile to Puritanism were above all liturgiology and ceremony,[132] but in only four out of the eleven years of the Personal Rule were any of them Vice-Chancellors (Wren in 1629, Laney in 1633, William Beale in 1635 and Cosin in 1640). The forces of those who were united in their suspicions of popery were represented by Love of Corpus (Vice-Chancellor in 1634), Brownrigg (1638 and 1639), Holdsworth of Emmanuel (1641), Bainbridge (1628), Batchcroft, Sibbes and Samuel Ward. Some heads avoided identification with either faction.

There were from time to time sermons in support of controversial ceremonies. In 1634, for example, Edward Martin's curate, Peter Hausted, preached an outspokenly anti-Puritan sermon attacking lecturers and irreverence in church, and defending bowing towards the altar.[133] He was summoned before the consistory court, but Vice-Chancellor Love's term of office had all but expired, and he was acquitted, William Beale presiding. At the opposite extreme, in May 1632, Nathaniel Barnard preached against innovations and neglect of preaching. He was imprisoned after a hearing in the High Commission, but he had 'courted disaster'[134] by expressing the hope that the queen might be converted, and by asserting that treason against the state was worse than treason against the royal blood. From time to time other sermons exposed the rival factions among the Heads,[135] but the archives suggest that only a few sermons out of the hundreds preached in the 1630s gave offence.

The records of the university court reveal proceedings in only two cases for preaching against the King's Declaration. The first concerned John

---

[128] Ibid., 254.
[129] Ibid., 268.
[130] Trevor-Roper, *Catholics, Anglicans and Puritans*, 81–2.
[131] J. D. Twigg, 'The University of Cambridge and the English Revolution', Cambridge University Ph.D. thesis, 1983, 9.
[132] Trevor-Roper, *Catholics, Anglicans and Puritans*, 78 (Wren), 82 (William Beale) and 84–8 (Cosin).
[133] Twigg, 'University of Cambridge and the English Revolution', 10.
[134] For a hostile account of what he said, see British Library, Harley MS 7019, f. 54.
[135] Ibid., ff. 55–64.

Normanton, who in January 1633 preached 'touching irresistibility of grace'.[136] After protracted hearings, he eventually 'submitted himself, and promised to be very careful, that hereafter he should not utter or speak anything that may be subject to misapprehension'. Even more protracted proceedings concerned Thomas Riley. It was claimed that before preaching a sermon of 1636 he had 'made an addition contrary to the canon to the Queen's title', and followed it with 'divers bold, irreligious and undutiful expressions concerning some great persons of this kingdom'. He had next 'thrust himself into the controversy of the right and power of kings', and then prayed God to forgive us our original sins, contrary to the Catechism. In 1637, perhaps emboldened by the fact that no proceedings had been taken against him, he preached in the university church on 'the chief and principal of the controversies of predestination'. A summons followed to the Vice-Chancellor's court, but Riley was skilled in all the usual delaying tactics, and protracted appearances eventually petered out indecisively.[137]

Such evidence as has survived of Commencement theses supports the inference of a continuing, sometimes contentious debate, in which the balance of advantage swung from time to time, but not a theological revolution. It can hardly be said that 'Calvinism was effectively banished' at Cambridge any more than at Oxford, either from lectures or from the Commencement.[138] In 1630 Samuel Ward told James Ussher that he had continued to discuss grace and free will, and had countered protests by not mentioning Remonstrant authors by name.[139] As to the Commencement, he was vigilant in watching for any occasion to call 'off side'. When, in 1629, Edward Quarles proposed that all baptized infants were undoubtedly justified, Ward in his turn claimed that it should not be debated, as crossing the king's Declaration. He was not successful. The Heads accepted the orthodoxy of the question on the basis of the Prayer Book rubric deferring confirmation.[140] It would be going too far to conclude, however, that two incompatible theologies of grace were ranged against each other,[141] for Ward himself agreed that infants were justified in baptism; he quarrelled only with the inference that the doctrine of perseverance was thereby impugned. More significantly, he told Ussher that he believed 'Mr Hooker . . . doth truly explicate the nature of sacraments.'[142] In 1633 it was argued that good works were effica-

---

[136] Cambridge University Library, Baker MS xxxiii f. 226.
[137] CUL V.C. Court Archives, I, ff. 64, 69, 74, 82; CU Registry Guard Book, 18 (9).
[138] Tyacke, *Anti-Calvinists*, 49.
[139] Ussher, *Works*, XV. 500.
[140] Ibid., 504.
[141] Tyacke, *Anti-Calvinists*, 52.
[142] Ussher, *Works*, XV. 506.

ciously necessary to salvation: Ward's protest was ignored by the Vice-Chancellor, but in the following year he was able to ensure that a member of his own college defended the doctrine *Sola fides justificat*.[143] Point and counterpoint, thesis and antithesis: in 1635 the riposte was *Fides quae sola justificat non est sine spe et dilectione*, coupled with *Peccatum est adequata causa odii Divini*. It was sometimes a tetchy debate; never an 'Arminian' takeover.[144]

As at Oxford, publications of the university press were independent of episcopal censorship. Davenant's Commentary on Colossians was published in 1630, his *Praelectiones* in 1631 and his *Determinations* in 1634. Predestination was by no means a forbidden topic. John Gerhard's *Meditations* appeared in translation in 1627, to be reissued in 1631, 1634 and again in 1638: they included an orthodox Lutheran exposition which emphasized that predestination was in Christ and warned against security. There was some demand for Gerhard's books. His *Golden Chain* appeared in 1631. George Herbert's *The Temple* was published in 1634. In spite of differences of emphasis, they represented an eirenic, pastorally orientated consensus which the historian must set against that of continued controversy and conflict.[145]

The personal rule in retrospect

There is no evidence from the 1630s to alter the view that official policy intended neither to outlaw Calvinism nor to propagate Arminianism. The existing formularies were left unchanged. No new glosses were added to them. The intention was simply to quieten controversy, and Laud was right in claiming that policy was attended with gradually increasing success. Of course, it is fair to comment that even granting that thrust of policy, perceptions to the contrary might still have played an important role in the tensions that led to the Civil War.[146] In conclusion, therefore, perceptions of the personal rule in 1640–2 will be reviewed. It will be suggested that even after the summoning of the Short Parliament, and notwithstanding the extensive use of the fear of popery in anti-Laudian polemic, there were relatively few references to the doctrine of predestination as a bone of contention, whether at Westminster or in the localities.

---

[143] Ibid., 580. For Morton's defence of the necessity of good works, see his *Antidotum adversus Ecclesiae Romanae de merito proprie dicto ex condigno venenum* (Cambridge, 1638).
[144] For Davenant's comments on the 1633 questions, see Bodl. Lib., MS Tanner 71, 164.
[145] Information derived from R, Bowes (ed.), *A Catalogue of the Books printed at or related to the University . . . of Cambridge, 1521–1893* (1894).
[146] W. Lamont, 'The Rise of Arminianism Reconsidered: A Comment', *Past and Present* 107 (1985), 227.

'Arminianism', whether narrowly defined as a doctrine of predestination, or more widely used to mean popery, had sharply depreciated since 1628 as polemical currency. Accounts of the Short Parliament suggest that popery, the altar policy and the Book of Sports were all live issues, but Arminianism was not. There were no references to licensing policy, none to the suppression of Calvinism, no mention of the doctrine of predestination, or even any complaints about too great an emphasis on the sacraments. Francis Rous did use the word 'Arminian' once, but Pym did not, and it was not in Earle's list of grievances.[147] In the Convocation of 1640, John Davenant's suggestion that there should be a canon against Arminian books in addition to canon iv against Socinianism seems to have found no support among his fellow bishops.[148] Arminianism did not loom large even in the debates of the Long Parliament.[149] In the Grand Remonstrance, it appeared briefly in the preface, but not in the lengthy list of specific grievances that constituted the main text.[150] Even speakers who urged the abolition of episcopacy, like Sir Henry Vane,[151] could afford to ignore 'Arminianism', speaking instead solely in terms of popery, superstitions in worship and consequent alienation from churches abroad. The report of the House of Lords' committee on 'Innovations in Religion',[152] which was chaired by John Williams and whose signatories included Ussher, Featley and Prideaux, might have been expected to make more of Arminianism, but of the eighteen items under the heading of 'doctrine', only one mentioned it by name, one other complained of the impugning of certitude of salvation, and a third of universal grace. Predestination, even in the perceptions of academic theologians, played at most a minor role.

Proceedings against the clergy provide no evidence to change the verdict that Arminianism was insignificant as a parochial issue. The total number charged with it, even if it proves to be more than the twenty-five that research has so far unearthed, works out at only two or three per county. The details are often so incoherent as to be worthless.[153] In

---

[147] J. Maltby (ed.), *The Short Parliament (1640) Diary of Sir Thomas Aston*, (Camden Society, Fourth Series (1988), esp. 7 (Rous), 87 (Earle). There are no index references to Arminianism.

[148] E. S. Cope (ed.), *Proceedings of the Short Parliament of 1640*, Camden Society, Fourth Series (1977), 111.

[149] S. Lambert, 'Committees, Religion and Parliamentary Encroachment on Royal Authority in Early Stuart England', *English Historical Review* 105/414 (1990).

[150] S. R. Gardiner (ed.), *Constitutional Documents of the Puritan Revolution* (Oxford, 1906), 202–32.

[151] Sir Henry Vane, *His Speech in the House of Commons at a Committee for the Bill against Episcopal Government* (1641).

[152] *A Copy of the Proceedings of Some Worthy and Learned Divines* (1641), sig. A21f.

[153] Tyacke, *Anti-Calvinists*, 195, rightly cautions against reading too much into this evidence.

Lincolnshire, for example, there were only two complaints. Hugh Barcroft 'had delivered for a truth the popish and Arminion [*sic*] doctrine
that no man can be assured of his salvation in this life or as much in
effect', but it is clear that the real complaint was against his observance
of Prayer Book ceremonial, and his reading of the homily against rebellion
at the coming of the Scots.[154] The other offender was Thomas Gibson,
vicar of Horncastle, who had preached that a man sinning is reprobate
and repenting is elect: but here again the doctrinal issue was less prominent than ceremony, the reading of the Book of Sports, and 'scandaliz-
ing orthodox and godly men with nicknames of Zealots, Anabaptists,
Puritans and Brownists'.[155] In most cases the evidence offered in defence
is not available, and there is no means of estimating the validity of the
charges. One particular instance suggests they could be wide of the mark,
for it involved Thomas Bedford, a convinced disciple of Samuel Ward
and John Davenant. Bedford was lecturer at St Andrew, Plymouth, and
according to his own defence the charge rested purely on the prejudice
of a faction which had opposed his appointment.[156] It is evident from the
records as a whole that sabbatarianism and ceremony were the key issues.
Even where points of doctrine were involved, it could be argued that
Laudian theology was less likely to lead to division and disharmony than
its contrary. The continued demand for infant baptism reflected at no
doubt varying levels of sophistication a sacramental tradition to which
the doctrine that Christ died for all did more justice than godly exclusiv-
ity. A pastor who, like George Herbert's Country Parson, saw himself
as the father of the whole parish, and who, if any continued refractory,
was 'long before he proceed to disinheriting, or perhaps never goes so
far; knowing that some are called at the eleventh hour', represented a conservative paternalism with the same underlying theology.

It was in the universities rather than in the parishes that predestination
had been contentious, and perceptions of what had been happening there
in the 1630s are especially valuable. The most aggressive anti-Puritan at
Cambridge was undoubtedly William Beale, but there was no hint of
predestinarian issues in the charges made against either him or John Cosin
in 1641. It was said that he applauded the papists as the king's truest subjects and affirmed 'Puritans to be traitors (or at least as bad as traitors)'.

---

[154] J. W. F. Hill, 'The Royalist Clergy of Lincolnshire', *Lincolnshire Architectural and
Archaeological Journal* 2/1, NS (1940), 44–56.
[155] Ibid., 57, 63.
[156] A. G. Matthews (ed.), *Walker Revised* (Oxford, 1948), 108. Thomas Bedford was the
author of *Luther's Predecessors* (1624) and *The Sin unto Death* (1621), a Paul's Cross Sermon of 1621 which referred to Calvin as the 'Coryphaeus of our divines' and attacked those
of 'Arminius's brood' (though it praised Hemmingsen). His notes of a defence against the
charge of Arminianism are to be found in Bodl. Lib., MS Tanner 285, 64^v.

He was charged with assisting Cosin in promoting 'Jesuitical, Popish and Canterburian religion'. Ceremonial conformity was undoubtedly the key issue.[157] The evidence offered to the House of Commons Committee of *Innovations in Religion and abuses in Government in the University of Cambridge* offers a much wider range of complaint, but in spite of the author's obvious desire to tell the committee what it wanted to hear, little space was given to predestination. 'Arminianism' was mentioned just once,[158] but in none of the 'scandalous sermons uncensored' dealt with in detail did predestination play any significant role: Turnay's of 1633 had concerned the nature of faith; both Hausted's of 1634, which had attacked irreverence and lecturers, and Normington's, which was 'deservedly suspected of Popery', were at bottom anti-Puritan; while Adams and Sparrow had both defended auricular confession; so had William Norwich of Peterhouse along with, it was said, penance and justification for works.[159] There were, to be sure, two brief references to Willington of St John's and Pullen of Magdalene as having both defended 'falling from grace', but no details were offered. Finally, Walton of Peterhouse had preached 'that the five points in controversy between the Remonstrants and Contra-Remonstrants did not belong to the foundation'.[160] Pullen and Normanton were also featured in the list of *Offensive Disputations Determinations and Questions*: Normanton was said to have carried about with him 'an extract of Calvin's errors . . . which in all companies he read to the disgrace of him', while Pullen had denied that baptism depended on predestination.[161] In both sections, 'Popery' was the key issue, Arminianism at best an also-ran; underlying the document as a whole was a preoccupation with liturgical change in the colleges.

Predestination figured hardly at all in the proceedings taken against individual bishops. Neile and Montagu both died in 1640, and it is impossible to say what charges, if any, would have been made against them. The articles of impeachment against Wren ignore 'Arminianism' altogether. Ceremony, chancels, Communion tables, rails, catechizing, the reading of the Book of Sports, the alleged silencing of preachers, the prohibition of extempore prayer dominate the charges.[162] The pamphlet literature

---

[157] *Articles Exhibited in the Parliament against William Beale . . .* (1641). *The Articles or Charge Exhibited in Parliament against D. Cozens of Durham* (1641). The contrast with Smart's attack on Cosin and other Durham clergy in 1630 (*Correspondence of John Cosin*), I. 161–99) is striking.

[158] Harley Mf 7019, f. 70.

[159] Ibid., ff. 53–61.

[160] Ibid., f. 63. Tyacke concludes (*Anti-Calvinists*, 57 n. 135): 'During the 1630s the preaching of Arminianism apparently went unchecked.'

[161] Harley MS 7019, f. 66.

[162] Christopher Wren, *Parentalia, or memoirs of the Family of the Wrens* (1750), 73–114.

tells the same story. *Wren's Anatomy* concerned itself with ceremony and silencing ministers.[163] 'Arminianism' was part of the polemic, but always in the context of altars, images and popery. Robert Baillie was a noted anti-Laudian whose *An Antidote Against Arminianism*[164] did concern itself with predestination, but he admitted that English Arminians abhorred the extravagancies of Vorstius and Socinus, 'yet their heart is hot inflamed after the abominations of Rome'. His *Life of William Laud*[165] attempted to convict Laud himself of Arminianism, but the only evidence adduced in support was that he had 'scraped out with his own hand' the phrase 'Father of thine elect' from the Prayer Book. At Laud's trial the charge was a virtual non-runner.[166]

The origins of the English Civil War, which broke out in 1642, are complex and in some respects remain elusive. It is no part of the purpose of this study to deny the part played by religious issues. The tensions between Lutheran and Reformed, or between the Protestant right and the Protestant left, had long been felt throughout Europe, but only in England had there been an attempt from the first to accommodate both within the borders of a single state.[167] That task became more difficult after the accession of James I to the English throne, for on the one hand Scotland offered encouragement and reinforcement to the left, while on the other, the declining political threat from Catholics, coupled with an increasingly confident Counter-Reformation, beckoned an adjustment on the right. Involvement in the Netherlands further complicated the precarious balance James eventually achieved, which in retrospect it is possible to see was altogether destroyed in the immediate aftermath of the Synod of Dort as the outbreak of the Thirty Years War raised militant Protestant expectations, and the negotiations for the Spanish match dashed them. Paradoxically, and for reasons quite unconnected with the doctrine of predestination, when war did come against Spain, the clergy of Durham House were able to consolidate their political ascendancy, and during the Personal Rule king and hierarchy combined in unprecedented campaigns to enforce ceremonial uniformity both in England and Scotland.

Yet theology had a momentum of its own. The story told here suggests that as far as predestination is concerned, the threat to the doctrinal balance came in the late Elizabethan period, and was concentrated in the

---

[163] *Wren's Anatomy, Discovering his notorious pranks and shameful wickedness; with some of his most lewd facts, and infamous deeds* (1641).

[164] R. Baillie, *An Antidote against Arminianism* (1641).

[165] R. Baillie, *The Life of William Laud, Now Lord Archbishop of Canterbury Examined, wherein his principal Actions, or Deviations . . . are traced and set down* (1643).

[166] 'I have nothing to do to defend Arminianism, no man having yet charged me with the abetting any point of it.' Laud, *Works*, V. 267.

[167] G. F. Nuttall and O. Chadwick, *From Uniformity to Unity, 1662–1962* (1962), 5–6.

universities. On the whole, the crown and its advisers operated responsibly to cool passions, and to perpetuate the Church of England's well-recognized *via media*. A notable exception was James I's flirtation with Contra-Remonstrant polemic, in contrast to the mediating role he played at Hampton Court, and in sharp conflict with his consistently Laudian churchmanship. Even then, however, English theology retained an independent momentum. In spite of the influence of their archbishop, the clergy sent to Dort deserved well of their church in respect of the peace they advocated, the moderation they espoused, and the latitude of doctrine they endorsed. Notwithstanding their efforts, they returned to an increasingly polarized church, again made worse by James I's involvement in the Montagu case. Lacking his father's adroitness and his love of politics, and incapable of being all things to all men, Charles I sought a real compromise rather than a cosmetic adjustment. Whatever his failings, his settlement of predestinarian disputes in 1628 was a result of consensus, and its operation under the Personal Rule was so manifestly fair, and seen to be fair, that by 1640 it could be appealed to even by John Davenant as a ground of reassurance to Puritan ministers suspicious of the oaths required of them.[168] The religious tensions of 1640–2 had little to do with the doctrine of predestination.

---

[168] *Bishop Davenant's Answer unto the Queries propounded by certain Ministers concerning Ye Oath in Ye Sixt Canon*, printed in M. Fuller, *The Life, Letters and Writings of John Davenant*, DD, 1572–1641 (1897), 540–53, esp. 542.

Select bibliography

The place of publication is London unless otherwise stated.

PRIMARY PRINTED WORKS

A., J. *A Historicall Narration of the Judgement of . . . English Bishops, Holy Martyrs and others . . . concerning God's Election and the Merit of Christ his Death* (1631).

A Copy of an Answer unto a Certain Letter (The Netherlands(?), 1563(?)).

A Copy of the Proceedings of Some Worthy and Learned Divines touching innovations in the Doctrine and Discipline of the Church of England (1641).

Abbot, George. *The coppie of a letter . . . showing reasons which induced the king's majestie to prescribe directions for preachers* (Oxford, 1822).

Quaestiones sex, totidem praelectionibus . . . discussae (Oxford, 1598).

Abbot, Robert. *The Third Part of the Defence of the Reformed Catholic against Dr Bishop's Second Part of the Reformation of a Catholic* (1609).

De Gratia et Perseverantia Sanctorum; Exercitationes aliquot (1618).

In Richardi Thomsoni Anglobelgici Diatribam de amissione et intercisione justificationis et gratiae animadversio brevis (1618).

Acta Synodi Nationalis . . . Dordrechti habitae annon 1618 et 1619. Accedunt plenissima de quinque articulis theologorum judicia (Dordrecht, 1620).

Ames, William. *Medulla theologiae* (Amsterdam, 1627).

Andrewes, Lancelot. *Works,* ed. J. P. Wilson and J. Bliss, Anglo-Catholic Library (11 vols., Oxford, 1841–54).

The Answere of the Vice Chancellor . . . and other Heads of Houses in the Universitie of Oxford . . . to the Humble Petition of the Ministers of the Church of England (Oxford, 1603).

Anti Montacutum: An appeale or remonstrance against R. Mountagu (1629).

Arminius, James. *Works,* tr. and ed. J. and W. Nichols (3 vols., 1825–75).

Articles Exhibited in the Parliament against William Beale (1641).

The Articles or Charge Exhibited in Parliament against D. Cozens of Durham (1641).

Articuli Lambethani (1651).

A Transcript of the Registers of the Company of Stationers, 1554–1640, ed. E. Arber (5 vols., 1875–94).

Balcanqual, Walter. *A Joynt Attestation, avowing that the discipline of the Church of England was not impeached by the Synode of Dort* (1626).

313

314   Select bibliography

Ball, John. *A Treatise of Faith* (1631).
Ball, T. *The Life of the renowned Dr Preston . . . writ in the year 1628*, ed. E. W. Harcourt (Oxford, 1855).
Baro, Peter. *In Jonam prophetam praelectiones* (1579).
De fide, eiusque ortu & natura explicatio (1580).
A special Treatise of God's Providence (1580).
Summa trium de Praedestinatione Sententiarum (Harderwijk, 1613).
Baudius, Dominicus. *Epistolarum Centuriae Tres* (Leiden, 1620).
Baynes, Paul. *A Commentary on the first chapter of the Ephesians* (1632).
Ballarmine, Robert. *Disputationes . . . de controversiis Christianae Fidei adversus huius temporis Haereticos* (Ingoldstadt, 1601).
Beza, Theodore. *A Book of Christian Questions and Answers . . . translated into English by Arthur Golding* (1574).
A Brief Declaration of the chief points of Christian Religion, set forth in a Table, tr. W. Whittingham (1575?).
The Treasure of Truth, touching the groundworke of man his salvation . . . with a brief summe of the comfortable doctrine of God his providence, comprised in 38 short Aphorisms, written in Latin by Theodore Beza, and newly turned into English by John Stockwood (1576).
Quaestionum et responsionum Christianarum libellus, 5th edn (2 vols., Geneva, 1577, 76).
Tractationes Theologicae (3 vols., Geneva, 1570–82).
Birch, T. (ed.) *The Court and Times of Charles I* (2 vols., 1849).
The Court and Times of James I (2 vols., 1849).
Boughen, Edward. *Two Sermons, the first preached at Canterbury. The second, at Saint Paul's Crosse* (1635).
Brandt, G. *The History of the Reformation . . . in and about the Low Countries, from the beginning of the Eighth Century, down to the famous Synod of Dort . . . translated from the Low-Dutch* (4 vols., 1720–3).
Bucer, Martin. *Psalmorum libri quinque . . . enarrati* (1554).
Metaphrasis et Enarratio in Epistolam D. Pauli Apostoli ad Romanos (Basle, 1562).
Praelectiones . . . in Epistolam . . . at Ephesios . . . habitae Cantabrigiae in Anglia anno MDL et LI (Basle, 1562).
Bullinger, H. *A Confutation of the Pope's Bull . . . together with a defence of the said true Christian Queen, and of the whole realm of England* (1572).
Henrici Bullingeri Commentarii in omnes Pauli Apostoli Epistolas (Zurich, 1582).
The Decades of Henry Bullinger, ed. T. Harding (5 vols. in 4, Parker Society, Cambridge, 1841–52).
Burton, H. *A Plea to an Appeale: traversed dialoguewise* (1626).
Israel's Fast. Or, a meditation upon the seventh chapter of Joshuah (1628).
The Seven Vials or A Brief and Plain Exposition upon the 15: and 16: chapters of the Revelation (1628).
Calvin, J. *Opera quae supersunt Omnia* (14 vols., Brunswick, 1863–1900).
Institutes of the Christian religion, ed. J. T. McNeil, tr. F. L. Battles, Library of Christian Classics (2 vols., 1961).
Cardwell, E. (ed.), *A History of Conferences and other Proceedings connected with the Book of Common Prayer, 1558–1690* (Oxford, 1840).

Synodalia (A Collection of Articles of Religion, Canons and Proceedings of Convocation in the Province of Canterbury, 1547–1717) (2 vols., Oxford, 1842).

Documentary Annals of the Reformed Church of England (A Collection of Injunctions, Declarations, Orders, Articles of Enquiry, etc.) 1546–1716 (2 vols., Oxford, 1844).

Carier, Benjamin. *A Treatise written by M. Doctour Carier, wherein he layeth down sundry learned and pithy considerations, by which he was moved to forsake the Protestant Congregations* (Liège, 1614).

Carleton, Sir Dudley. *Letters from and to Sir Dudley Carleton, Knt, during his Embassy in Holland,* ed. P. Yorke (1775).

Carleton, George. *An Oration made at the Hague, before the Prince of Orange, and the Assembly of the High and Mighty Lords, and the States General, by . . . the Lord Bishop of Llandaff* (1619).

An Examination of those Things wherein the author of the Late Appeale holdeth the Doctrines of the Pelagians and Arminians to be the Doctrines of the Church of England (1626).

Casaubon, I. *Ephemerides,* ed. J. Russell (2 vols., Oxford, 1850).

Certaine Sermons or Homilies appointed to be read in churches in the reign of Queene Elizabeth (1623).

Chamberlain, J. *The Letters of John Chamberlain,* ed. N. E. McClure (2 vols., Philadelphia, 1939).

The Collegiat Suffrage of the Divines of Great Britaine concerning the Five Articles controverted in the Low Countries (1629).

Chouneus, Thomas. *Collectiones Theologicarum ex diversis authorum sententiis excerptae* (1635).

Clarke, S. *The Lives of Thirty-two English Divines* (1677).

Commons, House of. *Journals of the House of Commons.*

Conyers, James. *Christ's Love and Saints' Sacrifice, preached in a sermon at St Paul's Crosse* (1635).

Cope, E. S. (ed.), *Proceedings of the Short Parliament of 1640,* Camden Society, Fourth Series (1977).

Corro, Anthony. *A Theological Dialogue wherein the Epistle of St Paul to the Romans is expounded* (1575).

Corvinus, Johannes-Arnoldus. *Responsio ad Bogermanni annotationes, pro Grotio* (Leiden, 1614).

Cosin, John. *The Works of John Cosin,* ed. J. Sansom, Anglo-Catholic Library (5 vols., Oxford, 1843–55).

Correspondence of John Cosin, ed. G. Ornsby, Surtees Society, vols. 52 and 55 Durham (1869–72).

Cotton, Robert. *The Danger wherein the Kingdome now standeth, & the Remedie* (1628).

Cox, J. C. (ed.), *The Records of the Borough of Northampton* (2 vols., 1898).

Crosfield, Thomas. *The Diary of Thomas Crosfield,* ed. F. S. Boas (Oxford, 1935).

Davenant, John. *Animadversions upon a Treatise entitled God's Love to Mankind* (Cambridge, 1641).

Du Moulin, Pierre. *Anatomy of Arminianisme* (1620; 2nd edn, 1626; 3rd edn, 1635).

Duppa, Brian. *Articles to be enquired of throughout the diocese of Chichester* (1638).

Eliot, John. *Negotium Posterorum*, ed. A. B. Grosart (2 vols., 1881).

Erasmus, Desiderius. *Paraphrases upon the New Testament* (1548).

Featley, Daniel. *A Parallel of New-Old Pelagiarminian Error* (1626).

Pelagius Redivivus, or Pelagius raked out of the ashes of Arminius and his schollers (1626).

A Second Parallel, together with a writ of Error sued against the Appealer (1626).

Cygnea Cantio (1629).

Fell, Samuel. *Primitiae, sive Oratio habita Oxoniae in Nona Novembris et Concio Latina ad Baccalaureos die Cinerum* (Oxford, 1627).

Field, Nathaniel. *Some Short Memorials Concerning the Life of that Reverend Divine Doctor Richard Field*, ed. J. Le Neve (1716–17).

Field, Richard. *Of the Church* (5 vols., 1606–10).

Fletcher, Phineas. *The Way to Blessedness: A Treatise or Commentary on the First Psalm* (1632).

Frere, W. H., and C. E. Douglas (eds,). *Puritan Manifestoes* (1907).

Gardiner, S. R. (ed.). *Debates in the House of Commons in 1625,* Camden Society, NS 6 (1873).

Reports of Cases in the Courts of Star Chamber and High Commission, Camden Society, NS 39 (1886).

Constitutional Documents of the Puritan Revolution (Oxford, 1906).

Gilbie, Anthony. *A Brief Treatise of Election and Reprobation: Answers to the Objections of the Adversaries of this Doctrine* (Geneva, 1556).

Goodwin, Thomas. *The Happiness of the Saints in Glory* (1638).

Gouge, William. *A Short Catechism, wherein are briefly laid down the fundamental principles of the Christian religion* (1615; 7th edn, 1635 (STC 12130)).

Grotius, H. *Briefwisseling van Hugo Grotius,* ed. P. C. Molhuysen and B. L. Meulenbroek (11 vols., The Hague, 1928–81).

Hacket, J. *Scrinia Reserata: A Memorial offer'd to the Great Deservings of J. Williams . . . Archbishop of York* (1693).

Hakewill, George. *An Answere to a Treatise written by Dr Carier . . .* (1616).

Hales, John. *The Golden Remains of the Ever-Memorable Mr John Hales of Eton College: Letters from the Synod of Dort* (2nd edn, 1673).

Hall, Joseph, *The Works of Joseph Hall*, ed. P. Wynter (10 vols., Oxford, 1863).

Harmonia Confessionum Fidei Orthodoxarum, et Reformatarum Ecclesiarum (Geneva, 1581).

Harsnett, Samuel. *A Sermon preached at Paul's Cross,* appended to R. Stewart, *Three Sermons* (1656).

Hemmingsen, N. *Commentarius in epistolam Pauli ad Ephesios* (1576).

Commentarius in epistolam Pauli ad Romanos (1577).

Enchiridion Theologicum, praecipua verae religionis capita breviter et simpliciter explicata (1577).

Heylyn, Peter. *Observations on The History of the Reign of King Charles published by H. L. Esq.* (1656).

Respondet Petrus (1658).

Certamen Epistolare, or the Letter Combat, managed by Peter Heylyn, DD. (1659).

Historia Quinquarticularis, or a Declaration of the Judgement of the Church of England in the Five Controverted Points, Reproached in these Last Times by the Name of Arminianism (3 vols. in 1, 1660).

Cyprianus Anglicus, or, The History of the Life and Death of William [Laud] (1668).

Aerius Redivivus, or The History of the Presbyterians (2nd edn, 1672).

Ecclesia Restaurata, or The History of the Reformation of the Church of England by Peter Heylyn . . . with a life of the author by John Barnard . . . ed. J. G. Robertson (2 vols., Cambridge, 1849).

Hickman, Henry. *Historia Quinq-Articularis Exarticulata or Animadversions on Dr Heylyn's Quinquarticular History* (1673).

Hildersham, Arthur. *Lectures on Psalm LI* (1635).

Historical Manuscripts Commission. *Seventh Report, Appendix I (The Manuscripts of G. A. Lowndes Esq.)* (1879).

Eleventh Report, Appendix I (The Manuscripts of Henry Duncan Skrine) (1887).

Twelfth Report, Appendix, Part I (The Manuscripts of Earl Cowper, K.G.) (1888).

Thirteenth Report, Appendix, Part VII (Manuscripts of the Earl of Lonsdale) (1893).

House of Lords MSS, Vol. XI, Addenda, 1514–1714 (1962).

Hoard, Samuel and Henry Mason. *God's Love to Mankind, Manifested by disprooving his Absolute Decree for their Damnation* (1633).

Hooker, Richard. *The Works of . . . Mr Richard Hooker*, ed. J. Keble (3 vols., Oxford, 1836).

The Folger Library of the Works of Richard Hooker, gen. ed. W. S. Hill. (5 vols., Cambridge, Mass., 1972–).

Hooper, John. *The Early Writings of Bishop Hooper*, ed. S. Carr (Parker Society, Cambridge, 1843).

Hutton, Matthew. *Brevis et dilucida explicatio verae, certae, et consolationis plenae doctrinae De Electione, Praedestinatione ac Reprobatione* (Harderwijk, 1613).

Jackson, Thomas. *Works* (12 vols., Oxford, 1844).

James I, King. *His Majesty's Declaration concerning His Proceedings with the States General of the United provinces of the Low Countries in the Cause of D. Conradus Vorstius* (1612).

A Meditation upon the Lord's Prayer (1619).

The kings majesties letter to the Lords Grace of Canterbury, touching preaching, and preachers (1622).

ed. C. H. McIlwain, *The Political Works of James I* (1918).

Jewel, John. *Works*, ed. J. Ayre (4 vols., Parker Society (Cambridge, 1845–50)).

Kellison, Matthew. *The Gag of the Reformed Gospel* (Douai, 1623).

Kenyon, J. P. (ed.), *The Stuart Constitution*, 2nd edn (Cambridge, 1986).

Larkin, J. F. and P. L. Hughes. (eds.), *Stuart Royal Proclamations* (2 vols., Oxford, 1973–83).

Latimer, Hugh. *Sermons and Remains of Hugh Latimer,* ed. G. E. Corrie (2 vols., Parker Society, Cambridge, 1844–5).

Laud, William. *The Works of William Laud*, ed. W. Scott and J. Bliss, Anglo-Catholic Library (7 vols., Oxford, 1847–60).

Leedham-Green, E. S. *Books in Cambridge Inventories: Book Lists from Vice-*

Chancellor's Court Probate Inventories in the Tudor and Stuart Periods (2 vols., Cambridge, 1986).

Loe, William. *A Sermon preached at . . . the Funeral of . . . Daniel Featley* (Oxford, 1645).

Lords, House of. *Journals of the House of Lords.*

Maltby, J. (ed.), *The Short Parliament (1640) Diary of Sir Thomas Aston*, Camden Society, Fourth Series (1988).

Montagu, R. *A Gagg for the New Gospell? No. A New Gagg for an Old Goose: or, An Answer to a Late Abridger of Controversies* (1624).

Appello Caesarem: A Just Appeal from Two Unjust Informers (1625).

Articles to be enquired of throughout the whole diocese of Chichester (1631).

Articles of Enquiry and Direction for the diocese of Norwich (Cambridge, 1638).

Musculus, Wolfgang. *Common places of Christian Religion* (1563).

N., O. *An Apology of English Arminianisme* (St Omer, 1634).

A Necessary Doctrine and Erudition for any Christian Man (1543).

Neile, Richard. *Marcus Antonius de Dominis . . . his Shiftings in Religion* (1624).

Notestein, W. and F. H. Relf (eds.). *Commons Debates for 1629* (Minneapolis, 1921).

Nowell, Alexander. *Catechism,* ed. G. E. Corrie (Parker Society, Cambridge, 1853).

Original Letters relative to the English Reformation, ed. and tr. H. Robinson (2 vols., Parker Society, Cambridge, 1846–7).

P., C. *Judicium Theologicum de Discrimine inter Philippum Melanchthon & Allobroges in doctrina de praedestinatione* (n. p., 1622).

Parker, Matthew. *How we ought to take the death of the godly, a sermon made in Cambridge at the buriall of the noble clerk, D. M. Bucer* (1551).

'A Preface unto the Bible folowying', from the Bishops' Bible of 1568.

The Correspondence of Matthew Parker, ed. J. Bruce and T. T. Perowne (Parker Society, Cambridge, 1853).

Peel, A. (ed.). *The Second Part of a Register* (2 vols., Cambridge, 1915).

Pemble, William. *Vindiciae Fidei* (Oxford, 1625; 2nd edn, 1629).

Vindiciae Gratiae, A Plea for Grace, more especially the Grace of Faith, or Certain Lectures as touching the nature and properties of Grace and Faith, wherein, amongst other matters of great use, the main sinews of Arminius's doctrine are cut asunder (Oxford, 1627; 2nd edn, 1629; 3rd edn, 1635).

Perkins, William. *Works* (3 vols., Cambridge, 1616–18).

Pollard, A. W. and G. R. Redgrave. *A Short Title Catalogue of Books printed . . . 1475–1640* (2nd edn revised & enlarged, 2 vols., 1986).

Potter, Christopher. *A Letter . . . vindicating his sentiments touching the Predestinarian Controversies,* in *A Collection of Tracts Concerning Predestination* (Cambridge, 1719).

Praestantium ac Eruditorum Virorum Epistolae Ecclesiasticae et Theologicae, ed. C. Hartsoeker and P. Limborch (Amsterdam, 1684).

Preston, John. *The Doctrine of the Saints Infirmities* (1636).

Prideaux, John. *Certain Sermons* (Oxford, 1636).

Prynne, William. *The Perpetuitie of a Regenerate Man's Estate* (1626).

The Church of England's Old Antithesis to the New Arminianisme (1629); appeared 'much enlarged' as *Anti-Arminianisme* (1630).

God, No Impostor or Deluder: An Answer to a Popish and Arminian Cavil, in the defence of Free Will and Universal Grace (1629).

A Quench Coale (1637).

Rome's Masterpiece (1644).

Hidden Works of Darkness (1645).

Canterburies Doome (1646).

R., I. *The Spy, Discovering the Danger of Arminian Heresy and Spanish Treachery* (Amsterdam, 1628).

Ramsden, Henry. *A Gleaning in God's Harvest: Four choice handfulls* (STC 20660) (1639).

Reformatio Legum Ecclesiasticarum (1571).

Reeve, Edmund. *The Communion Book Catechism Expounded* (1636).

The Register of the University of Oxford, ed. A. Clark (4 parts, Oxford Hist. Society 10, 1887–9).

Rogers, Thomas. *The English Creede consenting with the True Auncient, Catholique and Apostolique Church* (1585–7).

The Faith, Doctrine and Religion professed, and protected in the Realm of England, expressed in 39 Articles (Cambridge, 1607).

Rous, Francis. *Testis Veritatis: The Doctrine of King James . . . Of the Church of England of the Catholicke Church, Shewed to bee One in the Points of Predestination, Free-Will, Certaintie of Salvation* (1626).

Rushworth, J. *Historical Collections* (7 vols., 1659–1701).

Sclater, William (the elder). *Sermons experimental: on psalmes cxvi & cxvii, published by his son W. Sclater* (STC 21844) (1638).

Shelford, Robert. *Five Pious and Learned Discourses* (Cambridge, 1635).

Shuckbrugh, E. S. (ed.). *Two Biographies of William Bedell* (Cambridge, 1902).

Sibbes, Richard. *The Riches of Mercy in Two Treatises* (STC 22501) (1638).

Two Sermons (STC 22519) (1638).

The Christian's end. Or, the sweet soveraignty of Christ over his members. Being the substance of Five Sermons (STC 224985) (1639).

Light from Heaven, discovering the fountaine opened . . . In four treatises (STC 22498) (1639).

The Returning Backslider, or a commentary upon the whole xiiii chapter of Hosea (STC 22500) (1639).

Sparke, Thomas. *A Brotherly Perswasion to Unitie and Uniformitie Touching the Received and Present Ecclesiasticall Government* (1607).

A Supplication to the King's Most Excellent Majesty: A Plea for Toleration for Catholics (1604).

Sutcliffe, Matthew. *A Brief Censure Upon an Appeal to Caesar* (STC 18032) (1626).

Taylor, Thomas. *The Practice of Repentance, laid down in sundry directions* (STC 23845) (1628; 2nd edn, 1629; 3rd edn, 1632; 4th edn, 1635).

The progress of Saints to Full Holiness, described in sundry apostolical aphorisms or short precepts tending to sanctification (STC 23850) (1630).

The Parable of the Sower and the Seed . . . To which is added, A Mappe of Rome, in five Sermons (STC 23842) (3rd edn, 1634).

Thomson, Richard. *Diatriba de Amissione et Intercisione Gratiae, et Justificationis* (Leiden, 1616).

Trent, Council of. *Canones et Decreta Concilii Tridentini*, ed. A. L. Richter (Leipzig, 1853).

Twisse, William. *A Discovery of D. Jackson's Vanitie* (Amsterdam, 1631).
   The Doctrine of the Synod of Dort and Arles reduced to the practice (Wing
   T. 3420; STC 24403) (Amsterdam, 1631).
   A Brief catechistical exposition of Christian doctrine (1632).
   Vindiciae Gratiae, Potestatis ac Providentiae Dei (Amsterdam, 1632).
Ursinus, Zacharias. *The Summe of the Christian Religion* (Oxford, 1591).
Ussher, James. *The Works of James Ussher*, ed. C. R. Elrington (17 vols., Dublin,
   1847–64).
Vermigli, Peter Martyr. *Loci Communes* (1576).
Vossius, Gerard. *Historiae de Controversiis quas Pelagius eiusque reliquiae
   moverunt Libri septem* (Leiden, 1618).
   G. J. Vossii et clarorum vivorum, ad eum Epistolae, ed. P. Colomesius (2 vols.
   in 1, 1690).
Ward, Samuel. *Gratia Discriminans: Concio ad Clerum habita Cantabrigiae* (1626).
Whitaker, William. *Praelectiones de Ecclesia* (Cambridge, 1599).
White, John. *The Way to the True Church, wherein the principal motives per-
   suading to Romanism are familiarly disputed . . . and driven to their issues,
   where this day they stick between the Papists and us* (1608).
   A Defence of the Way to the True Church against A.D. His Reply (1614).
Whitgift, John. *The Works of John Whitgift*, ed. J. Ayre (3 vols., Parker Society,
   Cambridge, 1851–3).
Willett, Andrew. *Synopsis Papismi* (1592, 1600).
Winwood, R. *Memorials of Affairs of State*, ed. E. Sawyer (3 vols., 1725).
Womock, Laurence. *The Examination of Tilenus before the Triers . . . to which
   is annexed the Tenets of the Remonstrants* (1658).
   *Arcana Dogmatum Anti-Remonstrantium, or the Calvinists' Cabinet Un-
   locked, in An Apology for Tilenus against a pretended vindication of the Synod
   of Dort* (1659).
Wotton, Anthony. *A Dangerous Plot Discovered . . . wherein is proved that R.
   Mountague . . . laboureth to bring in the Faith of Rome and Arminius* (1626).
Wren, C. *Parentalia, or memoirs of the Family of the Wrens* (1750).
Yates, John. *Ibis ad Caesarem, or A Submissive Appearance before Caesar* (1626).
Zürich Letters, ed. and tr. H. Robinson (2 vols., Parker Society, Cambridge,
   1842–5).

SECONDARY WORKS

Adams, H. M. *Catalogue of Books Printed on the Continent of Europe 1501–1600
   in Cambridge Libraries* (2 vols., Cambridge, 1967).
Allison, C. F. *The Rise of Moralism* (1966).
Armstrong, B. *Calvinism and the Amyraut Heresy* (Madison, 1969).
Ashton, R. *The English Civil War: Conservatism and Revolution* (1978).
Babbage, S. B. *Puritanism and Richard Bancroft* (1962).
Backus, I. ' "Hercules Gallicus" et La Conception du Libre Arbitre dans le Com-
   mentaire sur la quatrième évangile de Martin Bucer', in I. Backus *et al.* (eds.),
   Martin Bucer, Apocryphe et Authentique, Cahiers, Revue de théologie et de
   philosophie 8 (Geneva, 1983).

Baker, J. Wayne. *Heinrich Bullinger and the Covenant: The Other Reformed Tradition* (Ohio, 1980).

Bangs, C. *Arminius: A Study in the Dutch Reformation* (Nashville, 1971).

Bartlett, K. R. 'The Role of the Marian Exiles', in P. W. Hasler (ed.), *The House of Commons 1558–1603* (3 vols., 1981).

Betteridge, M. S. 'The Bitter Notes: The Geneva Bible and its Annotations', *Sixteenth Century Journal* 14/1 (1983).

Booty, J. E. *John Jewel as Apologist of the Church of England* (1963).

Bowes, R. (ed.), *A Catalogue of the Books printed at or related to the University . . . of Cambridge, 1521–1893* (1894).

Bray, J. S. *Theodore Beza's Doctrine of Predestination* (Nieuwkoop, 1975).

Bromiley, G. W. *Baptism and the Anglican Reformers* (1953).

Bush, S. Jr and C. J. Rasmussen. 'Emmanuel College Library's First Inventory', *Transactions of the Cambridge Bibliographical Society*, 8/5 (1985).

Cochrane, A. *Reformed Confessions of the Sixteenth Century* (1966).

Cogswell, T. *The Blessed Revolution: English Politics and the Coming of War, 1621–1624* (Cambridge, 1989).

Collinson, P. *The Elizabethan Puritan Movement* (1967).

Archbishop Grindal, 1558–1583: The Struggle for a Reformed Church (1979).

Godly People: Essays on English Protestantism and Puritanism (1983).

'The Jacobean Religious Settlement: The Hampton Court Conference', in H. Tomlinson (ed.), *Before the English Civil War* (1983).

'England and International Calvinism, 1558–1640', in Menna Prestwich (ed.), *International Calvinism* (Oxford, 1985).

Cranfield, N. and K. Fincham. 'John Howson's Answers to Archbishop Abbot's Accusations at his "Trial" before James I at Greenwich, 10 June, 1615', in Camden Miscellany 29 (1987).

Cremeans, C. D. *The Reception of Calvinistic Thought in England* (Urbana, Illinois, 1949).

Cust, R. *The Forced Loan and English Politics, 1626–1628* (Oxford, 1987).

Cust, R. and A. Hughes. (eds.). *Conflict in Early Stuart England: Studies in Religion and Politics, 1603–1642* (1989).

Daly, J. 'Cosmic Harmony and Political Thinking in Early Stuart England', *Transactions of the American Philosophical Society*, 69/7 (1979).

Danner, D. G. 'The Contribution of the Geneva Bible to the English Protestant Tradition', *Sixteenth Century Journal*, 12/3 (1981).

de Burigny, M. *The Life of Hugo Grotius* (1754).

den Tex, J. *Oldenbarnevelt* (2 vols., Cambridge, 1973).

Dent, C. M. *Protestant Reformers in Elizabethan Oxford* (1983).

Dickens, A. G. *The English Reformation* (1964).

Dixon, R. W. *History of the Church of England* (6 vols., 1878–82).

Donnelly, J. P. *Calvinism and Scholasticism in Vermigli's Doctrine of Grace* (Leiden, 1976).

Dugmore, C. W. *The Doctrine of Grace in the English Reformers* (Hulsean Lectures, 1960, unpublished).

Duke, A. 'The Ambivalent Face of Calvinism in the Netherlands, 1561–1618', in Menna Prestwich (ed.), *International Calvinism 1541–1715* (Oxford, 1985).

Elton, G. R. *The Parliament of England, 1559–1581* (Cambridge, 1986).

Fincham, K. 'Prelacy and Politics: Archbishop Abbot's Defence of Protestant Orthodoxy', *Historical Research* 61 (1988).

Fincham, K. (ed.), *The Early Stuart Church* (forthcoming).

Fincham, K and P. Lake. 'The Ecclesiastical Policy of King James I', *Journal of British Studies* 24 (1985).

Foster, H. D. 'Liberal Calvinism: The Remonstrants at the Synod of Dort in 1618', *Harvard Theological Review* 16 (1923).

Frere, W. H. *The English Church in the Reigns of Elizabeth and James I* (1911).

Fuller, M. *The Life, Letters and Writings of John Davenant, DD, 1572–1641, Lord Bishop of Salisbury* (1897).

Fuller, T. *History of Cambridge*, ed. M. Prickett and T. Wright (Cambridge, 1840).

The Worthies of England, ed. P. A. Nuttall (3 vols. 1840).

The Church History of Britain, ed. J. S. Brewer (6 vols., Oxford, 1845).

Abel Redevivus: or the dead yet speaking, new edn, with notes by W. Nichols (2 vols., 1867).

Gardiner, S. R. *A History of England from the Accession of James I to the Outbreak of the Civil War* (10 vols., 1883–4).

Gaskell, P. *Trinity College Library* (Cambridge, 1980).

Gardy, F. *Bibliographie des Œuvres . . . de Théodore de Bèze* (Geneva, 1960).

Gee, H. *The Elizabethan Prayer Book and Ornaments* (1902).

Grayson, C. 'James I and the Religious Crisis of the United Provinces, 1613–1619', in D. Baker (ed.), *Reform and Reformation: England and the Continent, c. 1500–c. 1750*, Studies in Church History: Subsidia 2 (Oxford, 1979).

Guthrie, J. *The Life of James Arminius, translated from the Latin of Caspar Brandt* (1854).

Haigh, C. (ed.). *The Reign of Elizabeth* (1984).

Hardwick, C. *A History of the Articles of Religion* (3rd edn, Cambridge, 1859).

Haugaard, W. P. *Elizabeth and the English Reformation* (Cambridge, 1968).

'John Calvin and the Catechism of Alexander Nowell', *Archiv für Reformationsgeschichte* 61 (1970).

Hill, J. W. F. 'The Royalist Clergy of Lincolnshire', *Lincolnshire Architectural and Archaeological Journal* 2/1, NS (1940).

Hill, W. S. 'Doctrine and Polity in Hooker's Laws', *English Literary Renaissance* 2/2 (1972).

Hill, W. S. (ed.). *Studies in Richard Hooker: Essays Preliminary to an Edition of His Works* (1972).

Hoenderdaal, G. J. 'The Debate about Arminius outside the Netherlands', in Th. H. Lunsingh Scheurleer and G. H. M. Posthumus Meyes (eds.), *Leiden University in the Seventeenth Century* (Leiden, 1975).

Hudson, W. *The Cambridge Connection and the Elizabethan Settlement of 1559* (Durham, North Carolina, 1980).

Hutton, S. 'Thomas Jackson, Oxford Platonist and William Twisse, Aristotelian', *Journal of the History of Ideas* 39 (1978).

Hutton, W. H. *William Laud* (1895).

Inter-Collegiate Catalogue of Continental Books held in Oxford Libraries.

Johnson, A. F. 'The Exiled English Church at Amsterdam and its Press', *The Library*, Fifth Series 5/4 (1951).

Jones, N. L. *Faith by Statute: Parliament and the Settlement of Religion, 1559* (1982).

Kendall, R. T. *Calvin and English Calvinism to 1649* (pb. edn, Oxford, 1979).

Ker, N. P. 'Oxford College Libraries in the Sixteenth Century', *The Bodleian Library Record* 6 (1957–61).

Lake, P. *Moderate Puritans and the Elizabethan Church* (Cambridge, 1982).
'Calvinism and the English Church', 1570–1635' in *Past and Present* 114 (1987).
Anglicans and Puritans? Presbyterianism and English Conformist Thought from Whitgift to Hooker (1988).

Lamb, J. *An Historical Account of the Thirty-nine Articles* (Cambridge, 1829).

Lambert, S. 'The Printers and the Government, 1604–1637' in R. Myers and M. Harris (eds.), *Aspects of Printing from 1600* (Oxford, 1987).
'Richard Montagu, Arminianism and Censorship', *Past and Present* 124 (1989).
'Committees, Religion and Parliamentary Encroachment on Royal Authority in Early Stuart England', *English Historical Review* 105/414 (1990).

Lamont, W. *Marginal Prynne* (1963).
'The Rise of Arminianism Reconsidered: A Comment', *Past and Present* 107 (1985).

Lawson, J. P. *The Life of William Laud* (2 vols., 1829).

Le Bas, C. W. *The Life of Archbishop Laud* (1836).

Lockyer, R. *Buckingham: The Life and Political Career of George Villiers, First Duke of Buckingham, 1592–1628* (1981).

Loyer, O. *L'Anglicanisme de Richard Hooker* (2 vols., Lille, 1979).

McClelland, J. C. 'The Reformed Doctrine of Predestination according to Peter Martyr', *Scottish Journal of Theology* 8 (1955).

McConica, J. 'Humanism and Aristotle in Tudor Oxford', *English Historical Review* 94 (1979).

McLachlan, H. J. *Socinianism in Seventeenth Century England* (Oxford, 1951).

Maclure, M. *The Paul's Cross Sermons, 1534–1642* (Toronto, 1958).

Madan, F. *Oxford Books* (2 vols., Oxford, 1895).

Malcolm, N. *De Dominis (1560–1624): Venetian, Anglican, Ecumenist and Relapsed Heretic* (1984).

Malone, M. T. 'The Doctrine of Predestination in the Thought of William Perkins and Richard Hooker', *Anglican Theological Review* 52 (1970).

Manschreck, C. L. *Melanchthon, the Quiet Reformer* (New York, 1958).

Matthews, A. G. (ed.), *Walker Revised* (Oxford, 1948).

Møller, J. G. 'The Beginnings of Puritan Covenant Theology', *Journal of Ecclesiastical History* 14 (1963).

Morgan, I. *Prince Charles' Puritan Chaplain* (1957).

Morris, John. 'Restrictive Practices in the Elizabethan Book Trade', *Trans. Cambridge Bibliographical Soc.* 4 (1967), 276–90.

Mozley, J. B. *A Treatise on the Augustinian Doctrine of Predestination* (1855).

Muller, R. A. 'Perkins' *A Golden Chaine*: Predestinarian System or Schematized *Ordo Salutis*?', *Sixteenth Century Journal* 11/1 (1978).

Neale, J. M. *Elizabeth and Her Parliaments* (2 vols., 1953–7).

New, J. F. H. *Anglican and Puritan: The Basis of their Opposition* (1964).

Nijenhuis, W. 'Variants within Dutch Calvinism in the Sixteenth Century', *Acta Historiae Neerlandicae* 12 (1979).
Adrian Saravia (c. 1532–1613) (Leiden, 1980).

Nouvelle biographie générale (46 vols., Paris, 1855–66).

Peters, R. 'John Hales and the Synod of Dort', in G. J. Cuming and D. Baker (eds.), *Councils and Assemblies*, Studies in Church History 7 (Cambridge, 1971).

Platt, J. 'Eirenical Anglicans at the Synod of Dort', in D. Baker (ed.), *Reform and Reformation: England and the Continent, c.1500–c.1750,* Studies in Church History: Subsidia 2 (Oxford, 1979).

Porter, H. C. *Reformation and Reaction in Tudor Cambridge* (Cambridge, 1958).

Rademaker, C. S. *The Life and Work of Gerardus Joannes Vossius, 1577–1649* (The Netherlands, 1981).

Reeve, L. J. *Charles I and the Road to Personal Rule* (Cambridge, 1989).

Russell, C. 'Parliamentary History in Perspective', *History* 61 (1976).
Parliaments and English Politcs, 1621–1629 (Oxford, 1979).
'The Parliamentary Career of John Pym, 1621–9', in *The English Commonwealth 1547–1640*, ed. P. Clark *et al.* (Leicester, 1979).

Russell, C. (ed.), *The Origins of the English Civil War* (1973).

Sargeaunt, W. D. 'The Lambeth Articles', *Journal of Theological Studies* 12/46 and 12/47 (1911).

Schaff, P. A. *History of the Creeds of Christendom* (1877).
The Creeds of the Evangelical Protestant Churches (1877).

Schwartz, H. 'Arminianism and the English Parliament, 1624–1629', *Journal of British Studies* 112/2 (1973).

Seaver, P. *The Puritan Lectureships* (Stanford, California, 1970).

Sellin, P. *Daniel Heinsius and Stuart England* (1968).
John Donne and 'Calvinist' Views of Grace (Amsterdam, 1983).

Shaheen, N. 'Misconceptions about the Geneva Bible', in F. Bowers (ed.), *Studies in Bibliography* 37 (1984).

Sharpe, K. 'Archbishop Laud and the University of Oxford', in *History and Imagination*, ed. H. Lloyd-Jones *et al.* (1981).

Shriver, F. 'Orthodoxy and Diplomacy: James I and the Vorstius Affair', *English Historical Review* 336 (1970).
'Hampton Court Revisited: James I and the Puritans', *Journal of Ecclesiastical History* 33/1 (1982).

Sommerville, J. P. *Politics and Ideology in England, 1603–1640* (1986).

Southgate, W. M. 'The Marian Exiles and the Influence of John Calvin', *History* 27 (1942).
John Jewel and the Problem of Doctrinal Authority (Cambridge, Mass., 1962).

Sprunger, K. *The Learned Doctor William Ames: Dutch Backgrounds of English and American Puritanism* (Chicago, 1972).

Stephens, W. P. *The Holy Spirit in the Theology of Martin Bucer* (Cambridge, 1970).

Strype, J. *The Life and Acts of John Whitgift* (3 vols., Oxford, 1821).
Annals of the Reformation under Elizabeth (7 vols., Oxford, 1824).

Sutherland, N. M. 'The Marian Exiles and the Establishment of the Elizabethan Regime', *Archiv für Reformationsgeschichte* 87 (1987).

Thompson, C. 'The Divided Leadership of the House of Commons in 1629', in K. Sharpe (ed.) *Faction and Parliament: Essays on Early Stuart History* (Oxford, 1978).

Trevor-Roper, H. R. *Catholics, Anglicans and Puritans: Seventeenth Century Essays.* (1987).

Trinterud, L. *Elizabethan Puritanism* (New York, 1971).

Tyacke, N. R. N. 'Puritanism, Arminianism and Counter Revolution', in *The Origins of the English Civil War*, ed. C. Russell (1973).

'Arminianism and English Culture', in *Britain and the Netherlands*, ed. A. C. Duke and C. A. Tamse, VII (1981).

Anti-Calvinists: The Rise of English Arminianism c. 1590–1640 (Oxford, 1987).

'Debate: The Rise of Arminianism Reconsidered', *Past and Present* 115 (1987).

Usher, R. G. *The Reconstruction of the English Church* (2 vols., New York, 1910).

Venema, C. P. 'Heinrich Bullinger's Correspondence on Calvin's Doctrine of Predestination, 1551–1553', *Sixteenth Century Journal* 17/4 (1986).

Wallace, D. *Puritans and Predestination: Grace in English Protestant Theology* (Chapel Hill, 1982).

White, P. O. G. 'The Rise of Arminianism Reconsidered', *Past and Present* 101 (1983).

'Debate: The Rise of Arminianism Reconsidered', ibid, 115 (1987).

Willson, D. H. 'James I and his Literary Assistants', *Huntington Library Quarterly* 8 (1944–5).

Wood, A. *The History and Antiquities of the University of Oxford*, ed. John Gutch (2 vols., 1792–6).

UNPUBLISHED THESES

Adams, S. 'The Protestant Cause: Religious Alliance with the West European Calvinist Communities as a Political Issue in England, 1585–1630', Oxford University D.Phil. thesis, 1973.

Burchill, C. J. 'Girolamo Zanchi in Strasbourg, 1553–1563', Cambridge University Ph.D. thesis, 1979.

Davies, J. E. 'The Growth and Implementation of Laudianism with special reference to the Southern Province', Oxford University D.Phil. thesis, 1987.

Foster, A. 'A Biography of Archbishop Richard Neile, 1562–1640', Oxford University D.Phil. thesis, 1978.

Godfrey, W. R. 'Tensions within International Calvinism: The Debate on the Atonement at the Synod of Dort, 1618–19', Stanford University Ph.D. thesis, 1974.

Hewlett, A. D. 'The University of Oxford and the Church of England in the time of William Laud', Oxford University B.Litt. thesis, 1934.

Keep, D. J. 'Henry Bullinger and the Elizabethan Church', Sheffield University Ph.D. thesis, 1970.

Macauley, J. S. 'Richard Montague, Caroline Bishop, 1575–1641', Cambridge University Ph.D. thesis, 1964.

McElroy, K. 'Laud and his Struggle for Influence, 1628–1640', Oxford University D.Phil. thesis, 1943.

Milton, A. 'The Laudians and the Church of Rome, c. 1625–1640', Cambridge University Ph.D. thesis, 1989.

Olander, P. M. 'Changes in the Mechanism and Procedure for Control of the London Press 1625–1637', Oxford University B.Litt. thesis, 1976.

Raymer, V. E. 'Durham House and the Emergence of Laudian Piety', Harvard University Ph.D. thesis, 1981.

Schaff, M. E. Van der. 'The Theology of Thomas Jackson (1579–1640): An Anglican Alternative to Roman Catholicism, Puritanism and Calvinism', Iowa University Ph.D. thesis, 1979.

Shriver, F. 'The Ecclesiastical Policy of James I: Two Aspects: the Puritans (1603–5) – the Arminians (1611–25)', Cambridge University Ph.D. thesis, 1967.

Twigg, J. D. 'The University of Cambridge and the English Revolution', Cambridge University Ph.D. thesis, 1983.

Index

Abbot, Archbishop George, 10, 160, 162–3, 167–9, 177, 180, 188, 191 n., 199 n. 103, 210 n., 276–7, 283, 300–1; censorship under, 287–93; and the Directions to Preachers, 211–12, 214, 223, 238–9, 245; sequestration of, 247–8, 277 n; restoration of, 250; and the Declaration prefixed, 251, 254

Abbot, Bp Robert, 157–9, 169, 172, 173, 188, 277

adiaphora, 63, 163; *see also* fundamentals

Allen, William, 126

Ambrose, St, 69, 72, 78, 87

Ames, William, 289, 298

Amsterdam, 22, 23, 38, 160, 298

Amyraut, Moyse, 298 n.

Anabaptism, Anabaptists, 43, 44, 48, 93, 211; refuted by Articles of Religion, 52, 53–4, 56, 58

Andreae, Jacob, 98 n., 101 n., 115, 278 n.

Andrewes, Bp Lancelot, 1, 11–12, 73–4, 91, 103, 117–18, 208, 209 n., 216, 223, 243, 245; and the doctrine of assurance, 103, 109, 121; visited by Georg Doublet, 205–6; and the Five Articles, 212–13, 240; and Hugo Grotius, 163, 166, 205–6; on the Lambeth Articles, 107–10, 117; on perseverance, 109, 167–8; predestination not to be preached, 118

Antichrist, doctrine of the Pope as, 9, 19, 204, 216, 218, 224–5, 240, 247, 273

Antwerp, 93; Synod of (1566), 23 n.

Aquinas, St Thomas, 72, 84, 114 n., 115 n., 125–6, 133 n., 154, 267

Archer, John, 301

Aristotle, 125–6, 263

Arminianism: defined and refuted by Prynne, 3–5; as defined and defended by Heylyn, 8, 39; essence of, 31, 230; in England, x, 140, 178, 208–9, 256; Hooker alleged to be the founder of, 124–5, 138; changing definition of, 1625–9, 247–8,

272; in the Netherlands, 175–6, 178–9; alleged publications of under Charles I, 294–8; *see also* Remonstrants

Arminius, James, xi, 22–38, 136, 157, 159, 169, 175, 178, 180; on assurance, 35–6; objections to Beza's doctrine of predestination, 25–31; on Calvin, 37–8; on the divine decrees, 31–2; on faith, 34–5; and the Fall, 25–6; on grace and free will, 32–4; on human reason, 25; on necessity and contingency, 26, 108; on redemption, 27–8, 31; and the will of God, 27, 29–30, 33

Articles of Religion, 153–4, 168, 172, 183, 188, 190–1, 202, 220–1, 225, 254, 296, 297; the Forty-two, 44, 49, 52–9, 63; the Thirty-nine, 39, 66–7, 116, 130–2; discussion of at the Hampton Court Conference, 141, 144–6, 147–8; Neile's appeal to, 273, 274, 275; Thomas Rogers's exposition of, 150–2; subscription to, 148 n.; *see also* Declaration prefixed

Arundel, Thomas Howard, twenty-first Earl of, 205, 283

assurance, theology of: Andrewes on, 103, 109, 121; Arminius on, 35–6; Articles of Religion silent on, 58; Bancroft on 145; Baro on 109, 112, 116; Barrett on, 102–3, 105; Beza on, 21; Bucer on, 45–6, 48; Calvin on, 21; at Synod of Dort, 186, 196–7; Hooker on, 128–9; Hooper on, 41; Hutton on, 121; Jackson on, 269; Jewel on, 72–3; Latimer on, 43–4; Laud on, 280–1, Overall on, 146–7; Perkins on, 121; Peter Martyr on, 51; Saravia on, 103; Council of Trent on, 53, 58; Vossius on, 207; Whitaker on, 109, 115 n., Whitgift on, 104, 106, 109

atonement, theology of, *see* redemption

Augsburg Confession, 53, 57, 58 n., 68, 78, 174

Augustine, St, 54, 77, 154, 235, 263; quoted

by Articles of Religion on free will, 54–5;
Baro's exposition of his theories of
predestination, 112–14; Beale and Ward
differ on, 234 n.; on concupiscence after
baptism, 72; appealed to by Dort
delegates against the Contra-
Remonstrants, 195, 198; Hooker's use of,
130, 131, 135–6, 139; Hutton's exposition
of, 119–21; interpretation of 1 Tim ii, 4
followed by Bucer, 46, Martyr, 50, and
Zanchi, 78, but not by Bullinger, 78;
Montagu on, 220–1; Musculus and, 86–7;
Overall appeals to against the
Remonstrants, 166; authority for those
who think predestination should be
preached, 64; on reprobation, 102–3, 108,
114, 275, 279; Thomson's use of, 170–4;
Vossius on 206–7
Authorized Version, 147, 174
Aylmer, Bp John, 132

Bacon, Sir Nicholas, 61
Baillie, Robert, 311
Bainbridge, Thomas, 208 n.
Balcanqual, Walter, 181–2, 187–8, 190, 192,
199–200, 208–9, 246 n.
Baldwin, Francis, 70
Ball, John, 292
Ball, Thomas, 243, 289
Bancroft, Archbishop Richard, 74, 95, 141,
144–5, 147, 150, 154
baptism, of infants, 48, 85, 309
baptism, theology of, xiii, 79, 144, 149, 152,
171, 182, 187, 228, 268–9, 276
Barcroft, Hugh, 309
Barker, Charles, 92
Barlow, Bp William, 140–1, 144, 152, 168
Barnard, Nathaniel, 305
Baro, Peter, 10, 89, 94, 117–19, 126, 134,
138–9, 142–3, 215, 274; on assurance,
109, 112, 116; career of, 110–11, 117; on
the divine decrees, 112; on free will, 112,
114; on grace, 112; on the Lambeth Ar-
ticles, 108–10; on redemption, 113, 116;
on reprobation, 112–14, 116; on the will
of God, 112–14, 116, 118
Baronius, Cardinal César 216–17, 283
Barrett, William, 3, 10, 101–7, 108, 111; on
Christian assurance, 102–3, 105; on faith,
102–3, 105–6; on reprobation, 102–3
Basil, St, 174, 216
Basle, 83
Baudius, Dominic, 169
Baynes, Paul, 289
Beale, Jerome, 208–9, 234 n.

Beale, William, 305, 309–10
Beaumont, Robert, 84
Becanus, Martin, 161, 217
Bedell, Bp William, 283
Bedford, Francis Russell, first Earl of, 250
Bedford, Thomas, 309
Bellarmine, Cardinal Robert, 24, 84, 98, 154,
156–7, 217, 267, 276, 277–80
Belgic Confession (1561), 22–3, 38, 103, 182,
201, 233–4
Berne, 85
Bertius, Peter, 157, 166, 168, 195 n.
Beza, Theodore, xi, 3, 13–22, 83, 85, 92, 96,
98–9, 104, 108, 112, 134, 159, 164, 170,
172, 184–5, 267–8, 278, 280; on limited
atonement, 21–2; debate on, under
James I, 153–4, 156–8; on the divine
decrees, 17–18, 19–20; on the English
Church, 69; on the Fall, 19; on the
preaching of predestination, 15, 21;
supralapsarianism of, 16–17; his table of
predestination, 13–15, 49, 288
Bible, English see under Authorized Version,
Geneva Bible, Rheims Bible
Bibliander, Theodore, 49, 77, 270
Bill, William, 62
Bilson, Bp Thomas, 144
Bishop, William, 157–8
Bogerman, John, 38, 182, 192, 194, 199, 201
Bohemian Confession, 174
Bolsec, Jerome, 76, 151
Book of Common Prayer, 6, 8, 39, 49, 52,
55, 61, 66, 69, 96–7, 138–9, 189–91, 254;
revision of in 1604, 144, 148–9
Bonaventure, St, 120
Borrhaeus, Martinus 84
Boswell, Sir William, 209
Boughen, Edward, 296
Bradford, John, 5
Bray, William, 294
Breitinger, Johann, 79
Bremen, 82, 187–8, 191
Brenz, Johann, 78
Brès, Guy de, 23 n.
Bridges, Gabriel, 205, 209
Brooke, Samuel, 298–9
Browne, Walter, 258
Bucanus, William, 207–8
Bucer, Martin, 8, 44–48, 59, 61, 78, 82, 89,
120, 173–4, 235; on assurance, 47–8; on
election, 45–7; on free will, 47; on
perseverance, 47–8; on reprobation, 45;
on sanctification, 47
Buckeridge, Bp John, 1, 10, 221 n., 223–4,
227, 241–3, 245, 247 n., 276, 296

Buckingham, George Villiers, first Duke of, 1, 205, 224, 226, 238–41, 243–4, 247–8, 249–50, 272

Buckner, Thomas, 287–8

Bullinger, Henry, 74–9, 84, 87, 93; differences with Calvin, 76–7; on election, 75, 79; influence in England, 80–1; and Second Helvetic Confession, 78

Burgess, Cornelius, xiii

Burleigh, William Cecil, first Lord, 61–2, 65, 93, 111, 115–17, 118, 242, 274

Burton, Henry, 233 n., 246, 264–70, 272

Calvin, John, 3, 49, 60, 70, 82, 84, 92, 93, 96, 102–3, 104, 112, 115, 124, 127, 139, 164, 170, 173, 174, 195, 224, 247, 266–8; Arminius on, 37–8; correspondence with Bullinger, 76–7; Heylyn on, 7–8; debate on under James I, 152–9; *Institutes*, 7 n., 53 n., 74, 76, 84, 125, 139, 153, 280 n., 288–9, 304

Calvinists, Calvinism: definition of, x, xii; at Cambridge in the 1590s, 101–2, 104, 107–10, 121, 125; alleged dominance of, x, 1–2, 7–10, 82–3, 88; in what sense defended at Dort, 183–4, 184–8, 192, 194, 200–1, 203–4; development of under Elizabeth, 90–9; attacked and defended in the 1620s, 204, 207–8, 217–18, 221–2, 224, 227–35; influence of at the Stuart court, 212, 239–40, 243–4, 247–8, 254; publications of under Charles I, 288–94, 298; *see also* Contra-Remonstrants

Cambridge University, 44, 46, 61, 142, 146, 169, 177–8, 208–9, 214, 234, 239, 246, 250, 282–3; Commencement theses at, 295, 306–7; library inventories at, 84–5, 90; predestinarian controversies in the 1590s, 101–7, 110–17, 121–3, 142–3; publications at, 289; religious controversy in the 1630s, 305–6, 309–10; support for Remonstrants at, 178, 204–5, 208–9, 214

Canons Ecclesiastical (1571), 67; (1604), 149

Canterbury, 126

Capito, Wolfgang, 78

Cardencia, Isaac de, 83

Carier, Benjamin, 152–3

Carleton, Sir Dudley, Viscount Dorchester, 144, 174–5, 180, 182–3, 187–8, 199–200, 209, 240, 249, 252, 254, 282

Carleton, Bp George, 180–1, 183, 185–7, 190, 192, 201, 234, 249, 282; reply to *Appello Caesarem*, 231–3

Carlisle, James Hay, first Earl of, 224, 226, 228, 230

Caron, Sir Noel, 160, 162–3, 176

Cartwright, Thomas, 6–7, 57, 96, 124, 132, 291

Cary, Bp Valentine, 248 n.

Casaubon, Isaac, 158–9, 163–4, 216–17

Casaubon, Meric, 205

Cassander, Georg, 232

Cassian, John, 216

Castorillius, John, 83

Catechisms, 289, 291, 296, 301; the Prayer Book Catechism, 73, 94, 191, 210–11, 226, 228; revision of in 1604, 147, 149; *see also* Nowell, Alexander

Catholicity, English Church's claim to, 62–3, 70–1, 74, 80, 143 n., 152, 232

Cecil, Robert, first Earl of Salisbury, 273

Chaderton, Laurence, 111, 122, 143

Chamberlain, John, 177

Champneys, John, 288

Charles I, xi, 2, 204, 209–12, 238; and 'Arminianism', 238–46, 248–55, 312

Cheke, Sir John, 61–2

Chown, Thomas, 296

Chrysostom, St John, 72, 84, 130 n., 216–17

Civil War, causes of, ix–x, 307–12

Clayton, Richard, 104

Coke, Sir Edward, 248, 272

Coke, Sir John, 230, 243, 250 n.

Cole, William, 83

Comber, Thomas, 208 n.

Confessional Harmonies, 23 n., 38, 150, 152, 180, 206, 232–3

Contra-Remonstrants, 122–3, 160–1, 162–3, 165, 175–6, 177, 179, 182, 184–7, 189, 192–3, 199–202, 235

Convocation (1563), 67; (1571), 67–8; (1586), 80–1; (1604), 149, 152; (1625), 241, 243; (1640), 308

Conyers, James, 296

Corro, Antonio del, 93–4, 142, 232

Corvinus, Jean-Arnold, 122–3, 234 n.

Cosin, Bp John, 205, 222–4, 224–6, 228, 243–4, 246, 248 n., 305

Cotton, Sir Robert, 249

Covenant theology, 74–5, 80, 88

Cox, Bp Richard, 61–2

Crackanthorpe, Richard, 257–8

Cranmer, Archbishop Thomas, 44, 48–9, 52–3, 61, 66, 127, 130

creabilitarianism, 16

Crosfield, Thomas, 283, 288 n.

Crowley, Robert, 288

Davenant, Bp John, 234, 245, 263 n., 295, 297–8, 307, 312; court sermon of (1630), 299–300; as delegate at the Synod of Dort, 180, 188–92, 199

Davenport, John, 289
death of Christ, theology of, *see* redemption
Declaration, of returned exiles in 1559, 63–5
Declaration prefixed to the Thirty-nine Articles, of 1628, 203, 250–4, 256, 295, 296, 298
decrees of predestination, 13–17, 44; Robert Abbot on, 157–8; Andrewes on, 212–13; Arminius on, 31–2; Baro on, 112; Beza on, 13–17; Davenant on, 295 n., Richard Field on, 156–7; Joseph Hall on, 234–6, 302; Jackson on, 262–3, 265–6, 267–8, 270, 295; Montagu on, 219–21; Overall on, 165–6; Vossius on, 285; 'unknown' according to Articles of Relgion, 57
Device for the alteration of religion (1558), 62
divine foreknowledge, *simplicis intelligentiae* and *visionis*, 133 n., 156, 165
Dominis, Marcus Antonius de, 201 n., 222, 231, 273
Donne, John, 211 n.
Dort (Dordrecht) Synod of, 1, 3, 4, 38, 175, 179–204, 207, 209, 213, 227, 230–1, 233–4, 242, 265, 274–6, 286; choice of Engish delegates, 179–83; on election and reprobation, 184–7; on extent of the Atonement, 187–92; on free will and conversion, 192–5; on perseverance and assurance, 195–9; condemnation of Remonstrants at, 199–210
Doublet, Georg, 205, 207–8, 214 n.
Duns Scotus, 125
du Plessis Mornay, Philippe, 208 n.
Duppa, Bp Brian, 302
Durandus, William, 84
Durham House, clergy of, 206, 214, 218, 223, 240–4, 257

Earle, Sir Walter, 308
ecumenism, 179, 183, 191
Edward VI, 8, 61
Egerton, Stephen, 149–50
election, theology of: Andrewes on, 107; Arminius on, 28, 31–2; Baro on, 113–14, 116; Beza on, 18, 20; Bucer on, 45–8; Bullinger on, 74–5; discussions at Dort on, 186–7; Hooker on, 135–6; Hooper on, 40–1; Hutton on, 119–20; Jackson on, 268–9; Lambeth Articles on, 107–8; Latimer on, 42; Montagu on, 219–20, 228–30; Neile on, 274; Peter Martyr on, 50
Eleven Articles (1561), 66
Elizabeth I, 60–1, 65, 80, 91–2, 101, 123, 138, 242, 304 n.
Episcopius, Simon, 181

Erasmus, Desiderius, 69, 127, 206; *Paraphrases* of, 54–5, 65, 75
Erpenius, Thomas, 205
Estye, George, 122
Exiles, Marian, 60–5, 68, 80, 115, 172, 174
experimental predestinarianism, 95, 145 n., 290

faith: Arminius on, 34–5; Articles of Religion on, 55; Barrett on, 102–3, 105–6; Beza on, 18, 20–1, Bullinger on, 75; Council of Trent on, 55; discussions at Dort on, 194–8; Homilies on, 55–6; Hooker on, 128–9; Hooper on, 40; Jackson on, 269; Jewel on, 72–3; Latimer on, 42–4; Peter Martyr on, 51; Thomson on, 170–2; Ursinus on, 88–9; Vossius on, 207; *see also* election, justification, works, theology of
Fall, the, 16, 85, 89, 131, 158, 192–4, 220–1, 260, 262; Arminius on, 25–6; Articles of Religion on, 53–4; Beza on, 19–20, 278; *see also* original sin
Farel, William, 76
Featley, Daniel, 73–4, 222, 231–2, 241, 246, 258, 288 n., 293–4, 308
Fell, Samuel, 246–7, 303
Felton, Bp Nicholas, 245, 248 n.
Field, Richard, 154, 156–7, 159
Field, Bp Theophilus, 245
Finch, Sir Moyle, 178
Five Articles, 176–7, 183–99; Andrewes on, 212–13; Neile on, 274–6; *see also* Remonstrance, Arminian, of 1610
Fletcher, Phineas, 291–2
Forced Loan, 240, 247–8, 255
Foxe, John, ix, 9
Foxe, Bp Richard, 69
Frankfurt, 63
Frederick, Elector Palatine, 239–40
Fuller, Thomas, 126, 299
fundamentals, 161–2, 164, 178–9, 225, 241–2, 244

Galloway, Patrick, 148 n.
Geneva, 60–1, 63, 70, 76, 84, 100, 124, 126, 172
Geneva Bible, x, 6, 74, 91–2, 97, 147
Gerhard, John, 307
Gibson, Thomas, 309
Gilby, Anthony, 92
Goad, Roger, 111, 116–17
Goad, Thomas, 181, 185, 222, 246 n.
Gomarus, Francis, 23–4, 58, 108, 160–1, 184–5, 187, 199, 202, 207
Goodwin, Thomas, 289, 292

Gottschalk of Orbais, 284–5
Gouge, William, 289
grace, 66; Arminius on, 33–4; Articles of
   Religion on, 54; Baro on, 112, 115; Beza
   on, 20–1; discussions at Dort on, 193–4;
   Hooker on, 131, 136–7; Hooper on, 40;
   Neile on, 274; Prynne on, 4–5; Whitaker
   on, 101; see also will, freedom of
Greville, Fuke, first Lord Brooke, 209
Grevinchovius, Nicholas, 181, 231 n.
Grindal, Archbishop Edmund, 6, 61–2, 82,
   93
Grotius, Hugo, 162–6, 167–8, 176, 179,
   191 n., 205–7
Gualter, Rudolph, 68, 84
Gualter, Rudolph (the younger), 83

Hacket, Bp John, 213
Haemstede, Adriaen van, 93
Hague, Colloquy of The, 189, 235
Hakewill, George, 153–5
Hales, John, 181–2, 187, 216
Hall, Bp Joseph, 250, 301–2; at the Synod
   of Dort, 180–1; supports inhibition of
   controversy, 244; his Way of Peace in the
   Five . . . Articles, 234–6, 247
Hampton Court Conference, 10, 95, 140–50,
   167, 233
Harding, Thomas, 70, 304 n.
Harsnett, Bp Samuel, 10, 99–100, 205 n.,
   212, 245, 300
Hausted, Peter, 305
Haywood, William, 296
Heath, Sir Robert, 250, 253–4
Heidelberg Catechism, 23, 38, 87, 175
Heigham, John, 218–22
Helvetic Confession (the Second, of 1566), 78
Hemmingsen, Niels, 89–90, 101 n., 112, 113,
   115, 118, 174, 215, 270
Henry VIII, ix
Henrietta Maria, ix, 239, 249, 255
Herbert, George, 307, 309
Heylyn, Peter, 6–12, 39, 60–1, 212, 249, 300
High Commission, Court of, 300–1, 303 n.,
   305
Hilary of Arles, St, 131
Hildersham, Arthur, 291
Hoard, Samuel, 297–8
Hoe, Matthias, 299
Holland, Henry Rich, first Earl of, 250
Holland, Thomas, 160
Holles, John, 255 n.
Homilies, Book of, 3, 8, 39, 49, 55–6, 130,
   183, 190, 210–11, 269, 270, 296
Hommius, Festus, 177 n., 304
Hooker, Richard, xi, 11, 96, 124–39, 174,

215, 232, 258, 306–7; on assurance,
   128–9; on Calvin, 96, 134 n., 139;
   response to A Christian Letter, 96,
   129–37; on contingency and necessity,
   133; on doctrinal authority, 127–8; on
   faith, 128–30; on free will, 130–1; on
   grace, 130–1, 135–8; on justification, 130;
   on the Lambeth Articles, 137–8; on
   redemption, 132, 135–7; on reprobation,
   133–6; conflict with Travers, 126–9; on
   the will of God, 132–5; Lawe of Ecclesiastical Polity, 124, 130, 133, 138–9,
   280 n.
Hooper, Bp John, 4, 5, 8, 39–41, 80, 127
Hotman, Jean, 83
House of Commons (1604), 149; (1624) 223;
   (1625), 240–1; (1626), 244; (1628), 248–9,
   272; (1629), 252–3
Howson, Bp John, 10, 157 n., 212, 241,
   247 n.
Huber, Samuel, 101 n.
Hubert, Conrad, 82
Humphrey, Laurence, 83, 93, 94
Hutton, Archbishop Matthew, 101, 107, 109,
   117–22, 133, 147, 281; on assurance,
   120–1; on Baro, 118–19; on election and
   reprobation, 119–20, 282 n.

Infralapsarianism, see sublapsarianism
Injunctions, Ecclesiastical of 1559, 65, 273
Irish Articles, of 1615, 3, 4, 10, 108 n., 252 n.

Jackson, Thomas, 248, 256–71, 272, 296;
   charged with Arminianism, 256–7, 263–4,
   269–70; on assurance, 269; on Calvin and
   Beza, 258, 266–8; early career and
   outlook, 256–60; on justification, 259–61;
   on necessity and contingency, 262–3;
   Neoplatonism of, 262–3, 270; on
   perseverance, 261; appeal to reason, 259,
   261–2; hostility to Rome, 256, 266–7, 271;
   William Twisse on, 257, 263–4
Jacob, Henry, 143
James I, xii, 1, 3, 10, 122, 277; on Arminius,
   159, 291; churchmanship of, 294–5,
   304 n.; and the Directions to Preachers
   of 1622, 210–13; at the Hampton Court
   Conference, 140–1, 143–9, 152, 167–8;
   and Richard Montagu, 217–18, 222–5,
   230, 232, 240; directions to Oxford
   (1616), 10, 277; policies in the 1620s,
   203–4, 207–8, 209–11; and predestinarian
   disputes in the Netherlands, 162–4,
   175–81, 188, 190; and the Vorstius affair,
   159–62
Jeffrey, John, 287

Jegon, Thomas, 117
Jerome, St, 69, 169
Jewel, Bp John, 11, 61, 69–74, 80, 83, 125,
    127, 130, 139, 258, 304 n.; on faith and
    works, 72–3; on nature and grace, 72;
    Paul's Cross sermon of 1559, 70; on
    redemption, 72; *Apology* of, 71, 183
John of Damascus, St, 114 n.
Junius, Francis, 97
Junius, Francis (the younger), 205, 284
justification, theology of, 39, 103, 105;
    Robert Abbot on, 158–9; Articles of
    Religion on, 55; Homilies on, 55–6;
    Hooker on 130; Jackson on, 259–61;
    Jewel on, 71–2; Marian exiles on, 64–5;
    Montagu on, 225–6; Thomson on,
    169–71, 172–3; *see also* faith

Kellison, Mathhew, 154
King, Bp John, 212
Kingsmill, Andrew, 84
Knewstub, John, 143
Knight, William, 204, 207–8, 209
Knox, John, 69

Lake, Bp Arthur, 182 n., 248 n.
Lambeth Articles, xi, 3, 5, 58, 101, 107–10,
    111, 116–17, 120, 122–3, 168, 176, 231,
    233, 241–2; references to at Hampton
    Court Conference, 145–6, 149; Hooker
    on, 137–8
Latimer, Bp Hugh, 8, 41–4
Laud, Archbishop William, xi, 1, 10, 95, 205,
    212–13, 218, 223, 276–86, 311; disclaims,
    'Arminianism', 249; on assurance, 280–1;
    defends Beza against Bellarmine, 278;
    censorship under, 293–9; on
    fundamentals, 280–1; on grace and free
    will, 280; and Grotius, 205 n., 284; on
    perseverance, 280, 282; on reprobation,
    278–80, 285; hostility to Rome, 280–1,
    282; prefers silence to controversy, 282,
    283–4, 286, 299; and Stuart court,
    239–43, 245–6, 247 n., 248, 252, 254–5;
    on the Thirty-nine Articles, 281; contacts
    with Vossius, 282–6
Laurence, Thomas, 295
Leicester, Robert Dudley, Earl of, 6, 94
Leiden, university of, 23, 103, 159–60, 162,
    169, 206–7, 216
libertas prophetandi (liberty of prophesying),
    24, 38, 162, 169, 286, 301
Leslie, Bp Henry, 248
Lindsell, Augustine, 223
Loe, William, 241–2
L'Oiseleur de Villiers, Pierre, 94

Lombard, Peter, 2, 84, 86, 87, 151
London, 92, 193–4, 300–1
Lubbertus, Sibrandus, 160, 199, 202
Lucy, Bp William, 204–5, 209
Luther, Martin, 57, 78, 82, 84, 93, 158, 171,
    235
Lutherans, and Lutheranism, 37, 52, 69,
    77–8, 83–4, 85, 98, 112, 114, 121, 130,
    183, 191, 198, 202, 219, 220–2, 225; *see
    also* Melanchthon

Maccovius, Johann, 7, 194
Madey, Meredith, 301 n.
Mainwaring, Roger, 248
Man, John, 85
Manichees, 27, 40, 134 n.
Marbach, Johann, 77, 79
Marshall, William, 84
Martin, Edward, 287–8, 305
Martin, Sir Henry, 246 n.
Martinus, Matthias, 182 n., 187–8, 191
Mary I, 49
Mary Queen of Scots, 49
Matthew, Archbishop Tobias, 143 n., 148 n.
Mawe, Leonard, 208
May, Sir Humphrey, 250 n.
May, William, 61
Maynard, Sir John, 250 n.
Mead, Joseph, 209 n., 250 n.
Melanchthon, Philip, 38, 51–2, 57, 77, 89,
    93, 112–13, 174; Bucer's use of, 45–6;
    Martyr's dissent from, 49
Meredith, Richard, 276
Middleburgh, 130
Millenary Petition of 1603, 10, 141–2, 143–4
Montagu, Bp James, 10, 178, 212
Montagu, Bp Richard, 2, 3, 11, 203, 214,
    302; early career of, 215–17; churchman-
    ship of, 217–19; and the *New Gagg*, 12,
    218–24; and the *Appello Caesarem*, 223,
    230–6, 288; discussions about at the York
    House Conference, 224–30; Charles I's
    attitude towards, 239–43, 245–6; Bp of
    Chichester, 249
Montbéliard, Colloquy of, 98, 278
Mountaigne, Bp George, 212, 243, 245,
    247 n.
Morton, Bp Thomas, 154–5, 160, 295 n.; at
    the York House Conference, 224–8
Moulin, Pierre du, 179, 183, 205–6, 208 n.,
    233, 289
Musculus, Wolfgang, 85–7
Musculus, Wolfgang (the younger), 83

Nassau, William of, Prince of Orange, 8, 179

Nazianus, St Gregory, 72, 216–17
Necessary Doctrine and Erudition of any Christian Man, 54, 56
Neile, Archbishop Richard, 1, 37, 223, 245, 247 n., 249, 257–8, 277; answer to charge of popery and Arminianism, 272–6
Neoplatonists, Neoplatonism, 139, 262–3, 270
Newcastle 257, 265
Normanton, John, 306, 310
Northampton, church at 91
Nowell, Alexander, Catechism of 8, 67, 91, 147

Ockham, William of, 84
Oecolampadius, John, 84
Oldenbarnevelt, Johan van, Advocate of Holland, 24, 160–4, 175, 276
Olevianus, Caspar, 23 n., 87
Oley, Barnabas, 258, 264, 270
Oliver, John, 292
Origen, 69, 72
original sin, 40–1, 49, 53, 66, 72, 120, 135 n.
Overall, Bp John, 11, 73, 117, 118, 165–7, 176, 191, 199, 215, 217, 276, 296; influence on Davenant at Dort, 190–2; correspondence with Grotius, 165–7; at the Hampton Court Conference, 146–7; favourable references to, in the attacks on Montagu, 232–3, 234–6
Oxford University, 9, 49, 69, 83, 87, 94, 125–6, 142, 158–9, 204, 208–9, 222, 241, 257–8, 277, 282–3; library inventories at, 83–4, 90; publications at, 289, 291, 304–5, 307; religious controversy at in 1630s, 303–5

Palatine Confession, 183
Pareus, David, 204, 207, 267
Parker, Archbishop Matthew, 61–2, 91, 130, 288 n.
Parkhurst, John, 69, 83
Parliament (1559), 60–1; (1604), 148–9, (1625–9), 238–9, 242, 244, 248–9, 252–3, 272, 287; (Short Parliament), 307–8; (Long Parliament), 308
patristic authorities, appeal to, 39, 69, 71–2, 125, 163, 165, 170, 174, 176, 215–16; rejected by Arminius, 24
Paul, St, 64, 76, 86–7, 109, 164, 170–1, 173, 207, 273; Arminius on, 28–31; Beza on, 16–18, 21; Hooker on, 127, 136
Paul's Cross Sermons, 70, 99–100, 132, 204, 273, 288 n.
Pelagius, Pelagianism, 3, 22, 27, 40, 53, 68, 85, 94, 155, 192–3, 206–7, 230, 231–2;

Baro charged with, 114–15, 118, 122; Hooker on, 131; Vossius' History of, 282–3; Whitgift's fear of, 122–3
Pemble, William, 289
Pembroke, Philip Herbert, fourth Earl of, 224, 226–7, 230, 243, 248, 250, 256, 283, 303
Perkins, William, 80, 89, 95, 98–9, 114, 121, 134, 152–3, 157, 170, 185, 224, 267, 288; Arminius on, 32–5; Heylyn on, 9
perseverance, theology of: Andrewes on, 109, 167–8; Arminius on, 36–7; Articles of Religion on, 56–8; Barrett on, 102–3; Bucer on, 47–8; discussions at Dort on, 195–9; Hooker on, 137; Hooper on, 41; Jackson on, 261; Jewel on, 73; Latimer on, 43–4; Laud on, 280, 282; Montagu on, 219, 220–1, 227–8; Neile on, 275; Overall on, 146–7, 166; Peter Martyr on, 51; Thomson on, 169, 171–3; Council of Trent on, 53, 58; Vossius on, 207; Whitaker on, 115 n.; Whitgift on, 104, 105–6, 108–9; discussions at York House on, 225–7
Peter Martyr, 8, 48–52, 65, 68, 69, 77–8, 82, 84, 104, 115, 169, 172, 173, 174; relationship with Calvin and Beza, 49; on election, 50; on grace, 51; on reprobation, 49–51; on the will of God, 50
Petition of Right, 272
Piers, Bp William, 303 n.
Pighi, Albert, 49, 50
Pilkington, Bp James, 61
Piscator, Johann, 122, 190, 194, 267
Plancius, Peter, 22–3, 37
Playfere, Thomas, 117
Polanus, Amandus, 235
Polemic: anti-Arminian, 2–5, 231–3, 308–9; anti-Calvinist, xi, 6–8; anti-Laudian, 311; anti-Papist, 13; anti-Protestant, 13, 152–3, 155; anti-Puritan, 309–10; Contra-Remonstrant, 160–1, 231, 312
Pory, John, 250 n.
Potter, Bp Barnaby, 254 n.
Potter, Christopher, 295 n.
Powell, Gabriel, 258
practical syllogism, 36, 95, 121; *see also* assurance
predestination, *see* divine foreknowledge, election, experimental predestinarianism, reprobation
Preston, John, 224, 227–30, 239, 243, 248, 250, 289, 293
Pretty, Samuel, 300–1
Prideaux, John, 181, 222, 277 n. 291, 303, 308

'Principal Heads of Religion' (1561), 66
Privy Council, 61, 245, 247, 250, 251
proclamations (1603), 143; (1604), 148, 296;
'for Peace and Quiet in the Church of
England' (1626), 245–7; calling in *Appello
Caesarem* (1629), 250, 256
Prosper of Aquitaine, St, 37, 119, 131–2,
135–6, 138, 171–2, 198, 207, 285
Prynne, William, xi, 2–6, 39, 58, 204 n., 223,
256, 271, 282, 287–8, 292
Pucci, Francesco, 93, 101 n.
Puritanism, x, 39, 57, 60, 100, 124, 138–9,
208, 210, 277 n.; doctrinal Puritanism, 11
n.; anticipated in 1559, 62; objections to
the Book of Common Prayer under
Elizabeth, 96–7; of Henry Burton, 264–8;
of Thomas Cartwright, 132; of *A Christian Letter*, 129–30, 131, 132–3, 139;
underlying the Millenary Petition, 142–4;
at the Hampton Court Conference,
144–7, 148–50; existence of acknowledged
by Field, 157; and unquestioned by
Romanists 217; attacked by Heigham and
disowned by Montagu, 217–22; at the
York House Conference, 224–6; existence
of denied by Carleton, 232–3
Pym, John 240 n., 248–9, 252

Ramsden, Henry, 293
redemption, theology of: Andrewes on,
109–10; Arminius on, 27–8, 31; Articles
of Religion on, 57, 66; Bancroft on, 145;
Baro on 112, 113–14, 116; Beza on, 22;
Bucer on, 45–7; Bullinger on, 74–5, 77,
79; Calvin on, 170 n.; discussions at Dort
on, 187–92; Harsnett on, 99–100; Hooker
on, 132, 135–6, 137; Hooper on, 39–41;
Jewel on, 72–3; Latimer on, 41–2; Laud
on, 285–6; Neile on, 274–5; Overall on,
165–6, 191–2; Peter Martyr on, 50;
Whitgift on, 109–10, 132; *see also* election
Reeve, Edmund, 296–7
Reformatio Legum Ecclesiasticarum, 49, 53,
54, 58
Remonstrance, Arminian, of 1610, 162,
176–7, 184; *see also* Five Articles
Remonstrants, 10, 122–3, 160–1, 162–8,
176–8, 181–8, 187–8, 192, 233–5, 242;
support for at Cambridge, 208–9, 214;
condemned at Dort, 199–201; *see also*
Arminianism, Arminians
reprobation, theology of: Robert Abbot on,
157–8; Andrewes on, 107–8; Arminius
on, 26–8, 32; Articles of Religion silent
on, 58; Baro on, 112–13, 116; Barrett on,

102–3, 104–6; Beza on, 7, 16–18, 19–20,
21–2; Bucer on, 45, 47; Calvin on, 58; at
the Synod of Dort, 184–6, 190; Hakewill
on, 154; Harsnett on, 99–100; Hooker
on, 133–6; Hooper on, 40; Hutton on,
119–20; Injunctions of 1559 on, 65;
Jackson on, 265–9; Latimer on, 43;
Lambeth Articles on, 107–8; Laud on,
278–80; Montagu on, 219–21; Musculus
on, 86–7; Neile on, 275; Perkins on, 98–9;
Peter Martyr on, 50–1; Whitaker on,
101–2, 105, 107–8, 114; Whitgift on, 104,
105–6
Reynolds, John, 93, 94, 125, 142, 144–5,
148–9, 150, 152, 258
Rheims Bible, 97
Rich, Sir Nathaniel, 252
Richardson, John, 283
Ridley, Bp Nicholas, 127
Riley, Thomas, 306
Roe, Sir Thomas, 253, 299
Rogers, Richard, 293
Rogers, Thomas, 150–2, 232
Rous, Francis, 232, 298, 308
Rous, John, 282
Royal Supremacy, ix, 241–2, 253–5
Rushworth, John, 204 n., 212

sacraments, theology of, 67, 70, 128, 139,
144, 149–50, 152, 171, 226, 228, 273,
306–7
Salmeron, Alphonso, 154
Sampson, Thomas, 83
sanctification, theology of, 47, 128, *see also*
works, theology of
Saravia, Adrian, 103, 121
Savile, Sir Henry, 216, 249 n.
Saxon, Confession, 174
Saye and Sele, William Fiennes, first
Viscount, 224, 226–8, 230, 243, 282, 290
Scaliger, Joseph, 125
Sclater, William, 292–3
Selden, John, 222
Senhouse, Bp Richard, 248 n.
Shelford, Robert, 294–5
Sibbes, Richard, 289–90, 293, 305
Sibthorp, Robert, 247–8
Simpson, Edward, 177–8
sin, origin of, 7, 45, 49, 156; *see also* Fall
Slade, Matthew, 160–1, 206
Snecanus, Gellius, 8n., 79, 101 n., 113
Socinianism, 160–1, 178, 200
Some, Robert, 104, 112, 122
Sophists, Sophism, 90
Sparke, Thomas, 143, 167
Sports, Book of, 308–9

Stapleton, Thomas, 98, 154
Star Chamber decree (1637), 292–3, 298
Stationers' Company, 292
Stoics, Stoicism, 40, 90, 170, 174
Stranger churches, 6, 92–5
Strasburg, 63, 69, 77–8, 79, 82, 172
Suffrage, the British, submitted to Dort, 11, 184, 186–7, 188, 192–7
sublapsarianism, 7, 16, 31, 184, 235, 275
supralapsarianism, 7, 15–16, 31, 57, 184–6, 235, 263, 290
Sutcliffe, Matthew, 231
Sylvanus, Johannes, 96

Taylor, Thomas, 290–1, 293
Tertullian, 26, 166, 169
Theodoret, Bp, 72
Thirteen Articles (1538), 53
Thirty-nine Articles, see Articles of Religion
Thysius, Anthony, 119 n., 122
Thirty Years War, ix, 10, 204, 214
Thomson, Richard ('Dutch Thomson'), 166, 168–74, 199, 216
Tomson, Laurence, 97
Traheron, Bartholomew, 76, 82, 90
Travers, Elias, 208 n.
Travers, Walter, 126–9, 132
Trent, Council of, 7, 52–3, 55, 58, 154, 221, 280
Twisse, William, 254 n., 257, 263–4, 298
Tyndale, John, 39, 80

Ursinus, Zacharias, 23 n., 87–9, 171, 289
Ussher, Archbishop James, 244–5, 263 n., 283, 284–5, 290, 308

Vane, Sir Henry, 308
Veluanus, Johannes Anastasius, 79
Veron, John, 288
via media, 5–6, 11–12, 124–5, 152–3, 158, 165, 167, 189 n., 202, 210–11, 216–17, 222, 235–6, 259–60, 269, 285, 312
Vincent of Lerins, St, xii
visitation articles, 212, 302–3
Vorstius, Conrad, 157, 159–62, 175, 201
Vossius, Gerard, 206–9, 282–5
Votier, Daniel, 301

Walton, Izaak, 124, 126, 132
Ward, Nathaniel, 223
Ward, Samuel, 234, 244 n., 282, 305, 306–7; delegate at Dort, 180, 188–9, 192, 197, 199
Warwick, Robert Rich, second Earl of, 224, 243

Westminster Confession, 254
Whitaker, William, xii, 4, 58, 101–2, 104–5, 107–10, 114–15, 118, 122–3, 137, 152–3, 185, 228 n., 267, 291
White, Bp Francis, 138 n., 215 n., 218, 224–5, 227–30, 232, 248
White, John, 155
Whitehead, David, 62
Whitgift, Archbishop John, 96, 100–11, 116–17, 119, 122–3, 124, 127, 132, 137, 147, 240
Whittingham, William, 13 n., 17 n.
Wiburn, Percival, 91
Wiggertsz, Cornelis, 8, n., 79
will, freedom of: Arminius on, 32–3; Articles of Religion on, 54, 66; Beza on, 20; Bucer on, 47; discussions at Dort on, 193–4; Hooker on, 130–1, 133; Montagu on, 220–1; Neile on, 274; Peter Martyr on, 51, Vossius on, 285
will of God: Andrewes on, 107–8, 118; Aquinas on, 114 n.; Arminius on, 27, 29–30, 33; Baro on, 112, 113–14, 116; Beza on, 16–20; Bucer on, 46; Harsnett on, 99; Hooker on, 132–5; Hutton on, 118, 120; Jackson on, 263–4, 268; Lambeth Articles on, 107–8, 109–10; Peter Martyr on, 49–50; Prynne on, 4; antecedent and consequent, 113–14, 116, 134; 'general' and 'occasioned', 132; 'positive' and 'permissive', 134; voluntas signi and voluntas beneplaciti, 50, 118, 120, 134
Willett, Andrew, 101 n., 129 n., 210 n.
Williams, Bp John, 213, 244, 308
Winwood, Sir Ralph, 160–2, 167, 175, 177
Wittenberg, 87
Womock, Laurence, 7 n., 184 n.
Wood, Anthony, 277 n.
works, theology of, 155, 158, 173, 273, 307 n.; Articles of Religion on, 55–6, 66; Beza on, 21; Bucer on, 47–8; discussions at Dort on, 194–7; Hooker on, 130–1; Hutton on, 121–2; Jewel on, 71–2; Latimer on, 43; Marian exiles on, 63, 64–5, 68; Peter Martyr on, 50–1; discussions at York House on 225–6; see also justification, sanctification
Wotton, Anthony, 230–1
Wren, Christopher, 205
Wren, Bp Matthew, 208 n., 295, 305, 310–11
Wright, Bp Robert, 296
Württemberg Confession, 66
Wykes, Thomas, 293 n.

Yates, John, 223, 233
York House Conference, 224–30, 243
Young, Dr John, 188–9

Zanchi, Girolamo, 77–8, 79, 82, 113, 154,
    172, 235
Zurich, 49, 60, 63, 65, 71, 77, 79, 83, 87
Zwingli, Ulrich, 80, 84, 267
Zwinglianism, 8, 80